Mental Health
in America

MENTAL HEALTH IN AMERICA

Patterns of Help-seeking from 1957 to 1976

Joseph Veroff
Richard A. Kulka
Elizabeth Douvan

Basic Books, Inc., Publishers

NEW YORK

Library of Congress Cataloging in Publication Data

Veroff, Joseph, 1929–
  Mental health in America

  Companion volume: The inner American / Joseph Veroff,
Elizabeth Douvan, Richard A. Kulka.
  References: p. 342
  Includes index.
    1. Mental health—United States—History. 2. Help-
seeking behavior—United States—History. 3. Community
mental health services—United States—Utilization—
History. I. Kulka, Richard A. II. Douvan, Elizabeth Ann
Malcolm, 1926–   III. Title.
RA790.6.V48   362.2'0973   80–68959
ISBN: 0–465–04479–4   AACR2

This book is dedicated to
Professors Daniel Katz and Gerald Gurin,
esteemed colleagues, models of skill,
integrity, and humanity.

Contents

Acknowledgments

LARGE SCALE social research is by nature collaborative. It depends on the specialized contributions of many individuals, coordinated and integrated with each other.

We have enjoyed an exceptional series of collaborations in the course of conducting our research and writing this book. We have learned and increased our understanding in all of these relationships. We have found great personal pleasure in them as well.

In designing the 1976 replication study we consulted Gerald Gurin and Sheila Feld, co-authors of the 1957 study, our friends and colleagues over the years. Their advice, encouragement, and collegial support, given graciously and generously, are among the very great rewards the project held for us. Angus Campbell, long time director of the Survey Research Center (SRC) and distinguished social scientist, urged us to do the replication study and shared findings as they came in with characteristic enthusiasm.

Colleagues in SRC's service sections made their critical contributions with the professionalism and helpful personal styles we are lucky enough to be able to assume—Irene Hess in sampling, John Scott and Tracy Berckmans in the field section, Joan Scheffler in Coding.

David Klingel and Mary Ellen Colten helped through the whole process of the study as active discussants and constructive, keen critics. Dave also managed data, solved incredible technical problems, taught us and our students the latest analytic techniques, and maintained morale in tough times.

The study was funded by NIMH, under Grant MH26006. Herbert Coburn, who headed the section that reviewed and advised us on the proposal, was always constructive and thorough in his work and was extraordinarily helpful to us.

We applied for and received an NIMH training grant, MH14618, for doctoral and postdoctoral scholars to work on the project as they developed survey skills. With this group of remarkable young colleagues we shared for five years a seminar and a working life that was rich in intellectual and personal rewards, perhaps the most ideal work situation imaginable. This book owes much to their enspiriting talk and we thank all of them: Helen Weingarten, Charlene Depner, Toni Antonucci, Steven Dubnoff, Anne Locksley, Alfreda Iglehart, Lynn Kahle, Fred Bryant, Janet Kohen, Sandra Stukes, Jeanne Lemkau, James McRae, Karen Mikus, Aloen Townsend, Betty Jones, Lois Tamir, Luis

Rubalcava, Kathleen Pottick, Elysse Sutherland, Robert Taylor, Susan Goff, David Reuman and Susan Contratto.

Other colleagues who contributed in various significant ways include: Michael Gorodetsky, David Featherman, Richard Price, Kenneth Heller, Joann Veroff, and Warren Norman.

Mary Loewen, Toby Teumer, and Sue Ellen Hansen typed, coordinated, formatted and corrected various versions of the manuscript. They kept things organized and sane which could easily have gotten out of control. They brought care and creative solutions to numerous problems; they offered spirit and good will throughout.

Mental Health
in America

Chapter 1

INTRODUCTION

THIS BOOK describes and analyzes the way Americans have sought help in dealing with mental health problems during the last quarter of a century. How willing have we been to seek professional help? Who among us have actually sought such help, why, and how did it work out? Why have some people not sought help, when they thought they could have profited from consulting an expert? And why have some people been opposed to seeking help under any imaginable circumstance? These and related questions shape this volume, the second that reports findings from two national studies of the life experiences of Americans, one carried out in 1957 (Gurin, Veroff, and Feld, 1960) and the other in 1976. The first volume (Veroff, Douvan, and Kulka, 1981) integrated findings about people's view of their own mental health and covered a wide range of experiences of American adults in their everyday lives, their feelings of well being, and how they coped with worries and periods of unhappiness.

This volume continues the analysis of change in American coping styles. Examining patterns of formal help-seeking, we shift attention in this volume to the fact that we have come to rely more and more on experts in dealing with personal problems and life crises. This has been an important change; it is a result of both increased governmental support for services, and of changing values about seeking help from experts.

This book also describes ways in which formal help-seeking has remained the same in the years between the two studies. Like Book 1, *The Inner American*, this book will give attention to stability in our experience as well as change.

We shall be discussing two representative samples of adult Americans (twenty-one and older)—2,460 in 1957; 2,267 in 1976—and we shall be discussing what has remained stable and what has changed in Americans' search for help with personal problems. Most studies of populations seeking the advice of mental health experts usually fall short of a complete picture of American help-seeking because they deal only with the treated groups who cannot be easily compared to any untreated groups. In our study, we shall report results of a household survey. However, we use a survey research interview which has its own limitations for accurately assessing peoples' orientation to professional help. In later sections of this chapter we describe our precautions in asking questions and coding and analyzing information in order to maximize the validity of these methods. We feel we have valid appraisals of the way people feel about the professional help they have actually used, help they might have used, or help they think they would use if circumstances were appropriate. Our analyses both provide documentation and descriptions of those feelings and also enable us to investigate theoretical issues raised in interpretations.

Help-Seeking Patterns in American Life

While we briefly explore the way people use informal interpersonal supports in their family and friendship networks in order to handle stress, we shall concentrate on professional helpers such as doctors, clergy, psychiatrists, psychologists, and social workers. We seek answers to such questions as: what proportion of the adult population has actually consulted a professional about some problem that has arisen? For those who have never sought professional help, we ask whether their not doing so reflects a lower level of stress and problems, a tendency to deny problems, a personal and social integration which offers sufficient strength and resources to solve problems without turning to professionals, or fear of stigma associated with professional help-seeking. Would such people use a professional if they faced a problem too large and disruptive for their own powers? Can they imagine facing a problem for which seeking professional counsel would be the best course of action? If not, why not?

For people who have gone to professionals for advice and help, we pose another set of questions: How did they happen to go to the particular person or agency? Were they referred or did they find out about the help source from the media or some other source? What kind of help did the professional offer them? Did the respondent feel that such help was effective in mastering the personal problem or crisis? Would they use it again?

In our analyses, we try to answer such questions, and, in each case, we ask also whether things have changed over the twenty-year period between our studies. Did more people use professionals in 1976 than in 1957? Did people who did *not* use professionals in 1976 resemble their 1957 counterparts in things such as their level of experienced stress and problems, their social background or current status, their fear of being stigmatized? Did people who went to professional counselors in 1976 go for the same kinds of problems that led people to professionals in 1957 or has growing acceptance of the idea of professional counsel meant that people in 1976 sought such help for problems that would not have led them to professionals in 1957. Did 1957 respondents have to be subjected to much more serious states of stress before they would choose professional help? Did they go to the same kinds of professionals or different ones in the two years? Did they evaluate the help they received similarly?

In this volume, we use data on informal coping and social support only to illuminate issues of formal help-seeking: Do people seek professional help because they do not have friends and family to provide informal support? Or are people who use professional help also likely to talk to friends? In social science circles, there has arisen a widespread interest in informal social-support networks as a panacea for the isolation and general psychological difficulties that are presumed to have intensified during recent social history. We shall look at how extensive these helping networks are in people's everyday experience. Thus, we use information about informal support to understand the context and alternatives to formal help-seeking. For this purpose, we shall also refer back to some of the findings from Book 1 regarding styles of coping with everyday life (for example, denial, praying) as they shed light on formal help-seeking.

We expected that the use of professionals would increase from 1957 to 1976, and that people's awareness of appropriate professionals would be both more widespread in the population and more sophisticated. Our culture underwent many changes during this period of the recent past and many of the changes could be thought of as enlarging a psychological orientation toward experience and increasing sophistication about psychological resources.

CHANGES FROM 1957 TO 1976

Optimism About the Experts

Following World War II, the avant-garde and then the majority of Americans developed a new basis for evaluating themselves and other people. This basis was psychological adjustment. The good life increasingly derived definition from internal criteria—"peace of mind," contentment, excitement, joy, fulfillment. Goal fulfillment came to depend on such internal psychological states rather than consensually validated and objective goals such as success and achievement.

This shift in goals represented the outcome of historical and cultural

forces that evolved during the second world war and the postwar decades. Surely affluence must be counted among the most powerful of
these forces. When people struggle to survive, they have little time or
energy for a search for fulfillment and peace of mind. External reality—the struggle to wrest a livelihood from a difficult environment—
compels attention and absorbs consciousness. Self-consciousness and
self-development are luxuries to people whose whole effort and attention are demanded for survival.

Revolutions in transportation and communication also contributed
to the inward turn. When a population is rooted and stable, the self is
defined in large measure by one's position in a community and one's
stable relationships and interactions with familiar others. When, on
the other hand, we move and live mainly in a world of strangers, we
gain both the opportunity to define ourselves in a variety of ways as a
matter of choice, and the burden of discovering which of the possible
self-definitions correspond somehow to the "authentic" self. Mobile
people must establish themselves again and again in strange communities. This necessity broadens choice and makes for uncertainty.

The media offer images and ideals for uprooted persons to use in
designing and crafting a self—ways of behaving, being, believing, and
feeling. At the same time, the media support values and criteria developed in conjunction with mobility and affluence. In earlier eras, the
cultural hero was the man of action taming the West; in our era he is
more likely to be presented as the individual searching for meaning
and self-definition by self-exploration, fantasy, and self-expression.
Woody Allen gives us a hero who has all the success and achievement,
the money and fame, a person could dream of, and who, at the same
time, struggles with unsatisfactory relationships and a twenty-year
psychoanalysis. One critic has asserted that Allen treats life as a dis-
traction from psychoanalysis and the search for self. The critic contrasts this stance with the traditional (and more common) search for
self-definition *through* life and relationships.

The contrast is illuminating about modern life and about some of
the effects of the era of psychology. The present-day hero searches for
the self by reliving experience in a contractual relationship with a professional, a relationship which is, by definition, removed from "real
life" and artificial in the sense that the feelings and emotions it con-
tains are not indigenous to it but belong to other primary relationships in the real world. The "transference relationship" is an epiphe-
nomenon, a series of shadows on the wall of the consulting room cave.
By grappling together with the shadows, the patient and the expert try
to bring the patient's perception and response into a closer relationship with reality, to match his internal representations with the actual
occurrences and objects they portray. But that reality is always restricted to the shadows, for life itself is excluded from the consulting room.
Psychoanalysis (and psychiatry) is the only form of psychic healing

that attempts to cure people by detaching them from society and relationships. All other forms—shamanism, faith healing, prayer—bring the community into the healing process, indeed use the interdependence of patient and others as the central mechanism in the healing process. Modern psychiatry isolates the troubled individual from the currents of emotional interdependence and deals with the trouble by distancing from it and manipulating it through intellectual/verbal discussion, interpretation, and analysis.

In these characteristics—isolation, detachment, intellectual/verbal analysis—psychoanalysis represents quintessential science. Its popularity marks the movement of the scientific revolution to the last frontier—the sphere of human behavior and the thickets of the human soul—and represents, above all, a remarkable faith in and optimism about the power of science. Its emergence as the model of human counsel marks modern sensibility and displaces a religious/moral model.

The traditional moral or religious framework defines personal problems and interpersonal difficulties as problems of will, intent, morality, and spirit. As such they are different in *kind* from problems in other realms, such as mechanics or economics. They do not follow scientific rules and are susceptible to solution by the application of will if they are susceptible to any solution. They can never be known or treated as effectively by an outsider as they are by the person who experiences them, and it is the function of that person to apply will, effort, and personal resources to solve the dilemma. The role of a counselor (clergy, older friend, parent) is secondary to the action of the principal. The counselor can comfort by expressions of concern, sympathy, support, and by faith in the troubled person's ability to solve or transcend the problem troubling him or her. But the work of solving, transcending, or "forgetting" the problem can only be carried out by the troubled person.

In the modern "era of psychology," personal problems are brought under the rubric of science. They are seen as sharing with mechanical, medical, or economic problems the rules of science—cause and effect, logic—and are susceptible to change through technology. If one has an emotional problem or a problem in one's marriage or with one's child, the problem arises from causes in one's own background or behavior and the behavior of the other person involved. These causes are definable and can be diagnosed and altered by appropriate expert intervention. The spread of science to this last frontier followed from and reflected secular trends in the culture. As religion receded from center stage, from a position of dominance in the realm of human affairs, science moved in.

The role of counselor now assumes more importance and an aura of special skill. It is no longer the patient who has that special knowledge and grasp of the problem that alone leads to solution. It becomes the expert, trained in the complex and convoluted ways of the human mind, the dense meanings in human interaction, who now stands in a special relation to the problem and is able to design and direct solutions. The counselor's power comes in part precisely from separation from the problem—in contrast to the situation in the religious and moral model in which it is the patient's immersion in the problem that was thought to give exclusive purchase on its solution. When cure lies in rational, logical analysis, and derivation of meaning and understanding, the distant observer, the uninvolved person, is most likely to see the way. To be effective, the healer must have skill and training, but, most of all, needs objectivity and the emotional distance of an outsider. Solutions in the religious and moral approach rest on the most intimate grasp of the problem and the sense of the individual in all his complex reality—his strengths and weaknesses, resources and limitations, opportunities for diversion and supports from others, and the willful application of personal power. In the scientific scheme, solutions come as a result of distance, analysis, comparison, generalization, and guided intellectual understanding, the explication of meaning. For all of these activities, the expert, not the patient, is specially qualified.

The displacement of religious and moral counselors by trained, scientific experts is only one of the signs of science's triumph in its last frontier. Experts took over the role of psychic healer, but they also assumed a much broader and more important role in directing the behavior, goals, and ideals of "normal" people. They became the teachers and norm-setters who would tell people how to approach and live life so as to avoid ending up as patients. They would provide advice and counsel about raising and responding to children, how to behave in marriage, and what to see in that relationship. They warned of mental health symptoms and told us how to recognize them and what to do about them.

Science moved in because people needed and wanted guidance. The mobility which had disrupted traditional community ties left young couples alone in their child raising, without the support of older kin and friends. Increasing education contributed to secularization and loss of religious faith and also to a transfer of faith to science and rationality. All of these developments set the stage for a greater influence of science on the realm of human behavior and human affairs. Scientific experts offered new norms and guidelines to replace traditional personal, community, and religious-moral standards.

This triumph of science reflects, among other things, American optimism about the power of knowledge and technology. If we can just discover what causes a problem, we are sure that sooner or later science will develop the tools for solving it. The idea of unlimited progress—the heritage of our frontier mentality—dominated our national consciousness until very recently and by the simplest of mechanisms reinforced our faith in science. Science worked.

Pessimism About the Experts

Very recently, under the force of cataclysmic changes in our national and international situation, we have begun to see that science too has limits. We have come to see that technology can certainly destroy us all but that it may not be able to win wars or friends or even create a liveable environment. We have come to realize that technology carries costs and uses resources that are not limitless. As humanists, we recognize that science has allowed us to get to the moon but has not advanced the quality of human life and harmony more than an iota, if at all. The minds that solve the overwhelming technical problems of launching us into space have not been able to resolve conflicts between nation-states.

The reaction against science, the new skepticism, has affected our response to behavioral science and experts as well. Historians looking back now see the experts—epitomized by Benjamin Spock—as presumptuous, naive, shallow, foolish, and destructive in much of their advising and counseling. Christopher Lasch (1977) and others contend that the self-assured and self-important experts robbed parents of their belief in themselves and so added to the deterioration of legitimate authority, the. effectiveness of parents, and family cohesion and viability. Historians and social critics have begun debunking and demythologizing psychiatry, "scientific advice" about human behavior and problems, and the "experts" who have arrogated tc themselves the role of norm-setters.

More moderate critics have also become skeptical of the promise of social science and/or the value of psychiatric intervention. Even within the field, the earlier limitless optimism has given way to more moderate goals and a greater appreciation for the complexities of human relationships and human behavior, including the behavior of psychiatrists. Blum (1978) in an extraordinary work in the sociology of knowledge, has demonstrated that psychiatrists, like ordinary people, are susceptible to changing times. By demonstrating historical changes in definitions and criteria used and diagnoses made by psychiatrists and social scientists, Blum examined the field's claim to objectivity and concluded that these expert judgments, just like all human judgments, are vulnerable to many forces other than the objective reality of the situation or the behavior being judged.

Psychiatrists and psychotherapists have contributed to the growing skepticism about the value of long-term individual treatment by experts as a reasonable approach to mental healing. The family therapy movement, with intellectual impetus provided by Bateson and his colleagues (1956), questioned the unit of analysis of problems, asserting that problems were usually located in the space between people, in relationships, and would be more reasonably addressed by treating the relationship rather than the individual. Szasz (1974) and Laing (1967) claimed that official definitions of pathology were political, not scientific, and, in the final analysis, were also wrong. Choice of psychiatry as a speciality among medical students has declined dramatically, despite the fact that its economic rewards are among the highest in the medical professions—comparable with surgery and ophthalmology.

Finally, patients and political activists have contributed to the doubts about the validity of psychiatry. Secularization and suspicion of authority have prepared the ground for lawsuits against therapists who promise, or seem to promise, more than they deliver. The women's movement has sensitized female patients to psychiatrists' sexist practices and misuse of power. Suits for sexual harassment and exploitation of female patients have lowered the reputation of psychiatry.

Long-term individual therapy reached its peak of popularity about the time of the original study (1957) on which this book is based. From the end of the second world war until the mid-sixties, psychoanalysis spread in practice and popularity. Beginning with *Lady in the Dark* in 1944 and continuing through a whole series of films about Freud's life and/or the application of his theories, the theory and practice of psychiatry were popularized. Woody Allen has dramatized the most explicit and exaggerated regard for the practice, yet his portrayals always bear an ironic cast and also, by now, seem rather old-fashioned in the faith they convey. The era of omnipresent psychology has passed.

Aside from political and theoretical objections, practical issues encouraged skepticism about psychiatry's control of the helping functions. For if mental health professionals were to solve all personal and interpersonal problems by long-term intervention, then clearly an enormous number of professionals would have to be trained, a number that would outstrip the capacity of training institutions and would, in addition, represent an investment of an extravagant proportion of the nation's productive resources.

In the face of these pressures, the mental health establishment proposed two changes in facilities: first, the use of paraprofessionals and professionals outside the standard psychiatric fields, such as family doctors, lawyers, clergy, was encouraged. Psychiatrists and other mental health professionals would train these nonspecialist groups who, in turn, would deliver care directly. The second change was the community mental health movement, and it implied a belief in people's ability to manage ordinary problems on their own, since mental health clinics were to serve mainly as support in crisis management. This change also implied a shift in view about the origins of mental illness. Unlike traditional psychiatric theories' view that mental illness originated in psychic conflicts created or planted in childhood, the crisis intervention approach views psychic disturbance as deriving much more heavily from contemporaneous reality problems. Unemployment, the care of a chronically ill family member, a hyperactive child, eviction, a suit for nonpayment of taxes, or business failure—these are the events and crises that precipitate breakdown in psychological health, and these are the events which emergency support must help the individual negotiate or withstand. Once through a crisis, the person or family is presumed capable of managing life independently.

More recently still, the establishment has discovered in informal social support a new panacea. Numerous studies have reported that people who survive crisis without breakdown are people who have friends and kin they can call on for support and advice when problems arise (Heller, 1979). These findings have been interpreted to mean that social support aids survival (rather than that strong people attract friends and social support), and the building and nurturing of support networks has become a new field of action for mental health workers.

Even this idea of informal support is urged and promoted by experts, who are busy establishing the norm that it is "good" to have friends and kin ties because having them will protect your mental health and strengthen you to face crisis. One can imagine people scurrying around the neighborhood to make friends in order to be healthy, something like graduate students who distribute sign-up sheets for "spontaneous" discussion groups before an examination.

Not only had the experts become somewhat disillusioned with community mental health services but they also became increasingly aware that only in their everyday life circumstances would most people find the supports they need for well being. Psychological support must come through families, friendships, and even membership in community groups or neighborhoods that provide the indirect buttress people need for dealing with life problems. Antonovsky (1972) has analyzed "resistance resources" people invoke when they cope with stressful life events such as death of a loved one, loss of a job, or other disruptive events. These resistance resources are found in: the structure of social roles that provide alternatives for adapting to new situations; specific ties to others who provide care when disruptions occur; and general community ties to people that provide reassurance during times of trouble.

Many social researchers and theorists have now suggested that social support may be the critical factor in adaptation to crisis (Mechanic, 1976; Cobb, 1976; Caplan, 1974; Kahn and Quinn, 1977), although Heller (1979) has aptly pointed out that there is no clear evidence that social support causally reduces strain or distress. Most of the studies that have related social support to reduced strain may also be interpreted to mean that people who are copers are also people who easily enlist social support. It is perhaps too glib to assume that those who receive social support become better copers. Nevertheless, attention to informal social support is a critical new perspective that community psychology has brought to the consideration of the way people adapt to crisis.

So, despite growing skepticism about the intervention of professionals with therapeutic intent, mental health experts play a continuing role as norm-setters. It is perhaps the most startling symptom of the loss of community integration, the extent of alienation, that at least some people need experts to tell them that having friends will help them endure the hardships and tragedies of life. Most people probably don't need to be told. It may be mostly the experts who find this eye-opening information.

Before we examine the findings of our two studies, it is important for the reader to understand the methods used to obtain the data. Let us turn to the steps in the survey method. Below we repeat almost verbatim from Book 1 (pp. 25–34), since the methods used to collect and analyze the data apply equally to both studies. Occasionally we substitute material that illustrates the topics of this volume rather than the first.

Methods

DESIGN OF THE INTERVIEW SCHEDULE

The 1976 interview schedule appears as appendix A. Wherever possible exact wording of questions and structure of interviewing from the 1957 schedule were retained on the 1976 schedule. The first schedule followed the researchers' interest in obtaining multiple assessments of multiple areas of subjective well being and ways of handling problems. The flow was from general open-ended questions about feelings of well being in the first part[1] to more specific questions about mental health and help-seeking toward the end. Within any specific section of the interview there occurs the same funneling from general questions to specific ones. Furthermore, very personal questions (e.g., probing for whether a person sought help) were cushioned by asking for hypothetical responses first.

[1] The study was introduced as a study of modern living. The very first questions are neutral in both studies: inquiries about use of leisure time and socializing occur first. For a random two-thirds of the sample in both years, a story-telling procedure designed to measure human motives (Veroff, et al., 1966) intervened between these questions and the first ones asking about general feelings of well being (worries, happiness, etc.). The story-telling procedure is a neutral procedure. Most people enjoy it. It is rationalized to respondents as a measure of how people interpret situations as they come up in everyday life.

The funneling procedure means that responses to open-ended questions about well being are not influenced by the content of more specific questions. One can never totally control the bias that inevitably exists in the order of questioning, but funneling the entire interview from very general to very specific mental health questions and funneling within a given topic from open-ended to specific questions maximizes the validity of spontaneous responses.

Obviously people may be defensive in response to questions that ask them to evaluate their own lives. The strategy of using multiple assessments, besides conforming to the multiple criteria approach, helps us estimate how much defensiveness may be operating. We would expect some correlation between multiple measures of adjustment in a given area. Should one type of question provoke too much defensiveness, we would be alerted by its pattern of relationship to other measures. There should be some convergent validity.

To offset defensiveness we asked some questions in written form when it was clear respondents were able to read and use a checklist. This was true for the symptoms and certain personal questions about marriage on the 1976 survey (see appendix A, item D4).

Many open-ended questions were used. This is unusual in national surveys of this kind. Such questions permit us to evaluate the spontaneous reactions of people to general questions about their lives. What a difference it makes to ask about the problems for which someone has sought professional help. Asking what the problem was, rather than asking the person to answer yes or no to a list of problem types (a personal problem, a work problem, marital problem, and so forth). People do not usually categorize their problems so neatly and might become defensive if forced to do so.

Because they were irrelevant to some of the mental health issues of the 1970s, some questions asked in the 1957 survey were not repeated in the 1976 questionnaire. Other questions of 1957 were retained for the 1976 survey in spite of lack of clarity, because they were so important to our evaluation of change. For example, one of the 1957 symptom questions, "Do you ever drink more than you should?" is ambiguous, but we did not change it because we wanted comparative information.

After consultation with social scientists new questions were devised for the 1976 survey about subjective well being and styles of coping with problems. These were absent from the 1957 survey and should be included in the 1976 even if no comparison between the two survey years would be possible. Our inclusion of questions about help-seeking for situational crises (appendix A, question M7–M10) is the most important example of this new type of question. Another example is a set of items designed to assess feelings of depression (appendix A, question D4). As these new questions are introduced in discussion, they will be presented in detail.

THE INTERVIEWING SITUATION

Both the 1957 and 1976 studies followed the standard procedures used by the Survey Research Center. Interviewers have a backlog of experience gained from other surveys; they are permanent employees who are utilized for different surveys as they come up. Most of them are women (97 percent), white (87 percent) and over thirty-four (87 percent). Thus, the typical interviewer is a white middle-aged woman. They are trained to convey to the process a sense of legitimacy and are given further legitimacy by a letter that precedes direct contact with respondents. One may question the self-presentations men fashion when interviewed by women. However, more serious questions can be raised about such self-presentation to a male interviewer when questions focus on personal problems and distress. There is reason to think that female interviewers elicit more honest responses to such questions. In the 1976 survey, an effort was made to match black interviewers with interviewees drawn from predominantly black neighborhoods.

All interviewers are provided written instructions for each question. These inform them of special probing that may be required for a given question or special responses to give to questions a respondent might have about a particular item. The instructions also help establish a working alliance between the interviewer and the researchers.

While regional conferences were held throughout the country for all the interviewers involved in the 1957 survey, a conference at the University of Michigan was held for the field supervisors only in the 1976 survey. The personal nature of this survey was new to interviewers in 1957; by 1976, they were used to asking questions of that nature. Both sets of interviewers were impressed with the unusual value of the survey; the interviewers for the new (1976) survey were made especially aware of the potential to assess social change. Consequently, morale among interviewers was good, and judging from the answers to a questionnaire sent to respondents after the interview, we conclude that rapport between interviewers and respondents was perhaps higher than in the average survey interview. Outright refusal to be interviewed in 1957 was 9 percent of the designated sample. This figure nearly doubled by 1976 and reflects the general trend toward reluctance to participate in any interview. All surveys in the 1970s encountered this problem. We will discuss this issue in more detail in the section on sampling.

To introduce the interview, the following statement was read to respondents in both 1957 and 1976:

The Survey Research Center has been asked to make a study of the stresses and strains of modern living. There have been a lot of changes in our way of living over the past fifty years or so. These changes have brought this country to the highest standard of living in the world. But a great many people are concerned about whether or not there are problems involved in the rapid pace of our present life. Doctors, educators, religious leaders, and other experts are interested in finding out how people feel about this question.

Of course, this interview is completely voluntary. If we should come to any question you don't want to answer, let me know and we'll skip over it. I think you'll find the questions interesting and will want to give them careful thought.

Interviewing for both studies occurred during the summer months and in years when many people were aware of economic recession. The economic outlooks for 1957 and 1976 were not exactly comparable, but the general mood reflected a depressed phase of the economic cycle.

Though the average length of the interviews was ninety minutes, only a handful of interviews were cut short because of this unusual length for a national survey interview. Because of this length there might have been a slightly higher refusal rate in the two studies compared to other national surveys. When respondents heard the anticipated amount of time required for interviewing, they might have been slightly more prone to refuse to be interviewed in both 1957 and 1976. We have no way to tell how many nonresponses were refusals to be interviewed because of the time required or because of general unwillingness. The respondents did note in postinterview questionnaires that the interview was lengthy but most found it interesting, probably because of its personal nature. In an effort to make the interview shorter, we asked certain less central questions of only two-thirds of the sample. The same procedure was used in 1957. In all but a few cases questions discussed in this report are those asked of the total population. Exceptions are indicated as they appear.

SAMPLING

The national samples interviewed for the two studies were drawn in accordance with a multistage probability area design (see Kish and Hess, 1965).[2] This procedure identifies primary sampling points within the coterminus United States. These consist of: standard metropolitan areas, single counties, and certain county groups within each region of the country. Successive subdivisions of these sampling points are made in keeping with the sampling probabilities proportionate to their populations initially, and with equal probabilities in the final stages. At the last stages, addresses are identified and selected, and

[2]Details are available in appendix B. It should be noted that the sampling standard error is somewhat larger than conventional ones because a study of this sort is based upon a multistage area sampling design as opposed to simple random sampling. The design effect for this survey is minimal; the ratio of variances of the complex to the simple random sampling is close to one.

finally a single household resident among eligible members is randomly chosen to be interviewed. No substitutions are permitted.

Since the sampling procedure restricts the survey to private households, it excludes the following people: those residing in military establishments, hospitals, educational, penal, and religious institutions; hotels, larger rooming houses, logging and lumber camps. Thus, we omit from our sample a great many people who are transient and probably a good many who would choose responses to our questionnaire that would indicate considerable distress.

For the initial survey, 84 percent of the designated respondents were interviewed; for the 1976 survey, 71 percent were interviewed. This reduced rate is a serious problem. When the original study was conducted, national surveys had remarkably small nonresponse rates. By 1976, however, all surveys were having significant problems. In our case, the nonresponse rate comes close to being intolerable. When response rates are over 20 or 25 percent, the representativeness of the sample must be questioned. While we shall analyze our sample against census data and find that the sample does not deviate radically from the population on critical demographic measures, in the final analysis we cannot be completely sure of the sample's representativeness because the variables on which it is most likely to deviate are ones which are not measured in the census.

The fact is that all surveys are now in serious trouble. Our world has changed in many ways which militate against the household survey's success. American people have become much less trusting and open with strangers, and, even more important, many American households are deserted during the daytime hours ordinarily used to interview or to contact households and arrange interview appointments. With wives and mothers at work, no one is home to be contacted. And evening hours when respondents are more likely to be at home are not the most desirable times for interviewers to be alone on the streets or making first approaches unannounced to strange households. There are more nonresponses in densely populated metropolitan centers. The nonresponse rate for New York City in the 1976 survey was 40 percent. It was 55 percent in Los Angeles. Refusals also occur more often in these same areas. More older than younger people refuse to be interviewed. People living alone often refuse to be interviewed.

The problem is formidable and the decision of many survey research workers to shift from personal face-to-face interviews to telephone surveys is understandable in light of these changes in the culture.

We conducted analyses of our sample in comparison to 1976 Current Population Survey[3] data and have assured ourselves that the sample in

[3] The Current Population Survey, carried out monthly by the Bureau of the Census for the Bureau of Labor Statistics, samples 55,000 households in a multistage sampling of an updated listing from the latest census (1970). For each variable we used the available monthly statistic that was closest in time to the months our survey began.

TABLE 1.1

Comparison of Respondent Characteristics of the 1976 Study Sample with the 1976 Current Population Survey Estimate of the United States Population

| | 1976 Study Sample | | 1976 |
Respondent Characteristic	Percentage of Unweighted Sample	Percentage of Weighted[b] Sample	Current Population Survey Estimate of United States Population,[a] as a Percent
Sex			
Women	58	56	53
Men	42	44	47
	100%	100%	100%
Age			
21–24	11	11	11
25–34	25	25	23
35–44	17	17	17
45–54	14	16	17
55–64	15	16	15
65 and over	18	15	17
	100%	100%	100%
Race			
White	86	87	88
Black	11	10	10
Other	3	3	1
	100%	100%	100%
Marital Status[c]			
Married, separated	67	74	72
Single	11	11	14
Widowed	14	9	9
Divorced	8	6	5
	100%	100%	100%
Regions[d]			
New England	6	6	6
Middle Atlantic	15	16	18
East N. Central	18	18	19
West N. Central	10	11	8
South Atlantic	15	15	16
East S. Central	8	7	6
West S. Central	11	10	10
Mountain	3	3	4
Pacific	14	14	13
	100%	100%	100%
Education[e]			
Grade school	19	18	21
Some high school	15	15	15
High school grad.	34	35	36
Some college	17	16	17
College graduate	15	16	15
	100%	100%	100%

TABLE 1.1 *(continued)*
Comparison of Respondent Characteristics of the 1976 Study Sample with the
1976 Current Population Survey Estimate of the United States Population

	1976 Study Sample		1976
Respondent Characteristic	Percentage of Unweighted Sample	Percentage of Weighted [b] Sample	Current Population Survey Estimate of United States Population,[a] as a Percent
Household Income			
Under 3,000	8	—[f]	8
3,000–4,999	10	—[f]	10
5,000–6,999	9	—[f]	9
7,000–9,999	14	—[f]	12
10,000–14,999	21	—[f]	19
15,000–24,999	26	—[f]	27
25,000 and over	12	—[f]	15
	100%		100%

[a] Unless otherwise noted, the U.S. population figures are for adults twenty-one years and over, which matches the age range of the 1976 study sample. For sex, age, race, and region, the CPS data came from the July 1976 Current Population Surveys. For marital status and education, they came from the March 1976 survey. And for household income, the estimate was from March 1977 FPS, because at that time this was the respondent's estimated family income for "the previous year" and thus would overlap with the family income estimates for our survey which asked for estimates of "this year."

[b] Weighted by number of eligible respondents in the dwelling unit.

[c] CPS data for persons twenty years and over.

[d] Excluding Alaska and Hawaii.

[e] Data for persons twenty-five years and over in all estimates.

[f] It is not appropriate to weight household income by the number of eligible respondents in the household or dwelling unit.

the 1976 study does not deviate grossly from these census data in any of the critical social characteristics for which comparisons can be made: sex, age, race, marital status, region, education, and family income. Details of these comparisons are presented in table 1.1.

CODING

The choice in 1957 of highly detailed, elaborate coding schemes for open questions stood us in good stead when the 1976 coding began. For example, there were twenty-eight coding distinctions drawn in the code for responses to the question asking about the nature of the problem for which professional help was sought. Had a different choice been made in 1957—for example, for more abstract, general, or inclusive code categories—the problem of comparability of coding in the two studies would have been much thornier and would have required specific training to insure that coders could reproduce the judgments made in 1957. The 1976 coders could follow the detailed categorization scheme established in 1957 with no apparent difficulties. The specificity of the code designations assured comparability over time as well as high intercoder agreement.

In all open questions, the code provided a general "other" category for responses that could not be fitted into one of the more specific categories. Whenever an answer was thus coded, the answer was recorded verbatim on a card. In those instances where "other" cards accumulated in unusual numbers, we perused them carefully to see whether new categories could be formed to accommodate answers occurring frequently. In a few cases, new categories clearly emerged from the 1976 interviews. That is, some answers were common enough in 1976 to warrant a category that had not been necessary in 1957.

One example (and there was only a handful of such cases) will illustrate this situation. In answer to a question about problems respondents had encountered in raising their children, a new response category was necessary to accommodate answers about the special problems of raising children without the help of a father. The increased number of female, single adult households in 1976 had clearly raised the incidence of such problems to the point where we needed a category that had not been necessary in 1957.

In most of the chapters that follow, the first presentation will be year comparisons. The question of change or stability in percentages will be emphasized rather than absolute percentages. A cautionary note is in order regarding all results comparing 1957 to 1976. When we discuss the results, we shall often talk about the change or stability of results as if there were no intervening fluctuations. It could very well be that had we sampled the population in the 1960s or the early 1970s we would have seen change between 1957 and the 1960s, but no change thereafter. Or, when we see lack of change, there may have been change between 1957 and the 1960s but a reversion to the 1957 distribution in 1976. Without data for the 1960s and early 1970s we are in some technical error in referring to change or lack of change. For ease of analysis and interpretation we ignore these possibilities, and we may be wrong in some instances.

When we present comparisons for 1957 to 1976, we are able to ask a more analytic question: Can we attribute change or stability to critical demographic shifts from 1957 to 1976? We were a much more highly educated population in 1976; we also had proportionately more very young and very old birth cohorts in 1976 than we had in 1957, when the middle-aged cohort was proportionately larger. These substantial education and age shifts may be correlated with changes in the psychological reactions that we uncover. Furthermore, if we controlled for these demographic shifts, maybe some new year changes would have come to light that were not apparent in the overall year comparisons.

As a result, we needed a technique for analyzing year changes while simultaneously controlling for age and education differences. We used for this purpose a relatively new multivariate analysis technique, log-linear hierarchical modeling (Goodman, 1978), which allowed us to test the effect of time on a measure of well being or on the use of informal help, above and beyond the effect of demographic changes which have occurred in the population during the same time period.[4]

The necessity of some such technique will perhaps be clarified by an example. Let us use findings about the use of formal help in times of stress. In 1976, the use of formal help was much more common than it was in 1957. This is, of course, an interesting fact which tells us something important about American society. It is a fact of particular interest to mental health practitioners and the mental health movement. Following the 1957 study, community mental health policies were instituted by the government to redress inadequate resources and differential access to resources for mental health care. For in 1957, use of formal help—and particularly those formal resources designated as specific mental health resources (psychiatrist, social worker, mental health worker)—was primarily characteristic of people who had more education and higher incomes. Subsidiary findings supported an interpretation of the income influence on use as a problem of access. That is, mental health resources were scarce and costly, and people who had low incomes could not use them even when they might have wanted to or considered them important.

The fact, then, that use was way up in 1976 and that the relationship of use to income was down can at least be seen as reflecting the effectiveness of the community mental health movement. Educational programs, the introduction of inexpensive facilities, and third-party payment programs have encouraged the use of these resources and have spread that use to low-income groups which previously could not afford them.

Important though this may be, it is not the full picture of what had happened in the area of use during the twenty years between our studies. For the population also changed in many other ways during these years, and some of the changes are directly relevant to (indeed, confounded with) this series of findings. For one thing, the population in 1976 was much more highly educated than it was in 1957. Since education was (and still is) related to the use of resources, the increase in use of formal help might be simply a reflection of the larger proportion of educated people in the 1976 sample. This is not to say that the change is any less real or that it would lose interest for practitioners and policy makers if such were the case. The increased demand for service is just as real whether it is simply the result of a more educated populace or of a change in cultural norms about seeking

---

[4]The technique is described further in chapter 3, when results of its use are first reported, and in considerable detail in appendix C.

help—a diminished fear and resistance to the act of help-seeking which has affected the whole population rather than the highly educated alone.

But to be intellectually satisfying, the picture must be clarified. We would like to know not just that help-seeking was more common in 1976, but also whether the change is only a reflection of the general educational level of the population or is a consequence of a change in cultural norms about help-seeking. We want, then, to test for the effect of the generation—the passage of time from 1957 to 1976—over and above educational changes in the population. It is precisely for such purpose that log-linear hierarchical modeling is designed, and it is for this that we use it.

For any analysis of overall year differences there follows a presentation of the log-linear hierarchical modeling via Everyman's Contingency Table Analysis (ECTA) which looks at year differences in a given measure of help-seeking in a further cross-classification by education and age differences. (In addition we cross-classify the data by sex differences to see whether some of the results were more or less true for men or women.) This will allow us to do two things: (1) qualify results in our report of year differences either by saying that they are not apparent when the controls are introduced or by seeing that they are only apparent in certain groups; (2) see year differences that emerge only when controls are introduced.

The multivariate analysis permits us to see interaction effects: results that hold only for or are especially strong in certain subgroups based on sex, age, education, or year. For example we shall find that although consulting a doctor for a personal problem decreased between 1957 and 1976, there had taken place a substantial decrease only among young people. For older people, if anything, consulting a doctor had increased. These interactions are complicated to think about, but are among the most exciting results we report because they point to changes in some groups and not others. These differential results are often more meaningful than overall effects.

Multivariate analyses are also the starting points for our discussion of sex, age, and education differences within each chapter. They draw attention to results that should be emphasized considering how these social characteristics are related to various aspects of coping behavior and help-seeking.

In chapters 3 and 7 we will present data available only in the 1976 survey. Here too we rely on the cross-classification analysis but without year effects. We still underplay absolute percentages and emphasize comparisons among groups in discussing results.

Preview of the Book

In the next chapter, as background to information about help-seeking, we summarize study findings about the life experience and subjective mental health of American adults, which have been presented in detail and represent most of the content of Book 1, *The Inner American.*

These contents are grouped under topics which represent different points during people's experiences and are based on their evaluations of their own lives and adjustment. The topics covered are: feelings and sources of well being, self-perceptions, marriage, parenthood, work, and symptoms of stress.

Two major contents can be distinguished in this list: those which focus on individual characteristics and are traditional ways of assessing individual psychological adjustment (for example, feelings of well being and symptoms of stress) and those which focus on the individual in major life roles (the definition, fit, experience, and evaluation of marriage, parenthood, and work).

This summary of the state of people's adaptation, satisfaction, and problems in life provides background for analysis of coping behavior and help-seeking. When we look at formal help-seeking, we shall use measures of subjective adjustment to explain differences in the use of professional help (that is, people who experience more problems or greater stress will more often have sought professional help) or as control variables in certain analyses (for example, do young people use professional help more than older people, given a comparable level of stress?).

Following this portrayal of the general subjective experience of the population, in chapter 3 we proceed to an analysis of people's methods of handling personal difficulties. Here the emphasis is on the use of social resources.

Chapter 2

SUBJECTIVE MENTAL HEALTH 1957-1976

HELP-SEEKING is not random; it is one of a number of acts which may follow from an individual's detection of a problem in some aspect of her/his life—some psychological trouble such as anxiety or depression, an interpersonal difficulty that is troubling and intransigent, some problem at work or in the family, a crisis brought on by illness or death.

To place help-seeking in context and to introduce measures of subjective mental health to be referred to in later analyses, we shall summarize findings about various aspects of life experience and subjective mental health. The analyses we summarize here are the focus of Book 1, *The Inner American*, where they are presented in detail.

Our studies concern normal people who take up the business of life each day. We did not intend our studies to analyze pathology or evaluate and diagnose the population in a technical or clinical sense. We asked, rather, how people experience their own lives, and we assumed that that experience would be complex and many faceted. The fact that a person experiences a period of serious problems as a parent does not necessarily mean that he or she will have symptoms of anxiety or depression, or even that the person is unhappy or worried about other aspects of life—work, marriage, relationships with friends, and so forth.

We assumed, then, a multifaceted approach to subjective mental health. We focused questions and analyses about the following aspects of life experience: general well being, perceptions of self, marriage, parenthood, work, and symptoms. Do they turn to other people, kin or friends, for advice and support? For this analysis, we shall review relevant data from Book 1 and then present some information about social support available only in the 1976 study. We shall also briefly review Book 1 results which compare people's use in 1957 and 1976 of psychological devices such as denial or self-distraction (for example, "I try not to think about it" or "I get busy with some other activity when I have a problem I can't solve"), as well as people's use of prayer or direct, individual action in their efforts to solve problems.

Chapter 4 examines formal help-seeking; it focuses on attitudes toward hypothetical use of a professional helper. Chapter 5 deals with people's readiness for self-referral and their own help-seeking patterns (whom they consulted, what they sought help about, whether they thought the help was effective and why). Chapter 6 looks at a critical group in both 1957 and 1976: people who thought they could have used help but for one reason or another did not actually do so. In chapter 7, we present an analysis of help-seeking for situational crisis (as distinguished from personal problems). This analysis, unlike the others, cannot include changes that took place during the twenty years because the questions were asked only in 1976. Finally, in chapter 8, we correlate use of professional help with indicators of available mental health resources in particular communities and geographic locations. In chapter 9, we summarize and integrate the major elements in this analysis of professional help-seeking and the way in which it has changed during the recent past.

The summary which follows adheres to these divisions. In each section, we provide examples of questions used to obtain the information in that area. We summarize findings, particularly findings about change and stability over the twenty year interval of our studies. We are especially interested in interactions in the analysis of changes over time; instances in which a particular group (for example, the young, the highly educated, women) shows unusual change not matched in other groups. Such interactions can point to particular historical changes that have affected only subgroups in the population and they may help us refine our understanding and interpretation of historical change. Finally, the analyses summarized also include relationships between mental health variables and age, sex, and education. Following these summaries of individual areas, we will present a brief discussion of certain major integrative themes drawn from analysis in several areas.

Much of what follows is taken directly or paraphrased from Book 1.

Having attempted in Book 1 to achieve the clearest, most succinct statements of our findings and interpretations, we find it difficult and artificial to try to change our language. So, we ask indulgence from those who have read Book 1 and repeat our story for those who meet our studies for the first time in this volume.

Well-Being

We found many year differences (i.e., changes from 1957 to 1976) in the sense of well being which hold across sex, age, and education levels. Among the most important were the following: increased worry and readiness to admit having problems in 1976; increased experience of independence as a source of happiness; community, national, and world problems as a more common source of unhappiness; and jobs as a source of worry. We found other trends: slight decreases in happiness and morale about the future; decreased reference to the self as a source of unhappiness and a corresponding increase in reference to the self as a source of happiness.

These changes over the twenty years are independent of the obvious increase in people's educational level and changes in the age distribution which occurred in the same time period. We often find education and age main effects occurring at the same time that we get universal changes between 1957 and 1976. This gives rise to the assumption that shifts in feelings of well being, (for example, increase in worries, decrease in being "very happy," decrease in morale) are a function of specific historical changes independent of changes in demographic characteristics of the American population that have occurred during the same time span. People obviously respond to the issues of the 1960s and 1970s, such as role transitions for women, environmental problems, or fluctuations in the economy. These uncertainties are reflected in greater concern about community and international issues, greater concern about job problems and self-realization, and less concern about material problems. The generational shift from concerns about health to more interpersonal matters suggests that we have moved from uncertainties about physical well being to more concern about psychological aspects of our lives.

Sample Questions on Well-Being

Everybody has some things he worries about more or less. What kinds of things do you worry about most?

Do you worry about such things a lot, or not very much?

Now I'd like you to think about your whole life—how things are now, how they were ten years ago, how they were when you were a little (boy/girl). What do you think of as the happiest time of your life?

How about the way things are today—what are some of the things you feel pretty happy about these days?

Everyone has things about their life they're not completely happy about. What are some of the things that you're not too happy about these days? (PROBE FOR FULL RESPONSES.)

Taking things all together, how would you say things are these days— would you say you're *very happy, pretty happy,* or *not too happy* these days?

Compared to your life today, how do you think things will be five or ten years from now—do you think things will be happier for you than they are now, not quite as happy, or what?

We were impressed with how few interactions by survey year occur in analyses of well being over the generation. Only the following important results indicate changes in the *pattern* of well being between 1957 and 1976: In 1976, worries are more prominent in the young compared to other groups; the college educated young in 1976 are especially likely to say that childhood was the most unhappy period of their lives; in 1957 young people mentioned children as a source of happiness more than any other age group. Both worrying and expressing happiness about children are especially characteristic of the middle aged in 1976. When we control for parent status, however, the last two results are less clear cut and seem to be a function of the higher proportion of nonparents among the young in 1976.

The press to advance women's status in American society seems to have had only minimal effect on the differential well being of men and women. Women and men still approach issues of well being differently, with women consistently more negative than men in their assessments. This consistent difference in attitude between men and women is one of our most important findings. We see it as reflecting women's greater intraceptiveness as well as the more interdependent nature of their lives. The influence of education on well being persists over the generation. Our results suggest that the better educated, though more likely than the less educated to seek professional help, perceive themselves as well off in most measures of well being. In examining particular qualities of experience, the better educated focus on personal aspects of happiness and unhappiness and causes of worry, while the less educated focus more on economics and specific role requirements. The least educated (grade school) emphasize basic issues of survival, perhaps even more strongly than in 1957, as fewer and fewer people have such minimal education.

Life-cycle factors structure experiences of happiness, unhappiness, and worry. Further, most life-cycle differences are parallel in 1957 and 1976. We found little evidence of cohort effects. Regardless of year, we find strong differences in the way young, middle-aged, and older people experience the quality of their lives, their evaluations of well being, and sources of gratification and frustration. Older people are clearly less happy than middle aged or young people, though the pattern of differences varies for men and women. Older people do not view their past lives as having overwhelmed them at any point, either by causing nervous breakdown or confronting them with ill fortune. They evaluate the past in very different terms than younger people who see their past as a source of distress and see the present and future as times for recouping, maintaining, and securing happiness. Older people do not anticipate the future as a better or happier time. Their life is here and now or in the past. Middle-aged people are particularly sensitive to current experience as rich and interesting.

Perceptions of Self

Pressure for intraception in an increasingly educated population has encouraged stronger, more differentiated self-perceptions. Most changes over the generation indicate positive effects on self-perception. Many more people take a positive view of the self and are sensitive to psychological aspects of their strengths and qualities. One can think of these changes as reflecting a more integrated identity, a stronger sense of the self as a unique being with individuated ways of responding to the world. Whereas we were as a people somewhat more bound and defined by social roles in 1957, we seem to have moved toward a more personalized self-consciousness in 1976.

Sex differences were not large in either era. We found some slight evidence of muting of sex differences between 1957 and 1976. Age roles continue to affect people's view of themselves, not so much in specific role terms, but in the aspects of life experience integrated at different stages in the life cycle. Older people are less concerned than young people about affiliative issues and more concerned about the moral side of life. Middle-aged people are very aware of role achievements.

SELF-PERCEPTION: Sample Questions

People are the same in many ways, but no two people are exactly alike. What are some of the ways in which you're different from most other people?

Many people when they think about their children, would like them to be different from themselves in some ways. If you had a (son/daughter— SAME SEX AS R), how would you like (him/her) to be different from you?

How about your good points? What would you say were your strongest points?

Educated people in our society are now less concerned than they were in 1957 about social aspects of identity. In 1976, the college educated in particular were less likely to see themselves needing social power or social acceptance than they were in 1957. These results suggest that as the more educated develop individuated, personalized integrations, they also turn away from social relationships as the base of self-definition. These changes may have some negative consequences, but these do not emerge in measures of self-esteem in our study. College-educated respondents tend to be somewhat more ambivalent in their self-presentations, as well as more positive. This ambivalence may perhaps stem from turning too much to the self as a measure of adjustment and turning away from rewards available through roles. Thus, we see growing self-differentiation imposing certain costs. Nevertheless, our data suggest that, in the main, in 1976 people held more integrated concepts of themselves and of their strengths and weaknesses, than did the population in 1957.

The Marriage Role

A dramatic change occurred between 1957 and 1976 in men's and women's tolerance of the idea of a young person choosing not to marry. This loosening of the requirement of marriage to achieve valid adulthood undoubtedly has had and will continue to have profound effects on other reactions to marriage. The number of divorced people who do not remarry has clearly increased. Divorce has become more acceptable as an alternative to a bad marriage. In 1976, married people view divorce as a solution to problems, though husbands continue to feel somewhat better about their own marriages than wives do and are less positive about divorce than women are.

The increased understanding that marriage can be restrictive or negative in its consequences does not mean that Americans in 1976 felt that marriage was unimportant in their lives. Indeed, with parenthood, marriage was generally held to be more significant than either work or leisure pursuits. Reports of marital happiness and unhappiness are more critical than any other factor in accounting for overall well being. Thus, while Americans have become increasingly aware and tolerant of alternatives to marriage, they have not lost sight of the psychological importance of marriage.

Indeed, the fact that divorce has become more available as an alternative, helps to account for the finding that marriages were judged happier in 1976 than they were in 1957. Unhappy marriages dissolve more often now, leaving only the reasonably happy ones intact to be judged. Most people see their marriages as happy. Not that Americans in 1976 did not see problems in married life: we note a substantial increase in recognition of problems, especially in relationships. But our 1976 measures suggest that while married people recognize con-

---

MARRIAGE: Sample Questions

Now I'd like to ask you some questions about marriage:

First thinking about a (man's/woman's—SAME SEX AS RESPONDENT) life. How is a (man's/woman's—SAME SEX AS RESPONDENT) life changed by being married? (PROBE FOR FEELINGS.)

Suppose all you knew about a (man/woman—SAME SEX AS RESPONDENT) was that (he/she) didn't want to get married. What would you guess (he/she) was like? (PROBE FOR FULL RESPONSES.)

We've talked a little about marriage in general. Now, thinking about your own marriage, what would you say are the nicest things about it? (PROBE: Anything else?)

Every marriage has its good points and bad points. What things about your marriage are not quite as nice as you would like them to be? (PROBE FOR FULL RESPONSES.)

Taking things all together, how would you describe your marriage— would you say your marriage was *very happy, a little happier than average, just about average,* or *not too happy*?

Even in cases where married people are happy there have often been times in the past when they weren't too happy—when they had problems getting along with each other. Has this ever been true for you?

Many (men/women—SAME SEX AS RESPONDENT) feel that they're not as good (husbands/wives) as they would like to be. Have you ever felt this way? What kinds of things make you feel this way?

flict and resentments, experience tension about sexual issues, failures in understanding, such problems are neither frequent nor corrosive in most marriages. Marriage was seen as equitable for both partners by 85 percent of American husbands and wives.

Sex, age, and education differences in marital reactions generally persist across the generation. Comparisons of men and women speak much more to their similarities than to their differences, although some findings point to greater marital satisfaction among husbands than among wives. In the 1976 measures, this was most clearly high-lighted in wives' more frequent experience of irritation and resent-ment. Older couples continue to have fewer problems and conflicts but also, as 1976 measures showed, an accompanying reduction in ex-changes of physical affection with age. As couples get older they seem to reduce the intensity of their relationships, perhaps reflecting both diminished sexuality and the reduced requirements, as men and wom-en no longer struggle with childrearing or juggle family and work roles.

Education differences in marital well being are clear and strong. Compared to their less educated counterparts, highly educated hus-bands and wives evaluate most aspects of their marriages positively. At the same time, they are less likely to deny the existence of prob-lems in marriage. Thus, we find the more educated in our society more actively engaged in the interpersonal accommodations of marriage and more often enhancing the quality of their marriages. The mar-riages of the less educated may be in double jeopardy. Their lack of education often bars them from jobs and money which might contrib-ute to marital well being, and also often bars them from interpersonal and psychological understandings that can enliven and enrich marital interaction.

Parenthood

Complex changes in norms followed in the wake of universal access to cheap and effective birth control. Among the momentous changes which occurred were a re-evaluation of traditional family forms and viewing of marriage, conception, and child birth as *choices* to be made among alternatives, options to be weighed and balanced against other possible life choices. While earlier generations took marriage and par-enthood for granted as necessary parts of adulthood, such unconsid-ered assumptions now gave way to processes of choice, deliberation, and decision. Once parenthood is viewed as a choice, the experience is compared to the outcomes of other possible choices and some metric (personal satisfaction, cost-benefit, and so forth) must be found on which alternative outcomes can be scaled.

At the same time that strong pronatal norms were breaking up, secularization of the culture and dilution of traditional authority contributed to a change in attitudes toward child raising. While earlier generations stressed role aspects of parenthood and drew sharp lines between the roles of parent and child, later generations adopted the more psychological, interpersonal orientation urged by child-raising experts in which warm interpersonal interaction, empathy, and caring (rather than clear differentiation of authority and power between parent and child) were seen as the medium for insuring effective socialization.

Parents in 1976 stressed relational, interpersonal aspects of parenthood more than their counterparts in 1957. Those parents most actively and closely involved in the work of daily parenting, most directly in "the thick" of parenthood (women, young parents, fathers who are in the family rather than separated or divorced) stressed relational aspects of the role, particularly when referring to problems and insecurities in the role. Older parents, at a stage in life where they can see the results of their parenting, alluded to the interpersonal pleasures and satisfactions of parenthood but phrased problems and inadequacies more often as problems of material resources rather than as interpersonal problems. We interpret these age findings as reflecting both the stringent economic conditions many older parents confronted when their children's economic needs were largest and also some tendency

---

PARENTHOOD: Sample Questions

And now I'd like to ask you some questions about children:

First, thinking about a (man's/woman's—SAME SEX AS RESPONDENT) life, how is a (man's/woman's—SAME SEX AS RESPONDENT) life changed by having children? (PROBE FOR FEELINGS.)

What would you say is the nicest thing about having children? (PROBE FOR FULL RESPONSES.)

How do you feel about couples who decide to have no children at all?

Most parents have had some problems in raising their children. What are the main problems you've had in raising your child(ren)? (PROBE FOR FULL RESPONSES.)

Many (men/women—SAME SEX AS RESPONDENT) feel that they're not as good (fathers/mothers—SAME SEX AS RESPONDENT) as they would like to be. Have you ever felt this way?

on the part of older people to distance themselves from the intense emotional and interpersonal problems of parenthood.

In 1976, women also alluded more frequently to problems of supporting and providing for children—more than they did in 1957. Since this increase runs counter to the change for men and the general trends in our data which reflect a lessening of economic worries, we suggest that in this case the increased economic/material concern shown by mothers may be a reflection of the larger number of women who are raising children in single-parent households. Comparison of mothers who are divorced and separated with those who are married lends support to this interpretation.

Men in our society appear to find close interpersonal relations with their children especially problematic. They less often point to this aspect of the role as "the nicest thing" about parenthood and speak more often of lack of closeness with their children as a problem they have encountered or a source of feelings of inadequacy about their performance as parents. Since 1957, parenthood seems to have increased as a source of relationship strain for men—more so than for women. We see this differential change as reflecting the loss of authority which fathers in particular have experienced.

We find one exception to this erosion of men's parental authority from 1957 to 1976: divorced fathers now seem more involved with their children, more concerned about their personal relationship with them, and less concerned about their capacity to command respect than in our previous study. Nevertheless, even if divorced fathers are closer to their children than they once were, they are still very concerned about affiliative issues in parenting.

The Work Role

Results describing year, age, sex, and educational differences in work salience and job reactions are straightforward. Men and women's involvement with individual accomplishment in work has increased over the generation, but their involvement with the intrinsic interest of work and its affiliative rewards have decreased. These and the distinctly greater commitment of women to work in 1976 are the critical differences between our findings in 1957 and 1976.

Several consistent differences between younger and older respondents' reactions to work occur. The pattern of results helps us answer the following questions: How do people adapt to their work setting? How do they adjust their aspirations? How does involvement in work situations come to reflect aspirations? Quite clearly, younger workers are more distressed in their work, more aware of their own shortcomings, and more sensitive to difficulties. The young seek greater gratification from their work life. In contrast, older people are more often locked into a work to which they have already adapted and hence tend to make the best of what they have.

WORK: Sample Questions

Taking into consideration all the things about your job, how satisfied or dissatisfied are you with it?

What things do you particularly like about the job?

What things don't you like about the job?

If you didn't have to work to make a living, do you think you would work anyway?

How much does your job allow you to make a lot of decisions on your own? Would you say *a lot, somewhat, a little,* or *not at all?*

How much *ability* do you think it takes to do a really good job at the kind of work you do?

How good would you say you are at doing this kind of work—would you say you were *very good, a little better than average, just average,* or *not very good?*

Our results suggest that the power of work adaptation is profound. There is some indication that older people in the current generation are more aware of dissatisfactions at work, reflecting perhaps a phasing out of the work role and a new commitment to leisure, influenced by an increased cultural emphasis on retirement.

Profound differences between the college educated and the less educated in their reactions to work also yield insights about the questions raised. Probably all people in our society hope work will serve to fulfill their desires for interesting and exciting experience. But the college educated are perhaps especially likely to view work in this way, to reflect upon work experiences, and to savor them. The more educated may also be more ego involved in work satisfaction or dissatisfaction because they have been socialized to expect *highly personal* expression in work.

Sex differences in certain stereotypic reports of job satisfactions and dissatisfactions (men are more oriented to power, achievement, and economic matters, and women more to affiliation) are not particularly surprising, but nevertheless significant because they derive from national survey data. These differences suggest that men and women adapt to work settings in different and characteristic ways. Perhaps the most surprising of all our results is the finding that men are *less* ego involved in work than women. This is striking in light of interpretations that assume work to be more self-defining for men.

At the heart of this apparent discrepancy, of course, is our broader definition of ego involvement, conceived as *any* aspect of work which clearly engages the sense of self. Having no special bias in using only achievement or power aspects of work to define "ego involvement," we included affiliative pleasure from work in our definition of ego involvement, and women are much more involved in the social fabric of work. Women are well aware of the fact that work allows them to achieve a better adaptation to the larger social order than does staying at home with children and/or being a housewife. Demoralization frequently accompanies the housewife role, because in modern society we seem to overvalue performance in the job arena. This recognition, if anything, makes women *more* ego involved in being in the work setting, in spite of the fact that they are usually assigned to lower status jobs. Men rather routinely accept the fact that their place is in the work setting, and hence are perhaps somewhat less ego involved in work once they are there.

Men are perhaps increasingly learning about the affiliative nature of work. One of the most important differences in expressed satisfactions in work across the generation is that men as well as women are more uncertain about affiliative relationships in the job setting. Men's increasing attention to affiliative aspects of work may foreshadow a critical new psychological adaptation to work in the future, one that may foster a true egalitarian exchange between men and women as they teach one another the joys of individuation *and* communion in the workplace.

Symptoms of Stress

Analysis of the symptoms checklist for both the 1957 and 1976 surveys underscores a thesis offered in *Americans View Their Mental Health*, which, however, went unheeded in ensuing efforts to utilize symptoms in diagnosing mental health "problems": mental health is multidimensional, and adequate assessment of it must be based on multiple measures. We have isolated three factors that clarify some of these dimensions: ill health, psychological anxiety, and immobilization. These dimensions are replicated in four factor analyses done separately for men and women's symptoms reported in 1956 and in 1976. Depending on which dimension is examined, we emerge with different portrayals

SYMPTOMS OF STRESS: Sample Questions

How often have you had the following?:	NEARLY ALL THE TIME	PRETTY OFTEN	NOT VERY MUCH	NEVER
Do you ever have any trouble getting to sleep or staying asleep?				
Have you ever been bothered by nervousness, feeling fidgety and tense?				
Are you troubled by headaches or pains in the head?				
Do you have loss of appetite?				
How often are you bothered by having an upset stomach?				
Do you find it difficult to get up in the morning?				

How often have you had the following:	MANY TIMES	SOME-TIMES	HARDLY EVER	NEVER
When you feel worried, tense or nervous, do you ever drink alcoholic beverages to help you handle things?				
Have there ever been problems between you and anyone in your family (spouse, parent, child, or other close relative) because you drank alcoholic beverages?				
When you feel worried, tense or nervous, do you ever take medicines or drugs to help you handle things?				

Have you ever felt that you were going to have a nervous breakdown?

of which group experienced greater distress. Generally, 1976 respondents are higher than the 1957 respondents in ill health and psychological anxiety but not in immobilization. The same pattern holds for sex and education comparisons: women and the less educated are higher in ill health and psychological anxiety but not in immobilization. While older people are clearly higher in ill health symptoms than younger people, they are lower in immobilization symptoms and no different in psychological anxiety symptoms. Young people in 1976 have increased in psychological anxiety relative to young people in 1957.

The additional 1976 symptom items dealing with substance-use further underscore the need for different measures: men use alcohol for tension release, and find that drinking causes family problems more often than it does for women; women use medicine or drugs to relieve tension more frequently than men do. Drinking to relieve tension is primarily a symptom of the middle aged and more educated. While the less-educated and older people are more likely than younger people to use medicine or drugs, this is largely attributable to the greater frequency of physical health problems among the uneducated and older groups.

Social Correlates of Subjective Mental Health

The three characteristics systematically analyzed throughout Book 1—sex, age, and education—clearly are vital factors differentiating people's subjective mental health.

Sex differences on many measures suggest that women experience considerably more strain in their lives, although there are no large sex differences in measures of morale or self-esteem. These findings can be interpreted as showing both that men are more reticent about voicing complaints about their lives, and that the major role assignments of women to parenting and men to work carry with them different degrees of vulnerability.

A number of features of subjective life characterize the way different age groups view their mental health. Younger men and women quite naturally look to different gratification and frustration in accounting for their inner life and have different time perspectives in making their evaluations. Younger people experience more strain, while older people are more adapted to what life holds for them. In this sense, younger people are more distressed, but, in another sense, they are more open to change and more optimistic about change in the future.

Education differences in subjective well being are very powerful.

The more educated clearly have more resources for well being; the less educated experience greater demoralization. People with different educational attainments also focus on different facets of well being: the least educated, on health and economic issues; the moderately educated, on family roles; the most educated, on their jobs, their communities, and issues of self-fulfillment.

Integrating Themes

We tried in Book 1 to bring into focus certain themes that appeared in various areas of the analysis. These were conclusions and predictions developed in the course of analysis which arose again and again as we reviewed findings in many areas of the studies. For the present volume, we shall restate these themes: What has changed in our experiences and outlook on our lives? And what has remained stable?

CRITICAL CHANGES

We noted three critical changes in the psychological adjustments of Americans from 1957 to 1976. In more detailed discussions in Book 1, we present support for each systematically, some results that are very striking and some that show smaller differences but nevertheless add weight to our generalizations. These three themes are listed and only briefly amplified here.

Increased Concern About an Uncertain Future

A number of results suggest that there has been a generational shift in the degree to which people feel they can rely on the future as a time to expect improvement or at least stability in their lot. The most profound consequences of this uncertainty occur in young people, who have a longer future at stake, more of their future depending on commitments they make in their present lives.

The Movement from Social to Personal Integrations of Well Being

We were struck by an important change in the responses of the new generation: there has been a shift from a *socially* integrative paradigm for structuring well being to a more *personal* or *individuated* paradigm for structuring and judging well being. We see the 1957 population taking much more comfort in culture and the 1976 population gathering strength more from their own more personalized adaptations to the world. We see this theme in three types of changes that have occurred in people's responses to questions about their well being and

coping styles: (1) the diminution of role standards as the basis for defining adjustment; (2) increased focus on self-expression and self-di-
rection in life; and (3) a shift in concern from organizational to interpersonal integration.

An Increase in the Psychological Approach to Understanding One's Own
Behavior

It is clear from data in Book 1 that men and women have become
much more psychologically oriented in their thinking about themselves and their lives. The most dramatic findings illustrating this
come from two sources: the increase in formal help-seeking, which we
will see vividly in this volume and the decrease in the denial of problems in one's life roles. We do not interpret the latter to mean that the
problem nature of these roles has necessarily increased, but that *denial*
of problems was more common in 1957. Sensitization to problems often reflects an increased psychological orientation to the context of
problems.

COHORT EFFECTS

While we examined social change we were sensitive to the fact that
what we see as change might very well be a result of the movement of
cohorts through time, as well as the introduction of a different birth
cohort. Some changes observed may be the result of the diminished
ranks of the older cohort in the earlier study and/or the introduction
of a new cohort in 1976, rather than changes within people moving
through time over the generation. Analyses were examined for such
potential cohort effects. The themes we have just discussed apply to all
of the birth cohorts examined and represent general cultural shifts
rather than changes specific to one or two cohorts.

There are, however, some results which are perhaps better interpreted as cohort phenomena rather than as general cultural change. Two
of these results have to do with help-seeking; another has to do with
people's orientation toward children; the fourth, with people's orientation toward marriage; the last, with women's orientation toward
work.

Most important for this volume is the fact that young people in 1957
who became the middle-aged people in 1976 and middle-aged people
in 1957 who became the older people in 1976 were relatively constant
in their use of informal help for handling worries and unhappiness.
That is, if we examine the percentage of people who turn to friends
and family in periods of unhappiness or worry, we find percentages
constant in cohorts who were young in 1957 (and middle aged in
1976), and those who were middle aged in 1957 (and old in 1976). This
suggests that help-seeking orientations may remain relatively constant
as coping styles. Why then did we find such a remarkable shift in

overall population comparisons? Probably because the general cultural shift toward interpersonal sharing as a way to seek support for difficulties was especially consonant for the very youngest groups in the new generation and was especially dissonant for the much older groups in 1957 who were fewer in numbers in 1976. Though we obviously have a cultural shift in the view of informal support as a way to cope with problems, we thus also have evidence of some consistency in people's coping styles once they adopt them during their youth.

With regard to formal help-seeking, we also find an interesting cohort effect, which will be emphasized further in this volume. People who were middle aged in 1957 were just as likely to seek professional help in 1976 as they were in 1957. In other words, the general cultural shift toward formal help-seeking does not seem to have affected that group of people who were middle aged in 1957 and became the elderly in 1976. They seem to have been immune to the increased cultural dependence on expert guidance for dealing with psychological problems. The young cohorts thus seem to have been most easily socialized to the new norm which encouraged turning to mental health specialists. While we will see a large general change in formal help-seeking, we should remember that the change seems to have affected younger people in particular.

STABILITY IN WELL BEING FROM 1957 TO 1976

Although we emphasized in the first volume measures that differed in 1976 compared to 1957, we were equally impressed with the remarkable consistency in the way men and women responded to questions about their well being in 1957 and 1976. Overall, changes are small and in many instances there is no change at all.

With hindsight we can rationalize this lack of change, but we were initially surprised by it, particularly in certain instances. One of these was the lack of change in men's overall job satisfaction. By and large, people in 1957 and 1976 gave very comparable responses about how satisfied or dissatisfied they were with work. There was also essentially no change in the psychological value of the work role for men.

Another surprising consistency was the relatively stable distribution of responses in both years to questions about inadequacy in the spouse role. We had thought that the increased focus on interpersonal life and the increased difficulties of marriages in American society would have consequences on the confidence people felt about their performance as husbands and wives. This seems not to be the case. Although there was a large increase in perceived problems in marriage, there was no comparable increase in inadequacies experienced in performing the marital role.

Many other measures of subjective well being showed no difference between 1957 and 1976. People's happiness, satisfaction, feelings of competence or incompetence, and self-esteem are perhaps ultimately dependent on what is available at a given point of history. Thus, if there is a greater burden on people to perform a role such as marriage or parenthood in the normative climate of the society, people quickly adapt to that and judge their satisfactions or dissatisfactions relative to other people who are performing within that normative climate. The power of reference group adaptations to norms is especially important in how people evaluate their own self-esteem, their own feelings of happiness and unhappiness.

One might think that there are certain kinds of stresses in our social environments which change so dramatically that they induce problems of adaptation for everyone, and hence induce dramatic changes in psychological strain. Evidently we have not reached a point of stress so extreme that adaptation to reference group perspectives does not occur. Sociohistorically, 1957 was a different context for evaluating well being than was 1976. And it is within those contexts that psychological adjustment occurs.

Chapter 3

SOCIAL SUPPORT FOR CRISIS

HUMAN BEINGS in all societies automatically cope very well with the everyday problems of living. Our social selves have learned rules for behaving appropriately in response to most difficulties we confront. When it gets too cold, we put on more clothes; when too hot, we wear less. When we begin to feel lonely, we seek company; when the world is too much with us, we retreat from it. We even learn to deny problems that we cannot do much about. These rules for coping may vary from society to society, or group to group, as we demonstrated in analyses in Book 1 of how people differing in sex, age, and education respond to distress. Furthermore, our 1957 and 1976 comparison in Book 1 of how people handle worries and periods of unhappiness suggests that these rules may vary over historical periods. In 1957, men and women turned to prayer to help them handle periods of unhappiness much more than they did in 1976. Americans in earlier times were taught to believe in the effectiveness of prayer. It became a way of dealing with problems that was second nature to them. Our institutions were then geared to faith that religion could help solve problems. In contrast, people in more recent generations have become skeptical about the efficacy of seeking divine intervention. Other styles of coping have evolved.

In the analyses in Book 1 of changes in the way Americans cope with personal distress we were impressed with the shift that had occurred from formal ritualized ways of handling difficulties to more informal ways that require more personal initiative. We refer to a general pattern of findings showing that people in 1976 compared to those in 1957 were not only less inclined to utilize prayer as a coping strategy, but also somewhat less dependent on their families in general, and their husbands or wives in particular. The 1976 respondents were less likely to participate in formal organizations and ritualized visits with family or friends, and they were less likely to turn to marriage as an institutionalized social arrangement. They obviously were coping with the vacuum that the absence of these formal situations had created by searching out others (friends, various family members, and professional helpers). They were evolving new, more personalized forms of support.

Informal support-seeking is the dominant mode of coping used by people in the current generation. This will be an important fact to remember as we approach the main topic of this volume—formal help-seeking. Nevertheless, it is also important to keep in mind that this coping style refers to how people handle everyday problems, worries, or very general periods of unhappiness. It is not concerned with what people do during severe crises or after facing long-term serious problems, which are the life situations that most often prompt people to seek professional help. Instead, we enquire here about the informal support systems people in 1976 used to handle their stressful life events—support systems that may have buttressed, augmented, or served as substitute for the professional help people might otherwise have sought for aid with personal problems.

In this chapter we find that Americans' use of family and friends for help in crises is widespread. Many social researchers and theorists have suggested that this kind of social support may be the chief way that people use to adapt to crisis. (Mechanic, 1974; Cobb, 1976; Caplan, 1974; Kahn and Quinn, 1977). There is no clear evidence, however, that social support causally reduces strain or distress (Heller, 1979). Research that links social support to reduced strain may be easily reinterpreted: People whose distress can be easily managed are also people who readily enlist social support. Those who receive social support may be better copers. Nevertheless, the nature of social support during crises, whether or not it actually reduces strain, will be germane to understanding people's ways of coping with problems for which they may eventually seek professional help.

This chapter is devoted primarily to a brief set of analyses of the informal help people use to handle crises. How many people do those seeking help enlist, if any? Do they also seek formal help? Who among the married people depend solely on their wives or husbands? How much of people's support system is family based? To answer these questions, we analyze 1976 data only. We introduced in the 1976 interview questions about support networks—both informal and formal helpers—respondents used the last time a "bad thing" happened to them. (See chapter 2 of Book 1 for analysis of people's evaluation of such stress in their life—how often "bad things" occurred and the specific nature of the last "bad thing.") We will refer to these events as crises. For 1976 respondents only, we derived assessments of styles of social support for help in dealing with a crisis from the following series of questions:

Over their lives most people have something bad happen to them or to someone they love. By that I mean things like getting sick, losing a job, or being in trouble with the police. Or like when someone dies, leaves, or disappoints you. Or maybe just something important you wanted to happen didn't happen. Compared with most other people you know, have things like this happened to you a lot, some, not much, or hardly ever? When things like these happen to you, have there been times when you found it very hard to handle? That is, when you couldn't sleep, or stayed away from people or felt so distressed or nervous that you couldn't do much of anything?

(If yes to previous question) Would you say you felt that many times, or just once in a while?

Now think of the last time you felt that way. What was it about? How long ago did that happen?

(If no to previous question) Now think of the last time something really bad happned to you. What was it about? How long ago did it happen? When things like that happen some people like to talk it over with other people (at this point the respondent was handed a card with a list of people on it which included: husband, wife, son, daughter, father, mother, brother, sister, other relatives or family member, friend, neighbor, coworker). Did you talk to any of *these* people about the matter? For each person choose the one description that fits them best. If more than one person you talked to fits the same description (like a friend or relative), please tell me.

Now how about these people? Did you talk with any of these people about that matter (again a card was handed to the respondent which included the following names: psychiatrist, psychologist, social worker, counselor, doctor, nurse, clergyman, teacher, police, lawyer, other professional). Again for each person choose the one description that fits them best. If more than one person you talked to fits the same description, please tell me.

In this series of questions the respondent listed the people turned to in times of crisis. From the responses, we derived measures of the quality of social support people have available for dealing with life crises. In a future work we will analyze the data about the resources utilized in more detail. In this book, we are particularly interested in the general nature and types of informal and formal resources people use. Five assessments were made: number of informal resources used (from none, to three or more); number of formal resources used (from none, to two or more); pattern of informal and formal resources (both formal and informal resources used, only formal resources used, only informal resources used, neither formal nor informal resources used); spouse mentioned (for married people only); family mentioned. These assessments give us a basis for evaluating the social supports utilized by people in dealing with stressful events.

Social Support: 1976

Table 3.1 brings together major results indicating people's use of social support in 1976 for times of crises. In many ways they confirm findings discussed in Book 1 regarding the distinctive coping styles for worries, periods of unhappiness, and personal problems. Most people rely on some family members or friends for support during crises (only 16 percent say they spoke to *no* family or friends). At the same time they frequently also turn to professional help (42 percent utilized one or more professional helpers for their last crises), but only 3 percent spoke only to a formal helper. People in crises depend on the spouse a great deal (67 percent of the married people mention their spouses), but clearly many mention someone in addition to their husband or wife. Forty-two percent of respondents mention family members as a source of help, and an equal proportion (42 percent) rely only on nonfamily for help. Americans thus depend on a diverse set of helpers for aid in personal crises. From results analyzed in Book 1, we assume that both the variety of informal resources and the combined use of both informal and formal resources have increased.

These are the overall findings. To gain a better understanding of them, we subjected them to multivariate analyses. As in Book 1, we used log-linear cross-classification analyses (Goodman, 1978) taking into account age, education, and sex differences, and interactions of these factors. Since these data were available only in 1976, year differences in multivariate treatments, so important to analyses of coping style in Book 1 and professional help-seeking in this volume, cannot be considered. In place of year effects, we included another variable: whether the person felt overwhelmed or not by the events. The wording of the inquiry about social support was slightly different for people who said they felt overwhelmed by a recent crisis than for people who said they did not. The slightly different contexts for raising the question about social support may have had some bearing on the types of support engaged, and thus we used it as a control variable.

The multivariate treatment in this and subsequent chapters asks essentially, do you need the effects of any of the variables used to cross-classify respondents with respect to a given measure (social support

TABLE 3.1

Support for Times of Crises (1976 only)

	Percentage
Number of Informal Resources	
None	16
One	28
Two	22
Three or more	34
	100%
	(2,116)
Number of Formal Resources	
None	58
One	26
Two or more	16
	100%
	(2,115)
Pattern of Formal/Informal Resources	
Both formal/informal	39
Only formal	3
Only informal	45
Neither formal/informal	13
	100%
	(2,114)
Spouse Mentioned (married only)	
Yes	63
No	37
	100%
	(1,328)
Family Mentioned	
Yes	42
No	58
	100%
	(2,116)

NOTE: Numbers in parentheses are total number of persons who reported experiencing a crisis and responded to the questions about resources.

assessment in the present case) to reproduce observed cell frequencies? Does knowing the sex, age, education, or the degree to which a person felt overwhelmed by crises help predict how many people will appear in a given cross-classification cell? Or, is the knowledge of the general distribution of any of the variables all that you need? Such analyses also permit evaluation of whether the combined effect of two or more variables (interaction) is needed to reproduce the cross-classification. For a further amplification of the procedures (ECTA program for hierarchical log-linear analyses of cross-classification data) see appendix C.

Table 3.2 summarizes the multivariate treatment of the five measures of social support. This summary will be used as a basis for considering sex, age, and education differences.

TABLE 3.2

Summary of Multivariate Analyses of Support for Handling "Bad Things That Happen" (1976 only)

Support for Handling "Bad Things That Happen"	Relationship(s) Required[a] to Reproduce Observed Cross-Classification of Measures by Age × Education × Overwhelmed (yes/no) × Sex				
	Main Effect[b]				Interaction
	Age	Education	Overwhelmed	Sex	
Number of Informal Helpers Sought	Y<MA<O	G<H<C	yes>no	M<F	
Number of Formal Helpers Sought		G<H,C			
Patterns of Formal/Informal					
Both sought		G<H<C			
Formal only	Y>MA>O	G<H<C			
Informal only		G>H>C		M>F	
Neither					
Spouse Sought (married only)	Y<M,O				
Family					

[a] In this and subsequent tables, a listed relationship is "required" in one of two possible senses: (1) any main effect indicated by an entry or any interaction(s) listed, is part of a log-linear hierarchical model (Goodman, 1978), which produces expected frequencies that do not significantly deviate from those actually observed (X^2, $p > .05$); or (2) main effect listed, although contained within a required interaction listed in (1) has a significant effect (lambda, $p < .01$) above and beyond its role in the interactions. The elements of the log-linear hierarchical model listed represent the most parsimonious model over and above a base model, which includes all the two way relationships for the demographic variables (age, education, year, sex), plus all the interactions of these demographic variables.

[b] In this and subsequent tables, entries describe relationships by following designations: for age groups, Y=21 to 34, MA=35 to 54, O=55+; for education groups, G=grade school, H=high school, C=college; for year, 57=1957, 76=1976; for sex, M=men, F=women. Group(s) to the left of the < symbol are less than the group(s) to the right of that symbol; group(s) to the left of the > symbol are greater than the group(s) to the right of that symbol.

SEX DIFFERENCES IN SOCIAL SUPPORT

Multivariate analyses of social support in crisis yielded two significant differences as between men and women.

First, men less frequently engage more than one friend or member of the family in times of crises. Fifty-nine percent of women engage two or more helpers; 50 percent of the men do. Since there are no differences in married men and women's predilections to seek support from each other (61 percent of men talk to their wives; 64 percent of women talk to their husbands), we conclude that some of these results may be due to the fact that men rely solely on their wives more than women do on their husbands. Women talk to more people, and, in doing so, they talk to a more diverse set. We suggest that this may be one major reason why women seek professional help more frequently than men. They talk to more people, are adapted to that general way of coping, and are more likely to be referred to professional resources as a result.

Second, men more often talk to no one about crises—neither formal nor informal helpers. This is true of 18 percent of American men compared to only 10 percent of American women. This pattern was repeated in the responses to two 1976 questions about potential and actual support from friends and relatives:

1. Now think of the friends and relatives you feel free to talk with about your worries and problems or can count on for advice or help—would you say you have *many, several, a few,* or *no* such friends or relatives?

2. How often, if ever, have you talked with friends or relatives about your problems when you were worried or asked them for advice or help—*very often, often, sometimes, rarely,* or *never?*

To the first question, 62 percent of men reported "a few" or "no" friends or relatives they could count on. This was true of 53 percent of women. To the second question, 55 percent of the men say "rarely" or "never" had they talked with friends or relatives about problems or asked for advice or help. This is true of only 33 percent of the women. In identifying admitted isolates, we find that 15 percent of the men and only 7 percent of the women say they had never asked for help or spoken of their problems with friends or relatives.

Men are clearly more isolated in times of crisis than are women; they are also less social in general. In Book 1 we noted that men reported visiting with people less often and were less oriented to people in many of their responses (for example, working women were more likely than working men to mention people as a satisfaction in their work.) Women's affiliativeness thus placed them in a good position to ask for and get help in times of crisis. Men seem to be more isolated in crisis because they spend less time and energy building relationships in everyday life.

These results will be important to keep in mind as we approach the differential readiness for self-referral in men and women, a topic emphasized in chapter 5. Men's greater independence makes them less apt to define problems as requiring help. A large part of the reason that they see their problems as not requiring outside help may be because they tend to keep problems and crises to themselves. They may consult people only when matters get out of hand. Men who seek treatment are likely to be more desperate than are women who do so. More frequent informal talk about crises with friends and family might help men define less severe problems as requiring help and make them as likely as women to seek out professional help at some earlier point.

It is important in this regard to note (table 3.3) that women are more likely to use professional help than men only in those crises identified as interpersonal problems (divorce, a breakup in a relationship) or reactions to death. With regard to external problems (legal issues, money, job, or school difficulties), men are actually more likely than women to seek a formal helper. And, most important, when people identify crises as mental health adjustment problems, men are again more likely than women to seek professional help. We shall find further evidence of this pattern dealt with in chapter 4 among certain groups of men and women.

AGE DIFFERENCES IN SOCIAL SUPPORT

In Book 1 we presented results demonstrating that young people rely more on informal support for their troubles than old people, who more often turn to prayer. Furthermore, older people more often belong to community organizations which provide group support—sup-

TABLE 3.3
Sex Difference in the Consultation of Formal Helpers for Crises (by type of problem, 1976 only)

Type of Problem	Men		Women	
	Number	Percentage	Percentage	Number
External (legal, work, school, money)	184	43	34	129
Interpersonal	154	30	40	308
Death	253	26	36	427
Health	166	70	68	250
Mental Health	37	60	52	52

port that young people may need less, since they have access to help from friends and family.

In many ways results that summarize age group differences in seeking support for handling crises (see table 3.2 and table 3.4) replicate the pattern discovered in Book 1. Young people are more likely than older people to use only informal help for their problems, and within informal help sources, the young are more likely to depend on friends, neighbors, and associates rather than family members. These findings undoubtedly reflect the fact that young adults are in a transitional period between family of origin and family of procreation— when friends are more important. This also reflects the historical shift in family relationships that has occurred in American life—from an extended family system to the nuclear family.

One further significant age difference in support systems for crises situations is indicated in tables 3.2 and 3.4: Young people are less likely than older people to consult a formal help source. While this result may seem to follow from the fact that young people rely heavily on informal helpers, it actually is contrary to results about professional help-seeking for personal problems noted in Book 1 and emphasized in chapter 5 of this volume. That is, young people are oriented to seeking formal help for personal problems. What is the reason for this apparent contradiction? Critically important is the difference between asking about "personal problems" and "crises." We recall that the question under help-seeking discussed in this chapter asked sources of help when "bad things happen." Younger and older people may very well think of very different "bad things" when they answer the question. Therefore, we found it critical to control for the type of crisis for which people sought help. Seventy-five percent of these respondents' crises fell into four major categories: achievement problems (work or

TABLE 3.4

Selected Age Differences in Types of Social Support Used to Cope with Bad Things Happening (1976 only)

	Age					
Measure	20 to 29 (%)	30 to 39 (%)	40 to 49 (%)	50 to 59 (%)	60 to 64 (%)	65+ (%)
Number of Formal Helpers						
None	67	57	55	55	48	58
Pattern of Formal/ Informal Help						
Informal only	55	46	45	41	38	36
Family Sought						
Yes	33	43	45	46	52	42
Total Number	515	435	321	321	152	370

school problems); interpersonal problems (relationship difficulties, marriage problems); health problems; and death of significant others. We used these four distinctions as controls when examining age, sex, and education differences in those seeking help. The multivariate analyses yielded a significant effect involving an interaction of age by type of problem. The data reported in table 3.5 show that the lesser use of formal resources by young people is confined to issues of death and health. Young people less often turn to formal resources for periods in their life when they encounter death of a significant other or a health crisis. Since so many older people talk about these particular crises, overall, young people report less formal help-seeking for "bad things." When the crisis that young and old people mentioned is an achievement problem (such as the loss of a job or some difficulty in setting performance goals) or an interpersonal problem (such as break-up in a relationship), no age difference in the use of formal resources emerge (see table 3.5). In fact, in the age group twenty-one to twenty-nine, only 16 percent said they turned to no formal resources in times of interpersonal crisis. This type of problem may be closer to what people think of when asked about personal problems and help-seeking—the topic of chapter 5.

In light of these findings, we decided to also use multivariate analysis cross-classifying sex, age, and education and type of problem with styles of informal and formal help-seeking for "bad things" that happen (see table 3.5). In this analysis, age remains an important factor but in a complex way. Using only informal resources for dealing with crisis seems to be especially characteristic of younger people when they face death or health problems, a little less distinctive in connection with interpersonal crises, and not at all distinctive for younger people in problems of achievement. Fifty-nine percent of the youngest age groups (twenty-one to twenty-nine) turned only to informal resources in times of death of significant others, while 43 percent of the oldest group talked to only informal resources under these circumstances. Comparable differences appear for *informal* help-seeking about health and interpersonal crises, but in this case it is only the youngest group who differ from all other age groups (see table 3.5). This analysis demonstrates that the general proclivity of younger people to talk their problems over with friends and relatives is partially a function of the kinds of crisis they usually face. Were older people equally concerned with achievement and interpersonal crises, they too might seek informal guidance. This analysis also demonstrates that younger people probably still rely very heavily on parents for support, especially in times of death in the family and health crises. We refer back to Book 1 results for sources of help during periods of unhappiness and recall that younger age groups, as might be expected, do rely more heavily on parents than older people do. When they deal with personal or interpersonal problems, difficulties with parents may be one of

TABLE 3.5

Age Differences in Type of Social Support Used to Cope with Bad Things Happening
(by type of problem, 1976 only)

		Age					
Type of Problem	Type of Social Support	21 to 29 (%)	30 to 39 (%)	40 to 49 (%)	50 to 59 (%)	60 to 64 (%)	65+ (%)
Achievement	0 Formal Sources	71	72	71	83	60	70
	Only informal	58	63	58	67	50	60
		(65)	(43)	(31)	(18)	(10)	(10)
Interpersonal	0 Formal Sources	16	27	29	19	24	24
	Only informal	62	45	47	51	53	46
		(164)	(115)	(58)	(67)	(17)	(41)
Death	0 Formal Sources	71	70	66	73	55	66
	Only informal	59	57	56	52	41	43
		(127)	(112)	(106)	(106)	(64)	(165)
Health	0 Formal Sources	45	26	31	25	13	34
	Only informal	38	26	30	17	10	20
		(65)	(78)	(67)	(81)	(31)	(93)

NOTE: Numbers in parentheses are total number of persons in each group.

the problems. Consultation with professionals may then be more relevant.

EDUCATION DIFFERENCES IN SOCIAL SUPPORT

A major interpretation in Book 1 regarding informal help-seeking was that people of lower status (less education) have less varied resources available for help in time of crisis. This interpretation is further extended in analysis of the number of informal helpers utilized when bad things happen. People of high status mention more than two informal helpers more frequently than people of lower status (see table 3.6). Twenty-six percent of those with grade school education compared to 40 percent of college graduates mentioned more than two helpers to be called upon for support in times of crisis. Conversely, 26 percent of grade-school educated people were unable to call on any helpers at all in times of crisis, and this was true of only 11 percent of college graduates.

The least educated also reported a more limited range of helpers. Grade-school educated people reported using both formal and informal helpers significantly less often than other groups and reported neither kind of help more often (see table 3.6). The grade-school educated are also less likely to mention two or more formal helpers. All of

TABLE 3.6

Selected Education Differences in Types of Social Support Used to Cope with Bad Things Happening (1976 only)

	Education				
Measure	Grade School (%)	Some High School (%)	High School Graduate (%)	Some College (%)	College Graduate (%)
Number of Informal Helpers					
None	26	19	14	14	11
Three or more	26	31	34	40	40
Number of Formal Helpers					
Two or more	10	15	18	17	16
Pattern of Formal/ Informal Help					
Both sought	35	40	38	41	38
Formal only	5	2	4	3	1
Informal only	38	41	47	45	51
Neither	22	17	11	11	10
	100%	100%	100%	100%	100%
Total Number	348	325	716	395	324

these results confirm the general pattern: Less educated people have the least developed support system in times of crises.

These findings are weakened somewhat when we control for the type of problem mentioned. More educated people tended to mention achievement and interpersonal crises proportionately more often than less educated people, who in turn are more likely to mention death of a significant other and health crises. When we control for type of problem, as we did in table 3.7, the education differences in patterns of social support for these crises vary somewhat.

For death and health crises there is a distinct relationship between education and having neither formal nor informal resources available. Twenty-four percent of the grade-school educated people reported having neither formal nor informal resources available for loss by death, while only 14 percent of the college graduates referred to no resources at all. With regard to health, there is a similar pattern: 13 percent of the grade school educated reported having no formal or informal resources for health issues; 2 percent of college graduates had no formal or informal resources in situations involving ill health. A similar but a less definite pattern exists for achievement problems. For interpersonal problems, however, it is much less clear cut.

What about the fact that less educated people are more likely to mention no formal resources to aid them in dealing with difficult situations? Is it true about all types of problems? Table 3.7 shows that it is especially true for people who mention achievement problems. For interpersonal problems, problems rising out of death and problems rising out of health, however, the education groups are very similar.

Thus, our control in cross-classification for types of problem makes an important difference in how much education affects patterns of formal and informal resources used. Although the less educated more often reported no resources at all, either formal or informal, the results are especially striking with regard to achievement related problems. By contrast, the *more* educated referred to *no* formal resources at all much more frequently than the less educated in speaking of health related problems.

Thus we must be sensitive to the fact that different status groups will probably accept the idea of professional help or actually use it depending on the nature of the problem they face. We shall deal with "personal problems" in the next chapter. For these we find many differences in the use of formal helpers among education groups. We should keep in mind when we discuss education differences that these may also reflect differential orientations to seeking help for only certain kinds of problems.

TABLE 3.7

Education Differences in Types of Social Support Used to Cope with Bad Things Happening
(by type of problem)

Type of Problem	Type of Social Support	Education				
		Grade School (%)	Some High School (%)	High School Graduate (%)	Some College (%)	College Graduate (%)
Achievement	0 formal resources	75	84	84	62	68
	Neither formal nor informal resources	42	11	10	4	2
		(12)	(27)	(50)	(48)	(39)
Interpersonal	0 formal resources	64	68	60	67	62
	Neither formal nor informal resources	14	18	10	12	5
		(52)	(68)	(166)	(95)	(81)
Death	0 formal resources	71	68	66	67	66
	Neither formal nor informal resources	24	18	12	14	14
		(143)	(107)	(229)	(111)	(89)
Health	0 formal resources	31	26	30	26	45
	Neither formal nor informal resources	13	7	3	7	2
		(75)	(62)	(148)	(98)	(53)

NOTE: Numbers in parentheses are total number of persons in each group.

SOCIODEMOGRAPHIC FACTORS IN SOCIAL SUPPORT

We selected two measures of social support—number of informal helpers and the pattern of informal/formal helping—for more extensive analyses of potential sociodemographic correlates. In these analyses, the same factors explored in Book 1 for sociodemographic correlates of subjective mental health were again selected. These give us a range of possible effects. We shall test the relationship of social support to: economic position (income); role-statuses (occupation, employment status, marital status, and parental status); geographical environmental factors (region, population density); group identification (race, religion); social background (size of birthplace, father's occupation, broken home background); and social integration (church attendance).[1]

Cross-classification of each of the two measures of social support with each of the aforementioned factors also included classification by sex, age, and education. Thus we tested the effects of these sociodemographic variables independent of sex, age, and education effects. Complicated interactions were detected.

Table 3.8 summarizes major results from these multivariate analyses. For each measure we have checked the demographic or social characteristic for which a significant effect occurs, independent of sex, age, education, and their interactions.[2] For each check there is an abbreviated summary of the nature of the effect. For example, the first effect checked in the first column as a significant main effect is employment status of women under number of informal helpers. It is summarized as "working> all others" indicating that working women have significantly more informal helpers than nonworking women. We should point out that there are a only a few significant interactions. We shall discuss only those which are easily understood and meaningful.

Significant main effects are also tabulated in distributions in tables 3.9 and 3.10. In these and other parallel tables in this book we box findings that we especially highlight in our discussion.

Economic Position

In Book 1, we concluded that the poor have styles of coping with problems that reflect considerable resignation—they pray rather than talk to friends or family members about problems, unlike the more affluent who pray less and talk more. In table 3.8, we also see a result which substantiates this pattern. Among low-income people, there is an especially high proportion who talk to neither formal nor informal

---

[1] For a full discussion of these factors, and how they were assessed, see chapter 8 of Book 1.

[2] An effect is checked if it is needed in the model that best reproduces the contingency table. It is also checked if it is nested in an interaction needed in a model. In the latter case, its net effect must be significant at $p < .01$ by a lambda comparison.

resources about problems. Nearly one out of five of the lowest income people are in this group (see table 3.10). This suggests that among the poor those who do not use professional services are not compensating with informal support.

The poor, however, do not simply have fewer informal supports. The results are more complex than that. Table 3.8 indicates a complex and important interaction: People who have family income discrepant with their educational background—in other words those who are experiencing some status inconsistency—do not have as large support systems for crisis as those who experience status consistency. These results are plotted in table 3.1. Those with grade school education and moderate to high income, those with high school education and either very low or very high income, and those with college education whose incomes are moderate to low, all report smaller support systems than their counterparts whose education and income are consistent. It may be that people with these inconsistent statuses are marginal people. Their reference groups are confused. Their neighborhoods may contain people with whom they feel uncomfortable. For these reasons they may have fewer chances to build extensive support systems. Lack of money per se is not directly connected with the size of support system available. Indeed, one can imagine poor enclaves whose members are very supportive of each other. Carol Stack (1974) discussed such a group of poor black people in Oakland, California. People can exchange services rather than money. Not that all poor people live in such groups. We suspect that many poor people do not live in such enclaves, which would account for the fact that so many poor people report neither formal nor informal support in crisis.

Role Status

Either being employed, married, or a parent has important effects on the nature of people's support systems for crises. These results are summarized in tables 3.8, 3.9, 3.10.

First we note that women who are employed are more likely than full-time housewives and unemployed women to have large social networks for crises (see table 3.9). This is an important finding. It persists whether one considers married women or only mothers. It is clear that employed women have many more opportunities to form bonds of social support than women who do not work. One's circle of friends is enlarged when one goes to work. This larger circle is not only available to the working woman, but the circle of friends is also more likely to be aware when crises occur and to initiate support if the woman herself does not request it. The circle members may also be a critical referral source for formal help.

Secondly, it is clear that married men and women, compared to any of the nonmarried people, are more likely to have a large support system and to use only informal helpers in that support system. Both of

TABLE 3.8

Summary of Multivariate Analyses of Two Measures of Social Support for Crises

| | 1976 Measures | | | |
| Sociodemographic Characteristic | Number of Informal Helpers Used in Last Crisis | | Pattern of Informal/Formal Help Used in Last Crisis | |
	Main Effect	Interaction	Main Effect	Interaction
Economic Position				
Income		(X) with education Income consistent with education = large social network	(X) Low income> Med., High: % neither informal nor formal help	
Role Status				
Employment status	(X) women only: working>all others			
Marital status	(X) married> others> single	(X) with education single grade school educated <all other	(X) married> all others: % only informal divorced>all others: % only formal	(X) with sex
Parental Status	(X) parents> nonparents		(X) parents> nonparents: % using both formal and informal help	
Geographic Social Environment				
Region	(X) Border states <others<Pacific		(X) West North Central, Solid South, Border states>all others: % neither informal nor formal help	
Population Density	(X) rural<others <small city			
Group Identification				
Race				(X) complicated interactions with age
Religion	(X) Baptists<others <Lutherans (Jews see one person>others)			

NOTE: ⊗ indicates that a significant effect exists in the multivariate analysis. The effect is briefly described.

TABLE 3.9

Selected Sociodemographic Comparisons in Number of Informal Helpers Used in Last Crisis

Sociodemographic Characteristic	(N)	Number of Informal Helpers Used in Last Crisis				
		None (%)	One (%)	Two (%)	Three or more (%)	Total (%)
Working Status						
(Women Only)						
Employed	578	12	27	21	40	100
Housewife	482	13	29	24	34	100
Retired	119	24	24	23	29	100
Unemployed	61	15	15	36	34	100
Marital Status						
Married	1,313	14	28	22	36	100
Single	242	19	32	19	30	100
Widowed	300	22	23	23	32	100
Divorced/Separated	259	18	32	19	31	100
Parental Status						
Parents	1,613	15	28	22	35	100
Nonparents	261	24	24	22	30	100
Region						
New England	132	15	26	23	36	100
Middle Atlantic	311	12	31	21	36	100
E. N. Central	383	12	28	24	36	100
W. N. Central	216	22	27	20	35	100
Solid South	546	21	32	18	29	100
Border states	158	24	30	20	26	100
Mountain states	73	10	29	30	31	100
Pacific states	297	12	20	25	43	100
Population Density						
Metropolitan areas	156	14	32	25	29	100
Suburbs	329	12	30	18	39	100
Small cities	441	15	23	22	40	100
Towns	686	18	28	24	30	100
Rural areas	504	19	29	19	33	100
Religion						
Baptists	446	20	33	21	26	100
Methodists	226	21	25	19	35	100
Lutherans	138	17	23	16	44	100
Presbyterians	94	13	20	28	39	100
Fundamentalists	195	12	32	21	35	100
Other Protestants	248	15	22	24	39	100
Catholics	473	15	27	22	36	100
Jews	56	5	47	18	30	100
No preference	207	16	26	26	32	100

TABLE 3.10

*Selected Sociodemographic Comparisons in Patterns of
Formal/Informal Help-Seeking for Last Crisis*

Socio-demographic Characteristic	(N)	Patterns of Help Sought for "Last Crisis"			
		Both Formal or Informal Help Sought (%)	Only Formal Help Sought (%)	Only Informal Help Sought (%)	Neither Formal nor Informal Help Sought (%)
Income, in dollars					
<4,000	280	41	6	35	18	100%
4,000 to 7,999	362	37	3	42	18	100%
8,000 to 9,999	185	33	5	52	10	100%
10,000 to 12,499	226	43	2	40	15	100%
12,500 to 19,999	489	38	2	50	10	100%
20,000 and over	435	39	2	48	11	100%
Marital Status					
Married: Men	615	38	2	44	16	100%
Married: Women	696	38	2	51	9	100%
Single: Men	121	28	0	49	23	100%
Single: Women	121	26	4	60	10	100%
Widowed: Men	43	46	0	19	35	100%
Widowed: Women	257	44	4	36	36	100%
Divorced/Separated: Men	87	37	10	39	14	100%
Divorced/Separated: Women	172	49	6	36	9	100%
Parental Status					
Parents	1,611	42	3	43	12	100%
Nonparents	261	30	5	46	19	100%
Region					
New England	132	38	4	47	11	100%
Middle Atlantic	310	40	2	48	10	100%
E. N. Central	382	45	4	43	8	100%
W. N. Central	215	32	1	76	20	100%
Solid South	546	36	3	43	18	100%
Border states	158	34	5	42	19	100%
Mountain states	73	40	1	51	8	100%
Pacific states	297	42	3	46	9	100%

TABLE 3.11

*Status Consistency (Education-Income) and Percentage Having Large Social
Network[a] For Coping with Last Crisis (among 35 to 54 year olds)*

		Percent Consulting Three or More Informal Helpers when "Last Bad Thing Happened"			
		Status Consistency in Income Compared to Education		Status Inconsistency in Income Compared to Education	
Education	Income Level, in dollars	Percentage	(N)	Percentage	(N)
Grade School	<8,000	30	40		
	>8,000			17	23
High School	>8,000< 20,000	41	194		
	<8,000 (low)			34	67
	>20,000 (high)			32	94
College	>20,000	41	116		
	<20,000			38	88

[a] Consulted three or more informal helpers when last "bad thing" happened.

these findings corroborate our conclusions about the greater overall social support available to married people but it also suggests that nonmarried people might be the greatest users of formal help-seeking. In fact, among divorced people, we find the highest proportion of people who turn only to formal helpers. This is significant. Among single people, however, are many isolates, people who seek out neither formal nor informal resources (see table 3.10). The unmarried often worry that their status leads others to avoid them. And it may. Social contacts for informal support are built most easily by married people. Divorced people may experience some overt avoidance from both family and friends, which may be why we and Callaghan (1978) find that divorced individuals are particularly likely to use formal help as their sole support during crises. The latter result seems to be particularly true for males. Single people are most likely to experience complete lack of support during crises (this is particularly true for uneducated people). Perhaps it is not because the single person is avoided, but because few other people take direct responsibility for the single person, and thus, cannot become aware of emotional crises the single person faces. In passing, it is interesting to note that widows and widowers are not unusual with regard to the presence or absence of social support. Although many turn to neither formal nor informal support, this result is not significant with age and education controls.

Third, parents are more likely than nonparents to have support systems for crises, including both formal and informal helpers. They also clearly have more informal helpers (see tables 3.8, 3.9, and 3.10). Being a parent puts a person automatically in touch with institutions (schools, hospitals, and so forth) that are accessed by nonparents. Friendships among parents develop as result of their children's friendships. In Book 1, we found that parents are more likely to experience strain than nonparents, but without lowered morale. The availability of social support may be the reason that strain is not translated to decreased morale. Undoubtedly, some of parents' interest in formal help comes from difficult relationships or problems with children. It may also be easier to seek out help for a child than for one's self.

Geographic Social Environment

Regional[3] and population density differences in social support exist, although they do not all lend themselves to easy interpretation (see tables 3.8, 3.9, and 3.10). People living in rural areas clearly are more

---

[3] The states in the sample representing each region are as follows: New England (Connecticut, Maine, and Massachusetts); Middle Atlantic (New Jersey, New York, and Pennsylvania); East North Central (Illinois, Indiana, Michigan, Ohio, Wisconsin); West North Central (Iowa, Kansas, Minnesota, Missouri, Nebraska, South Dakota); Solid South (Alabama, Arkansas, Florida, Georgia, Louisiana, Mississippi, North Carolina, South Carolina, Texas, Virginia); Border (Kentucky, Maryland, Oklahoma, Tennessee, Washington, D.C., West Virginia); Mountain (Arizona, Colorado, Idaho, New Mexico, Utah); Pacific (California, Oregon, Washington).

likely than others to say they seek no informal helpers, and for that matter, no formal helpers as well. Rural men and women are apparently more isolated in their crises. This conclusion is based on a significant rural-urban difference in number of informal helpers (table 3.9) as well as very low use of helpers among border state residents, a distinctly rural region, and low use of both informal and formal helpers in rural regions (West North Central, Solid South, and Border states). These latter results appear in table 3.10.

In contrast, the Pacific states and small cities are social environments in which people are especially prone to call upon a number of people for social support during crisis (see table 3.9). In the case of the Pacific States, we suggest as we did in the first volume that the West Coast, and especially California, lead the country in avant-garde ways of dealing with personal issues. Talking over your problems with friends, neighbors, and relatives has become a fashionable style. Visitors to the West Coast are often taken aback by the instant intimacy that is part of the prevailing style and encourages support seeking from many resources when "bad things" happen.

The fact that small cities have a preponderance of people who talk to many others reflects a somewhat different phenomenon. The small city may be the ideal setting for establishing an integrated social support system—neither too small and isolated, as are small towns, rural areas, or suburbs; nor too large, as are metropolitan areas.

These results together suggest that population density in our places of residence, along with the general social environments that characterize the regions of the country we live in may be critical factors in formal help-seeking as well. They are clearly factors affecting informal help. Since different regions and places of different population density undoubtedly have different available facilities for mental health consultation, we may expect that these social environmental variables will be potent factors in people's readiness for self-referral to professional resources. We approach this problem directly in chapter 8 when we consider the relationship of available facilities to people's help-seeking patterns.

Religion

Three religious groups stand out as having special orientations to social support. Baptists are low in number of informal helpers sought in crises; Lutherans are high; and Jews tend to talk to only one informal helper (see table 3.9). Two of these results correspond to other findings about social support discussed in Book 1. First, Baptists include many Southern rural poor, and we may thus interpret their lack of support on bases other than religious identification. Secondly, because Lutherans tend to establish insulated subsocieties in American social life, they have well-established bases for informal group support. Both of these interpretations are discussed in more detail in Book 1.

It is only the greater dependence of Jews on a single support that requires special interpretation in this volume. One can conjecture that this support is the spouse. Among married people who mention only one resource for crises, only the Lutherans compare with Jews in the very high reliance on spouses (81 percent). In general, Jews are more likely (79 percent) than other groups of married people (62 percent) to mention their spouse as a resource. In Book 1, we found among Jews marital happiness to be a factor that brightened an overall gloomy appraisal of well being. We suggest that Jewish husbands and wives provide the support that alleviates that gloom. There may be another explanation. We find Jews to be ready users of professional helpers. If as a group they are prone to use formal help, then consultation with just one person about a crisis may quickly lead to a professional referral instead of to further social support from family members or friends.

The preceding results are the major findings linking sociodemographic characteristics to the two measures of support-seeking for crises, with sex, age, and education as controls. We should point out that various social background characteristics—size of birthplace, father's occupation, and broken home background— had little relationship to the measures. We are led to believe that seeking informal support for crises may come out of people's current social environment rather than out of their past socialization. It is for this reason that we are surprised that church attendance has little effect on measures of social support. Why should not those who attend church more often have more available informal supports for crises? We should remember, however, that church attendance also reflects religious commitment. Indeed, in Book 1 we found that people who attend church frequently are likely to pray when unhappy. We thus suggest that for some people dependence on spiritual guidance for crises may dampen any reliance on people as support in crises. Shared commitment to prayer with other church members may, however, be symbolically very supportive. No words need be exchanged between people when they share a religious faith that strengthens them in adapting to the stresses of life.

Is a Larger Support System Better for Subjective Mental Health than a Smaller One?

From one set of analyses in Book 1, we concluded that the style of seeking support for troubles was not clearly correlated with indicators of subjective mental health, but the trends were mildly affirmative of the value of support for well being. In this volume, we pose a slightly different question: Is an extensive support system better for subjective mental health than a more restricted one? Do people who turn to more rather than fewer people in times of crises experience fewer psychological difficulties?

To answer this question we correlated the measure of social support (number of informal helpers) to five measures of well being discussed fully in Book 1—psychological anxiety (a summary score of reported symptoms of nervousness, tension, and sleeplessness); ill health (a summary score of reported symptoms of general bad health); happiness (responses to a simple question about how things are these days, whether the person is "very happy," "pretty happy," or "not too happy"); self-esteem (a summary score of reported good feelings about oneself, based on questions used by Rosenberg, 1965); and zest (a sum-

TABLE 3.12

Relationship of Number of Informal Resources to Selected Measures of Well Being (1976 only)

		Number of Informal Resources Used in Crisis				
Measure of Well Being	(N)	None (345) %	One (582) %	Two (453) %	Three (326) %	Four or more (389) %
Psychological Anxiety						
Percent very high[a]		16	19	19	17	15
			$X^2{}_{(16)}^b = 18.80$, N.S.[c]			
Ill Health						
Percent very high		18	16	18	15	11
			$X^2{}_{(16)} = 22.40$, N.S.			
Happiness						
Percent not too happy		14	12	13	9	8
			$X^2{}_{(8)} = 11.92$, N.S.			
Self-Esteem						
Percent low		34	36	34	31	27
			$X^2{}_{(8)} = 13.49$, $p < .10$			
Zest						
Percent low		39	37	34	34	30
			$X^2{}_{(8)} = 10.41$, NS			

[a] For simplicity critical comparisons are tabulated in each row of this table.

[b] X^2 is computed on *entire* classification of measure of well being, degrees of freedom in parenthesis indicate levels used.

[c] Not significant.

mary score of reported feelings of involvement with life, feeling useful, and so forth, based on items from the Zung scale of depression,
1965). The results of these correlations are reported in table 3.12; trun-
cated sections of cross-tabulations accentuate critical results.

We have only very weak trends in table 3.12 indicating that there is
little overall connection between the support index and measures of
psychological well being. The most notable result is a slight correlation between low self-esteem and having no informal helpers. Yet this
correlation, along with other slight trends, dissolves when multivariate analyses control for sex, age, and education. There is then little
evidence of a relationship between the number of informal resources
people report using in times of crises and their general subjective
mental health. At least the size of a person's support system and his/
her reports of well being is not correlated very strongly in the national sample.

Summary

Americans use informal help extensively for coping with crisis. More
people use informal helpers than formal helpers. Very few use neither; even fewer use only formal help. Americans' informal helping
systems have a large component of family members but also a compar-
ably large component of nonfamily members. As we approach the
study of formal help-seeking, we are impressed with that fact. Those
who do not seek professional help, do not necessarily go unaided by
others. Further we should remember that in many cases where formal
help is utilized, a set of informal helpers are also consulted and used
for support.

Men are less likely than women to have a wide network of helpers.
Men are more isolated from either informal or formal resources. We
suggest that men may be less prone to seek formal help because they
avoid talking over their crisis with friends and family. If they did call
on informal support more frequently, they might more quickly define
their crises as suitable for professional consultation.

Young people are much more oriented toward using informal help
than are older people. So are the more educated, who have a more
complex and larger support system. In both age and education comparisons, however, controls for type of crisis make an important difference. When the crisis concerns achievement, for example, age differences in support-seeking disappear. When the crisis is about
interpersonal matters, education differences decrease. Nevertheless,
we should remember that younger and more educated people general-

ly have more elaborate networks of informal helpers than do older and less educated people.

Sociodemographic analyses yielded significant findings about social support systems, the more important ones suggesting that people in certain role statuses in the society—having a job, being married, and having children—provide automatic access to support that is less available to people who lack such statuses.

Chapter 4

THE
HYPOTHETICAL
USE OF
PROFESSIONAL
HELP

IN DISCUSSING the way people use formal resources to cope with problems encountered in everyday living, we assume that dramatic changes have taken place during the past two decades. By any standard, the period from 1957 to 1976 has been marked by tremendous growth in support for mental health services, manpower training, research, and education. To the extent that efforts to make mental health services more accessible to all members of society have been successful, their impact should be reflected in our data. And indeed we found that in 1976 more people from all strata of society had sought professional help for personal problems, but some groups had sought help more than others, and it will be of considerable interest to know which ones had done so. Numerous studies conducted over this same period document remarkably persistent relationships between help-

seeking attitudes or behaviors and a broad range of sociocultural variables (see Mechanic, 1975). Therefore, in keeping with a dominant
theme developed throughout this book, this and the following chapter
will present instances of change in formal help-seeking patterns between the two surveys, juxtaposed against stable patterns of help-seeking behavior in certain groups over the generation.

As in 1957, a major objective of the 1976 study was to assess the
distribution of actual and potential use of professional resources, and,
drawing on our replication design, to discover patterns of persistence
and change in those distributions during the past twenty years. In our
1960 monograph, this assessment relied exclusively on the general
concept of "readiness for self-referral"; that is, a person's willingness
to admit the need to seek help for his or her problems (or those of
someone close), as opposed to mere intellectual or hypothetical acceptance of the notion that professional help is an appropriate solution to
personal problems (see Gurin, Veroff, and Feld, 1960, pp. 255–258). In
this volume, we again rely primarily on the conceptualization and
measurement of readiness for self-referral to describe patterns of stability and change in the actual or potential use of formal resources
(chapter 5), but we shall supplement our use of the readiness for self-
referral index with two other kinds of measures: the hypothetical use
of professional help and professional help-seeking for crises.

Although intellectual or hypothetical acceptance of a modern mental health point of view—that difficult personal problems should be
referred to specialized professional sources for treatment—must clearly be distinguished from personal or emotional acceptance, that is,
readiness to look at oneself and some of one's own problems within
such a framework, knowledge about the former is not without value
in a study seeking to assess changes in the potential as well as the
actual use of professional resources. Thus, before we turn to analyses
of changes in the distribution of readiness for self-referral in chapter
5, we shall briefly explore differences in such "intellectual" acceptance of professional help-seeking by examining responses to a question structured around potential use of professional help for a hypothetical personal problem:

Problems often come up in life. Sometimes they're personal problems—
people are very unhappy, or nervous and irritable all the time. Sometimes they're problems in a marriage—a husband and wife just can't get
along with each other. Or, sometimes it's a personal problem with a child
or a job. I'd like to ask you a few questions now about what you think a
person might do to handle problems like this. For instance, let's suppose
you had a lot of personal problems and you're very unhappy all the time.
Let's suppose you've been that way for a long time, and it isn't getting
any better. What do you think you'd do about it?

Spontaneous mention of a formal help source and type of professional help were coded from answers to this question, which also
served as a lead-in question for those that were used to derive the
readiness for self-referral index, described in chapter 5.

A second measure used to supplement the readiness for self-referral
index addresses a somewhat different distinction. The term "personal
problem(s)" when used in a question about professional help-seeking
has for many people the connotation of emotional distress caused by a
personality problem or a problem in interpersonal relationships. An
increasingly popular alternative way of conceptualizing psychological
distress is as "normal" reactions to some external crisis, such as death
or severe illness of a significant person in one's life, something that
happens to a person rather than something that is an outgrowth of
one's own personal malfunctioning. Analyses of the use of formal resources as a response to such externally-caused distress are based on a
series of questions asked in 1976. These are presented in chapter 7.

In this chapter, we shall examine year differences in hypothetical
use of professional help for a personal problem, along with sex, age,
and education differences. None of these analyses was examined in
our 1960 monograph (Gurin, et al.) primarily because a hypothetical
question of the sort posed must always evoke, to some degree, an "intellectual" rather than a "personal" response. As we shall see later,
responses to this question are in fact only slightly related to indicators
of the actual use of formal help. Nevertheless, they are informative
about people's acceptance of professional help as a possible resource
for aid in dealing with mental health problems. Changes in the pattern of responses to this question from 1957 to 1976 may be utilized as
one index of social change in public attitudes toward mental health
problems and mental health professionals.

Year Differences

Year differences in the spontaneous mention of a professional help
source in response to our hypothetical question are presented in table
4.1 and reveal a substantial increase in acceptance of professional help-
seeking over the twenty years. While one-third of the respondents in
1957 mentioned seeking help from a professional as a possible way of
dealing with a hypothetical personal problem, this proportion rose to
almost one-half by 1976. Moreover, the multivariate analyses summarized in table 4.2 indicate that this increase in acceptance of mental
health resources for solving problems is independent of changes in
age and educational level of the population over the same period.

Nevertheless, other data presented in table 4.1 indicate that this in-

TABLE 4.1

Year Differences in Hypothetical Use of Professional Help

Hypothetical Use of Professional Help	Year of Interview			
	1957		1976	
	Net[a] (%)	Gross[b] (%)	Net[a] (%)	Gross[b] (%)
Spontaneous Mention of Professional Help Source (percent yes)	—[c]	33	—[c]	46
Source Mentioned				
Clergy	55		27	
		18		13
Doctor	32		28	
		11		13
Psychiatrist/psychologist	17		22	
		6		10
Marriage counselor	8		4	
		3		2
Other mental health source	7		17	
		2		8
Lawyer	4		1	
		1		<1
Other professional help source	7		26	
		2		12
Total	—[d]	—[d]	—[d]	—[d]
Total Number	819	2,460	1,046	2,264

[a] Percentage base: those mentioning a professional help source.

[b] Percentage base: the total sample.

[c] All respondents mentioned a professional help source.

[d] Columns total more than 100 percent (or more than the percentage mentioning professional help) because some respondents mentioned more than one source.

creased readiness to use professional resources does not apply uniformly to all types of professional help. Note that year differences in the proportions of respondents mentioning each type of help resource are presented in two different ways: (1) the "gross" rate, or the proportion of the total sample and (2) the "net" rate, or the proportion of only those who say they would seek formal help. The "gross" rate assesses the potential readiness of the population at large to use each type of professional help. The "net" rate gives us some indication of the relative readiness to use each type of help source among a more select group, those generally oriented to seeking help.

Though data derived from these two different percentage bases need not always be consistent, in this case they are, with only one exception. Most evident in these comparisons is a general decline from 1957 to 1976 in the mention of clergymen, in conjunction with a slight increase in the mention of psychiatrists and psychologists and a nota-

TABLE 4.2

Summary of Multivariate Analyses of Hypothetical Use of Professional Help

Hypothetical Use and Sources Mentioned	Main Effects[b]				Relationship(s) Required[a] to Reproduce Observed Cross-Classification of Measures by Sex × Age × Education × Year
	Sex	Age	Education	Year	Interactions
Mentioned Professional Help Source Source Mentioned:[c]	M<F	MA>Y>O	G<H<C	57<76	Age × Year
Clergy	—	—	H>G,C	57>76	Sex × Age or Age × Year
Doctor	—	Y,MA<O	G,H,>C	—	Sex × Age × Education, Sex × Age × Year, and Education × Year or Sex × Age × Year and Age × Education × Year
Psychiatrist/psychologist	—	—	G,H<C	—	
Marriage counselor	—	Y>MA>O	—	57>76	
Other mental health source	—	—	G,H<C	57<76	Sex × Age
Lawyer	M>F	Y<MA<O	G>H,C	57>76	Sex × Age or Age × Education
Other professional help source	—	Y,MA>O	G,H<C	57<76	

NOTE: An entry with a — indicates that no significant relationship exists.

[a] See Footnote[a] of Table 3.2 for an explanation of "Required."

[b] See Footnote[b] of Table 3.2 for a description of "Main Effects."

[c] Analyses based on those respondents mentioning a professional help source ("Net" use in Table 4.1).

ble increase in "other mental health sources" (for example, social workers, counselors, "therapists," "someone at the mental health center") and other professional help sources. Most of the latter responses were essentially of the form: "I'd seek professional help" (without specification). Although some of these undoubtedly refer to more "general purpose" professional resources, the term probably serves as an idiom for any of a broad array of mental health professionals. In addition, while the multivariate analyses summarized in table 4.2 suggest that modest year differences in the mention of psychiatrists or psychologists may be accounted for by changes in age or education, the other major results which underlie the apparent shift toward more specialized professional resources in 1976 are largely independent of such demographic changes. The one finding which runs counter to this general increase in the hypothetical use of professional mental health sources is the decline in mention of marriage couselors. This result may be understood by recalling that the 1976 sample had proportionately fewer married respondents. As a result, the hypothetical problem considered by the 1976 sample was less likely to have been structured around marriage. We will have another interpretation of this result in chapter 5, page 87.

Multivariate Analyses: Sex, Age, and Education

Juxtaposed against these general year trends, however, are a number of significant sex, age, and educational differences in the hypothetical use of professional resources. There are also a few complicated interactions, some involving findings that qualify general year differences noted previously.

Consider first differences in the spontaneous mention of professional help. As indicated in table 4.2, all three demographic measures are independently related to the hypothetical use of formal resources. As in 1957, women and the more educated are still more likely than men and the less educated to mention use of professional help as a resource for personal problems. Although the multivariate analysis indicates that middle-aged respondents are those most likely to think of professional help resources and older people least likely, we must qualify this statement because of a significant year by age interaction.

Table 4.3 highlights that interaction, in which we see that the marked year increase in the mention of formal resources which had earlier been noted is evident primarily in comparisons of adults aged thirty-five and over with their counterparts in 1957. Young respondents in 1976 by contrast were only slightly more likely than young adults twenty years earlier to mention a professional help source (46

TABLE 4.3

Age Related to Mentioning a Professional Help Source for
Hypothetical Personal Problems (by year)

	1957		1976	
Age	Number	Percent Mentioning Professional Help Source	Number	Percent Mentioning Professional Help Source
21 to 34	759	42	814	46
35 to 54	1,007	35	698	54
55 and older	682	23	750	40

percent versus 42 percent). As a result, a substantial gap between the young (twenty-one to thirty-four) and old (fifty-five and over) which was evident in 1957 had closed considerably by 1976, when in fact more middle-aged adults mentioned a professional than either the young or old. In conjunction with more detailed age and cohort analyses presented elsewhere (Kulka and Tamir, 1978), these results suggest that cross-sectional age differences in orientation toward the use of formal help in 1976 were less a function of age per se than of the particular historical periods in which various cohorts represented by those age groups were born, raised, and socialized.

Within this broad pattern of differences in orientation toward professional help are a sizeable number of sex, age, and educational differences (many involving complex interactions) in the particular types of formal sources mentioned. We are able to consider only a few of these here. Particularly important are interactions that lead us to qualify any general year trends noted in the previous section.

Most noteworthy among these is the significant age by sex interaction underlying the decreased mention of clergy as a potential source of help. This interaction reflects a disproportionate decrease in the selection of religious counselors by young people in 1976, who were about one-third as likely to mention such sources in 1976 as their age counterparts in 1957. Although in 1957, adults of various ages were about equally likely to suggest the use of clergy, by 1976 young people were significantly less likely to do so than adults thirty-five and over. This disproportionate decline among the young in their orientation toward consulting clergy for help with personal problems is consistent with parallel declines within this group in church attendance and the general use of prayer for coping with periods of worry and unhappiness (described in Book 1). The young in the 1970s clearly did not view the church and the clergy as a major resource for aid in handling problems.

Significant declines in the mention of doctors—the other major "general purpose" help source—are also particularly characteristic of the young, although the interaction in this case is substantially different for men and women. The number of young women who mentioned doctors declined somewhat less than the number of young men who did so. Other age changes by year are also different for the two sexes: older men and middle-aged women decreased in their mention of physicians and middle-aged men and older women increased. The net result is a consistent positive relationship in 1976 between age and mentioning a doctor as a possible source of help for both men and women. No such clear relationship existed in 1957. As in the case of the analysis of the hypothetical use of the clergy, we found in 1976 a crystallization of differences between the old and young in orientation toward doctors. Where age differences were once slight, if they existed at all, there are now clear tendencies for younger people to be the least oriented toward doctors and clergy as potential helpers, and for older people to be the most oriented.

The significant complex interaction (age by education by year) noted for doctors in table 4.2 reflects a parallel trend for differences among educational groups. Although these relationships are age dependent in a complex manner, significant decreases among the college educated in mentioning physicians as appropriate help sources in conjunction with equivalent increases among the grade-school-educated produced in 1976 a distinct negative relationship between education and the mention of doctors, where none had been evident in 1957. Thus, changes over the past two decades have resulted in even more exaggerated age and education differences in the readiness to mention the less specialized professionals—clergy and doctors—as sources of help for personal problems.

In contrast, social status differences in the mention of more specialized mental health professional resources did not change over the two decades. In both 1957 and 1976, college-educated adults were significantly more likely than the noncollege educated to mention a psychiatrist/psychologist or "other" mental health professionals as a potential resource for handling a personal problem.

In summary, our examination of the hypothetical acceptance of the notion that professional help is an appropriate channel for the solution of personal problems revealed a substantial increase in people's acceptance of mental health professional help over the two decades. People are now more willing to accept the view that emotional problems should be referred to more specialized professional resources (mental health specialists) for treatment rather than to more general purpose professional help sources, such as doctors or clergy. Underlying this general trend, however, were some distinct patterns of differential change between 1957 and 1976 among different age and education groups. While there was a reduction of age differences in the general mention of professional resources, there was an increase in age and education differences in mentioning the clergy and the medical profession as potential sources of psychological help. Younger and more educated people have no doubt become even more oriented than they once were to specialized sources of help in dealing with potential problems. The young and more educated in 1976 did not see themselves as turning to a particular type of mental health resource in contrast to their counterparts in 1957. Nevertheless, they are now much more distinctly oriented to mental health helpers in general in lieu of doctors and the clergy.

Taken as a whole, these data clearly imply a substantial shift over the twenty years in the distribution of public attitudes toward the use of professional help and, especially, mental health resources. This will be a useful background for investigating other possible changes in patterns of professional help-seeking over the same period. Recall, however, that intellectual acceptance of the idea that professional help is an appropriate solution for potential emotional problems is hardly synonymous with a willingness to consider going for professional help for actual problems encountered. Fortunately, it is precisely this willingness to utilize professionals to help manage problems in one's own experience that was directly assessed as the readiness for self-referral, to be discussed in chapter 5.

Chapter 5

FORMAL
HELP-SEEKING

AMONG THOSE who felt a need for professional help in 1957, there was clearly a greater access to it for the more affluent and educated members of American society. This was one of the most important conclusions in *Americans View Their Mental Health.* Along with a number of other conclusions compiled by the Joint Commission on Mental Illness and Health in 1960, it supplied the impetus for many programs enacted by Congress in the 1960s and 1970s to make mental health resources more accessible to all people. In particular, community mental health centers were created throughout the country. We, therefore, approach the results presented in this chapter with an understanding that they may be used not only to gauge changes in our acceptance of the mental health movement, but also to evaluate the impact of programs introduced to make mental health resources available to the general population. Our evaluation, however, can only be indirect. We did not ask people directly about community mental health centers or any other program introduced since 1960. Nevertheless, in assessing changes from 1957 to 1976 in the proportion of people who used various professional help sources, we have information that indicates something about the effectiveness of such programs. And, as we shall see, it seems clear that these programs have been effective. Although there are many results in the 1957 to 1976 comparison that might be used by mental health practitioners and social engineers as a basis for introducing new programs or changing old ones, most of the results indirectly affirm the value of what has been done over the past generation to make psychological services more generally available for Americans.

Readiness for Self-Referral

In *Americans View Their Mental Health*, responses about the formal help-seeking process were organized around the concept of *readiness for self-referral*. Although we considered other ways of structuring the information, this orientation seemed as viable for the analysis of change from 1957 to 1976 as it did for 1957 alone. Essentially, it conceives of people as ordering themselves on a continuum of readiness to seek professional help for a personal problem from being extremely accepting to being extremely resistant. This continuum is represented in figure 5.1. Because the continuum summarizes not one but many psychological issues, it is not always clear cut where certain people belong on this continuum. Two intertwined psychological processes especially contribute to some complexity in how ready people are to seek professional help: realizing that one can have the kind of personal problems appropriate for seeking outside help; and realizing that professional helpers, and not friends or family or oneself, are effective and available resources for help. These processes are not always differentiated and indeed they are somewhat intertwined in our designation of people's position along the readiness for self-referral continuum, as indicated in figure 5.1.

Let us briefly outline our ordering of people on the continuum of readiness for self-referral. We consider people who do not think they could ever have a psychological problem relevant for help as being on the resistant side of the readiness dimension. We make a further distinction between those who emphasize an ideological self-help position from those who simply see themselves as capable of managing their own lives. The first group we view as the most resistant of all.

We further assume that the group most ready to accept professional help were those who actually used some professional help; next most ready were those who said they could have used help but for some reason did not; third most ready, those who could imagine themselves needing help even if they had not used help or did not think they could have at some time in the past. The ordering of people on the continuum naturally has potential slippage. For example, some people who used professional help might have been forced into it by circumstances; or, some people who said they could imagine themselves as having a problem for which help would be relevant might be strong self-helpers when problems actually arose. Nevertheless, the general ordering diagrammed in figure 5.1 has a clear logic and remains a

FIGURE 5.1

Schematic Designation of the Readiness for Self-Referral Continuum

Group 1	Group 2	Group 3	Group 4	Group 5
Person *has used* professional help for personal problems	Person sees that he could have used professional help for a personal problem	Person can imagine himself/herself *as potentially having a problem for which professional help would be useful*	Person cannot imagine himself/herself *as potentially having a problem for which professional help would be useful*	Person strongly endorses self-help

Extremely
Accepting
of
Professional Help

Extremely
Resistant
to
Professional Help

psychologically meaningful way to organize our analysis of formal help seeking in the 1957 to 1976 comparisons.

MEASURES

The question assessing potential use of professional help for a hypothetical personal problem served as a frame of reference for the questions assessing the readiness for self-referral. The former defined "personal problems" which was then carried forward in measuring the readiness for self-referral. These hypothetical personal problems were described as: being "very unhappy, or nervous and irritable all the time," a husband and wife not getting along with each other, a problem with a child or a job.

    1. How about you—have you ever gone anywhere like that for advice and help with any personal problems?

    2. (If answered "No" to 1.) Can you think of anything that has happened to you, any problems you have had in the past, where going to someone like this might have helped you in any way?

    3. (If answered "No" to 1 and 2.) Do you think you could ever have a personal problem that got so bad that you might want to go someplace for help—or do you think you could always handle things like that yourself?

In spite of their common frame of reference, however, the question analyzed in the previous chapter and the preceding set of questions clearly address different aspects of people's orientation to the use of professional help. The former asks whether a person would seek professional counsel if he or she had such a problem; the latter asks whether the person has even considered going for professional help as relevant and appropriate for problems actually encountered or can visualize such help-seeking for an actual future problem.

From the answers to these three questions, the index of readiness for self-referral defining the five groups listed in figure 5.1 was derived as follows:

Group 1. *Has used help* (answered "Yes" to question 1). These were people who had actually gone for some kind of professional help at some time in their lives.

Group 2. *Could have used help* (answered "Yes" to question 2). These were people who saw professional help as relevant for some problems they had faced though they did not actually go.

Group 3. *Might need help* (answered "Yes" to question 3). These were people who did not see help as relevant for any problem they had encountered but saw it as something they might possibly need some time in their lives.

Group 4. *Self-help* (answered "No" to question 3 but with no special emphasis on self-help: e.g., "I could handle it myself," "I think I could handle it myself"). These were people who rejected the possibility of ever having a problem that they could not handle with their own resources.

Group 5. *Strong self-help* (answered emphatic "No" to question 3: e.g., I'm sure I could manage my own problems," "I'd never go to anyone for help"). This group is similar to Group 4, but with a clearer emphasis on self-help as an adopted position.

While these questions are more likely to evoke a "personal" response than the question considered in chapter 4, some measurement ambiguities still remain. A projected future situation posed in the question that distinguishes groups 3, 4 and 5, is still a hypothetical question, and thus may evoke defensive responses to some degree.

READINESS FOR SELF-REFERRAL IN 1957 AND 1976

Year differences in the distribution of readiness for self-referral are presented in table 5.1. Overall, as one might anticipate, there was a substantial increase in readiness for self-referral over the twenty-year period from 1957 to 1976. The proportion of the adult population reporting actual use of professional help almost doubled (from 14 percent to 26 percent) and the proportion who felt that they could always handle problems by themselves declined from 44 percent in 1957 to 35 percent in 1976. Moreover, multivariate analyses involving age and education reveal that these increases in self-referral were independent of changes in sample composition for the two survey years.

Although we are impressed with the increase in professional help-seeking, we are equally impressed with the still substantial group of

TABLE 5.1
Distribution of Readiness for Self-Referral,
1957 and 1976

	Year	
Readiness for Self-Referral	1957 (%)	1976 (%)
1. Has used help	14	26
2. Could have used help	9	11
3. Might need help	27	22
4. Self-help	34	29
5. Strong self-help	10	6
6. Not ascertained	6	6
Total	100%	100%
Total Number	2,460	2,264

Americans (35 percent) who resist the idea that they may at some time in their lives be unable to manage life on their own and would have to seek professional counsel.

What styles of adaptation are employed by people who rule out formal help-seeking as a possible means of coping? It is of particular interest because of different explanations that may be offered for rejection of formal help. If we knew that those committed to self-help utilized informal helpers more frequently than other groups, or that they denied their difficulties, or that they independently coped directly with problems, we would be able to interpret their commitment more clearly. We would also be able to locate in these analyses people who are particularly unconnected with both informal and formal support systems.

To assess coping styles, we returned to measures used in Book 1—ways people report handling worries and periods of unhappiness. Are they passive (do nothing), do they pray, do they cope directly (do something about it), seek informal help? These responses are tabulated in table 5.2 separately for people ready for professional help versus those committed to self-help. The tabulation reveals little difference between the groups. Multivariate analyses controlling sex, age, education, and year yield no differences between the two groups. With the control for education an important phenomenon is revealed and tabulated in table 5.3: less educated people are more likely to be passive about periods of unhappiness when they are committed to self-help. This suggests that denial as a method of dealing with troubles may be more common among uneducated people who are opposed to professional help-seeking.

How large was the group who refused both professional help and informal help when they are troubled? Had the size of this group changed at all between 1957 and 1976? The closest we can come to such an estimate for both years is to identify a group of people who were committed to self-help not only in their responses to the question that probed about their willingness to consider professional help but also in their responses to questions about talking over worries. We may call this group the "loners," since they were clearly operating very much on their own. This group was a very small part of the American population in 1957 (10 percent) and even smaller in 1976 (7 percent). Multivariate treatment of these data shows that this difference is significant, accompanied by significant sex, age, and education effects (loners are more likely to be older, men, and grade-school-educated). Any suggestion that our society during this past generation has so developed that people are totally cut off from social connection—

TABLE 5.2

Styles of Adaptation to Worries and Unhappiness Among People Ready for Professional Help and People Committed to Self-Help (by year)

	1957		1976	
Measure	"Ready" for Professional Help	Self-Help Committed	"Ready" for Professional Help	Self-Help Committed
Adaptation to Worries				
Passive	32	36	25	27
Prayer	17	15	13	16
Coping	15	14	16	18
Seek informal help	25	25	38	30
Other	7	5	5	4
Not ascertained; inappropriate	4	5	3	5
	100%	100%	100%	100%
Adaptation to Periods of Unhappiness				
Passive	22	25	22	24
Prayer	33	32	23	25
Coping	7	7	8	7
Seek informal help	21	19	29	27
Other	10	9	14	10
Not ascertained; inappropriate	7	8	4	7
	100%	100%	100%	100%
Total Number	1,372	1,088	1,480	814

TABLE 5.3

Percentage of People Ready for Professional Help and People Committed to Self-Help Who Handle Periods of Unhappiness by Passive Coping

	Percent Passive in Coping with Periods of Unhappiness							
	1957				1976			
Education	"Ready" for Professional Help		Self-Help Committed		"Ready" for Professional Help		Self-Help Committed	
Grade school	19	(406)[a]	25	(396)	21	(191)	27	(189)
High school	22	(674)	25	(511)	20	(709)	22	(404)
College	20	(294)	18	(163)	23	(543)	25	(215)

[a] Numbers in parentheses are the total number for each cell.

either formal or informal—in times of trouble is counterindicated by these data.

Americans have clearly increased their readiness to seek help from professionals. We can ask two critical questions of these global changes in readiness for self-referral: (1) have they occurred uniformly in different groups? and (2) do they reflect different psychological orientations of people who have sought help in the two years? Before we examine these two questions, however, let us briefly compare the readiness index with our measure of the hypothetical use of professional help, as a way to emphasize the distinction between the two measures.

READINESS FOR SELF-REFERRAL AND THE HYPOTHETICAL USE OF
PROFESSIONAL HELP

Table 5.4 reveals a significant, though modest, relationship between readiness for self-referral and the hypothetical use of formal help in both survey years. Respondents who mentioned the use of professional help as a solution to a hypothetical personal problem were more likely to have actually gone for help and more likely to admit that they might need such help in the future than those who did not mention a professional resource for the hypothetical problem. Within this

TABLE 5.4

*Hypothetical Use of Professional Help Related to
Readiness for Self-Referral (by year)*

| | Hypothetical Use of Professional Help | | | |
| | Yes | | No | |
Readiness for Self-Referral	1957 (%)	1976 (%)	1957 (%)	1976 (%)
1. Has used help	19		11	
		33		19
2. Could have used help	9		9	
		12		10
3. Might need help	29		25	
		24		20
4. Self-help	33		35	
		23		35
5. Strong self-help	6		13	
		4		9
6. Not ascertained	4		7	
		4		7
Total	100%	100%	100%	100%
Total Number	819	1,046	1,641	1,218

general trend, however, two more specific patterns are worth noting because they illustrate clearly the inherent tension between intellectual versus personal acceptance of professional help as appropriate for personal problems.

First, the data presented in table 5.4 confirm our basic assumption that a respondent may say that he would seek professional help if he had an emotional problem while feeling that there is no possibility that he ever would actually have such a problem. In fact, more than a quarter of the respondents in both surveys who said they would seek professional help if they had a serious personal problem subsequently rejected the possibility of ever having a problem that they could not handle by themselves. Or, viewed from the opposite perspective, a third or more of the adults who felt that they could always handle such problems by themselves, nevertheless see formal resources as appropriate for such problems. Thus, those endorsing a "self-help" position with regard to personal problems may be thought of as consisting of two distinct subgroups: those who reject the possibility of ever having an unmanageable emotional problem (29 percent and 35 percent in 1957 and 1976, respectively) and those who actively resist the idea of seeking help in principle—a distinction one should keep in mind for subsequent analyses of "self-help" respondents.

Second, having established empirically our basis for distinguishing between intellectual and personal acceptance of professional help-seeking, we are now ready to consider evidence implying that discrepancies between intellectual and personal attitudes in this area may have *diminished* somewhat between 1957 and 1976. Notably, our log-linear analyses reveal a significant interaction by year in the relationship between the hypothetical use of help and readiness for self-referral, such that the relationship between the two was stronger in 1976 than in 1957 when the effects of sex, age, and education are controlled. The essence of this change can be seen in the comparisons between those mentioning a formal help source in response to our hypothetical question in 1957 and their counterparts in 1976. Fewer of them now take a self-help position on the readiness for self-referral index (note boxed area in table 5.4). Thus, by 1976 we see a greater congruence between people's "personal" and "intellectual" responses to the potential use of professional help for an emotional problem. One possible interpretation of this set of results is that there has been a reduction in the stigma attached to recognizing personal problems that might or should be referred to a professional. In 1976, more people perhaps translated their acceptance of professional help for a hypothetical problem into readiness to see their own problems as relevant for help-seeking.

READINESS FOR SELF-REFERRAL AND SUBJECTIVE ADJUSTMENT

In this section, we will examine relationships between readiness for self-referral and the multiple measures of subjective adjustment considered in chapters 2 through 7 in Book 1. As in the 1960 monograph, we are interested in the extent to which different ways of structuring subjective mental health translates into a readiness to rely on professional help resources. Given the particular concern of this volume, we are especially interested in the stability or change in these relationships between 1957 and 1976, and the extent to which they are or are not independent of or contingent on the sex, age, and education of our respondents. As a result, our examination of these data is based primarily on multivariate analyses of these relationships, which incorporate controls for sex, age, education, and year in the manner described in chapter 3.

In these analyses, we shall not be relating the experience of a particular problem or a specific index of distress in any given adjustment area to the actual use of help or readiness to use help for the particular problem represented by that index. Only a handful of people indicating distress on a given measure would have specifically gone for help for the problem indexed by that measure. Thus, when we find in these analyses that a given index of subjective adjustment is related to self-referral, we will regard the result to mean that the general type of distress represented by the index may underly a person's willingness to use or consider using a professional resource for a personal problem.

Because of the great number of adjustment indicators considered in this section, only basic data are summarized here.

General Adjustment

Relationships between readiness for self-referral and various measures of general adjustment are remarkably stable from 1957 to 1976. People who experience high levels of general distress—whether as unhappiness, worrying, nervous breakdown, dissatisfaction, or lack of zest—are especially predisposed to make use of professional help. They have more often actually gone for help and less often adopt a self-help attitude with regard to a future problem than people who do not report high levels of distress. Moreover, the differential relevance for self-referral of different sources of distress is also consistent in both survey years. People whose unhappiness is expressed in terms of problems in interpersonal relationships (unhappiness with marriage, children, family, or nonfamily relationships) are more accepting of professional help for themselves than are people whose unhappiness is seen in more external terms, such as unhappiness over economic and material problems or ill health. Each of these relationships remains when sex, age, and education are controlled, although several manifest interactive effects with one or more of these control variables.

The one relationship which was significantly different in 1976 from 1957 was between self-referral and feelings of an impending nervous breakdown. Essentially, people who in 1976 reported having felt an impending nervous breakdown were much more likely than people who reported such feelings in 1957 to accept the possibility that they might have a problem that would require professional help. This is the only general adjustment indicator that is more strongly related to self-referral in 1976 than in 1957. As we shall see later, this is also the only indicator among all our subjective adjustment measures which is related to use of help by those who defined a problem as relevant for professional help.

In striking contrast with this dearth of interactions by year are a sizeable number involving age. All reflect the same basic pattern: in contrast to younger and older people, middle-aged men and women who experience distress as unhappiness (particularly, unhappiness about relationship problems), dissatisfaction, or lack of zest are especially ready to accept professional help for their personal problems. For example, half of those aged thirty-five to fifty-four in 1976 who reported finding their lives not very satisfying had actually gone for help compared to a third of young respondents and less than 20 percent of older people who had expressed similar dissatisfaction. That feelings of general adjustment appear to have a special relevance for self-referral behavior among middle-age adults may well reflect differences in time perspectives used for evaluating well being by people of different ages, as discussed in chapter 2 of Book 1. That is, to the extent that middle-aged people are more oriented toward the present in evaluating their well being than either the young or old, it is not surprising that these indicators of present well being have somewhat greater relevance for help-seeking than they do for the more future-oriented young or the more retrospective old.

Self-Perceptions

Significant relationships between perceptions of the self and readiness for self-referral suggest that those who are open to appraising themselves are also open to seeking help for personal problems. Although the relationships underlying this theme are relatively weak, they are evident for all the self-percept measures, persist when controls for sex, age, and education are introduced, and are generally consistent in 1957 and 1976. Specifically, people who see themselves as different from others, those who mention strong points, and those who mention shortcomings are all more likely to have sought formal help, while people who do not view themselves as different, as well as those who deny either strong points or shortcomings, are more likely to appear in the "self-help" or "strong self-help" categories. In combination, these results suggest that the most salient factor of self-perception conducive to self-referral may well be the capacity for self-appraisal and introspection. The negative or positive tone of one's self-assessment may be less important.

Consistent with this interpretation are relationships observed with two more direct measures of the positive-negative dimension of self-percepts—degree of self-acceptance and self-esteem (the latter measured in 1976 only). Although a general negative association between degree of self-acceptance and readiness for self-referral is evident (those more positive in their self-percepts are more likely to be "self-help"), within this general trend we find that it is not the respondents coded "negative" but those coded "ambivalent" in self-perceptions who are most open to the use of formal help. Moreover, those with low self-esteem are those least oriented to the use of professional resources, although multivariate analyses reveal that this relationship is significant only for women. Thus, as observed in 1957, "what seems to be important . . . is not a purely negative appraisal, but the ability to 'weigh' the self, to look at the self in a way that encompasses both positive and negative attributes" (Gurin, Veroff, and Feld, 1960, p. 264).

Adjustment in Marriage

Relationships between readiness for self-referral and the several measures of adjustment in marriage are consistent with the pattern discerned previously for measures of general adjustment. That is, people who experience distress in marriage—whether expressed in terms of unhappiness, feelings of inadequacy, the experience of problems, or irritation—appear more open to the use of professional help than those who do not experience such distress. These findings are similar for 1957 and 1976 and, except for the measure of marital happiness, are independent of the influence of sex, age, and education. Among our different indicators of marital distress, only an index of marital harmony (combining Frequency of Chatting and Frequency of Physical Affection, assessed only in 1976) failed to show a relationship with self-referral. A significant interaction observed between education and the measure of marital happiness suggests that marital unhappiness is especially likely to bring grade school-educated people to a professional helper. Among the grade school-educated, those who report being "not too happy" in marriage are almost six times as likely to have sought formal help as the "very happy." This compares to a ratio of about two to one among the more educated.

Do we have any indication from the data that people who structure marital problems in one way or another are more or less ready to seek help for personal problems? Yes, but these results apply primarily to the 1957 respondents, who were more likely to be open to professional help-seeking if they structured what was "not so nice" about their marriage in terms of deficiencies within the marital relationship rather than in terms of situational factors, or their own or their spouse's inadequacies. These results essentially disappeared in 1976, which is curious. We might have assumed the opposite—that more people who saw relationship unhappiness in marriage in 1976 would translate such feelings into problems needing professional help. The fact that it applies only in 1957 suggests the following: when admitting to relationship difficulties was less normative (as it was in 1957), such feelings could easily arouse people's help-seeking propensities; when admitting to these feelings was more normative (as it was in 1976), they could be "lived with," as part of what marriage is all about. Furthermore, a more acceptable route in 1976 for dealing with relationship problems in marriage was divorce. This can, obviously, eliminate any need for marriage counseling. Perhaps this kind of analysis may also explain drop-off in the mention of marriage counselor as a source of help in response to the question about hypothetical personal problems, discussed in chapter 4.

Adjustment in Parenthood

Relationships between readiness for self-referral and adjustment in the parental role parallel those observed with respect to marriage. Although people's attitude toward parenthood bears no relationship to self-referral in either survey year, possibly due to the indirect nature of the question used to assess this construct, both the experience of problems with children and feelings of parental inadequacy reveal clear relationships in both 1957 and 1976 (independent of controls for sex, age, and education), indicating that those experiencing distress in the parental role are more ready to accept the use of formal resources.

With regard to content of parental distress, the results are once again mixed. While content of felt inadequacies shows no significant relationship with readiness in either year, there is a consistent relationship between content of parental problems and self-referral in both surveys. Parents who speak of a relationship problem with a child are much more open to professional help than are parents who structure their parenting problems as issues of finances, physical caretaking, or other external difficulties.

Job Adjustment

Findings indicating the significance of job adjustment for readiness for self-referral are sparse. Of the three indicators of distress in the job role, only one—the experience of work problems—in both survey years bears a consistent relationship with self-referral, which persists when sex, age, and education are controlled. No significant relationship between feelings of inadequacy on the job and self-referral appears in either 1957 or 1976, and an apparent U-shaped relationship between use of help and job satisfaction, evident in 1976 alone, disappears when controls are applied. Similarly, no significant relationships exist between the type of work problem people mention and their help-seeking readiness. Any significant results relating sources of job dissatisfaction to readiness to seek help disappear in the face of controls.

Symptom Patterns

Given the widespread diagnostic use during the past twenty-five years of symptom checklists as devices for estimating the untreated psychiatric disturbance in the community, and thus the need for mental health services (see Tischler, et al., 1975), it would be surprising if the symptom factors delineated in chapter 7 of Book 1 were not related to readiness for self-referral. And, indeed, relationships between readiness for self-referral and each of the symptom measures (including those assessed only in 1976) conform to expectations.

Although in both survey years symptoms of psychological anxiety and immobilization show a somewhat stronger relationship to self-referral than symptoms of ill health, a log-linear analysis examining all three factors in combination (conducted because of the relatively high intercorrelations among these measures, as presented in chapter 7 of Book 1), reveals that each of the relationships is independent of the other two. All three symptom factors bear a strong positive relationship with readiness for self-referral, as do the three additional symptom items added in 1976 to assess the use of alcohol and medicine or drugs to relieve tension and the prevalence of alcohol-related family problems. In each case, those reporting higher levels of distress are more likely to have actually sought professional help than those scoring low on these indicators and are less likely to reject the possibility of ever needing such help in the future.

These results are remarkably stable and clear cut. Multivariate analyses reveal no significant interactions by year; relationships are remarkably similar in 1957 and 1976. Furthermore, no noticeable attenuation of these relationships occurs when sex, age, and education are controlled, and, except for a complex and uninterpretable interaction involving immobilization, there is only one other noteworthy interaction with these three other control variables. Specifically, the relationship between ill health and help-seeking behavior is stronger for high-school educated people than either the grade-school or college educated. Otherwise, the pattern of relationships described here between symptom measures and readiness for self-referral is consistent across various sex-age-education subgroups.

Overall, then, these data provide little support for common assumptions that: (1) psychological symptoms are more relevant to self-referral than symptoms expressed in physical terms; and (2) that a particular type of symptom of distress is differentially related to self-referral among different sex, age, and education groupings.

Summary

From the analysis of relationships between readiness for self-referral and each of the measures of subjective adjustment described in this section, a rather consistent pattern of findings has emerged. Indicators of distress assessed in a variety of ways—general unhappiness, symptoms of physical and psychological strain, the experience of problems or feelings of inadequacy in family roles, and a number of other measures of subjective mental health—are characteristic of people who accept the idea of dealing with personal problems they have experienced or can imagine experiencing by using professional help. There is also some evidence that readiness for self-referral is associated with being introspective about the self and with the tendency to structure unhappiness and difficulties in family roles in interpersonal terms.

There are two important exceptions to these conclusions. First, distress about work is minimally related to readiness for self-referral. Evidently, adaptation to work is a psychological process which if unsuccessful is as likely to stimulate thoughts of self-help as of seeking help from professionals. Indeed one might surmise that people often diagnose their own psychological problems at work as being ones which require that they "get themselves together" or find other work or another job. This option of leaving a job as a solution to a work problem may possibly reduce the association between work distress and readiness for self-referral.

There is a second noteworthy exception to this conclusion. Unlike married people in 1957, husbands and wives who structured marital problems in interpersonal terms in 1976 were no more oriented to help-seeking than those who structured their marital problems in other ways. Our interpretation of the result—that divorce is now seen as a readily available solution to interpersonal troubles in marriage—is not unlike our interpretation of why distress in the job generally does not enlist the readiness for self-reference. When there is a clear option to leave the situation which induces distress, people will often take that alternative and sidestep professional help.

The multivariate analyses controlling for sex, age, education, and year suggest that the connections between readiness for self-referral and both the level of distress experienced and the way distress is structured, are equally applicable to men and women, to different age and education groups, and to different historical eras. Thus, consistent relationships observed here argue that if people from many different backgrounds and life situations are distressed in certain ways or structure their experience of distress in certain ways, there is a fairly universal tendency to accept the idea that personal problems in one's life may require help from some professional.

While analyzing factors underlying the readiness for self-referral, we have indirectly described people who are committed to self-help. If we translate results just enumerated into the reverse—the subjective adjustment of people committed to self-help—we come up with the following description of people who cannot imagine ever using professional help for personal problems that might arise in their lives. Relative to those people who are ready to seek professional help, they are happy in general and in their marriages, optimistic about the future, free of worry and symptoms of anxiety, ill health and immobilization, see few problems in marriage or raising their children, have less frequent feelings of inadequacy in family roles, are more self-accepting of their perceived differences from others, and understand their family problems in impersonal terms. Those who hold emphatic moral positions about self-help are also unable to be introspective about their strengths, weaknesses, or differences from others. All of these results are reflections of significant differences obtained through multivariate analyses controlling for sex, age, education, and year.

There are three equally plausible explanations for such a pattern of findings about people who reject the possibility of professional help: (1) they are well integrated members of our society whose easy adjustment makes it impossible for them to imagine difficulties in their personal lives that might require professional attention; (2) they deny distress; (3) they are particularly unpsychological in their approach to experience. All of these explanations are probably applicable. All are important to bear in mind when we think about this sizeable group who persistently follow the American ideal of making the best out of what life has to offer while confronting difficulties without institutional support.

SOCIAL AND DEMOGRAPHIC DIFFERENCES IN READINESS FOR SELF-REFERRAL

In turning to an examination of relationships between social or demographic characteristics and readiness for self-referral, we now enter a domain in which there has been considerable research activity over the past two decades. As part of a broad and substantial literature on the use of health and welfare services (Aday and Eichhorn, 1972; Andersen, Kravits, and Anderson, 1975; Anderson and Andersen, 1972; McKinlay, 1972; Mechanic, 1976, 1978), behavioral scientists have repeatedly shown that persons seeking help for psychological problems from specific resources or professional resources in general have sociocultural characteristics that differ from those of persons in their respective communities who do not (e.g., Asser, 1978; Brown, 1978; Gourash, 1978; Greenley and Mechanic, 1976a, 1976b; Gurin et al., 1960; Huffine and Craig, 1974; Kadushin, 1969; Kessler, Reuter, and Greenley, 1979; Linn, 1967; Mechanic, 1975; Ryan, 1969; Scheff, 1966). The research literature is rich with studies reporting that one sociodemographic variable or another (for example, sex, age, social class, place of residence) is related to the use of professional help. As Mechanic

(1969a) has noted, however, much of the data linking sociocultural factors to help-seeking behavior is limited because the studies were conducted ten to twenty or more years ago and/or based on small samples unrepresentative of the general population. From this point of view, a relationship between a given sociocultural characteristic and help-seeking observed in the mid-1950s or mid-1960s does not imply the persistence of such a relationship into the 1970s or 1980s. Accordingly, our 1957 and 1976 comparisons of these relationships offer a rare opportunity to assess the stability of the correlations between a broad array of social characteristics and the use of professional help.

We approach these comparisons with certain broad expectations. In Book 1, we examined relationships between several demographic characteristics and selected ways of expressing and defining distress; in the preceding section of this chapter we have described relationships between the measures of distress and self-referral. From these two analyses, one might reasonably expect a greater psychological readiness to use professional help among those subgroups of the population who tend to express their problems in ways which in turn are most highly related to self-referral.

Sex, Age, and Education

From the 1960 volume we knew that people's sex, age, and education were important characteristics underlying their readiness for self-referral in 1957. These findings were so important and powerful, that in the preceding section we routinely applied controls for sex, age, and education to establish the independence of relationships between measures of subjective adjustment and self-referral from these three important social characteristics. Results from the 1976 survey clearly tell us that sex, age, and education continue to be powerful factors in people's readiness for self-referral in 1976 (table 5.5). There are also some changes in these relationships which provide insight into the significance of education and age over the generation. Table 5.5 shows that all three variables are clearly and consistently related to self-referral in both survey years. Women, young people, and the more educated have all more frequently gone for help in the past and less often adopt a self-help position with regard to problems anticipated in the future. Moreover, a multivariate analysis relating each of these factors to self-referral accompanied by year indicates that sex, age, and education are all independently related to the self-referral index.

This same analysis, however, also calls our attention to a significant education by year interaction which specifies a distinct difference between the two surveys in which aspects of self-referral tend to differentiate the higher and lower educational groups. Note in table 5.5 that the relationship between education and having actually sought help is significantly weaker in 1976 than in 1957. That is, as compared to college graduates, the grade-school educated were less than one-third as

TABLE 5.5

Sex, Age, and Education Related to Readiness for Self-Referral (by year)

| | Readiness for Self-Referral | | | | | | | | | | | | | | | |
Social Characteristic	Has Used Help 1957 (%)	Has Used Help 1976 (%)	Could Have Used Help 1957 (%)	Could Have Used Help 1976 (%)	Might Need Help 1957 (%)	Might Need Help 1976 (%)	Self-Help 1957 (%)	Self-Help 1976 (%)	Strong Self-Help 1957 (%)	Strong Self-Help 1976 (%)	Not Ascertained 1957 (%)	Not Ascertained 1976 (%)	Total Percentage 1957	Total Percentage 1976	Total Number 1957	Total Number 1976
Sex																
Male	11	22	7	10	27	22	37	33	12	8	6	5	100	100	1,077	960
Female	17	29	10	11	27	22	32	27	9	5	5	6	100	100	1,383	1,304
Age																
21 to 29	18	28	12	16	31	19	30	28	5	4	4	5	100	100	453	553
30 to 39	17	32	11	15	29	23	31	23	7	4	5	3	100	100	584	463
40 to 49	16	32	7	10	27	23	36	24	10	6	4	5	100	100	515	341
50 to 59	11	26	9	6	27	22	32	31	14	8	7	5	100	100	390	342
60 to 64	5	19	7	7	23	24	40	37	17	9	8	7	100	100	153	166
65+	7	13	7	6	19	21	42	39	15	11	10	4	100	100	353	397
Education																
Grade school	8	16	8	4	25	21	36	40	14	10	9	10	100	100	802	380
Some high school	14	27	10	11	26	21	34	27	10	7	6	9	100	100	511	347
High school graduate	17	26	9	12	27	20	33	31	9	6	5	7	100	100	674	766
Some college	18	29	9	14	33	22	33	27	4	4	3	5	100	100	247	411
College graduate	26	32	10	13	27	26	29	19	5		3	4	100		210	

likely to have sought help in 1957, but half as likely in 1976. In contrast, the gap between these education groups in assuming a self-help stance is wider in 1976 than in 1957. Thus, within the same table, we have evidence for a convergence of these distinctive subgroups of the population with regard to the actual use of help in conjunction with an increased polarization (see Glenn, 1967) of these educational groups with respect to the potential use of formal help. And, in both cases these changes are independent of the general decline in the number of grade-school educated adults in the population during the past twenty years.

To the extent that efforts to extend awareness and availability of mental health sources to all members of our society during the past few decades have been successful (see Rosen, 1977), a reduction of education differences in actual help-seeking between 1957 and 1976 is to be expected. But what of the sharpening of the relationship between education and adopting a self-help position? This is not as readily anticipated. Looking carefully at the boxed percentages in table 5.5, we see a disproportionate increase in self-help orientation among the grade-school educated, and a disproportionate decrease among college graduates. Perhaps these results reflect the general increased isolation of the grade-school educated from those in other educational groups. Having less than a high-school education is, of course, much more uncommon than it was twenty years ago and apparently reflects a degree of marginality not so clearly implied in previous times. Moreover, in the not too distant future there may very well not be anyone left in the adult population who has not been educated beyond grade school, thereby eliminating a major source of resistance to the use of formal resources. It may be, however, that with the gradual elimination of a grade-school-educated class, the difference between the high-school and college educated will become even more pronounced, a forecast which seems at least as tenable from the results considered here.

In contrast, differences in self-referral between men and women and among various age groups are essentially the same in 1976 as they were in 1957. This is also generally consistent with what might be expected from relationships observed earlier between sex and age and measures of subjective adjustment, in that women and younger people are more likely than men and older respondents to experience and/or structure their distress in ways that are relevant for self-referral. They are more psychologically oriented about themselves. In our discussion in Book 1 of sex differences in subjective mental health, we also concluded that women are more vulnerable to strain because they shoulder more emotional responsibility for others than do men.

Although beyond the scope of our discussion here, we have shown elsewhere (Kulka and Tamir, 1978) that underlying the apparent stability of the relationship between age and self-referral across year are some distinctive year by *cohort* interactions. There are some differential shifts over the twenty-year span among age cohorts in their psychological readiness to use help. In the present context, perhaps the most important conclusion from that analysis is that the sets of cross-sectional age differences in self-referral observed here, rather than being a function of maturation or aging per se, are probably a function of the eras in which people were born and lived.

Other Social Characteristics

Table 5.6 presents relationships between readiness for self-referral and the sixteen social characteristics. Thirteen of these were described in detail and examined in chapter 8 of Book 1, including measures of socioeconomic position, geographical social environment, group identification and institutional integration, social background, and role status.[1] Three additional characteristics were selected, especially for our description of sociodemographic differences in self-referral.

One of the variables added was a measure of relative family income (low, middle, high), derived by trichotomizing income distributions in each survey year to produce essentially equal proportions of the 1957 and 1976 samples in each category.[2] By supplementing the constant dollars measure of income used in Book 1 with this alternative income variable, we were able to compare more directly the significance of relative versus absolute earning power for self-referral.

Also added were a measure of how long a respondent had lived in his or her present community (*time in community*), used to assess the influence of geographic mobility on self-referral, and a *region of* birth (*place*) measure, an additional indicator of early childhood background which may also be informatively used to contrast with region of current residence.

As in Book 1, each social and demographic characteristic was first used in a simpler analysis of readiness for self-referral and then in a more complicated analysis. The simpler analysis asked two questions: Is a given social characteristic a significant contributor to the cross-classification of readiness for self-referral, independent of the survey year? and is its relationship significantly different in 1976 compared to 1957? Sometimes a relationship present in one year would be absent in the other; sometimes it would be stronger in one year or the other.

---

[1] The age of youngest child measure shown in table 5.6 represents an elaboration of the simple parental status variable used in Book 1. Parents are further differentiated here according to their approximate stage in the parental life cycle. Following the pattern set in Book 1, this combined measure of parental status and age of youngest child, along with measures of occupation and marital and employment status, is examined separately for men and women in the analysis presented here.

[2] For 1957, relative income brackets were: (1) less than $3,000 (28 percent), (2) $3,000 to $5,999 (42 percent), and (3) $6,000 and over (30 percent). Comparable income brackets for 1976 were: (1) less than $7,000 (27 percent), (2) $7,000 to $17,499 (44 percent), and (3) $17,500 and over (29 percent).

TABLE 5.6

Social and Demographic Characteristics Related to Readiness for Self-Referral (by year)

Social or Demographic Characteristic	Readiness for Self-Referral													Total Percentage		Total Number	
	Has Used Help		Could Have Used Help		Might Need Help		Self-Help		Strong Self-Help		Not Ascertained							
	1957 (%)	1976 (%)	1957 (%)	1976 (%)	1957 (%)	1976 (%)	1957 (%)	1976 (%)	1957 (%)	1976 (%)	1957 (%)	1976 (%)	1957	1976	1957	1976
Income—relative																
Low	11	25	10	9	24	19	35	32	12	8	8	7	100	100	666	578
Middle	14	28	10	12	27	19	35	30	9	7	5	4	100	100	1,002	921
High	18	26	8	11	28	28	31	25	10	5	5	5	100	100	722	608
Income—1976 dollars																
Under 4,000	10	24	10	7	25	21	35	32	11	8	9	8	100	100	407	295
4,000 to 7,999	15	25	9	10	25	17	34	34	12	7	5	7	100	100	549	380
8,000 to 9,999	13	28	10	14	28	18	36	30	8	7	5	3	100	100	389	195
10,000 to 12,499	12	26	12	12	25	20	37	29	8	7	6	4	100	100	323	245
12,500 to 19,999	17	28	8	13	28	22	31	27	10	6	6	4	100	100	536	518
20,000 and over	20	26	6	10	31	28	31	26	9	4	3	6	100	100	186	474

TABLE 5.6 (continued)
Social and Demographic Characteristics Related to Readiness for Self-Referral (by year)

Social or Demographic Characteristic	Has Used Help		Could Have Used Help		Might Need Help		Self-Help		Strong Self-Help		Not Ascertained		Total Percentage		Total Number	
	1957 (%)	1976 (%)	1957 (%)	1976 (%)	1957 (%)	1976 (%)	1957 (%)	1976 (%)	1957 (%)	1976 (%)	1957 (%)	1976 (%)	1957	1976	1957	1976
Occupation (if employed)—men																
Professionals, technicians	20	31	8	8	27	24	35	27	8	5	2	5	100	100	116	132
Managers, administrators, proprietors	9	25	9	12	29	18	35	34	12	5	6	6	100	100	116	122
Clerical workers	13	22	6	14	35	26	28	21	18	12	—	5	100	100	54	42
Sales workers	21	26	6	14	28	18	34	33	4	—	7	9	100	100	53	43
Crafts workers	11	17	7	13	24	20	37	38	12	9	9	3	100	100	211	177
Operatives	9	22	9	8	28	24	38	37	9	6	7	3	100	100	161	119
Service workers	10	15	12	11	28	22	35	32	10	11	5	9	100	100	60	46
Laborers, non-farm	13	18	—	15	32	24	32	34	17	6	6	3	100	100	47	33
Farmers	5	10	6	13	25	16	45	55	14	6	5	—	100	100	86	31

Occupation (if employed)—women

Professionals, technicians	21	32	14	17	34	30	29	17	2	1	—	3	100	100	56	114
Managers, administrators, proprietors	26	49	—	10	29	17	37	17	5	2	3	5	100	100	38	41
Clerical workers	29	35	9	13	25	21	25	24	5	2	7	5	100	100	131	191
Sales workers	[9]	42	12	12	30	15	28	27	12	—	9	4	100	100	33	26
Crafts workers	—	46	37	18	13	—	38	9	12	18	—	9	100	100	8	11
Operatives	11	27	8	7	38	14	33	31	3	10	7	11	100	100	73	73
Service workers	24	30	13	15	19	14	30	29	9	5	5	7	100	100	119	137
Laborers, non-farm	34	80	—	20	—	—	33	—	33	—	—	—	100	100	3	5
Farmers	22	27	—	—	—	37	34	18	33	9	11	9	100	100	9	11

Size Place of Residence

Metropolitan areas	21	24	11	14	21	20	27	30	11	4	9	8	100	100	325	166
Suburbs	13	30	10	10	25	23	33	25	14	6	5	6	100	100	326	350
Small cities	16	30	7	12	27	20	38	26	6	7	6	5	100	100	385	461
Towns	14	25	8	10	28	22	33	28	12	8	5	7	100	100	704	737
Rural areas	10	20	11	10	28	22	36	37	9	6	6	5	100	100	720	550

TABLE 5.6 (continued)
Social and Demographic Characteristics Related to Readiness for Self-Referral (by year)

Social or Demographic Characteristic	Has Used Help 1957 (%)	Has Used Help 1976 (%)	Could Have Used Help 1957 (%)	Could Have Used Help 1976 (%)	Might Need Help 1957 (%)	Might Need Help 1976 (%)	Self-Help 1957 (%)	Self-Help 1976 (%)	Strong Self-Help 1957 (%)	Strong Self-Help 1976 (%)	Not Ascertained 1957 (%)	Not Ascertained 1976 (%)	Total Percentage 1957	Total Percentage 1976	Total Number 1957	Total Number 1976
Region of Residence																
New England	15	31	3	8	23	27	43	25	13	6	3	3	100	100	181	140
Middle Atlantic	15	25	7	9	23	22	36	27	13	8	6	9	100	100	445	340
East North Central	13	29	11	11	28	20	32	30	8	6	8	4	100	100	441	409
West North Central	15	20	6	10	28	20	33	38	13	9	5	3	100	100	275	238
Solid South	13	22	10	9	28	22	34	31	9	7	6	3	100	100	648	577
Border States	11	26	16	12	27	22	30	32	7	4	9	9	100	100	115	172
Mountain States	10	31	8	11	26	20	42	30	8	3	6	4	100	100	104	74
Pacific States	18	30	11	17	29	22	27	21	9	5	6	5	100	100	251	314

Time in Community of Residence

Less than 1 year	21	34	9	16	28	19	31	26	5	3	6	2	100	100	149	123
1 to 2 years	16	28	14	18	26	19	33	21	5	9	6	5	100	100	216	207
3 to 4 years	16	37	14	13	23	16	34	29	9	1	4	4	100	100	190	213
5 to 9 years	16	22	8	9	28	28	29	27	13	8	6	6	100	100	355	319
10 to 19 years	13	28	9	12	28	20	36	26	10	7	4	7	100	100	452	367
20 years and over	13	22	7	9	26	22	36	34	11	7	7	6	100	100	1,061	1,016

Religion

Baptist	11	22	11	9	28	22	33	34	10	7	7	6	100	100	525	473
Methodist	14	23	8	11	25	26	39	29	9	6	5	5	100	100	398	246
Lutheran	14	28	8	12	32	18	31	31	10	6	5	5	100	100	200	147
Presbyterian	14	30	9	7	26	25	33	27	16	7	2	4	100	100	162	101
Fundamentalist	13	28	13	10	30	17	29	33	7	7	8	4	100	100	222	207
Other Protestant groups	15	27	7	11	26	22	37	24	9	4	6	8	100	100	242	269
Catholic	16	22	7	11	26	24	35	29	11	8	5	6	100	100	542	504
Jewish	21	51	7	9	21	16	23	17	17	8	11	5	100	100	91	57
No preference	16	28	12	15	19	21	30	26	11	2	12	3	100	100	57	225

TABLE 5.6 (continued)

Social and Demographic Characteristics Related to Readiness for Self-Referral (by year)

| | Readiness for Self-Referral | | | | | | | | | | | | | | | |
| | Has Used Help | | Could Have Used Help | | Might Need Help | | Self-Help | | Strong Self-Help | | Not Ascertained | | Total Percentage | | Total Number | |
Social or Demographic Characteristic	1957 (%)	1976 (%)	1957 (%)	1976 (%)	1957 (%)	1976 (%)	1957 (%)	1976 (%)	1957 (%)	1976 (%)	1957 (%)	1976 (%)	1957	1976	1957	1976
Church Attendance																
More than once a week	17	32	9	7	29	20	30	29	10	5	5	7	100	100	295	259
Once a week	15	25	7	8	29	23	34	31	9	7	6	6	100	100	834	559
A few times a month	13	28	9	9	27	22	36	28	10	8	5	5	100	100	536	390
A few times a year	13	23	11	13	24	22	35	32	12	5	5	5	100	100	562	634
Never	11	25	11	14	23	22	34	25	11	9	10	5	100	100	218	392
Race																
White	14	27	9	11	27	22	34	29	10	6	6	5	100	100	2,170	1,953
Black	14	22	11	7	25	18	32	34	10	10	8	9	100	100	190	245

Father's Occupation

Professionals and technicians	28	30	9	13	19	30	**28**	**21**	**13**	1	3	5	100	100	136	152
Managers, administrators, proprietors	20	25	8	15	26	23	**30**	**25**	**10**	3	6	9	100	100	271	274
Clerical and sales workers	13	31	12	10	26	26	**35**	**20**	**9**	8	5	5	100	100	120	114
Crafts workers	14	30	9	8	28	19	**32**	**30**	**12**	9	5	4	100	100	362	402
Operatives and service workers	15	28	11	12	29	20	**33**	**27**	**6**	9	6	5	100	100	321	330
Farmers and farm workers	10	19	8	8	28	23	**36**	**37**	**11**	8	7	6	100	100	903	500
Laborers (non-farm) and private household workers	14	26	8	11	19	19	**35**	**36**	**18**	6	6	2	100	100	128	110

Region of Birth

East	14	27	6	10	26	23	39	25	10	8	5	7	100	100	541	495
Midwest	14	27	10	11	28	23	33	30	10	6	5	3	100	100	735	656
Solid South	**13**	**22**	10	8	28	21	34	34	9	7	6	8	100	100	641	552
Border States	15	25	14	13	28	19	27	33	9	5	7	5	100	100	176	228
West	**22**	**35**	9	16	26	21	32	20	4	5	7	3	100	100	164	198

TABLE 5.6 (continued)
Social and Demographic Characteristics Related to Readiness for Self-Referral (by year)

| | Readiness for Self-Referral | | | | | | | | | | | | | | | |
| | Has Used Help | | Could Have Used Help | | Might Need Help | | Self-Help | | Strong Self-Help | | Not Ascertained | | Total Percentage | | Total Number | |
Social or Demographic Characteristic	1957 (%)	1976 (%)	1957 (%)	1976 (%)	1957 (%)	1976 (%)	1957 (%)	1976 (%)	1957 (%)	1976 (%)	1957 (%)	1976 (%)	1957	1976	1957	1976
Size Place of Childhood Residence																
Country or farm	11	24	8	8	28	23	34	32	12	7	7	6	100	100	989	745
Town (less than 50,000)	17	26	9	10	27	23	33	29	8	7	6	5	100	100	568	536
Small city (50,000 to 99,999)	16	25	11	14	26	18	35	31	8	7	4	5	100	100	362	413
Large city (100,000 or over)	18	29	8	12	26	22	32	26	11	5	5	6	100	100	468	527
Broken-Home Background																
Parents divorced or separated	25	29	15	16	23	22	27	26	6	4	4	3	100	100	123	191
Parent(s) died	14	20	11	7	29	22	28	33	11	7	7	11	100	100	351	243
Intact home	13	25	8	11	27	22	35	30	11	7	6	5	100	100	1,915	1,742
Marital Status—men																
Married	10	18	7	8	27	23	39	36	12	9	5	6	100	100	908	697
Single	15	23	11	16	27	22	28	31	11	3	8	5	100	100	82	130
Widowed	9	19	6	13	26	24	36	20	6	15	17	9	100	100	47	46
Divorced or separated	23	46	15	17	28	14	20	16	7	3	7	4	100	100	40	87

Marital Status—women

Married	14	28	10	11	28	25	33	25	10	5	5	6	100	100	963	739
Single	25	21	9	18	33	20	21	25	8	10	4	6	100	100	76	126
Widowed	13	19	7	7	26	20	36	37	9	8	9	9	100	100	233	262
Divorced or separated	41	54	20	14	15	11	14	16	5	3	5	2	100	100	111	175

Age of Youngest Child in Home (parental status)—men
Youngest child in home is:

Preschool	13	21	10	9	28	17	37	38	8	9	4	6	100	100	284	161
School age	12	21	4	9	28	25	38	34	10	7	8	4	100	100	272	228
Age 17 or over	8	17	2	6	21	24	37	34	21	13	11	6	100	100	62	67
No children in home	7	22	7	10	25	21	37	31	17	10	7	6	100	100	223	254
Has no children	10	23	10	14	27	22	35	30	11	5	7	6	100	100	229	249

Age of Youngest Child in Home (parental status)—women
Youngest child in home is:

Preschool	18	35	12	12	30	21	31	24	6	4	3	4	100	100	319	196
School age	22	37	9	15	30	22	27	18	7	3	5	5	100	100	342	326
Age 17 or over	17	24	10	8	18	24	37	32	12	5	6	7	100	100	108	117
No children in home	12	23	10	7	23	19	33	35	14	8	8	8	100	100	329	375
Has no children	14	26	11	14	27	24	35	25	8	5	5	6	100	100	277	286

TABLE 5.6 (continued)
Social and Demographic Characteristics Related to Readiness for Self-Referral (by year)

Social or Demographic Characteristic	Has Used Help 1957 (%)	Has Used Help 1976 (%)	Could Have Used Help 1957 (%)	Could Have Used Help 1976 (%)	Might Need Help 1957 (%)	Might Need Help 1976 (%)	Self-Help 1957 (%)	Self-Help 1976 (%)	Strong Self-Help 1957 (%)	Strong Self-Help 1976 (%)	Not Ascertained 1957 (%)	Not Ascertained 1976 (%)	Total Percentage 1957	Total Percentage 1976	Total Number 1957	Total Number 1976
Employment Status—men																
Employed	11	22	7	11	28	22	37	34	11	7	6	4	100	100	924	753
Retired	3	16	6	4	19	24	41	30	19	15	12	11	100	100	108	155
Unemployed	4	31	8	13	28	10	36	38	12	3	12	5	100	100	25	39
Employment Status—women																
Employed	22	34	10	14	27	20	29	24	6	3	6	5	100	100	457	599
Housewife	13	25	11	9	27	26	33	28	11	6	5	6	100	100	876	504
Retired	7	17	10	12	27	14	37	38	3	12	16	7	100	100	30	126
Unemployed	37	31	5	8	16	22	21	18	16	9	5	12	100	100	19	65

NOTE: A dash indicates that the percentage is less than one-half of 1 percent.

Sometimes a relationship in one year distinguished groups only with respect to whether professional help was actually used; and in another, only with respect to how strong a self-help position was taken. The more complicated analysis asked whether the patterns found in the simpler analysis were independent of sex, age, and education.

Socioeconomic Status: Income

We found that analyses using two alternative income measures produced slightly different results, although they were essentially consistent in their implications. For both indicators, table 5.6 demonstrates the reliable (though modest) relationship found between family income and the self-referral index in both years, although the relationship described slightly different phenomena occurring in 1957 and in 1976. In 1957, respondents earning high incomes were more likely to have sought help than those with low incomes, a difference which essentially disappeared in 1976. In contrast, income differences in self-referral found in 1976 reflected a tendency for persons with low incomes to adopt a self-help position with regard to future problems more often then wealthier respondents, a trend that was not statistically reliable in 1957.

When controls for sex, age, and education were included, however, we found that even the income differences in help-seeking noted for 1957 were not independent of the relationship of income to education. Evidently, the affluent who were help-seekers in 1957 were also more educated. Income did not seem to play a role beyond this, and it clearly had no role at all in help-seeking ratios in 1976.

One significant finding does emerge between income and the readiness for self-referral when the controls are applied. An examination of the data by sex reveals that, independent of education, for women but not for men, there was a negative relationship between relative income and adopting a self-help position. Furthermore, this relationship tended to be stronger in 1976 than in 1957, although this interaction was not quite significant. Thus, the general trend noted previously for low income people in 1976 to be especially rejecting of professional help as a way to solve present or future personal problems (the self-help position) was most marked for women. Often women who are in a low-income status are on their own. Many divorced or separated are in low-income groups, as we saw in Book 1, chapter 5. So are widows. There has also been a greater political emphasis during this generation on women being able to cope on their own. Perhaps this emphasis imparted by the women's movement made women living on their own in 1976 more eager to reject help for personal difficulties and to manage life independently, even if they have low incomes. A look ahead at the relationships of marital status to self-referral corroborates this interpretation. From 1957 to 1976, only married women showed a reduction in self-help responses. Those in nonmarried statuses show either no change or a marked espousal of self-help.

Overall, then, income differences in the actual use of help, primarily a function of education, have essentially disappeared between 1957 and 1976, while differences among income groups in self-help orientation, at least partially independent of education and observed particularly among women, have increased over the same period.

Socioeconomic Status: Occupation

Without exception, when age and education are controlled, relationships between occupational status and self-referral for both men and women disappear, suggesting that any differences indicated in table 5.6 are a function of education rather than of variation among the occupations held by men and women in our society.

Without the controls, a classic manual–nonmanual occupational dichotomy (see Vanneman and Pampel, 1977) existed for men in both 1957 and 1976. Men in white-collar jobs in 1976 were more likely than those in blue-collar jobs to have used help (27 versus 18 percent) and less likely to adopt a self-help position with regard to potential use of help (35 versus 45 percent). Comparable proportions in 1957 were 15 versus 10 percent for actual use of help and 44 versus 48 percent for self-help.

For women, two results bear singling out. First, there was a very substantial increase in help-seeking among saleswomen in 1976 (42 percent) compared to 1957 (9 percent). Secondly, women who were manual workers in 1976 are clearly more self-help oriented (35 percent) than women white-collar workers (23 percent), a contrast that did not exist in 1957. Both results are perhaps interpretable as due to different age or educational distributions in these occupations for 1976, since controlling for age and education removes the effects. Nevertheless, these are interesting descriptive characteristics of these women's occupations in 1976.

Geographic Social Environment: Place of Residence,[3] Region, and Time in Community

In contrast, indicators of geographic social environment all showed significant relationships with readiness for self-referral independent of controls for sex, age, and education. Each, however, was different in 1976 than it was in 1957.

From 1957 to 1976, there was a general reshuffling among people from different types of urban-rural environments in their tendencies for self-referral. Specifically, there was a marked increase in formal help-seeking among adults living in suburban areas. In addition, a notable decrease in self-help orientation among men and women living

[3] See footnote 3 on page 60 of chapter 3 for a detailed list of states grouped in each region.

in small cities was balanced by parallel increases for those in big cities and rural areas. The net result was a somewhat different type of rural-urban difference in 1976. Presumably reflecting dramatic changes in the population composition of our urban areas during the two decades, people in suburban areas and small cities (rather than big city residents) are those most psychologically prepared to use professional help, while those living in rural areas are the least prepared. Although such differences reflect, at least in part, differences in socioeconomic status among those living in these areas, that these results are essentially independent of age and education implies that such factors as the differential availability of resources in these areas may also have an important effect.

Demographic changes in the population at the regional level also seem to account for there being a number of differences in the region—self-referral relationship in 1957 and 1976. Although a number of regions are apparently distinctive in their pattern of self-referral in one year or the other, these differences disappear with the sex, age, and education controls. Nevertheless, net of these controls, a consistent relationship between region and self-referral remains, indicating that adults residing in the South are particularly low in actual help-seeking while residents in the Pacific states are especially high. People in the West North Central are particularly high in their self-help orientation. It may be asked, are these regional differences concordant with the subjective adjustment differences found for these regions? To an extent they are. The South is somewhat nonpsychological in general responses to questions about sources of well being. By contrast, the West is very psychologically oriented, and if focusing on the self psychologically predisposes people to seek help, as results noted in the previous section relating measures of subjective adjustment to patterns of self-referral suggested, these regional differences make sense. Since we had no good psychological portrait of the West North Central states from the same analysis, the results fit only stereotypes of self-sufficient mid-Westerners. We have little data to explain this regional effect.

Relationships between time in community of residence and readiness for self-referral also vary significantly by year, independent of controls for age and education. Compared to somewhat inconsistent trends for 1957, geographically mobile people in 1976 were clearly more likely to have sought help and less likely to adopt a self-help position than those who have resided longer in their communities. These results may well reflect the same findings we have noted about place of residence. Geographically mobile people in 1976 undoubtedly included many who had moved away from the larger cities to smaller cities and the suburbs, the places where we found people most ready for referral in 1976, and perhaps the places where the facilities were more accessible. Analyses in chapter 8 may clarify this interpretation.

Group Identification and Integration: Religion, Church Attendance, and Race

Turning now to findings presented in table 5.6 concerning group identification and integration, we first observe a significant relationship between religion and self-referral, which is essentially the same in 1957 and 1976 and independent of our controls. Most notably, in both years, Jews are clearly the group most oriented to seeking professional help; 21 percent in 1957 and over 50 percent in 1976 had actually gone for help. Baptists are consistently the group least oriented to seeking professional help. The results concerning Baptists perhaps reflect the tendencies of this largely Southern conservative group to not be imbued with the psychological approach to experience. In our discussion in chapter 8 of Book 1 we described how Baptists differed from other religious groups in their subjective mental health. In a similar way, we may utilize conclusions about Jews in Book 1 to help us interpret their distinctive propensity to seek professional help for personal problems. Jews, we said, were quick to be aware of their feelings—and especially their psychological pain. If mental health professionals are technicians who deal with feelings, and if many of these professionals are themselves Jews (as is the case), then it is not usually difficult for Jews to take the step of consulting a professional for a personal problem. Jews freely admit to psychological pain; they are aware that many Jews are involved as professionals; and so they are able to view help-seeking without the stigma other groups might apply to such behavior and even with some positive group support.

Similarly, with respect to church attendance, high church attenders in both survey years seem slightly more open to using professional help. Furthermore, the link between frequency of church attendance and readiness to accept formal help is found more frequently among older people than among those under fifty-five. The pattern may reflect the fact that the devout elderly have become especially tied to the church and established trusting relationships with the clergy. As a result, at times of personal crises, they are able to more readily turn to the clergy for advice.

In contrast with these religion differences in patterns of self-referral is the absence of differences in self-referral by race. No significant relationship was evident at all in 1957, and although whites in 1976 appeared slightly more oriented to the use of help than blacks, this modest difference disappeared when education is controlled. These small disparities are thus more a function of socioeconomic status than of black-white differences.

Social Background

Father's occupation, region of birthplace, place of childhood residence, and broken home background were each related to the readiness for self-referral. Some consistent relationships between readiness for self-referral and these social background indicators persist in the face of multivariate controls. Notable among these are relationships between father's occupation and self-referral, which differ significantly, however, between the two survey years. Reminiscent of a pattern consistently observed in this chapter is a leveling of differences in the actual use of help when the highest status background (people whose fathers were professionals) is compared to a generally lower status background (people whose fathers were farmers) across the two survey years.

In 1957, the high status group was almost three times as likely to have sought help when contrasted to the low status group (28 percent to 10 percent); in 1976, this ratio was cut to less than two to one (30 percent to 19 percent). By contrast there has been a sharpening over the generation in the differences between high and low status groups in their self-help orientation. In 1976, adults from low status backgrounds (their fathers were farmers or blue-collar workers) were much more likely to take a self-help position about potential professional help-seeking than adults from high status backgrounds (their fathers were white-collar workers). This discrepancy was much less apparent in 1957 (see boxed sections of table 5.6). Since these results are apparent even when the respondent's own education is controlled, one's social status background and one's current social status each appear to contribute to the polarization that now seems associated with taking a self-help position. In each case, we would speculate that the shrinking number of people who either come from or are in a clearly defined low status position makes that minority relatively isolated from general attitude changes in the society. This isolation may indeed induce rejection of, rather than convergence with, the dominant culture's acceptance of professional help. Suspicion festers in isolation. This may have happened to people who came from extremely low status groups in our society as the society became generally more educated and affluent.

Findings for region of birthplace essentially parallel those described for regional differences by place of residence, including a significant interaction by year which essentially disappears when sex, age, and education are controlled. Net of these controls, however, is one prevailing consistent pattern: adults born in the West are particularly high on the self-referral index, and those from the South particularly low.

In contrast, a person's place of childhood residence apparently has less general significance for self-referral than the current place of residence. While significant rural-urban differences by place of childhood residence occurred in the 1957 data, even these disappear when age and education are controlled.

Although a hint of interaction by year is evident in our findings with respect to broken-home background, the general pattern of re-

sults indicates that in both 1957 and 1976 people from a home disrupted by divorce more frequently sought help than those coming from a
home disrupted by the death of a parent and were slightly more likely
than those from intact homes to say they would potentially use help
for personal problems. In chapter 8 of Book 1, we learned that adults
from homes disrupted by divorce have experienced more distress and
often express their distress in the introspective, psychological terms
we found relevant for self-referral in the previous section. It is thus
not surprising to find them open to professional help.

Role Statuses

In looking at relationships between role statuses and self-referral,
analyzed separately for men and women, the most consistent relationships observed are those between marital status and readiness to seek
professional help. In both survey years, divorced or separated men
and women more often had gone for help (in 1976 reaching 46 and 54
percent, respectively!) and were less likely to reject the possibility of
needing help in the future than those in other marital statuses. Married men were consistently low on the self-referral index across the
two surveys. As we saw in chapter 3 on informal helping, married
men in our society, especially in 1976, depended much more on their
wives as their sole support system than wives depended on their husbands. This might be interpreted to mean that wives provide better
emotional supports for their husbands' problems than husbands do for
their wives'. We have no direct evidence on this, however. We do
know that women more frequently than men structure their marital
problems as a difficulty in the mate. If a good percentage of personal
problems for married people reflects these marriage problems, then it
might be surmised that a woman would have a harder time discussing
personal problems with her husband than vice versa. If the husband is
perceived to be the "cause" of the problem, she would more likely
turn for help to others, including professionals.

From 1957 to 1976, an important shift occurred in women's readiness for self-referral when single and married women were compared
(this was a significant interaction in the multivariate analysis). While
single women in 1957 reported a greater readiness to seek help than
married women, a striking reversal of this trend was evident in 1976.
Our discussion in Book 1 about the shift in norms about marriage focused in the 1976 sample on the greater acceptance of choosing not to
be married. This made the role of the single woman in particular
much less deviant and stressful in 1976. The phenomenon may well
account for a greater self-reliance about personal problems among single women in 1976 in contrast to single women in 1957. Single women
are one of the few groups who showed a decline in the actual use of
help from 1957 to 1976 (25 percent to 21 percent). Over the same period, married women doubled their use of professional help (14 percent

to 28 percent). This change resembles the general shift in the culture to the use of professional help. Although we see the reversal as stemming from the acceptance of their marital status that single women now have but lacked in 1957, it could also be a function of increased stress (see Gove, 1978) or vulnerability (see Kessler, 1979) that may have occurred in the lives of married women during this generation.

While each of these relationships between marital status and readiness for self-referral is maintained when age and education are controlled, that is not the case for relationships involving parental status and employment status. Although men and women with young children appear somewhat more willing to seek professional help than the childless or those with older children, these findings primarily reflect age differences among these groups. Similarly, significant differences in readiness for self-referral by employment status evident in table 5.6 (for example, the consistent tendency for retired men and women not to use professional help), all essentially vanish when age and education are held constant. These results should not be completely ignored. Clearly, parents during the early phases of the family life cycle are very open to professional counsel, and retired men and women are not. There are descriptive features of these groups that would be helpful in setting up help programs for them. Nevertheless, one should also be aware that young parents' openness and retired people's rejection of help-seeking may be as much a result of their age as their family or work status.

Summary

Although our examination of relationships between sociodemographic characteristics and readiness for self-referral offers a complex set of findings, a number of relatively firm conclusions may be derived from it. Although a number of exceptions are apparent, there is considerable stability in these relationships over the nineteen-year interval between the two surveys. Women, young people, and the higher educated are consistently high in readiness for self-referral; and, net of these three factors, urban or suburban residents, people who grew up or live in the Pacific states, Jews, high church attenders, children of professionals, adult children of divorce, and those divorced themselves are all relatively open to accepting professional help. We are impressed with the consistency of these results that indicate something critical about each of these social factors that may be relatively unchanging. Whether we considered the social environments of 1957 or of 1976, each of these demographic features was relevant to people's willingness to contemplate calling on outside help for personal problems and to actually seek such help.

No single explanation integrates the relevance of all of these diverse factors to people's readiness for self-referral. As each was presented in our analyses, we offered interpretations. As we look back over these interpretations, we see that we have used three basic kinds. First, some of these interpretations depended on our conceiving a social characteristic as reflecting a stress so powerful in a person's life that it overrides any reluctance people might characteristically have about help-seeking. People who, by some objective standard, experience a critical stress may automatically feel the need for help more than others and hence be quick to act on that need. We interpret the consistent findings for children of the divorced and those adults divorced themselves as examples of people who experience such clearcut stress that they have a very strong readiness for self-referral. We also view women's proclivity for help-seeking as partially reflecting greater social stress in their lives. Second, some of our interpretations depend on understanding a given social group as being so psychologically-minded that they become particularly open to psychological help. Sex, age, and education differences in help-seeking patterns were, to some extent, interpreted this way. So were results about Jews, urban or suburban dwellers, people who live in the Pacific states, and children of professionals. Finally, we have implicitly used a third but related interpretation to explain why some social characteristics are related to self-referral. This interpretation states that being a member of a certain social group exposes a person to help-seeking as an approved alternative, and that he or she will thus become favorably disposed toward that alternative. Mere exposure is part of this effect and reference group support is another. Let us call this the group exposure interpretation, one that we used or we could easily use in thinking of reasons why the college educated, Jews, people who live in the Pacific states, children of professionals, and frequent church attenders, are likely to be open to help-seeking. It can also be used to explain low readiness in people who live in small towns or in rural areas. They just have not had an opportunity to become familiar with the idea of professional help-seeking as an alternative for coping with personal problems.

So much for stability of relationships between sociodemographic factors and the readiness for self-referral. What about patterns of change in these relationships from 1957 to 1976?

The most dramatic pattern of historical change in the relationships between self-referral and demographic characteristics involves several indicators of social class or socioeconomic status (education, income, occupation, and father's occupation), all of which show a convergence among relevant subgroups between 1957 and 1976 in the actual use of help, in conjunction with a greater polarization of these social status groups during the same period with respect to the potential use of help. Although multivariate analyses reveal that educational differences are predominant in this pattern, suggesting a need for greater attention to the question of how education affects orientation toward personal problems and the decision to use professional help, the consistency of relationships in this pattern with all indicators of status should not be overlooked.

Echoing an observation made in the 1960 monograph (Gurin, et al.), we should emphasize that, whether stable or changed, not all of these relationships are readily amenable to explanation in terms of variations among subgroups in their psychological orientations or adjustment patterns in one year or the other (see Gurin, et al., 1960, pp. 285–286). Clearly some are, as we discussed previously. In most cases when a given population subgroup does manifest a pattern of adjustment predictive of high self-referral (for example, women, young people, Jews, and especially the higher educated), that particular group does indeed turn out to be relatively high on readiness for self-referral. Nevertheless, certain pairs of subgroups, while they sharply contrast in their patterns of self-referral, do not contrast in clear ways in how they express or structure distress (for example, rural versus urban residents, high versus low church attenders, residents of the West versus the South), thereby suggesting that other factors, conditions, and circumstances bear a significant relationship to readiness for self-referral. We must alert ourselves to possible explanations in terms of the group exposure effect, some of which we shall also see operating in the next section, in which we discuss stages of self-referral.

FACILITATING VERSUS PSYCHOLOGICAL FACTORS: STAGES OF SELF-REFERRAL

In attempting to specify some of these other determinants of readiness to use professional resources, Gurin, Veroff, and Feld (1960) found it useful to view self-referral behavior as a consequence of at least two sets of variables—psychological factors and facilitating or hindering factors:

> In addition to the psychological orientations and motivational factors that make a person receptive to the idea of going for help, there are numerous factors that may be viewed as hindering or facilitating the decision to go. Whereas psychological factors tend to point toward the use of help as desirable, facilitating factors point torward the use of help as available or accessible. Facilitating factors include the actual availability of the resources in the community, an individual's knowledge about the availability of the resources, and the extent to which going for help is "the thing one does" in one's social group. (p. 286)

As a means of clarifying this distinction between psychological and facilitating factors, they proposed that the measure of readiness for self-referral be conceived of not as a single index, but rather as a composite of three distinct decision points (see Kadushin, 1969): (1) whether or not a problem will be defined as a mental health problem (that is, as one relevant for professional help); (2) whether or not to go for help with the problem; and (3) the choice of where to go (that is, the selection of a particular help source). While recognizing that psychological and facilitating factors are interrelated, and have relevance at all three stages of the self-referral process, Gurin and his colleagues hypothesized that psychological factors are most clearly relevant at the first decision point (that is, the initial definition of a problem in mental health terms), while facilitating factors have increasing significance at the latter two decision points—the decision to go for help and the choice of a particular type of help source. And, consistent with this basic hypothesis, the authors of the 1960 volume found that certain demographic variables, assumed to reflect various combinations of psychological and facilitating factors, did indeed become more important at different stages of the self-referral process.[4]

Since this volume focuses on patterns of stability and change in help-seeking behavior over a generation, we offer two corollaries to this basic proposition that guided our own analyses: (1) the degree to which a given factor reflects either psychological and/or facilitating factors is subject to change over time; and (2) factors which serve primarily to facilitate or hinder the use of professional help are probably more readily susceptible to change by social policy than are psychological orientations and motivational factors.

In this section, and part of the next, we shall explore these basic assumptions by examining possible changes in help-seeking behavior for each stage of the self-referral process. In particular, we will examine relationships between social and demographic characteristics, assumed in 1957 to reflect distinctive combinations of these two sets of factors, and these three stages of readiness for self-referral. Before turning to these analyses, however, we shall first describe changes by year for the first two stages of self-referral.

Year Differences in Stages of Self-Referral

The first major decision concerns whether or not a particular problem is to be defined in mental health terms (that is, whether or not it

[4] This approach is supported in the work of Kadushin (1969). Furthermore, in the context of a larger theoretical framework, Andersen and his colleagues (Andersen and Newman, 1973, pp. 107–110; Andersen, Kravits, and Anderson, 1975, pp. 5–8, 14–15) present a quite similar model of individual determinants of health care utilization, which describes utilization as a consequence of: (1) the predisposition of the individual to use services (predisposing variables), (2) his or her ability to secure sevices (enabling variables), and (3) his or her illness level (illness variables). Specifically, predisposing variables in their model include demographic variables (age, sex, marital status, and neighborhood tenure), social structural variables (education, race, occupation, and religion), and beliefs (values, attitudes, and knowledge) about health and medical care, while enabling factors include both family resources (income, availability of health insurance, and type of access to regular source of care) and community characteristics (availability and cost of health services, region, and urban-rural differences). They do not make explicit, however, the possibility that a given individual characteristic may reflect both predisposing and enabling factors.

is perceived as relevant for professional help). In terms of the self-referral index, persons who have defined a problem in mental health terms are those who have either actually gone for help or who can think of a problem in the past for which they could have used help (Gurin et al., 1960, p. 258). Thus, to study the relationship between social class indicators and this first decision point of the self-referral process, we need only reexamine tables 5.1 through 5.6 and combine the percentages in the first two columns of those tables to determine the total proportion of any particular group who have defined a problem in their own experience as one appropriate for professional help. Thus, in table 5.1, we see a significant increase (14 percent) over the past two decades in the tendency of people to define problems experienced as mental health problems, rising from 23 percent in 1957 (14 plus 9) to 37 percent (26 plus 11) in 1976. Moreover, it is clear that this increase is almost entirely due to the increase in the actual use of professional help (noted previously) rather than to an increase in the report of problems for which such help would have been appropriate.

The second decision point concerns "the extent to which a mental health definition of a problem has been translated into a decision to go for help, that is, what proportion of the people who defined a problem in mental health terms has actually gone for help" (Gurin et al., 1960, p. 291). To answer that question, we consider only those respondents who have either gone for help or viewed some problem they have experienced as relevant for professional help, rather than the total sample interviewed. Once again, relationships relevant to this second decision are based on data presented in the first two columns of tables 5.1 through 5.6. Thus, figures in the first two columns of table 5.1 indicate that of those in 1957 who defined a problem in mental health terms, 61 percent actually went for help, while in 1976, 71 percent of those defining a problem in mental health terms actually sought help. Overall then, six out of ten Americans in 1957 translated a problem they had experienced as relevant for help-seeking into actual help-seeking behavior; by 1976, seven out of ten Americans made this translation. These differences are independent of sex, age, and education controls from multivariate analyses. While these data are based on lifetime prevalence rates which make such estimates somewhat tenuous, it might reasonably be argued that we are coming fairly close to maximizing utilization of professional help by persons who are at all receptive to the idea.

Subjective Adjustment and Stages of Self-Referral

Although these global changes by year in the first two stages of self-referral have some obvious significance as social indicator data, of greater interest perhaps are potential differences between the two survey years in relationships between these two decision points and selected adjustment and sociocultural variables, which may reflect factors underlying these basic changes.

First we shall briefly consider how factors of adjustment may be involved in the two decision points. Congruent with the pattern of relationships described earlier between measures of subjective mental health and the global index of self-referral, the majority of measures of general adjustment, adjustment in marriage, parenthood, and work, self-perceptions and symptoms are consistently related in both years to the first stage of self-referral—the definition of problems experienced in mental health terms. With very few exceptions, however, these adjustment measures are consistently related *only* to defining a problem as relevant for professional help, and not to the translation of this definition into an actual decision to go for help. Thus, differential relationships apparent in both surveys between our adjustment indicators and these two separate stages of the self-referral process strongly confirm their role as psychological or predisposing factors—indicators of an orientation that renders a person more receptive to the idea of going for help—rather than factors that hinder or facilitate one's decision to actually go.

Two notable exceptions to this general trend are presented in table 5.7: those who have felt an impending nervous breakdown or experienced symptoms of psychological anxiety are more likely both to have defined a problem in mental health terms and to have sought help for the problem. Moreover, in each case, the relationship between these indicators of subjective distress and the decision to seek help was *stronger* in 1976 than in 1957. This is particularly evident for people high in psychological anxiety, who in 1957 were no more likely than those low in psychological anxiety to translate mental health problems into help-seeking, but in 1976, they were clearly more likely to do so. The results are important because these two measures of psychological strain are possibly our most direct measures of a felt need for psychological services. To find that they are more clearly related to translating a problem into help-seeking in 1976 than they were in 1957 suggests there was a decline in stigmatization of those seeking professional counsel. In addition, other obstacles have probably been reduced. In any case, it is clear that there have been changes in the meaning of self-referral once a problem is recognized. It is now easier to translate the experience of distress into professional help-seeking than was the case a generation earlier.

Sociodemographic Characteristics Related to Stages of Self-Referral

In turning now to an examination of relationships between social and demographic characteristics and the first two decision points in the self-referral process, we will be able to assess more directly the basic assumptions underlying the distinction between psychological and facilitating factors: (1) that different characteristics take on greater

TABLE 5.7

Feelings of Impending Nervous Breakdown and Psychological Anxiety Related to Stages of Self-Referral (by year)

Measure of Subjective Adjustment	Mental Health Definition of Problem				Actual Use of Professional Help							
	Has Used or Could Have Used Help		Total Number		Has Used Help		Could Have Used Help		Total Percentage		Total Number	
	1957 (%)	1976 (%)	1957	1976	1957 (%)	1976 (%)	1957 (%)	1976 (%)	1957	1976	1957	1976
Felt Impending Nervous Breakdown												
Yes	44	65	464	472	67	81	33	19	100	100	205	308
No	18	29	1,992	1,785	58	64	43	36	100	100	362	515
Psychological Anxiety												
(Low) 5	12	19	432	217	64	64	36	36	100	100	50	42
6 to 7	19	31	704	537	63	74	37	26	100	100	136	165
8	22	38	419	412	58	65	42	35	100	100	91	158
9 to 10	29	39	517	692	60	65	40	35	100	100	151	270
(High) 11 to 20	36	48	380	377	60	81	40	19	100	100	138	182

TABLE 5.8

Sex, Age, Education, and Income Related to the Definition of Some Past Problem in Mental Health Terms and the Actual Use of Help Among Those Who Have Done So (by year)

Social or Demographic Characteristic[a]	Mental Health Definition of Problem				Actual Use of Professional Help							
	Has Used or Could Have Used Help		Total Number		Has Used Help		Could Have Used Help		Total Percentage		Total Number	
	1957 (%)	1976 (%)	1957	1976	1957 (%)	1976 (%)	1957 (%)	1976 (%)	1957	1976	1957	1976
Sex												
Men	18	32	1,077	960	60	68	40	32	100	100	194	304
Women	27	40	1,383	1,304	61	72	39	28	100	100	373	519
Age												
21 to 29	30	43	453	553	61	64	39	36	100	100	134	239
30 to 39	28	46	584	463	62	69	38	31	100	100	164	214
40 to 49	23	42	515	341	69	77	31	23	100	100	120	143
50 to 59	19	32	390	342	56	82	44	18	100	100	75	108
60 to 64	12	26	153	166	42	72	58	28	100	100	19	43
65 and over	14	19	353	397	53	67	47	33	100	100	49	76

Education

Grade school	16	21	802	380	48	80	52	20	100	100	127	78
Some high school	25	38	511	347	58	71	42	29	100	100	126	130
High school graduate	25	38	674	766	65	68	35	32	100	100	171	287
Some college	27	42	247	411	67	67	33	33	100	100	67	174
College graduate	36	44	210	347	72	73	28	27	100	100	75	153
Income—relative												
Low	21	33	666	578	52	74	48	26	100	100	138	192
Middle	24	40	1,002	921	58	69	42	31	100	100	238	369
High	26	37	722	608	71	70	29	30	100	100	184	227
Income—1976 dollars												
Under 4,000	20	31	407	295	50	77	50	23	100	100	80	91
4,000 to 7,999	24	36	549	380	61	72	39	28	100	100	132	135
8,000 to 9,999	22	43	389	195	58	66	42	34	100	100	87	83
10,000 to 12,499	24	39	323	245	52	68	48	32	100	100	77	95
12,500 to 19,999	25	41	536	518	68	68	32	32	100	100	135	213
20,000 and over	26	36	186	474	78	72	22	28	100	100	49	171

importance at the different decision points; and (2) that characteristics which strongly reflect psychological factors will be especially relevant at the first decision point (whether or not a problem is defined as a mental health problem), while those which strongly reflect facilitating or hindering factors will be particularly relevant to the actual decision to seek help and the selection of a particular help source (the latter to be examined in the next section of this chapter). As noted previously, the basic data underlying relationships relevant to these comparisons are presented in the first two columns of tables 5.5 and 5.6. The sum of the percentages in columns 1 and 2 identifies the people who have defined their problems in mental health terms; and the ratio of percentages in column 1 to that sum identifies the people who translated mental health problems into help-seeking. We shall analyze in some detail the relationships of sex, age, education, and income to these two recombined measures. For these social characteristics the new combinations of percentages are retabulated in table 5.8 and referred to in discussion. For other social characteristics, we discuss only broad issues and emphasize only those relationships which persist when controls for sex, age, education, and year are also taken into account in multivariate analyses (see table 5.10).

Sex, Age, and Education

Sex, age, and education all show distinctive patterns of association with these first two decision points in the self-referral process. Let us examine each in turn.

While sex differences in mental health problem definition vary significantly by education, it is clear that women both in 1957 and in 1976 define a problem in mental health terms more often than do men. The largest sex difference occurs among the high-school educated (see table 5.9). In 1976, for example, 43 percent of high school-educated women defined a problem of theirs in mental health terms; this compares to only 28 percent of the high school-educated men. By contrast, there are only small differences by sex among the college educated. In 1976, 42 percent of the college-educated men defined personal problems as relevant for help, nearly the same percentage as for college-educated women (45 percent). We are thus able to see that in spite of the proclivity of men not to evaluate the difficulties they experience in life as mental health problems, their exposure to a college experience seems to alert them to perceiving their problems as relevant for help-seeking.

In neither 1957 nor 1976 did men and women differ at the second decision point. Thus, although women more often define a problem as relevant for professional help, they are no more likely than men to translate a mental health problem definition into a decision to seek help. These data are thus consistent with a growing body of evidence suggesting that sex differences in professional help-seeking are pri-

TABLE 5.9

*Sex and Education Related to the Definition of Some Past
Problem in Mental Health Terms (by year)*

| | Mental Health Definition of Problem | | | |
| | Has Used or Could Have Used Help | | Total Number | |
Education (within Sex)[a]	1957 (%)	1976 (%)	1957	1976
Men				
Grade school	11		367	
		18		154
High school	18		461	
		28		424
College	30		242	
		42		378
Women				
Grade school	20		435	
		22		226
High school	30		724	
		43		689
College	32		215	
		45		380

[a] The "not ascertained" groups on education are omitted from this table.

marily due to a greater psychological propensity among women to see themselves as vulnerable and needing help (e.g., Kessler, Reuter, and Greenley, 1979).[5]

Independent of sex and education is a consistent negative relationship between age and mental health problem definition. Young adults in both survey years more often than the elderly defined problems they had experienced in mental health terms. Among those who defined a problem as relevant for help, however, older people were as likely as young adults to have actually sought professional help. Middle-aged adults, especially those forty to fifty-nine in 1976, were the most obvious users of help. These results suggest that the well-documented lower utilization of formal help sources by the elderly for emotional and mental health problems (for example, see Kramer, Taube, and Redick, 1973; Butler and Lewis, 1977; Eisdorfer and Stotsky, 1977) may be largely a function of factors which point to the use of help as desirable or appropriate rather than of factors relevant to the availability of professional resources. That middle-aged adults

[5] Gove (1978) cites these data from the 1957 survey (taken from Gurin et al., 1960) as evidence indicating that "when disorder is controlled, women are no more likely than men to perceive themselves as having a mental health problem or to seek professional help" (p. 192). While this basic proposition may or may not be true, it should be evident that these data are essentially irrelevant to its assessment.

TABLE 5.10

1957 and 1976 Comparisons of Significant Relationships of Sociodemographic Characteristics to Two Stages of Self-Referral

Social/Demographic Characteristic	Significant[a] Relationship at Stage 1: Defining Problems in Mental Health Terms			Significant[a] Relationship at Stage 2: Seeking Help for a Self-Defined Mental Health Problem		
	Significant Relationship in		Description of Relationship	Significant Relationship in		Description of Relationship
	1957	1976		1957	1976	
Sex	⊗	⊗	Women > Men[b]	—	—	—
Age	⊗	⊗	Young > Middle aged > Old	⊗	⊗	Middle aged > Young, Old
Education	⊗	⊗	Grade school < High school < College	⊗	—	Grade school < High school < College
Income	—	X	Low < Middle, High income	X	—	Low < Middle, High income
Occupation:						
Men and women	⊗	⊗	Semi-skilled < All others	—	—	—
Place of residence	⊗	⊗	Rural < Urbanized areas	⊗	—	Rural < Urbanized areas
Region	⊗	⊗	West > All other > Solid South	⊗	—	North East > All others
Time in community	—	⊗	Mobile > Permanent	—	—	—
Religion	—	⊗	Jews > Others > Baptists	X	—	Baptists, Fundamentalists < Others
Church attendance	—	—	—	⊗	⊗	High > Low church attenders
Race	—	X	Whites > Blacks	—	—	—
Father's occupation	⊗	⊗	White collar > Others > Farmers (fathers)	X	—	Professional father > Others
Region of birth	⊗	⊗	West > All others	X	—	West, East > Others

Characteristic						
Place of childhood residence	X	X	Rural < Others	—	—	—
Broken-home background	⊗	⊗ (Significantly weaker in 1976)	Divorced/Separated > Intact background	—	—	—
Marital Status:						
Men	⊗	⊗	Divorced/Separated > Others >	—	—	—
Women	⊗	⊗	Married	—	X	1957: Single women > All others 1976: Single women < All others
Parental Status:						
Men	X	—	No children, has preschoolers > Others	—	—	—
Women	—	X	Has young children > Others	—	—	—
Employment Status:						
Men	X	X	Retired < Others	—	—	—
Women	⊗	X	Employed > Housewives > Retired[c]	⊗	—	Employed > Housewives

NOTE: An — entry indicates that no significant relationship exists, an X that a significant relationship does exist, and an XX entry designates a significant interaction by year. A circled X (⊗) indicates that a significant relationship is maintained with controls for sex, age, education, and year.

[a] Needed in cross-classification analysis of the social or demographic characteristic × Stage 1 (or Stage 2) behavior × year.

[b] Important interaction by education: Minimally true of college educated.

[c] Important interaction by age: employed > housewife, especially for middle aged.

in 1976 were more likely than either young adults or the elderly to have translated a mental health problem definition into an actual decision to seek help (see Kulka and Tamir, 1978) is consistent with other research documenting greater levels of professional help-seeking during the middle years (Kramer et al., 1973; Shanas and Maddox, 1976). Tamir's analysis (1980) of men aged forty to forty-nine is that they experience a special kind of distress, one that causes them to reemphasize the importance of marriage in their lives. This reemphasis is exactly the kind of psychological orientation that we found particularly characteristic of people who accept self-referral for personal problems.

A consistent positive relationship between education and defining a problem in mental health terms was also apparent in both 1957 and 1976—higher-educated people more often define a problem as relevant for formal help—although, as noted, there is a significant sex by education interaction (table 5.9). For men, there are consistent increases in mental health problem definition at each educational level, while for women, only differences between the grade school and high school educated are significant. Thus, while college apparently serves to level out differences between men and women with regard to mental health problem definition (as noted previously), the consistent lack of a difference between high school and college-educated women implies less overall significance of higher education for the help-seeking orientations of women. One might conclude that just the experience of a high school education brings women into the psychological sphere of attending to personal issues as mental health problems. Another explanation is possible. Grade-school educated women in our society are likely to be closely identified with an ethnic group, either because they are first-generation immigrants or because they grew up in a restricted ethnic community. To the extent that in these communities, women clearly serve as a resource for the emotional support of others, such as being the psychologically strong person for a family, they have a stake in seeing themselves as able to manage their own problems and would therefore be likely to reject the idea that their personal problems would ever require professional help. Myerhoff's (1978) analysis of older Jewish women in *Number Our Days,* many of whom had minimal education, fits this characterization.

The most critical finding in the analyses of this section, however, is the significant education by year interaction in the use of help among those who define their problems in mental health terms. The relevant results are boxed in table 5.8. Among those defining a problem in mental health terms in 1957, more educated respondents were distinctly more likely to have actually gone for help than those less educated (ranging from 48 percent for the grade school educated to 72 percent among college graduates). Not even a hint of this relationship remained in 1976. (Comparable proportions are 80 percent and 73 percent, respectively). Thus, the significance of education for converting a mental health problem definition into an actual decision to seek help has declined significantly over the twenty-year period.

Essentially the same pattern exists when we consider the significance of income for the second stage of the self-referral process (see table 5.8). Among those who described some past problem as relevant for professional help, high-income persons in 1957 were more likely than low income persons to have actually sought help. This difference disappeared by 1976, thereby implying a decline in the significance of income (or other facilitating/hindering factors associated with income) for the decision to seek professional help. As noted elsewhere, (Kulka, Veroff, and Douvan, 1979), the 1957 relationship between income and use of help also disappears when education is controlled. The reverse is also true. Together, the results suggest that either may account for social status differences in the actual use of formal help, differences which in any case were no longer evident by 1976.

The implication of these results cannot be overemphasized. As we stated elsewhere (Kulka, Veroff, and Douvan, 1979), being of lower socioeconomic status (less educated or poorer) seemed to be an obstacle to help-seeking in 1957, but was not in 1976. These data may be interpreted as indicating that attempts since 1960 to make professional help more available or accessible to disadvantaged people have indeed been successful.

Other Social and Demographic Factors. The relationship between these two stages of self-referral (defining a problem in mental health terms plus seeking help after having defined the problem in that way) and other social and demographic characteristics were analyzed both for their overall contribution to significant differences in each of the years of the survey, plus their contribution independent of sex, age, education, and year differences. We summarize these results in table 5.10 by indicating whether a significant result was present in each of the two years, whether these results were independent of controls, and what the general finding was, if there was any significant result. Our analyses of sex, age, education, and income effects, discussed in the previous section, are also summarized in table 5.10. Those interested in the specific effect of any of these characteristics on the two stages of self-referral may refer to the table.

Of particular concern in table 5.10 is the extent to which the pattern of findings is consistent with the propositions offered at the onset of this discussion. Within the general framework distinguishing psychological from facilitating factors that may influence the two decision points in the self-referral process, the general hypothesis was that, while these two types of factors are clearly interrelated and any given variable may reflect aspects of both, facilitating factors tend to be relatively more operative at the second decision point than the first—that is, at the point of deciding to seek help rather than in the initial definition of the problem. Shortly we shall attempt to classify and interpret the differences in table 5.10 in terms of this hypothesis.

First, however, let us briefly consider evidence bearing on our two suggested corollaries to this general proposition, both relevant to expected patterns of change. First, we suggested that the degree to which a given characteristic tends to reflect primarily psychological or facilitating factors is presumably subject to change. Although evidence for this proposition is not overwhelming, a few of the relationships reported in table 5.10 are consistent with this assumption in that they appear most relevant at different decision points in 1957 and 1976. For example, while regional differences in 1957 were apparent only in the translation of recognition of a mental health problem into a decision to go for help (a pattern characteristic of facilitating factors), regional differences in 1976 appeared only for the tendency to structure problems in mental health terms (a pattern characteristic of psychological factors). Similarly, in 1957, education and rural-urban differences in self-referral appeared to involve both psychological and facilitating factors, each being significantly related to both of the first two stages of the self-referral process. In 1976, however, these two variables were related only to the initial stage of self-referral—a pattern most reflective of psychological factors—thereby implying a decline in the significance of education and the rural-urban distinction as indicators of facilitating factors.

Second, we suggested that factors which serve primarily to facilitate or hinder the use of professional help are probably more readily susceptible to change than psychological orientations and motivational factors. Results consistent with this assumption are much more evident in the analyses summarized in table 5.10. Ignoring relationships which were not independent of our controls (relationships which in most cases are probably more clearly interpretable in terms of age or educational differences), it is striking that in every instance where a significant difference appears in 1957 but is no longer evident in 1976, the relevant relationships involve the second rather than the first decision point in the self-referral process. Education, income, size of place of residence, region, and employment status (for women) all follow this pattern. Thus, under the assumption that facilitating factors are those most relevant to the latter stage of self-referral, a decline in the significance of these variables for that stage from 1957 to 1976 implies general decline in the significance of factors which serve to facilitate or hinder the use of help among those defining a problem in help-relevant terms. A decline in the significance of these variables for that stage from 1957 to 1976 implies that changes over the generation that facilitated the use of professional help made these characteristics less relevant to seeking help.

On the other hand, two other apparent changes over the same period seem to involve changes in psychological factors. Notably, region and religion, though essentially unrelated to defining a problem in mental health terms in 1957, both show significant relationships in 1976, implying an increase in the psychological significance of these factors for self-referral over the two decades. When we look closely at these effects it is clear that in 1976 Westerners and Jews were particularly likely to define a problem in mental health terms. For both groups, we believe that the group exposure effect we hinted at in discussing our results for readiness for self-referral may be the relevant "psychological" factor. Help-seeking is a common behavior in Western life and among Jews. Its very frequency in these groups may induce people to take a mental health perspective on their problems. Overall, however, the predominance of facilitating factors rather than psychological factors in the patterns of change observed in these relationships seems to be more striking.

Given these patterns of change, however, and the general hypothesis that the tendency to define a problem in mental health terms is relatively more affected by psychological and less by facilitating factors than is the decision to seek help, let us attempt to describe some of these sociodemographic differences (primarily as they appeared in 1976) in terms of this distinction between psychological and facilitating factors.

With the possible exception of age, in 1976 no sociodemographic factors emerged as clearly distinctive for both decisions, whereas in 1957 both education and size of place of residence did. In large part, this lack serves once again to emphasize an apparent decline from 1957 to 1976 in the significance of facilitating factors for self-referral. The case of age is possibly the exception which proves the rule in that the significant age difference which emerged in 1976 involves a greater tendency among a specific set of birth cohorts (those forty to fifty-nine) to translate a mental health problem definition into an actual decision to seek help. This increased tendency toward professional help-seeking among those reaching their middle adult years in 1976 suggests perhaps that this group may have been particularly susceptible to concerted efforts during the two decades to increase the knowledge, availability, and accessibility of mental health services. Nevertheless, the significance of age as a psychological influence still appears predominant. Younger and older people still appear to differ more in their psychological orientations toward problems than in how susceptible they are to information or social climates facilitating or hindering help-seeking decisions (see Kulka and Tamir, 1978).

If we turn our attention to factors that emerge more clearly at the first decision point than at the second, we see that sex, education, place of residence, region, community tenure, religion, father's occupation, region of birth, broken-home background, and marital status are all significantly related in 1976 to defining a problem in mental health terms but not to translating this definition into an actual decision to seek help. Thus, by numbers alone, it is clear that by 1976 sociodemogràphic differences in the self-referral process were largely a function of variation in factors that make a person psychologically receptive to the idea of seeking help rather than those which hinder or facilitate the decision to do so.

Repeating the pattern observed in 1957, women apparently differed from men primarily in the type of psychological orientation toward the self that leads to a definition of problems in mental health terms, rather than in the resources available to them, in their information about professional sources, or in the social norms influencing them once a problem has been recognized. It is also not surprising that education remained distinctive at the first stage of self-referral, since we have seen that education is still closely related to a psychological orientation to adjustment, an orientation which is clearly relevant for defining emotional problems in mental health terms. What is somewhat surprising, though enlightening, is that education differences no longer seem to be facilitating factors, suggesting a greater equivalence among education groups in knowledge about professional help sources, access to them, and/or attitudes about going to them.

Logically, community variables such as rural-urban characteristics or region of the country would primarily reflect facilitating factors, since these characteristics are directly associated with the availability and concentration of help-relevant resources or facilities as we shall document in chapter 8. And, indeed, in 1957 this was the case. By 1976, however, efforts to distribute mental health resources more equally throughout the nation had apparently met with some success, since these factors no longer appear to influence the decision to seek help among those who have defined a problem appropriate for such assistance. (We have a clearer test of this in chapter 8.) Rather, these two community variables (as well as time in the community) now appear to reflect differences in psychological orientations which either enhance or mitigate against the definition of problems as relevant for help—values, motives, or other predispositions which continue to distinguish urban from rural residents, Westerners from Southerners, and the geographically mobile from the nonmobile.

Similarly, differences in religion, social background, and marital status appear predominantly at the first decision point rather than at the second. Apparently, Jews versus Baptists, people whose fathers were professionals versus farmers, those growing up in the West versus elsewhere, adults from intact homes versus those broken by divorce, and the divorced versus other marital groups all differ more in their psychological orientations toward problems than in the availability of resources or information about them or in social climates which serve to facilitate or hinder their help-seeking decisions.

In contrast to this broad array of measures now related only to mental health problem definition, church attendance was the only factor that is clearly more operative in 1976 at the second decision point than at the first. Frequent church attenders in 1976 were no more likely than infrequent attenders to structure their problems in mental health terms, but they were more likely to seek help once the problem had been defined. This consistent difference apparently reflects both a greater availability of professional sources of at least one sort (religious counsel) for the religious person and the probable existence of a traditional climate of approval of their use.

Finally, in spite of plausible theoretical reasons for assuming their relevance to the self-referral process, it is worth noting that occupation, race, urban-rural background, parental status, and work status all bear no consistent relationship to either decision point when traditional controls for sex, age, and education are taken into account. This serves to remind us how powerful overall age and education differences are.

People Who Have Gone for Help

Having established the patterns of stability and change in the general use of professional resources during the past two decades, and in the social and demographic correlates of this general use of formal help for personal problems, we now turn our attention to an intensive analysis of some more specific aspects of the nature and process of professional help-seeking behavior by focusing exclusively on those people who have actually used formal resources to aid them in coping with problems they have experienced. Specifically, this discussion will be based on responses to the following set of questions, asked of respondents subsequent to those used to derive our index of readiness for self-referral.

As in the 1960 monograph, we approach our analysis of those people who have sought professional help and their responses to this series of questions with five basic practical and theoretical issues in mind: (1) Why did these people seek help; (2) Which sources did they consult; (3) How did they get to these sources of help; (4) Do they feel that they were helped; and (5) If so, in what ways do they feel that they were helped? We shall review the data for possible changes in each aspect of the use of help expressed in these interrelated questions, including potential differences in relationships among them (for example, relationships between kinds of personal problems and the sources of help used). Finally, we shall analyze the way that various social groups differ in the types of problems for which they seek help

Sometimes when people have problems like this, they go someplace for help. Sometimes they go to a doctor or a minister. Sometimes they go to a special place for handling personal problems—like a psychiatrist or a marriage counselor, or social agency or clinic.
1. How about you—have you ever gone anywhere like that for advice or help with a personal problem?
2. What was that about?
3. Where did you go for help?
4. [1957 only] How did you happen to go there?
   [1976 only] How did you know to go there? That is, how did you know about that (person/place)?[6]
5. What did they do—how did they try to help you?
6. How did it turn out—do you think it helped you in any way?[6]

and the particular sources to whom they turn for help. In these latter analyses, we shall be getting at the core of information that will help us understand the third decision point in the self-referral process.

WHY PEOPLE GO FOR HELP

What are the kinds of personal problems which people perceive as being serious enough to require the assistance of a professional resource? Given a sizeable increase between 1957 and 1976 in the proportion of respondents that have gone somewhere for help with a personal problem, one could make a plausible case for expecting some substantial change in the nature of problems for which people seek such help, in spite of evidence presented in Book 1 indicating only modest differences between the 1957 and 1976 surveys in the content of general well being (that is, unhappiness and worries). On the contrary, however, table 5.11 indicates that the particular problems for which professional help is sought were remarkably similar in 1976 to those reported in 1957. Although users of formal resources in 1976 were about twice as likely as those in 1957 to have sought help for a situational problem involving other people (for example, death or illness of someone close), the majority of problems cited still related to some type of interpersonal difficulty—predominantly problems in a current or prior marriage—with the proportion indicating problems in personal adjustment (for example, being unhappy, suffering from specific psychological symptoms) also remaining relatively stable.

Paralleling this relative stability in the specific content of problems for which professional help has been sought is a relative stability in inferred general causes or loci of these difficulties, that is, whether

[6]After much deliberation, we decided to ask this question somewhat differently in 1976 because a substantial number of people in 1957 gave responses inappropriate to our intended frame of reference (e.g., "in a taxi" or some restatement of the problem).

TABLE 5.11

Nature of Personal Problems for Which People
Sought Professional Help: 1957 and 1976

	Year of Interview	
Problem Area	1957 (%)	1976 (%)
Spouse; marriage	42	40
Child; relationship with child	12	10
Other family relationships—parents, in-laws, etc.	5	3
Job or school problems; vocational choice	6	4
Nonjob adjustment problems in the self (general adjustment, specific symptoms, etc.)	19	22
Situational problems involving other people (e.g., death or illness of a loved one) causing extreme psychological reaction	6	11
Nonpsychological situational problems	8	11
Other problem areas	4	5
Nothing specific; a lot of little things; can't remember	2	1
Not ascertained	1	4
Total	—[a]	—[a]
Total Number	345	580

[a] Indicates that percentages total to more than 100 percent because some respondents gave more than one response.

some personal failing, another person, a situational factor, or an interpersonal relationship is seen as the root of difficulty (table 5.12). Users of professional help in 1976 were not any more likely than those in 1957 to structure the locus of their personal problems in another person's difficulties or faults, or in the failures of an important interpersonal relationship. Nor were they more likely to structure their problems or to see their difficulties as directly lodged in their own deficiencies or behaviors. This perhaps undermines a stereotype created by the popular media. Our country has not become more densely populated over the generation with self-indulgent people seeking long-term treatment for neurotic personality failures about which they are all too ready to talk, if not boast.

There was only one significant change from 1957 to 1976. A proportionately greater number of Americans in 1976 went for help about problems they saw as situational, such as reactions to the death or illness of a loved one or a reaction to their own ill health or financial stress. This result implies that the decision to seek help for a personal problem may have been influenced over the generation by efforts in the community mental health movement to emphasize crisis intervention as a critical facet of their work. We suggest that psychological

TABLE 5.12

Perceived Locus of Personal Problems for Which
People Sought Professional Help: 1957 and 1976

| | Year of Interview | |
| | 1957 | 1976 |
Locus of Problem	(%)	(%)
Extreme psychological reaction to situational problems	8	13
Personal or interpersonal problem involving defect in self	23	25
Problem in other person, or interpersonal problem involving defect in the other	25	21
Interpersonal problem with defect viewed in the relationship, or locus of defect unspecified	32	31
Problem structured in impersonal, nonpsychological terms	12	9
Not ascertained	4	8
Total	—a	—a
Total Number	345	580

a Indicates that percentages total to more than 100 percent because some respondents gave more than one response.

reactions to such situational crises have become increasingly viewed as problems appropriate and sufficiently serious for professional counsel.

WHERE PEOPLE GO FOR HELP

Having recognized that a particular problem merits professional attention, a person in distress may choose among a broad array of professional counselors, including clergymen, psychiatrists, clinical psychologists, physicians, lawyers, marriage counselors, vocational guidance workers, social workers, and others. Thus, the third decision in the self-referral process described earlier (a choice relevant only among people who actually made a decision to go for help) involves the choice of where to go for help, that is, the selection of a particular help source. Of interest here, then, is the differential use of various professional help sources and, especially, the relative use of the clergy, the medical profession, the psychiatric profession, and other mental health sources.

The percentages presented by year in table 5.13 are the rates of utilization of professional sources approached for help by our respondents. The rates are expressed in the same two units distinguished in chapter 4: "net" rate of utilization of each type of help source among those who had actually gone for help (345 and 580 respondents in 1957 and

1976, respectively); and "gross" rates of utilization for each type of professional source in the total samples. Although table 5.13 shows that these gross rates of those consulting each of the major help sources[7] in 1976 were higher than in 1957 (except for lawyers and social service agencies[8]), the net rates reveal distinctive and interesting differences.

Notably, while proportions of those seeking help from the clergy, doctors,[9] or lawyers declined between 1957 and 1976 in net rate (the latter two differences being statistically significant), the proportions consulting a psychiatrist/psychologist, a marriage counselor, or other mental health professional or agency increased substantially in net rate during the two decades. Thus, while less than 30 percent of those persons seeking professional help for a personal problem in 1957 consulted a mental health source of one type or another, almost half (49 percent) of those who went for help in 1976 consulted a private practitioner or someone in an agency that could be described as a "mental health professional." In gross rates, the use of mental health professionals over the past twenty years or so has more than tripled (from 4 percent in 1957 to 13 percent in 1976), while more modest increases in the use of clergy and doctors occurred during the same period.

Thus, while the increased use of professional help by adults in 1976 reflects a greater overall use of virtually all specific types of help, increases in consultations with mental health professionals are especially striking, paralleling as they do a similar shift in orientation toward the potential use of these more "specialized" professional help sources (emphasized in chapter 4). There has been a considerable increase in the population's readiness to consult mental health professionals in times of crisis. Undoubtedly there has been sufficiently widespread knowledge about the availability or reported effectiveness of such professionals, that previous barriers to using them for crises have declined. As we shall see in the next chapter, there is still a sizeable group of people who say they refused to go to a professional for help because of the possible shame it would entail, but the people who

[7] It is important to note that we are dealing here with reported sources of help, and that public terminology with regard to the differentiation of these professionals is potentially quite loose, even in 1976. A general practitioner or other physician may have been incorrectly referred to as a "psychiatrist," while a psychiatrist may have been designated simply as a "doctor." The public image of various mental health professionals is likely to have been especially confused (cf. Elinson, Padilla, and Perkins, 1967). Although public sophistication in differentiating these sources is probably greater in 1976 than in 1957, it is likely that many persons still cannot distinguish between psychologists and psychiatrists, for example. Accordingly, those who mentioned seeing psychologists are grouped with those who mentioned psychiatrists and a variety of other mental health sources (for example, counselors, social workers, or agencies set up to handle psychological problems) are grouped under one generic category: "other mental health source."

[8] Welfare agency; employment bureau; any nonmental health social service.

[9] A physician or doctor not specifically designated as a psychiatrist was coded as a doctor.

TABLE 5.13

Sources of Help Used by People Who Have Sought
Professional Help for a Personal Problem: 1957 and 1976

| | Year of Interview | | | |
| | 1957 | | 1976 | |
Source of Help	Net[a] (%)	Gross[b] (%)	Net[a] (%)	Gross[b] (%)
Clergy	42		39	
		6		10
Doctor	29		21	
		4		6
Psychiatrist or psychologist	17		29	
		2		7
Marriage counselor; marriage clinic	4		8	
		<1		2
Other mental health source (specialist or agency)	10		20	
		1		5
Social service agency (nonmental health)	4		3	
		<1		<1
Lawyer	6		2	
		<1		<1
Other	12		7	
	—[c]	2	—[c]	2
Total		—[d]		—[d]
Total Number	345		580	
		2,460		2,264

[a] Percentage base: People who have sought professional help.

[b] Percentage base: All respondents.

[c] Indicates that columns total to more than 100 percent (or more than the percentage who sought professional help) because some respondents mentioned more than one source.

[d] Columns do not total 100% because those who did not seek help are omitted.

constituted that group in 1976 were slightly different from their counterparts in 1957.

In spite of the clear and important shift in 1976 toward the consultation of mental health professionals for personal problems, one cannot fail to be impressed by the continuing critical role that the clergy play in assisting many Americans in dealing with personal problems. As we shall see, the clergy are consulted not only for matters that are traditionally part of their functions as pastoral conselors (comforting those who mourn and advising those who confront illness), but also for interpersonal difficulties. Indeed, nearly half of the consultations with the clergy concerned marital issues. We thus should not forget in our emphasis on the mental health professions, that one out of every ten Americans in 1976 said that at one time or another they talked to their clergy about a personal problem.

TABLE 5.14

Type of Problem Brought to Different Sources of Help (All Responses) (by year)

Problem Area	Clergy		Doctor		Psychiatrist/ Psychologist		Marriage Counselor		Other Mental Health Source		Social Service Agency		Lawyer		Other	
	1957 (%)	1976 (%)	1957 (%)	1976 (%)	1957 (%)	1976 (%)	1957 (%)	1976 (%)	1957 (%)	1976 (%)	1957 (%)	1976 (%)	1957 (%)	1976 (%)	1957 (%)	1976 (%)
Spouse; marriage	47	45	41	27	40	38	92	92	64	40	14	21	62	50	32	37
Child; relationship with child	8	8	9	6	20	12	17	4	30	20	14	16	10	7	20	3
Other family relationships	6	4	6	3	3	4	—	2	3	4	—	—	5	—	—	3
Job or school	5	4	2	2	3	4	—	—	3	2	7	5	—	—	22	—
Adjustment problems in self (nonjob)	20	15	22	30	32	25	—	4	6	33	—	11	—	—	7	42
Psychological reaction to situational problem	6	14	5	19	7	10	—	4	—	4	14	5	5	7	5	16
Nonpsychological situational problem	3	9	13	19	—	6	—	2	—	7	43	37	14	21	12	8
Other problem area	7	5	3	5	2	5	—	2	—	4	—	5	5	7	—	3
Nothing specific; can't remember	3	2	1	2	2	1	—	—	—	—	—	—	—	—	5	—
Not ascertained	—[a]	5	2	1	—[a]	4	—[a]	—[a]	—[a]	2	7	—	—[a]	—	2	—[a]
Total	—[a]	—[a]	—[a]	—[a]	—[a]	—[a]	—[a]	—[a]	—[a]	—[a]	—[a]	—[a]	—[a]	—[a]	—[a]	—[a]
Total Number	144	226	99	124	60	167	12	49	33	113	14	19	21	14	41	38

NOTE: A dash indicates that the percentage is less than one-half of 1 percent.

[a] Indicates that percentages total to more than 100 percent because some respondents mentioned more than one problem area.

To gain further insight into reasons people may have for choosing among these various sources of help, we examined the kind of personal problems people brought to each of the sources of help (table 5.14). For the large part, men and women bring the types of problems to a given source of help that are appropriate to that source. Marriage counselors are predictably consulted almost exclusively for marriage problems; physicians and social service agencies are more likely than other professionals to be sought for nonpsychological situational problems (for example, illness viewed strictly in physical terms, financial problems); and people who consult "other mental health sources" (which include child guidance counselors and children's agencies) mention problems with a child more often than those who went to other sources. Thus, both in 1957 and 1976 these differences largely conform to an anticipated pattern.

Within this general pattern, however, there were some significant changes between 1957 and 1976 that are worth attending to. The clearest is the increased consultation of practically all help sources for either psychological reactions to situational problems or for nonpsychological situational problems. The incidence of consultation for these kinds of problems in 1976 was still not large, but the change from 1957 is noteworthy. Not a single mental health professional was mentioned by a respondent in the 1957 sample as having been consulted for a nonpsychological situational problem. In 1976, 6 percent of the psychiatrists/psychologists consulted and 7 percent of those categorized as "other mental health sources" were seen for such problems. Also evident among "other mental health professionals" is a substantial increase in their handling of problems of personal adjustment, which in previous years were predominant only among those consulting psychiatrists or psychologists. This substantial increase probably reflects increased numbers of professionals trained for agency work in community mental health centers as well as an increased public acceptance of these professionals, and their agencies as well, as major purveyors of personal psychological guidance. Partially offsetting these 1957–1976 increases was a decrease in the consultation of doctors and "other mental health specialists" for marriage problems. This implies perhaps a greater tendency to consult specialists—marriage counselors—for these difficulties.

Increased use of specialized resources can be seen indirectly in another analysis. We know that people who said that they had at some time or another felt that they were going to have a nervous breakdown were especially prone to seek help for personal problems. Whom did they consult in 1957 and 1976, if they did seek help about a personal problem?[10] The results are tabulated in table 5.15. There has

---

[10]Although we cannot say for sure that the help source specified was sought for controlling the feelings that the respondent had about a nervous breakdown, in a good percentage of the cases this was probably true.

TABLE 5.15

Sources of Professional Help Used by People
Who Had Felt an Impending Nervous
Breakdown (by year)

	Year of Interview	
Source of Help	1957 (%)	1976 (%)
Clergy	3	3
Doctor	77	52
Psychiatrist or psychologist	4	18
Marriage counselor	—[c]	—[c]
Other mental health source	3	10
Social service agency	—[c]	—[c]
Lawyer	1	—[c]
Other	11	17
Total	—[b]	—[b]
Total Number[a]	231	227

[a] Does not include the 233 people in 1957 and 245 in 1976 who had felt an impending nervous breakdown but did not mention referring the problem to any professional help resource.

[b] Indicates that percentages total to more than 100 percent because some respondents mentioned more than one source.

been a dramatic shift from all but total reliance on doctors to greater use of mental health specialists (psychiatrists/psychologists or other mental health sources) for those people who one time or another felt psychologically overwhelmed. One can conclude that people who define dysfunctions in psychological terms now are more likely to consult specialists in psychological issues.

One way to think of how such specialization crystallizes in people's minds is to ask whether those who go to certain help sources tend to locate the source of their problems in themselves, in another person, in a relationship or a situation. We have already seen how situational problems have become more characteristic of those consulting mental health professionals than they once were. These trends are evident again in table 5.16, in which we analyze the perceived loci of problems for which each type of help source was consulted in 1957 and 1976. From the pattern of findings we may draw a number of conclusions that are consistent in both survey years. Psychiatrists or psychologists were sought out by many people who perceived their problems as arising from a defect in themselves, whereas those consulting clergy and marriage counselors often attributed their problems to a defect in a relationship or to an unspecified locus. Neither of these, however, was so prominent as to indicate specialization. People seeking advice from a doctor were not particularly distinctive in localizing their diffi-

TABLE 5.16

Locus of Problem Brought to Different Sources of Help (All Responses) (by year)

	Source of Help															
	Clergy		Doctor		Psychiatrist/ Psychologist		Marriage Counselor		Other Mental Health Source		Social Service Agency		Lawyer		Other	
Nature and Locus of the Problem	1957 (%)	1976 (%)	1957 (%)	1976 (%)	1957 (%)	1976 (%)	1957 (%)	1976 (%)	1957 (%)	1976 (%)	1957 (%)	1976 (%)	1957 (%)	1976 (%)	1957 (%)	1976 (%)
Psychological reaction to situational problems	10	16	8	17	8	16	—	6	—	6	14	5	5	7	5	8
Problems involving defect in self	22	16	24	34	42	32	—	4	9	35	7	11	—	—	20	42
Problems involving defect in other person	23	19	25	25	30	23	33	12	49	27	7	42	33	29	32	32
Interpersonal problems involving defect in relationship or locus unspecified	41	35	30	15	27	30	67	71	46	35	7	5	19	36	20	16
Problems structured in impersonal, nonpsychological terms	6	8	13	17	—	4	—	4	—	4	50	32	33	21	22	8
Not ascertained	2	12	4	2	—[a]	5	—[a]	8	—[a]	4	14	5	10	7	5	3
Total	—[a]	—[a]	—[a]	—[a]	—[a]	—[a]	—[a]	—[a]	—[a]	—[a]	—[a]	—[a]	—[a]	—[a]	—[a]	—[a]
Total Number	144	226	99	124	60	167	12	49	33	113	14	19	21	14	41	38

NOTE: A dash indicates that the percentage is less than one-half of 1 percent.

[a] Indicates that percentages total to more than 100 percent because some respondents mentioned more than one problem area.

culties. Thus, even over a twenty-year span, the only help source that seems have been attributed to a true specialization is the marriage counselor, who is sought for problems which are rarely structured as a defect in a person but rather simply as marital troubles.

Within this general pattern, however, there is evidence of some significant change between 1957 and 1976. Once again, differences in the nature of problems brought to "other mental health professionals" play a prominent role in this pattern of change. Reflecting the 1957 to 1976 increase in personal adjustment problems noted previously, table 5.16 indicates that people who sought assistance from "other mental health professionals" in 1976 were more likely than those in 1957 to perceive a defect in the self and less likely to attribute their problems to defects in another person. As a result, the perceived locus of problems dealt with by these professionals in 1976 is hardly distinguishable from those characteristic of psychiatrists and psychologists. Another change is among the people who consulted social service agencies in 1976 contrasted with their counterparts in 1957. More of them in 1976 consulted these sources about a defect in another person. Such small numbers of people are in these groups for each year that we will not dwell on this finding, but only point it out. A final change to note is the reduction in the reporting of interpersonal difficulties as a presenting problem among those consulting doctors. No doubt this reflected some channeling of such problems to those perceived as more specialized in these matters: marriage counselors, other mental health professionals, and the clergy.

HOW PEOPLE CHOOSE HELP RESOURCES

In order to gain some additional understanding of motivating factors underlying the selection of a particular help source, we asked people how they happened to arrive at a particular source of help. As noted earlier (see footnote 6, p. 130), somewhat different questions were asked to determine such reasons for choosing professional help sources in the two surveys, so that responses to these questions in 1957 and 1976 are not strictly comparable, and comparisons by year should be interpreted with caution. Essentially, the question was rephrased in 1976 because many responses given in 1957 were not codeable as reasons for choosing a particular help source, thereby limiting severely the usefulness of the data. As can be seen in table 5.17, however, the reworded question used in the 1976 survey was only partially efficacious in remedying this problem. While the proportion of respondents giving a response which was not codeable as a reason is reduced to only 5 percent, 11 percent of the reasons for choosing a given source are still "not ascertained."

In spite of these limitations, however, some significant year differences are evident and appear to represent more than an artifact of the

TABLE 5.17

Reasons for Choice of a Particular Source of Help by People
Who Have Used Professional Help for a Personal Problem
(by year)

	Year of Interview	
	1957	1976
Reason for Choice of Source	**(%)**	**(%)**
Spontaneous Mention of Referral from Outside Source		
Referred by doctor	7	10
Referred by clergy	1	3
Referred by family or friends	8	18
Referred by school, court, other civic agencies	3	7
Referred by mass media (e.g., "I read about it.")	1	3
Other referral agent	7	8
No Spontaneous Mention of Outside Referral		
Personal relationship with help source	18	36
Help source functionally appropriate for problem	27	7
Other reasons	7	4
Reason not specified	34	5
Not ascertained	1	11
Total	—[a]	—[a]
Total Number	345	580

[a] Indicates that percentages total to more than 100 percent because some respondents gave more than one response.

way in which the questions are worded. Of particular note is a substantial increase in the proportion of people who mentioned an outside referral. Specifically, the proportion of those mentioning a referral source almost doubled (from 26 percent in 1957 to 47 percent in 1976), and while the proportion mentioning each type of referral source was higher in 1976, significant increases occurred in referrals from family and friends and from civic agencies. In contrast, referrals by clergymen to other formal help sources still remained rare, although they increased.

Among those who answered the question intended to probe for referral in terms of their own motivations for choosing a particular help source, there is a substantial decline in the proportion saying that they went to a particular person or agency because they felt that source was most appropriate for their problems. Twice as many people in 1976 mentioned a personal relationship with a professional helper as a reason for their choice of a given source. Overall, these changes suggest the increasing importance of informal social processes as significant factors underlying the choice of a given help source. Over half of the reasons given in 1976 for selecting a particular formal helper implicit-

TABLE 5.18

Reasons for Choice of Particular Source by People Who Have Used Professional Help for a Personal Problem (by year)

	Clergy		Doctor		Psychiatrist/ Psychologist		Marriage Counselor		Other Mental Health Source		Social Service Agency		Lawyer		Other	
Reason for Choice of Source	1957 (%)	1976 (%)	1957 (%)	1976 (%)	1957 (%)	1976 (%)	1957 (%)	1976 (%)	1957 (%)	1976 (%)	1957 (%)	1976 (%)	1957 (%)	1976 (%)	1957 (%)	1976 (%)
Referral from Outside Source																
Referred by doctor	1	1	1	3	30	17	—	8	18	15	—	11	—	—	—	5
Referred by clergy	—	—	—	2	2	2	9	10	3	4	—	—	5	—	—	—
Referred by family or friends	3	6	4	6	15	31	17	23	18	21	7	11	—	14	2	5
Referred by school, court, or other civic agencies	—	1	—	2	—	8	8	6	12	18	14	26	—	—	5	3
Referred by mass media	1	—	—	—	—	3	8	6	—	5	7	11	5	—	5	3
Other referral agent	2	1	2	2	7	10	8	19	16	14	29	5	5	—	5	6
No Mention of Outside Referral																
Personal relationship with help source	27	62	11	42	5	10	8	—	3	3	—	—	9	29	17	34
Help source functionally appropriate for problem	10	7	23	10	35	2	33	—	15	2	36	10	48	7	42	5
Other reasons	—	2	—	5	5	2	—	6	12	3	7	5	33	7	22	5
Reason not specified	56	6	59	10	—	2	—	—	—	1	—	5	—	14	2	—
Not ascertained	—	14	—	18	1	13	9	22	3	14	—	16	—	29	—	34
Total	100%	100%	100%	100%	100%	100%	100%	100%	100%	100%	100%	100%	100%	100%	100%	100%
Total Number[a]	144	226	99	125	60	167	12	49	33	114	14	19	21	14	41	38

NOTE: A dash indicates that the percentage is less than one-half of 1 percent.

[a] The number of people totals more than 345 and 580 (in 1957 and 1976, respectively) because people who mentioned more than one source of help are included in more than one column.

ly involved the influence of social network linkages (for example, informal referrals or a personal relationship), while in 1957, such factors were apparently much less salient in this decision process.

Moreover, as shown in table 5.18, with few exceptions, these significant patterns of change between 1957 and 1976 in reasons for choosing a particular resource tend to be surprisingly consistent. For example, fewer of those consulting each type of help source in 1976 said that they went to a particular person or agency because they felt that source of help was appropriate to their problem. There are, however, a few important exceptions. People who sought help from doctors and clergymen were much more likely in 1976 to have done so because of a personal relationship with a physician, minister or priest, while those who went to a psychiatrist were notably less likely to be referred by a doctor and more likely to be referred by family or friends in 1976 than in 1957.

As a result, some rather clear distinctions remain in these relationships between sources of help used and reasons for selection, suggesting some distinct differences in the paths by which people tend to reach these different professional sources. Remarkably consistent with the pattern evident in 1957, the path to a clergyman or doctor appears to be a direct one, rarely mediated by either a formal or informal referral, but often dependent upon a personal relationship. In contrast, psychiatrists (or psychologists), marriage counselors, other mental health specialists or agencies, and social service agencies are predominantly, and increasingly, approached after prior consultation with a referral source. Both formal and informal sources were equally important in the 1976 referrals, but social service agencies, as one might anticipate, still received the majority of their referrals from public institutions and other formal referral agencies.

DO PEOPLE FEEL THEY ARE HELPED?

That people seek professional assistance for their problems does not, of course, ensure that the counsel they receive will prove effective. Given some of the changes we have noted in the types of problems for which people seek help, in the perceived locus of such problems, and in the types of sources consulted, one might reasonably assume that encounters with professional helpers may be perceived as either more or less gratifying in 1976 than they were in 1957. Table 5.19 shows, however, that people who sought professional help for their problems in 1976 were no more or less likely than those seeking such help in 1957 to perceive such assistance as effective. Over two-thirds of the respondents in both survey years who received such professional counsel felt that it helped them with their problems, and less than 20 percent reported that it had failed to do so.

Although professional help sources were usually perceived as help-

TABLE 5.19

Perception of Helpfulness by People Who Have
Used Professional Help for a Personal Problem
(by year)

	Year of Interview	
	1957	1976
Perception of Helpfulness	(%)	(%)
Helped; helped a lot	58	56
Helped; qualified	14	19
Did not help	20	16
Don't know whether helped	1	2
Not ascertained	7	7
Total	100%	100%
Total Number	345	580

ful, at times they were not. For what kind of problem was consultation seen as inadequate? In both survey years, people who sought help for marital problems were significantly less likely than others to feel they were helped, though this was less true in 1976 than in 1957 (see table 5.20). Viewing the issue a little differently, we see in table 5.21 that, in both survey years, people who sought help for a problem structured as a defect in another person or in a relationship were less likely to feel that they were helped. If we put these two findings together, it may be suggested that marital problems presented to a help source as a problem in one's spouse or in one's relationship to one's spouse are often perceived as not being helped by professional consultation. If help-seeking is a step taken to preserve a marriage and the marriage, for whatever reasons, is not preserved, then it is difficult for the help-seeker to consider the consultation as helpful. It is difficult to tell how much the help source actually sanctions the dissolution of the marriage. There are undoubtedly some who take a clear position on the matter (to preserve a marriage at all costs, or to dissolve what is viewed as an unhealthy relationship), but, probably more often than not, therapeutic counsel accentuates the direction in which a marriage was going before the advice was sought. And it is those people who hoped to preserve a marriage by therapeutic intervention who are probably most disappointed when the help cannot magically reinstate the relationship.

These speculations about why help sources consulted for marital problems may frequently be judged as not helpful can be generalized to other kinds of problems. It seems reasonable to us that people who go for help with a very specific goal in mind, the successful attainment of which can also be externally validated, are people who may easily perceive consultation as unsuccessful when the goals are not

TABLE 5.20
Relationship Between Area of Problems and Perception of Helpfulness (by year)

How Much Helped	Marriage		Child		Other Family		Job/School		Adjustment in Self		Situations Involving Others		Non-psychological Situational Problems		Other	
	1957 (%)	1976 (%)	1957 (%)	1976 (%)	1957 (%)	1976 (%)	1957 (%)	1976 (%)	1957 (%)	1976 (%)	1957 (%)	1976 (%)	1957 (%)	1976 (%)	1957 (%)	1976 (%)
Helped, helped a lot	49	50	58	55	59	47	63	71	72	70	53	55	62	50	73	70
Helped (qualified)	12	22	15	26	23	16	16	10	14	10	26	18	14	21	—	15
Did not help	32	22	15	10	—	32	11	9	6	14	11	13	14	13	20	7
Don't know	1	2	5	4	—	—	—	5	5	1	—	3	—	3	—	4
Not ascertained	6	4	7	5	18	5	10	5	3	5	10	11	10	13	7	4
Total	100%	100%	100%	100%	100%	100%	100%	100%	100%	100%	100%	100%	100%	100%	100%	100%
Total Number	146	233	40	58	17	19	19	21	64	128	19	62	29	62	15	27

NOTE: A dash indicates that the percentage is less than one-half of 1 percent.

TABLE 5.21

Relationship Between Nature and Locus of Problems and Perception of Helpfulness (by year)

Nature and Locus of Problem

How Much Helped	Psychological Reaction to Situational Problem		Personal Problem—Defect in Self		Problem Involving Defect in Another		Defect in Relationship or Unspecified		Impersonal, Non-Psychological Terms	
	1957 (%)	1976 (%)	1957 (%)	1976 (%)	1957 (%)	1976 (%)	1957 (%)	1976 (%)	1957 (%)	1976 (%)
Helped, helped a lot	67	65	71	69	47	44	56	51	56	56
Helped (qualified)	18	12	14	11	14	28	13	21	15	17
Did not help	4	13	9	13	29	20	23	22	19	13
Don't know	—	1	4	1	2	3	1	2	—	2
Not ascertained	11	9	2	6	8	5	7	4	10	12
Total	100%	100%	100%	100%	100%	100%	100%	100%	100%	100%
Total Number	27	78	79	142	87	124	109	181	41	52

NOTE: A dash indicates that the percentage is less than one-half of 1 percent.

reached. Just as marriage counselors may be particularly vulnerable to this judgment, as previously noted, so may any help source asked to remedy a specific symptom (for example, obesity, enuresis, a school performance problem). If the consultation is about a general issue of well being, whether in one's self or in a relationship, then it is much easier to accept any consultation as helpful. People do not want to appear foolish; they do not want to admit, even to themselves, that investing time and/or money in professional help was of little value. It would take an extraordinarily inept practitioner to overcome the general bias of people toward viewing any consultation they have initiated as being helpful. Furthermore, most people perceive honest benefits in the process of talking through personal issues with someone removed from the person's ongoing crisis.

In this connection, those most likely to report that professional counsel had helped them "a lot" were those who sought help for a personal adjustment problem (table 5.20), those who, in other words, traced their difficulty to some general defect in themselves (table 5.21). These findings suggest that people who recognize that some general internal personal change in themselves is needed in order to alleviate their difficulties are those most amenable to accepting help in working out their problems or, at least, are most likely to believe that the professional counsel they received actually helped them. Moreover, except for a slight tendency in 1976 for those seeking help for other family problems to perceive the counsel they received as somewhat less effective than in 1957 and a reverse trend for those seeking help for marriage problems (noted previously), there are no significant changes by year to obscure this remarkably consistent pattern of findings.

Relationships between the particular sources of help selected and perceptions of the efficacy of their counsel (table 5.22) are also consistent by year. In both 1957 and 1976, people who went to marriage counselors and "other mental health professionals" were more likely than other help-seekers to deprecate the help they received. These are the very help sources who, we suggest, are consulted for easily specified goals—marriage problems (see table 5.14) or defects in a relationship or another person (see table 5.16). Surprisingly, this is not true of the clergy, in spite of the high proportion of people who seek them out for marital problems or defects in interpersonal relations. They are persistently viewed as a very helpful source. Two explanations may be offered why this may be so, both equally plausible. The clergy may be sought by people who are more committed to maintaining than to dissolving a marriage or an interpersonal relationship. As a result, consulting the clergy may be only a symbolic act of recommitment. Or the clergy, in fact, may be a particularly effective help source for a marriage or any other relationship in trouble. The counsel of the clergy has a moral force that would probably be directed toward healing

TABLE 5.22

Relationship of Source of Help Used to Perception of Helpfulness of Treatment (by year)

| | | | | | | | Source of Help | | | | | | | | | |
| How Much Helped | Clergy | | Doctor | | Psychiatrist/ Psychologist | | Marriage Counselor | | Other Mental Health Source | | Social Service Agency | | Lawyer | | Other | |
	1957 (%)	1976 (%)	1957 (%)	1976 (%)	1957 (%)	1976 (%)	1957 (%)	1976 (%)	1957 (%)	1976 (%)	1957 (%)	1976 (%)	1957 (%)	1976 (%)	1957 (%)	1976 (%)
Helped, helped a lot	65	58	64	64	49	62	25	25	34	46	50	42	43	43	44	55
Helped (qualified)	13	22	12	15	13	14	8	24	27	25	36	26	33	29	29	24
Did not help	18	11	14	9	23	20	67	51	30	21	14	21	14	14	20	8
Don't know	—	1	1	2	5	3	—	—	3	4	—	—	—	—	2	—
Not ascertained	4	8	9	10	10	1	—	—	6	4	—	11	10	14	5	13
Total	100%	100%	100%	100%	100%	100%	100%	100%	100%	100%	100%	100%	100%	100%	100%	100%
Total Number	144	226	99	124	60	167	12	49	33	113	14	19	21	14	41	38

NOTE: A dash indicates that the percentage is less than one-half of 1 percent.

rather than severing relationships. Mental health professionals do not so clearly exert such force. Their training often socializes them to be aware of how personal values may interfere with "proper" help. Of course, we should not ignore the assumption that people who select the clergy for counsel are themselves probably more susceptible to religious and moral evaluations of their behavior. We are clearly not endorsing the therapy used by one or the other type of help source. We are merely trying to understand why the clergy are so uniformly perceived as effective in spite of their work with some of the same problems for which mental health professionals have a lower rate of perceived effectiveness.

Two significant changes in the perceived helpfulness of various sources occurred between 1957 and 1976. One perhaps reflects a more complicated view of the clergy's helpfulness. In 1976, people evaluated the help they received from the clergy in more qualified terms. Compared to 1957, they gave neither as much unqualified endorsement nor as much unqualified devaluation of the help they received. The decrease in viewing the clergy as unequivocally helpful may come from some loss of faith in the religious evaluation of experience. For example, more people who now seek out a clergyperson for marital counseling may themselves be oriented toward divorce as a solution and hence find disquieting a conservative church position on divorce advocated by many ministers, rabbis, and priests. The decrease in viewing the clergy as unhelpful needs explanation also. Undoubtedly there has been some secularization of pastoral counseling over the past generation that might, in some instances, even support divorce. Certainly some such counselors would be more psychologically, rather than morally, oriented in the help given. When members of congregations talk to their clergy about personal problems and are made to feel guilty because of any moral inadequacy, they frequently retreat defensively from the clergy's counsel and scorn it as having no value. Our guess is that that kind of response occurred much more often for the 1957 respondents than for the 1976 respondents. The clergy have clearly become much more psychologically oriented, sometimes at odds with moral or religious positions they may hold. And this secularization of their counseling services lessens the poor reception they may have been accorded in an earlier time. Thus, we see paradoxical forces at work; one reduces the unqualified acceptance of pastoral counseling, the other reduces its unqualified rejection.

The only other significant change in the perceived effectiveness of help sources is a substantial increase in the perceived helpfulness of psychiatrists and psychologists, who in 1976, along with clergy and doctors, were widely recognized as the most effective sources of help. While this finding undoubtedly reflects a significantly greater acceptance of and belief in the particular types of treatment characteristic of psychiatric counselors, it may also reflect a greater willingness on the part of psychiatrists and psychologists to adapt their treatment styles to the particular needs of people in distress. One distinct possibility is that psychiatrists and psychologists have learned not to promise to meet specific goals. If, in the beginning of treatment, they make clear that only general personal change can result from treatment, then the psychiatrist or psychologist becomes less vulnerable to devaluation, as we discussed earlier.

How People Feel They Are Helped

In addition to asking respondents whether or not the treatment they received had been beneficial, we were also interested in potential differences in some of the general ways in which they felt that they had been helped. These included possible changes in relationships between these different kinds of perceived gains with both the sources of help selected and the degree to which respondents felt they were helped. In table 5.23, we see that there are indeed some significant year differences in the general kinds of benefits perceived.

The most dramatic increase was in the proportion of those indicating having been helped by talking or getting advice, which by 1976 accounted for over four out of ten effective help-seeking encounters. Significant, though less dramatic, increases were also evident in the proportions who said they were comforted by the help they received or who spoke in terms of a palliative change in either themselves or in a relationship. These increases were offset primarily by significant declines in the proportions of those who said that the therapy helped with the following: another person close to them; some nonpsycholo-

TABLE 5.23

Perception of Ways in Which Treatment Helped (by year)

	Year of Interview	
Type of Help	1957 (%)	1976 (%)
Helped in terms of comfort, ability to endure problem	12	17
Helped in terms of cure, change in respondent or relationship	15	21
Helped by working with other person in relationship	9	3
Helped by breaking, or by being given support for breaking, relationship (e.g., divorce)	6	5
Helped in nonpsychological aspect of problem	12	4
Helped by talking, advice; not ascertained how this helped	28	43
Helped in other ways	6	1
Not ascertained	12	6
Total	100%	100%
Total Number[a]	249	432

[a] Includes only people who said they were helped.

gical aspect of the problem; miscellaneous ways coded as "nonascertainable." Overall, then, significant patterns of change in how people felt they were helped seem to reflect an increasing preference for the more supportive functions of psychological counseling—talking, comfort, or advice—rather than the miracle-working functions—bringing about changes in the world or another person. In 1976, perceived supportiveness in one form or another constituted over 60 percent of the reasons that treatment was thought to be helpful. In 1957, the comparable percentage was only 40 percent.

As might be anticipated, however, such helping behaviors were not equally characteristic of different types of professional help sources, although there was somewhat greater uniformity in such helping styles among help sources in 1976 than in 1957. As shown in table 5.24, in 1957 the clergymen in particular were appreciated for their ability to offer comfort and for their capacity to provide a forum in which talking or giving advice could take place; doctors and psychiatrists were most often credited with having effected a cure. While doctors in 1976 were still perceived to have frequently brought about cures, ministers and priests in 1976 were rivaled by doctors in their ability to provide comfort and by all the mental health professionals in their ability to provide a forum for talking things out or getting advice. Thus, the perceived distinctive functions that the various professional helpers seemed to be performing in 1957 were becoming somewhat blurred by 1976. Doctors have probably become more psychologically oriented, and the mental health professionals more oriented to being supportive than to being change agents for psychological health, as they become increasingly aware that psychotherapy does not necessarily produce miracles. The mental health professions have probably become either more humble about their potential or more articulate about their supportive goals than they once were, and this changed appraisal has undoubtedly been picked up by their clients who have come to define effective treatment more and more in terms of support.

Is support thus seen as the basis for consultations that were especially effective in 1976? That turns out not to be clearly the case. In table 5.25, we distinguish the type of perceived help received among two groups: help-seekers who were unqualified about the efficacy of the help they received and those who offered some qualification. These two groups differed only in how much cure or change they thought was brought about, with more cure or change seen by people who unqualifiedly evaluated positively the help received in treatment. The two groups did not differ in how much perceived comfort they thought occurred. It is important to note, however, that perceiving comfort as the basis of the help received in treatment was less characteristic of the 1957 sample of people who spoke unqualifiedly about the helpfulness of treatment. We suggest, therefore, that people in

TABLE 5.24

Relationship Between Source of Help Used and Perception of Ways in Which Treatment Helped (by year)

					Source of Help											
	Clergy		Doctor		Psychiatrist/ Psychologist		Marriage Counselor		Other Mental Health Source		Social Service Agency		Lawyer		Other	
Type of Help	1957 (%)	1976 (%)	1957 (%)	1976 (%)	1957 (%)	1976 (%)	1957 (%)	1976 (%)	1957 (%)	1976 (%)	1957 (%)	1976 (%)	1957 (%)	1976 (%)	1957 (%)	1976 (%)
Comfort; ability to endure	23	18	9	24	11	16	—	4	—	11	—	8	6	—	3	13
Cure; change in respondent or relationship	8	15	27	25	22	28	50	17	15	24	—	8	—	—	10	27
Changed other	10	3	5	2	14	2	—	4	20	6	8	8	—	—	10	—
Breaking relationship	10	5	5	3	3	5	25	9	10	4	—	23	12	10	7	7
Nonpsychological aspect	6	3	11	8	5	—	—	—	5	2	58	38	31	20	23	—
Talking; advice	30	51	23	31	13	43	25	54	35	44	17	15	19	70	27	50
Other	4	—	9	1	8	—	—	4	—	—	8	—	13	—	13	—
Not ascertained	9	5	11	6	24	6	—	8	15	9	8	—	19	—	7	3
Total	100%	100%	100%	100%	100%	100%	100%	100%	100%	100%	100%	100%	100%	100%	100%	100%
Total Number[a]	113	180	75	98	37	126	4	24	20	80	12	13	16	10	30	30

NOTE: A dash indicates that the percentage is less than one-half of 1 percent.

[a] Includes only people who said they were helped.

TABLE 5.25

Relationship Between Perception of Helpfulness and
Perception of Ways in Which Treatment Helped (by year)

Type of Help	How Much Helped			
	Helped; Helped a Lot		Helped (Qualified)	
	1957 (%)	1976 (%)	1957 (%)	1976 (%)
Comfort; ability to endure	11	17	17	19
Cure; change in respondent or relationship	19	23	—	14
Changed other	8	2	13	6
Breaking relationship	7	5	2	5
Nonpsychological aspect	12	4	10	5
Talking, Advice	30	44	17	42
Other	5	1	12	1
Not ascertained	8	4	29	8
Total	100%	100%	100%	100%
Total Number[a]	201	326	48	106

NOTE: A dash indicates that the percentage is less than one-half of 1 percent.

[a] Includes only people who said they were helped.

1976 who went for help were very aware of the supportive nature of professional consultations, but that does not necessarily mean that they perceived such support as unqualifiedly helpful.

MULTIVARIATE ANALYSES OF PROBLEMS AND PATTERNS OF HELP-SEEKING

Earlier in this chapter (table 5.5), we observed that in both survey years proportionately more women than men, more younger than older persons, and more highly educated respondents than less educated respondents consulted a professional help source with a personal problem. And, for all of these groups, the 1976 sample had sought more help than the 1957 sample. Furthermore, in our investigation of the group of people who used help, a number of significant changes were noted between 1957 and 1976 in specific aspects of their help-seeking behavior. At this point in our discussion, we shall attempt to link these two lines of inquiry by examining multivariate relationships of sex, age, education, and year to these various aspects of the help-seeking. Initially, we are interested in the extent to which these multivariate analyses suggest a need to qualify our previous descriptions of year differences in dimensions of help-seeking. In addition, however, we are especially interested in possible sex, age, and educational differences in the particular kinds of problems with which people seek help, in the particular help sources they choose, and other aspects of the help-seeking process, including, as usual, a particular concern with potential differences in such relationships in 1957 and 1976.

Qualifications to Year Differences

Table 5.26 provides a summary of multivariate analyses describing the main and interactive effects of sex, age, education, and year for the problems and patterns of help-seeking examined in this section. A careful examination of that table suggests first that our prior descriptions of year differences in these various aspects of help-seeking require very few qualifications, since most of the year differences observed are independent of relationships involving sex, age, and education. To summarize, people in 1976 who reported having gone for help with a personal problem were: (1) more likely than those in 1957 to have gone for a situational problem involving other people (or a psychological reaction to a situational problem); (2) more likely to have consulted a psychiatrist or psychologist, a marriage counselor, or other mental health professional, and less likely to have chosen a doctor, lawyer, or other professional help source; (3) more likely to have cited a referral by family or friends, a school, court, or agency, or a personal relationship as a reason for choosing a particular source; and (4) more likely to say they were talked to, given advice and comfort, or cured by the help they received.

Supplementing these general patterns of change, however, are a few significant year differences which only occur or especially occur for men or women, or for one age group or another.

First, although the difference is quite small, women in 1976 were significantly less likely than twenty years earlier to seek help for problems related to their jobs or schooling (3 percent versus 0.3 percent); men in 1957 and 1976 were equally likely in both years to have gone for help with such problems (10 percent in both years).

Second, the significant decline noted previously in the use of physicians between 1957 and 1976 was evident predominantly among the young (those aged fifty-five and over were actually slightly *more* likely to consult doctors in 1976, though the difference is not significant). Thus, it is the young adults especially who turned less to these non-psychiatric specialists.

Third, two sex by year interactions, indicated in table 5.26, which occur among reasons for choosing a particular help source, suggest

TABLE 5.26

Summary of Multivariate Analyses Relating Sex, Age, Education, and Year to Problems and Patterns of Help-Seeking

Relationship(s) Required[a] to Reproduce Observed Cross-Classification of Measures by Sex × Age × Education × Year

Measure of Help-Seeking	Main Effects[b]				Interactions
	Sex	Age	Education	Year	
Problem Area					
Spouse; marriage	—	Y,MA>O	—	—	Sex × Age
Child; relationship with child	M<F	Y<MA,O	—	—	—
Other family relationships	—	MA>Y,O	—	—	—
Job or school	M>F	—	—	—	Sex × Age, Sex × Year, Age × Education
Adjustment problems in self (nonjob)	—	MA<Y,O	H<G,C	—	—
Psychological reaction to situational problem	M<F	Y<MA<O	—	57<76	—
Nonpsychological situational problem	—	Y<MA<O	G>H>C	—	—
Other problem area	—	Y>MA,O	—	—	—
Nothing specific; can't remember	—	—	—	—	—
Not ascertained	—	—	—	—	—
Nature or Locus of Problem					
Psychological reaction to situational problem	M<F	Y<MA<O	—	57>76	—
Problems involving defect in self	—	MA<Y,O	H<G,C	—	—
Problems involving defect in other person	M<F	Y<MA,O	—	—	—
Interpersonal problems involving defect in relationship or locus unspecified	—	Y>MA>O	G<H<C	—	Sex × Age
Problems structured in impersonal, nonpsychological terms	—	—	—	—	Sex × Age
Not ascertained	—	—	G>H>C	57>76	—
Source of Help (Among Those Who Used Help)					
Clergy	—	—	—	—	Sex × Age
Doctor	M<F	—	G,H>C	57>76	Age × Year
Psychiatrist or Psychologist	—	—	G<H<C	57<76	Sex × Age
Marriage counselor; marriage clinic	—	—	—	57<76	—
Other mental health source	—	Y,MA>O	—	57<76	—
Social Service Agency	—	—	—	—	—
Lawyer	—	Y<MA<O	—	57>76	—

	Sex	Age	Education	Year	Interaction Effects
Clergy	M<F		H,C>G	57<76	Age × Year
Doctor	—	MA>Y,O	G<H<C	57<76	Sex × Age
Psychiatrist or Psychologist	—	Y,MA>O	G,H<C	57<76	—
Marriage counselor; marriage clinic	M<F	Y,M>O	—	57<76	—
Social service agency	—	—	—	—	—
Lawyer	—	—	—	—	—
Other	M<F	—	G,H<C	—	—
Reason for Choice of Source					
Referral from outside source:					
Referred by doctor	—	—	—	—	Age × Education
Referred by clergy	—	—	—	57<76	—
Referred by family or friends	—	—	—	57<76	Sex × Age, Sex × Year
Referred by school, court, or other civic agency	—	Y,MA>O	—	57<76	—
Referred by mass media	—	—	—	—	Sex × Year
Other referral agent	—	—	—	—	—
No mention of outside referral:					
Personal relationship with help source	—	—	—	57<76	—
Help source functionally appropriate	—	—	—	57>76	—
Other reasons	—	MA>Y,O	—	—	—
Reason not specified	—	—	—	57>76	—
Not ascertained	—	—	—	—	Education × Year
Perception of Helpfulness					
Type of Help					
Comfort; ability to endure	—	Y,MA<O	—	57<76	Sex × Year
Cure; change in respondent or relationship	—	Y>MA>O	—	57<76	—
Changed other	—	—	G>H,C	—	—
Breaking relationship	—	—	—	—	—
Nonpsychological aspect	—	—	G>H,C	57>76	—
Advice	—	Y>MA>O	—	57<76	—
Other	—	—	—	—	—
Not ascertained	—	—	—	—	—

NOTE: A dash indicates that there is no significant effect.

[a] See Footnote [a] of Table 3.2 for an explanation of "Required."

[b] See Footnote [b] of Table 3.2 for a description of "Main Effects."

TABLE 5.27

Sex, Age, and Education Related to Source of Help Used (Net[a] and Gross[b] Use) (by year)

Social or Demographic Characteristic	Source of Help Used																			
	Clergy		Doctor		Psychiatrist/ Psychologist		Marriage Counselor		Other Mental Health Source		Social Service Agency		Lawyer		Other		Total Percentage[d]		Total Number	
	1957 (%)	1976 (%)	1957 (%)	1976 (%)	1957 (%)	1976 (%)	1957 (%)	1976 (%)	1957 (%)	1976 (%)	1957 (%)	1976 (%)	1957 (%)	1976 (%)	1957 (%)	1976 (%)	1957	1976	1957	1976
Sex (Net)																				
Men	42	36	23	16	21	32	4	11	9	19	2	4	7	3	13	5	—	—	116	207
Women	42	41	31	24	16	27	3	7	10	20	5	3	6	2	11	7	—	—	229	373
Sex (Gross)																				
Men	4	8	2	3	2	7	1	2	1	4	—[c]	1	1	1	1	1	—	—	1,077	960
Women	7	12	5	7	3	8	1	2	2	6	1	1	1	1	2	2	—	—	1,383	1,304
Age (Net)																				
21 to 29	49	42	27	12	9	29	5	7	6	22	5	3	2	3	11	5	—	—	82	153
30 to 39	31	31	36	20	22	32	3	9	15	24	3	4	1	1	11	3	—	—	101	147
40 to 49	46	41	23	26	23	33	5	10	11	20	5	1	10	3	11	7	—	—	83	110
50 to 59	38	39	29	22	16	21	—[c]	10	7	19	—[c]	8	17	4	21	10	—	—	42	88
60 to 64	38	45	38	19	25	36	—[c]	7	—[c]	16	—[c]	—[c]	—[c]	—[c]	25	10	—	—	8	31
65 and over	50	45	23	43	8	20	4	6	4	2	12	4	12	2	4	14	—	—	26	51
Age (Gross)																				
21 to 29	9	12	5	3	2	8	1	2	1	6	1	1	—[c]	1	2	1	—	—	453	553
30 to 39	5	10	6	6	4	10	1	3	3	8	1	1	—[c]	—[c]	2	1	—	—	584	463

40 to 49	7	13	4	9	4	11	1	3	2	7	1	—	2	1	2	2	515	341
50 to 59	4	10	3	6	2	5	—c	3	1	5	—c	2	2	1	2	3	390	342
60 to 64	2	8	2	4	1	7	—c	1	—c	3	—c	—c	—c	—c	1	3	153	166
65 and over	4	6	2	6	1	3	—c	1	—c	—c	1	1	1	—c	—c	2	353	397
Education (Net)																		
Grade school	41	25	27	7	16	2	13	8	15	10	2	7	15	8	—		61	62
Some high school	44	41	23	15	26	3	9	10	22	3	5	8	11	9	—		73	92
High school graduate	42	28	27	15	24	5	8	13	17	5	3	6	10	5	—		111	196
Some college	47	44	17	22	27	4	6	9	24	—c	5	4	9	9	—		45	117
College graduate	39	28	11	32	50	4	14	6	21	2	5	4	17	5	—		54	112
Education (Gross)																		
Grade school	3	7	2	5	1	3	1	1	1	2	1	—c	1	1	1	—	802	380
Some high school	6	11	6	2	7	—c	1	1	6	—c	1	1	2	2	—		511	347
High school graduate	7	11	5	3	6	1	2	2	4	1	1	1	2	1	—		674	766
Some college	9	11	5	4	8	1	2	2	4	—c	1	1	2	1	—		247	411
College graduate	10	9	4	8	16	1	5	1	7	—c	1	1	4	1	—		210	347

[a] Net use: percentages based on those who actually went for help.

[b] Gross use: percentages based on all respondents.

[c] Indicates less than one-half of one percent.

[d] Percentages total more or less than 100 percent because some respondents mentioned either more than one source or (in the case of gross use) no professional sources of help.

that increases from 1957 to 1976 in mentioning at least certain kinds of referral sources were more characteristic for men than for women. While both sexes were significantly more likely in 1976 to mention family and friends as referral agents, the increase is particularly dramatic for men, who were seven times more likely (3 percent versus 21 percent) in 1976 to mention an informal referral, while women were less than twice as likely (10 percent versus 17 percent). Similarly, while women in 1957 and 1976 were about equally likely to mention having been influenced by the mass media in their choice of a help source, men in 1976 were slightly more likely to mention the media.

In spite of these exceptions, however, one cannot help but be impressed by the overall consistency of year differences in the patterns of formal help-seeking across major population subgroups.

Let us now use the same multivariate analyses in table 5.26 to emphasize a number of consistent relationships of sex, age, and education with each of the different areas of help-seeking behavior. From time to time, we shall refer to table 5.27, which presents sex, age, and education differences in sources of help used.

Sex Differences in Help-Seeking Patterns

Although men and women did not differ dramatically in the kinds of problems for which they went for help, there are some significant differences. Men were significantly less likely than women to have referred problems involving a child (particularly in 1976) or a distressing situational problem (death or illness) and were significantly more likely in both years to have sought help for problems related to a job or their own schooling (again particularly in 1976). Men and women differed in their rate of referral of a marriage problem, but only among those aged twenty-one to thirty-four: young women more often than men tended to seek professional help for marital problems. This is undoubtedly the reason that young women were also more likely to consult a professional for a problem perceived as arising from a defect in a relationship. This difference was not apparent among other age groups. In fact, in 1976, older men were more likely to seek help for marital problems than were older women. We shall return to a discussion of this result in the next section in which we examine the differential help-seeking patterns of men and women as they reach different points in the life cycle.

Overall, however, differences in the types of problems referred to professionals by men and women, though not dramatic, appeared to reflect an influence of sex role differentiation in our society, one that persisted from 1957 to 1976. Women's roles orient them more toward the social and interpersonal aspects of living, while men's are more associated with striving for achievement and career success. Thus, it is not surprising that women (and especially young women) tended to seek help for interpersonal problems, and men, for problems involving their work or education. In light of changes in work-family pat-terns documented in Book 1, one might reasonably have expected somewhat greater similarity between men and women in 1976 in the kinds of problems they tended to perceive as relevant for help—a change which is not, however, evident in these data.

Men and women who have gone for help were, if anything, more alike in the particular sources of help they chose to consult than in the types of problems which they presented (see table 5.27 for these sex differences). Only two consistent differences are evident: compared to men, women more frequently consulted a nonpsychiatric physician for emotional problems, and, except among young adults, less fre-quently consulted a psychiatrist or a psychologist. Both of these differ-ences are minimal, but they do suggest that once men and women decided to seek help, more men than women ended up with specialists (psychiatrists, psychologists). In 1976, 32 percent of the male help-seekers saw a psychiatrist or psychologist, while only 27 percent of the women did. (The comparable percentages in 1957 were: 21 percent of the male help-seekers, 16 percent of the female.) Perhaps men who bring themselves to seek help were in much worse psychological shape than women who sought help. If so, men would be more likely to seek out the psychological specialists. On balance, however, the rel-ative lack of significant differences in the choice of a particular help resource between men and women who sought help is probably more worthy of note than these two modest relationships.

Since women are more frequent professional help-seekers than men, they normally end up consulting more help sources of many types in absolute terms (see the multivariate analysis of the fourth measure in table 5.26, and the "gross" differences for sex reported in table 5.27). More women than men consulted doctors, the clergy (except for the college educated), mental health agencies, and the other resources cod-ed as "other mental health sources," but only among young adults did women see more psychiatrists or psychologists than men. Thus, wom-en in both years avail themselves of all kinds of resources more than men. We should remember, however, that once men decide to go for help they seem generally to avail themselves of the same resources that women do, and, if anything are more likely to turn to a psychia-trist or psychologist.

Differences between men and women in their reasons for choosing a particular help source also tended to be slight and varied by year or, in one case, by age. In 1957, for example, women were slightly more likely than men to mention both a referral by family or friends and information provided by the mass media as their reason for selecting a particular help source. Neither difference persisted in 1976. In fact, we found that older men (fifty-five and over) were significantly more likely than women to mention an informal referral.

Age Differences in Help-Seeking Patterns

A number of significant differences among adults of different ages are apparent in table 5.26, a few of which involve significant interactions by sex. Perhaps the most noteworthy of such differences serves to clarify a pattern briefly mentioned in our discussion of sex differences in help-seeking patterns. Underlying a general trend for the young and middle aged to seek help for marital problems more often than older adults is an interesting sex by age interaction: while among women the tendency to seek help for a problem in marriage appears to decline rather consistently with age (as does their tendency to perceive problems arising from a defect in a relationship), among men, the reverse is true. Older men (the middle aged in particular) who seek help are more likely than the young to be seeking help for marital problems. And, as a result, in 1976, older men were actually more likely than women to seek help for marital problems. Although these data hardly constitute conclusive evidence, they are at least consistent with theories (Jung, 1933) and research (Gutmann, 1968; Neugarten and Gutmann, 1968) suggesting that a reversal of sex roles takes place during later adulthood. Men are thought to become more concerned with social and interpersonal aspects of living as they age and women more concerned with assertiveness and independence. Although older women are not more likely than older men to seek help for job- or school-related problems, some evidence of developmental reversals for the two sexes exists on this issue: middle-aged women, compared to other women, and younger men, compared to other men, are the most likely to seek help for job- or school-related problems.

There are other predictable changes in the nature of problems confronting adults, regardless of sex, as they proceed through the life course. It is not surprising, for example, that young adults are less likely than those thirty-five or over to seek help for a problem with a child. Those in the later age category are more likely to have school-age or adolescent children whose problems come to the attention of others. At the other end of the age spectrum, it is also not surprising that older compared to younger men and women more often seek help for situational problems. Many people who go for help about situational problems are seeking consultation about their depression or anxieties resulting from the death or illness of loved ones—events more frequent in the lives of middle-aged and older people.

Somewhat less obvious, from a life span development viewpoint, is why middle-aged adults are less likely to have consulted a professional about their personal adjustments or a problem perceived as arising from some personal defect. Recall, however, that such problems are largely defined in terms of not getting along, being unhappy, or suffering from a particular psychological or physical symptom, all particularly prominent among young adults and to a somewhat lesser extent among older men and women (see chapter 7, Book 1). Middle-aged people evidently structure the problems in their lives in more interpersonal or motivational terms. It is perhaps important for the help resources of those at middle aged to bear these results in mind. Although life-span developmental psychologists see middle age as a time for personal reassessment and a turn inward (Neugarten, 1968), this interiority is evidently not translated into specific help-seeking goals. The middle aged structure their problems externally or interpersonally.

In spite of these several differences in the types of problems adults of different ages tend to bring to professional counselors, differences in the particular sources of help they consult are not striking (see tables 5.26 and 5.27). In absolute terms, older people are proportionately less likely than younger adults to consult many resources. Surprisingly, this also includes the clergy. In net terms, or in looking at only those who have gone for help (see table 5.27 "net" age differences), however, many of these age differences are no longer apparent. There are some resources whom older as opposed to younger help-seekers are especially likely to consult: lawyers, but only in 1957; doctors, but only in 1976. What accounts for these results? The net use of lawyers for personal problems by the elderly in 1957 was not very frequent (only 17 percent among those fifty to fifty-nine, 12 percent among those sixty-five+), but was more apparent for them than for the younger age groups. The net use of lawyers by the elderly had clearly declined by 1976. The reverse was true for their use of doctors, increasing from a net 23 percent usage in 1957 to a net 43 percent usage in 1976 among those aged sixty-five and older. We have little doubt that these latter results could be accounted for by the introduction of Medicaid in the interim. In addition, however, we can see some of the shift to the use of doctors rather than lawyers in 1976 as a tendency among the elderly to be less inclined to externalize their personal problems. Lawyers take care of "outside" difficulties, (for example, arranging for or changing a will, preparing gifts or property transfers to children); doctors handle "inside" troubles even if they are often diagnosed and treated as physical problems. No doubt the elderly in 1976 were more sophisticated about defining personal problems in psychological terms than the elderly in 1957. This may account for the shift to greater use of doctors rather than lawyers in 1976.

The greater absolute use of psychiatrists and psychologists by middle-aged men and women (see the fourth measure in table 5.26 and table 5.26, and "gross" age differences in table 5.27) is a phenomenon that perhaps reflects the fact that the costs of these resources are not easily met by younger people (we find in a later section that people with higher incomes are more likely to use psychiatrists or psychologists.) Furthermore, the heavier use of psychiatrists or psychologists for personal problems among the middle aged is less apparent when "net" use is computed only among those who have sought help (see the third measure in table 5.26, and table 5.27, the "net" age results). In fact, the multivariate analyses confined to help-seekers only suggest that it is really both the middle-aged and the older groups of men who seek out psychiatrists or psychologists, and both the younger and middle-aged groups of women who do so (table 5.28). Common to both male and female help-seekers is a high preponderance of middle-aged people who turn to psychiatrists or psychologists, but this trend is also equally apparent among elderly men and young women.

We offer two major speculations about these complex and somewhat surprising findings. First, we might suggest that women start out at an early age worrying about their own general personal adjustment in the very psychological terms that match the psychological specialist's requirements for a "proper" case. As women age and manage the responsibilities of family life, they perhaps no longer think of their problems in self-doubting terms but more in situational terms. Men's doubts about themselves in internal psychological adjustment terms perhaps begin to surface mainly at mid-life and continue through old age. The crossover at mid-life for the perceived locus of men's and women's concerns—men becoming more internal, women less so—makes the differences between the sexes' use of psychiatrists or psychologists especially dramatic in old age (see table 5.28). In fact, looking at the 1976 data alone in table 5.28, we perceive that more women seek out the psychological specialists when younger, and fewer women than men seek them out when middle aged or older.

We offer a second set[11] of speculations about the sex-age findings in the use of psychiatrists or psychologists. Money may still be an issue in explaining these results for 1976. Early in their lives, single and divorced women without children may be particularly heavy users of psychiatrists and psychologists, because the money spent on these resources for self-improvement can be easily justified as instrumental to their social goals. One of the major developmental tasks for most young adults is to resolve heterosexual commitments—especially by securing a good marriage. Thus, single or divorced women of this age, since they are not usually expected to spend money in the mating and dating game, are free to invest money in themselves to aid them in their developmental task. Psychotherapy is congruent with their task. Young single and divorced men, by contrast, given the sex role rules of the society, often have to invest their money directly in the mating-dating competition. They spend money on entertaining women, or on such critical masculine symbols as a car or motorcycle.

---

[11] There is a third explanation worth pursuing, and that is to consider the easily available use of psychiatrists and psychologists through the Veterans Administration hospital services that may have existed for middle-aged men in 1957 who served in World War I and middle-aged and older men of 1976 who served in World War II or the Korean War. These are the very groups that show a surprising use of psychiatrists and psychologists.

TABLE 5.28
Age Differences in Use of Psychiatrists or Psychologists Among Those Who Used Help (by sex and year)

	Men				Women			
	1957		1976		1957		1976	
Age	Percentage	Number	Percentage	Number	Percentage	Number	Percentage	Number
21 to 34	12	42	23	78	12	87	32	155
35 to 54	27	59	41	83	20	105	27	136
55 and over	20	15	33	46	12	34	17	82
Age × Marital Status								
21 to 34 unmarried	0	11	22	37	11	27	46	63
married	16	31	46	26	12	60	22	55
35 to 54 unmarried	33	12	46	26	14	42	22	55
married	26	47	39	57	24	63	36	81
55+ unmarried	50	2	25	16	8	24	14	52
married	15	13	37	30	20	10	23	30

The act of spending money on women is itself often therapeutic for men's sense of doubt about their own progress in heterosexual commitment. These speculations are confirmed in table 5.28 in which we present the proportional use of psychiatrists or psychologists for unmarried versus married men and women in each age group. In both years, but especially in 1976, young unmarried women contrasted to young unmarried men were particularly heavy users of psychological specialists. These sex differences did not exist for the young married respondents.

In later periods of their lives, men who are not married are usually in much better financial situations than comparable women, and we suspect that it is among the older nonmarrieds that we would find particularly heavy use of psychiatrists or psychologists by men in contrast to women. This is confirmed in most instances in table 5.28.

Which are the less psychological and/or "cheaper" resources? From our analyses of the data, these resources could very well be the clergy. We find that young men and older women are distinctly more likely than other groups to turn to the clergy for personal problems (see table 5.29); close to half of the young male and older female help-seekers turn to the clergy. One possible explanation is that the clergy represent a group who are not going to push people into an intense examination of the self and how it should be changed, except on clear moral grounds, and perhaps that is why they are particularly attractive to younger men and older women. Reasoning from our other explanation, we might also suggest that seeking of help from the clergy does not present the financial obstacles that seeking help from mental health specialists does. Young men who are in the throes of family building and older women who are often in poor financial condition might then be especially interested in the clergy for counsel. Of course, both factors might be operating.

Even less in evidence were any differences between older and younger people in reasons they give for choosing a particular help source. In fact, except for a tendency for adults under fifty-five to have been referred more often by an "official" source, there were no consistent overall relationships of interest between age and reasons for selecting a given formal resource. And, only two interactive relationships appear.

Among the high-school educated (and only among this group), older people seeking help were more likely to have been referred by a doctor. While this trend is consistent with the greater exposure of older people to physicians, in general, why this difference is found only among the high-school educated is not clear. Research on health care utilization suggests that the grade-school educated tend generally to consult physicians less than the more educated (cf. Aday and Eichhorn, 1972) and for older college-educated people the path to a psy-

TABLE 5.29

Age Differences in Use of Clergy Among Those Who Used Help (by sex and year)

	Men				Women			
	1957		1976		1957		1976	
Age	Percentage	Number	Percentage	Number	Percentage	Number	Percentage	Number
21 to 34	52	42	41	78	40	89	34	155
35 to 54	37	59	35	83	38	105	41	136
55 and over	33	15	30	46	50	34	51	82

chological counselor may well tend to be a direct one, less likely mediated by their general sources of health care.

A second interaction involving age indicates a strikingly different pattern of informal referral by age for men and women. For men, mentioning family and friends as referral agents had a positive relationship with age, while, for women, the relationship was negative. Thus, once again, we find that older men and young women were those more likely to have reached a formal help source (often a psychiatrist and psychologist, as noted above) through an informal referral agent.

Although there were no significant age differences apparent in the extent to which people felt that their treatment was effective, table 5.26 indicates there was a relationship, consistent in both years, between age and the general ways in which people felt they were helped. Essentially, young adults were more likely to assert that they were personally changed by the experience or had been helped by talking or getting advice, while older people were more likely than the young or middle aged to emphasize that they were comforted by the help they received. Interestingly, this consistent pattern may reflect differences in the expectations that people of different ages bring to the psychological counselor as well as actual differences in the kinds of problems discussed.

Education Differences in Help-Seeking Patterns

A comparison of educational groups as to the kinds of problems that led to their seeking help yields very few differences and only one appears especially worthy of note. As shown in table 5.26, the high-school educated were significantly less likely to seek outside help for a problem defined as a personal adjustment problem (or as a defect in the self). That the high-school educated are less intuitive about their adjustment problems requiring help than the college educated is reasonable in light of evidence of the greater personal psychologizing among the college educated. But why less than the grade-school educated? One can only suggest that those with less status are often labeled as having personal inadequacies by those with more status. Over time these diagnoses may come to be self-attributions for those with less status. The moderately successful (high-school educated) may apply such self-attributions less often because other people may apply such diagnoses less often. We also find that the higher one's education, the less one refers to situational problems (such as a financial difficulty) as reasons for seeking help, a finding which probably reflects the fact that people of higher status realistically may experience fewer stressful external problems.

A comparison of education groups' absolute rates of consulting various sources of help (the fourth measure in table 5.26, and table 5.27, "gross" education differences) reveals that in every case where a significant relationship appears, it is the more educated (and, in particular, the college educated) who are more likely to consult any given help source. This is important. It tells us that the more educated are using more of all resources. When we look at only those who have sought help and where they have gone, a different pattern emerges (see the third measure in table 5.26, and table 5.27 on "net" education results). The only striking relationship between education level and the use of a particular help source was the greater use of psychiatrists or psychologists by the highly educated, a result which appeared in both 1957 and 1976. By 1976, in fact, 50 percent of the college graduates who sought help for a personal problem went to a psychiatrist or psychologist. In 1957, the comparable figure was 32 percent. Grade-school educated help-seekers were also particularly unlikely to seek out psychologists or psychiatrists. The other significant education difference in the use of a particular help source among help-seekers was evident only in 1976: the college educated in 1976 were distinctly less likely than those with less education to have consulted a doctor. This lesser net utilization of physicians, in conjunction with a trend in the same direction for the use of clergy (the other major nonmental health source) is a reflection of the greater overall tendency for highly educated respondents in 1976 to consult more specialized mental health sources for help with their personal problems.

Except for the results described earlier—among those aged fifty-five and over the high-school educated were significantly more likely to cite a referral by a physician—there were no significant relationships between education and either the reasons given for selecting a particular help source, or the perceived helpfulness of treatment. Finally, there was only a modest association with the general nature of the type of help received. Grade-school-educated respondents were more likely than those with more education to say that the treatment helped another person close to them or ameliorated some nonpsychological aspect of the problem, responses which followed from the fact that the grade-school educated did go more often for help for nonpsychological situational problems. Thus, we see that the less educated not only structure their problems and the help they receive somewhat differently—mostly in situational terms—but that they are also less likely to use psychiatric specialists, who as a group do not often structure the help they offer as dealing with problems defined in situational terms. Psychiatrists and psychologists are especially prone to examine internal dynamics, personal difficulties that may be amenable to change. We have no idea of what is cause, and what effect. It could be that the less educated structure their problems situationally and hence avoid psychiatric specialists, or it could be that they are more likely to go to other professionals who are more likely than psychiatrists and psychologists to help them structure their problems in situational terms. Both processes may be at work.

Other Sociodemographic Characteristics Related to the Source of Help Used

In the preceding major section of this chapter, we examined relationships between a variety of sociodemographic characteristics and the first two decision points in the self-referral process—the decision to define one's problems in mental health terms and the decision to go for help. We are now ready to determine which sociodemographic characteristics become particularly relevant at the third decision point—the decision of where to go for help. Before we began, we assumed that facilitating rather than psychological factors would be particularly relevant at this stage in the self-referral process, just as they were in the more general decision to go for help. How realistically available or accessible are the various resources for certain groups or a certain locale or community? How much do people know about various possibilities? These are clearly questions that deal with facilitative rather than psychological factors. A third question could be asked about the choice of a particular source of help: What social norms govern the use of one type of professional help as opposed to another? One can look at norm regulation of these choices as either facilitative or psychological. If members of one's reference group seek out psychiatric counsel for handling problems, it both psychologically primes one to see that alternative as valid and approved (hence a "psychological factor") and makes one more knowledgeable about available resources (a "facilitative" factor). We shall try to keep this distinction in mind as we approach the results.

In this section, we are concerned particularly with the differential choice of the clergy, the medical profession, the psychiatric profession, and other mental health resources among those who had actually gone for help. An analysis of the social and demographic distribution of these choices only within that group of respondents makes the findings relevant to the following critical question: where do people who are different in certain important respects go for help once they recognize that they have a problem requiring help? Table 5.30 presents relationships between selected sociodemographic characteristics and the sources of help that people used, excluding relationships for sex, age, and education, which have been presented in tables 5.26 and 5.27.[12] Recall that consistent differences involving sex, age, and education were relatively few. The most important of these were: (1) a greater tendency by women and older people to consult doctors, and (2) the greater use of psychiatrists by the more educated, as well as by older men and younger women.

Let us first consider a number of variables for which consistent relationships are *not* apparent in table 5.30. Essentially, except for a few scattered relationships which are neither unexpected nor particularly

[12] For a full description of these variables, see chapter 8 of Book 1.

TABLE 5.30

Social or Demographic Characteristics Related to Source of Help Used (Among People Who Have Used Help) (by year)

Social or Demographic Characteristic	Clergy 1957 (%)	Clergy 1976 (%)	Doctor 1957 (%)	Doctor 1976 (%)	Psychiatrist/ Psychologist 1957 (%)	Psychiatrist/ Psychologist 1976 (%)	Marriage Counselor 1957 (%)	Marriage Counselor 1976 (%)	Other Mental Health Source 1957 (%)	Other Mental Health Source 1976 (%)	Social Service Agency 1957 (%)	Social Service Agency 1976 (%)	Lawyer 1957 (%)	Lawyer 1976 (%)	Other 1957 (%)	Other 1976 (%)	Total Percentage 1957	Total Percentage 1976	Total Number 1957	Total Number 1976
Income—Relative																				
Low	39	38	24	29	10	24	0	2	15	19	10	6	15	3	13	7	—a	—a	72	142
Middle	53	42	30	22	11	26	6	8	9	22	2	2	6	2	10	6	—a	—a	139	254
High	32	36	31	15	29	36	3	15	8	16	2	2	2	2	13	7	—a	—a	130	159
Income—1976 dollars																				
Under 4,000	48	36	18	31	5	19	0	4	10	24	13	10	15	1	8	10	—a	—a	40	70
4,000 to 7,999	43	38	26	27	14	30	5	0	12	19	5	3	11	4	16	3	—a	—a	81	97
8,000 to 9,999	56	42	28	18	12	22	6	11	10	20	2	4	2	4	8	7	—a	—a	50	55
10,000 to 12,499	48	48	40	22	8	29	3	6	10	19	0	0	8	2	8	5	—a	—a	40	65
12,500 to 19,999	33	41	34	21	23	28	3	9	10	22	2	3	2	2	15	10	—a	—a	92	145
20,000 and over	29	35	24	15	45	36	3	17	3	15	3	2	0	2	8	5	—a	—a	38	123
Occupation—Men																				
Professionals	44	34	13	5	47	36	8	12	0	17	0	5	0	0	13	2	—a	—a	23	41
Managers	50	30	10	10	10	40	0	20	20	20	0	3	20	3	0	0	—a	—a	10	30
Clericals workers	86	44	0	0	0	0	0	11	14	44	0	0	0	0	0	0	—a	—a	7	9
Sales workers	27	46	27	9	18	36	9	9	0	18	0	0	9	0	18	9	—a	—a	11	11
Crafts workers	30	50	39	10	17	27	0	13	9	13	4	3	9	7	22	9	—a	—a	23	30
Operatives	43	23	28	27	21	35	14	8	7	27	0	15	0	4	14	8	—a	—a	14	26

TABLE 5.30 (continued)

Social or Demographic Characteristics Related to Source of Help Used (Among People Who Have Used Help) (by year)

Social or Demographic Characteristic	Clergy 1957 (%)	Clergy 1976 (%)	Doctor 1957 (%)	Doctor 1976 (%)	Psychiatrist/ Psychologist 1957 (%)	Psychiatrist/ Psychologist 1976 (%)	Marriage Counselor 1957 (%)	Marriage Counselor 1976 (%)	Other Mental Health Source 1957 (%)	Other Mental Health Source 1976 (%)	Social Service Agency 1957 (%)	Social Service Agency 1976 (%)	Lawyer 1957 (%)	Lawyer 1976 (%)	Other 1957 (%)	Other 1976 (%)	Total Percentage 1957	Total Percentage 1976	Total Number 1957	Total Number 1976
Service workers	83	29	0	14	0	0	0	0	17	14	0	0	17	29	0	29	—a	—a	6	7
Laborers	33	50	33	33	17	17	0	0	0	33	0	17	17	17	0	0	—a	—a	6	6
Farmers	0	33	50	67	25	33	0	0	0	33	0	0	25	0	0	0	—a	—a	4	3
Occupation—Women																				
Professionals	50	24	17	8	8	43	0	16	8	24	0	3	8	0	25	5	—a	—a	12	37
Managers	30	40	30	20	30	30	10	10	0	20	10	0	10	5	8	5	—a	—a	10	20
Clerical workers	40	39	37	31	16	28	8	8	11	18	3	3	5	0	16	8	—a	—a	38	67
Sales workers	67	27	33	36	0	18	0	9	0	27	0	0	0	0	0	27	—a	—a	3	11
Crafts workers	0	60	0	20	0	0	0	0	0	40	0	0	0	0	0	0	—a	—a	0	5
Operatives	38	40	50	20	13	15	0	0	25	25	0	0	25	5	13	0	—a	—a	8	20
Service workers	64	39	14	22	11	37	0	5	4	17	7	2	14	0	11	5	—a	—a	28	41
Laborers	0	25	0	25	100	0	0	0	0	50	0	0	0	0	0	0	—a	—a	1	4
Farmers	0	33	100	33	0	33	0	0	0	33	0	0	0	0	0	0	—a	—a	2	3
Size of Place of Residence																				
Metropolitan areas	40	23	18	13	12	33	10	15	19	26	6	3	2	5	21	3	—a	—a	68	39
Suburbs	35	30	28	21	37	39	0	8	12	21	5	2	0	4	9	10	—a	—a	43	104

Small cities	**57**	**45**	23	25	16	3	7	10	21	5	3	5	1	10	7	—[a]	—[a]	62	139
Towns	**47**	41	**36**	18	16	1	8	4	18	2	3	**10**	3	10	6	—[a]	—[a]	101	187
Rural areas	28	42	**35**	27	14	3	10	7	17	4	5	**10**	2	10	6	—[a]	—[a]	71	111
Region of Residence																			
New England	30	26	19	**37**	19	4	2	19	21	7	5	7	5	22	7	—[a]	—[a]	27	43
Middle Atlantic	39	34	18	21	21	6	8	13	15	9	5	2	4	10	4	—[a]	—[a]	67	85
East North Central	46	44	23	19	19	9	8	11	20	4	0	7	3	11	13	—[a]	—[a]	57	118
West North Central	55	47	**15**	**38**	**8**	3	12	15	20	5	7	10	3	15	11	—[a]	—[a]	40	147
Solid South	43	42	44	25	12	0	13	2	12	1	0	11	0	5	3	—[a]	—[a]	86	125
Border States	**23**	**47**	46	**29**	**13**	0	4	8	22	0	2	8	4	8	7	—[a]	—[a]	13	45
Mountain States	73	35	36	13	18	0	4	0	22	0	2	0	0	0	0	—[a]	—[a]	11	23
Pacific States	32	32	34	**39**	**27**	2	17	9	31	2	4	0	2	25	5	—[a]	—[a]	44	94
Time in Community of Residence																			
Less than 1 year	48	31	29	33	13	0	5	7	26	3	2	3	0	7	7	—[a]	—[a]	31	42
1 to 2 years	41	29	24	17	29	0	12	9	26	6	5	3	5	15	2	—[a]	—[a]	34	58
3 to 4 years	40	33	23	19	10	3	12	10	15	3	5	7	1	17	2	—[a]	—[a]	30	78
5 to 9 years	38	34	41	18	20	9	11	7	20	2	5	5	1	14	4	—[a]	—[a]	56	71
10 to 19 years	40	41	40	19	14	4	10	12	18	0	3	0	4	12	8	—[a]	—[a]	57	104
20 years and over	44	46	22	25	18	3	6	9	19	6	3	10	2	11	9	—[a]	—[a]	133	224

TABLE 5.30 (continued)

Social or Demographic Characteristics Related to Source of Help Used (Among People Who Have Used Help) (by year)

Social or Demographic Characteristic	Source of Help Used																			
	Clergy		Doctor		Psychiatrist/ Psychologist		Marriage Counselor		Other Mental Health Source		Social Service Agency		Lawyer		Other		Total Percentage		Total Number	
	1957 (%)	1976 (%)	1957 (%)	1976 (%)	1957 (%)	1976 (%)	1957 (%)	1976 (%)	1957 (%)	1976 (%)	1957 (%)	1976 (%)	1957 (%)	1976 (%)	1957 (%)	1976 (%)	1957	1976	1957	1976
Religion																				
Baptist	42	47	46	26	7	25	2	7	8	17	3	5	7	2	7	7	—[a]	—[a]	59	105
Methodist	53	46	18	27	16	27	4	4	6	18	7	2	13	4	15	11	—[a]	—[a]	55	56
Lutheran	39	46	32	22	18	24	0	10	11	17	4	5	4	2	14	11	—[a]	—[a]	28	41
Presbyterian	45	40	27	23	18	27	0	27	14	10	5	3	5	0	9	3	—[a]	—[a]	22	30
Fundamentalist	46	61	36	15	14	14	11	7	7	14	4	5	11	3	4	9	—[a]	—[a]	28	59
Other Protestants	26	28	17	25	29	35	6	13	17	16	6	3	3	3	17	6	—[a]	—[a]	35	72
Catholic	46	43	26	26	15	21	2	6	7	22	2	2	5	4	16	10	—[a]	—[a]	87	113
Jewish	11	10	32	3	32	59	11	7	21	31	5	3	0	0	5	3	—[a]	—[a]	19	29
No preference	22	14	11	13	56	45	0	6	11	31	0	3	0	2	0	3	—[a]	—[a]	9	64
Church Attendance																				
More than once a week	69	68	16	21	16	13	2	4	8	13	0	4	2	0	14	5	—[a]	—[a]	51	82
Once a week	48	53	33	21	14	22	1	8	9	17	5	2	6	4	11	9	—[a]	—[a]	126	140
A few times a week	37	39	30	23	17	25	3	11	7	18	3	5	7	1	16	6	—[a]	—[a]	70	109
A few times a year	24	25	30	24	16	35	11	10	16	22	6	3	6	2	11	9	—[a]	—[a]	71	148
Never	22	16	30	16	39	47	0	8	9	27	9	4	13	4	0	2	—[a]	—[a]	23	99

Race																		
White	41	30	21	19	29	4	9	8	20	4	3	6	2	12	7	—[a]	—[a]	305	518
Black	48	22	26	0	28	4	6	26	17	11	8	4	4	15	6	—[a]	—[a]	27	53
Father's Occupation																		
Professionals	47	16	13	21	46	11	17	13	17	5	4	8	0	24	7	—[a]	—[a]	38	46
Managers	38	32	16	26	37	4	5	11	24	2	2	11	3	9	6	—[a]	—[a]	53	67
Clericals and sales	31	31	14	13	23	6	9	25	17	6	3	6	0	6	0	—[a]	—[a]	16	35
Crafts workers	39	33	19	20	25	4	11	10	25	2	1	4	1	12	6	—[a]	—[a]	49	120
Operatives and service	48	35	22	19	27	0	5	6	17	6	10	0	4	8	9	—[a]	—[a]	48	92
Farmers	44	30	27	11	18	1	4	3	13	3	2	6	3	10	7	—[a]	—[a]	88	94
Laborers	44	28	31	11	31	6	14	0	24	6	7	6	0	17	0	—[a]	—[a]	18	29
Region of Birth																		
East	34	25	20	22	39	4	8	14	17	9	1	0	3	10	4	—[a]	—[a]	77	132
Midwest	49	22	24	17	22	4	10	9	24	3	3	10	2	12	10	—[a]	—[a]	102	174
Solid South	44	39	27	11	25	1	8	7	12	4	3	7	1	9	5	—[a]	—[a]	82	122
Border States	41	33	19	4	17	4	3	11	19	0	5	11	5	11	7	—[a]	—[a]	27	58
West	36	33	13	36	36	6	9	11	28	0	3	0	3	14	4	—[a]	—[a]	36	69
Size Place of Childhood Residence																		
Country or farm	47	26	22	11	23	1	7	5	14	4	3	7	2	11	6	—[a]	—[a]	104	175
Town	44	38	28	20	33	5	5	9	17	3	3	6	2	10	8	—[a]	—[a]	96	138
Small city	41	29	15	23	24	5	5	7	22	4	3	7	3	14	8	—[a]	—[a]	56	104
Large city	43	22	19	20	31	4	14	18	26	6	3	5	3	11	6	—[a]	—[a]	82	150

TABLE 5.30 (continued)

Social or Demographic Characteristics Related to Source of Help Used (Among People Who Have Used Help) (by year)

Social or Demographic Characteristic	Clergy 1957 (%)	Clergy 1976 (%)	Doctor 1957 (%)	Doctor 1976 (%)	Psychiatrist/ Psychologist 1957 (%)	Psychiatrist/ Psychologist 1976 (%)	Marriage Counselor 1957 (%)	Marriage Counselor 1976 (%)	Other Mental Health Source 1957 (%)	Other Mental Health Source 1976 (%)	Social Service Agency 1957 (%)	Social Service Agency 1976 (%)	Lawyer 1957 (%)	Lawyer 1976 (%)	Other 1957 (%)	Other 1976 (%)	Total Percentage 1957	Total Percentage 1976	Total Number 1957	Total Number 1976
Broken-Home Background																				
Parents divorced or separated	36	30	26	20	23	34	13	11	16	27	7	4	7	4	10	2	—[a]	—[a]	31	56
Parents(s) died	49	41	20	35	16	25	2	2	10	20	4	4	8	0	14	14	—[a]	—[a]	49	49
Intact home	42	40	30	20	17	28	2	9	9	20	4	3	6	2	11	6	—[a]	—[a]	258	441
Marital Status—Men																				
Married	40	41	29	16	21	34	4	10	9	17	1	6	7	2	9	5	—[a]	—[a]	91	128
Single	58	33	8	23	0	23	0	0	8	23	0	3	0	3	42	7	—[a]	—[a]	12	30
Widowed	50	33	0	22	25	44	0	0	25	0	0	0	25	0	0	11	—[a]	—[a]	4	9
Divorced or separated	56	25	0	10	44	33	11	23	0	23	11	0	11	8	11	5	—[a]	—[a]	9	40
Marital Status—Women																				
Married	37	41	39	24	18	26	2	8	9	17	3	1	3	2	7	8	—[a]	—[a]	135	203
Single	32	39	37	23	5	42	0	4	0	12	5	4	11	0	21	4	—[a]	—[a]	19	26
Widowed	57	52	10	48	10	16	3	0	3	8	10	12	3	0	17	8	—[a]	—[a]	30	50
Divorced or separated	49	34	20	14	18	31	7	10	22	29	4	4	13	3	18	6	—[a]	—[a]	45	94

Age of Youngest Child in Home (parental status)—Men
Youngest child is:

Preschool	58	50	26	9	18	24	3	15	5	9	3	12	0	6	3	3	—[a]	38	34
School age	24	41	33	14	24	37	3	14	18	22	0	2	9	2	12	4	—[a]	33	49
Age 17 or over	20	18	0	9	0	27	0	18	0	9	20	9	20	9	40	0	—[a]	5	11
No children in home	44	30	25	19	44	35	6	11	6	16	0	4	13	2	13	9	—[a]	16	57
Has no children	50	34	8	20	8	32	8	4	4	25	0	2	8	4	21	5	—[a]	24	56

Age of Youngest Child in Home (parental status)—Women
Youngest child is:

Preschool	43	46	38	19	10	25	2	6	17	16	2	2	2	2	10	4	—[a]	58	68
School age	41	34	28	28	19	26	7	9	16	23	5	2	2	3	8	4	—[a]	75	120
Age 17 or over	56	50	22	32	11	25	6	4	0	25	6	7	22	4	11	14	—[a]	18	28
No children in home	49	46	28	30	21	20	0	5	3	16	5	5	5	0	15	13	—[a]	39	84
Has no children	26	36	37	15	16	38	0	10	0	14	5	4	11	3	16	6	—[a]	38	73

Employment Status—Men

Employed	43	38	23	13	22	30	5	12	8	20	1	5	8	4	10	5	—[a]	106	165
Retired	0	29	67	33	33	42	0	4	33	13	33	0	0	0	0	8	—[a]	3	24
Unemployed	0	33	0	17	0	42	0	8	100	8	0	8	0	0	0	8	—[a]	1	12

Employment Status—Women

Employed	46	35	29	23	15	30	4	8	8	21	4	2	10	1	13	6	—[a]	102	205
Housewife	38	51	34	25	16	19	2	5	11	14	4	2	3	3	11	6	—[a]	118	126
Retired	50	43	50	0	0	19	0	5	0	14	0	2	0	3	0	10	—[a]	2	21
Unemployed	29	25	14	43	29	19	14	19	0	14	14	14	0	0	14	10	—[a]	7	20

[a] Indicates that percentages total more than 100 percent because some respondents mentioned more than one source.

enlightening,[13] occupation, community tenure, race, father's occupation, broken-home background, and marital, parental, and work status all bear no consistent relationship to the decision of where to seek professional help, especially when controls for sex, age, and education are taken into account. Nevertheless, as shown in table 5.30, a fair number of the other sociodemographic variables considered earlier in this chapter are related in interesting ways to this third decision point. Let us look at these closely. We select only those findings that survive the multivariate controls for sex, age, education, and year.

Income

Family income, for example, whether analyzed in either relative or constant dollar terms, is clearly related to the differential use of the various help sources by people who went for help. Perhaps the most striking finding is that wealthier respondents in both years were more likely than poorer ones to turn to a psychiatrist or psychologist for help in handling their personal problems. Note, however, that the relationship was considerably weaker in 1976 than in 1957. (Gamma values for the relative income measures are 0.48 and 0.18 for 1957 and 1976, respectively, and for the constant dollars income measure the relationship is not even statistically reliable for 1976.) Moreover, as noted elsewhere (Kulka, Veroff, and Douvan, 1979), while the relationship between income and the use of psychiatric treatment essentially disappeared in 1976 when education was controlled, the opposite was true in 1957, when, holding income constant, education was not significantly related to the selection of psychological specialists. Together, these results suggest that income per se played a less significant role in the use of these professionals in 1976 than it did in 1957.

Income played a significant role in the choice of two other professional groups in 1957, but not in 1976. In 1957, middle-income people were more likely than either high- or low-income respondents to have consulted a clergyman, but this relationship was no longer statistically reliable in 1976. Similarly, only in 1957 do we find that low-income respondents had more often consulted an attorney with their problems than high-income respondents. Thus, as in the case of psychiatrists and psychologists, we find income differences playing a significantly smaller role in influencing where people go for help. Where once only the rich could afford psychologists or psychiatrists, that seems to have become less true. Where once poor people could afford to talk only to a lawyer, that also seems to have become less so. Where once the clergy had a special hold on middle-income people, that is no

[13] For example, men in professional occupations in 1976 were less likely to seek help from doctors; adult children of unskilled workers were more likely in 1976 to report using social services; and divorced and separated men in 1976 and women in both years were more likely to have consulted a marriage counselor or other mental health source, respectively.

longer apparent. We can account for this pattern if we assume that a greater variety of resources became available for poorer and middle-income groups. Community mental health centers made available some free services. Insurance programs covered more and more of the costs of available psychological resources. In this regard, it is interesting to note that marriage counselors were selected more heavily by the wealthy in 1976 alone. Third-party payments for health insurance do not generally cover marriage counselors, and so they have become increasingly a resource for the well-to-do.

While these results suggest that we have generally removed income barriers to obtaining most types of professional help, one set of findings nevertheless suggests that the poor are channeled into what may be inadequate resources for psychological help. In both years, the very lowest income group was more likely to turn to a social service agency for personal problems than other income groups. These agencies are especially set up for the poor to handle problems connected with unemployment or welfare benefits. But it is important to keep in mind that the poor also convert these agencies into places where they discuss personal problems. Situational problems of employment and money are interwoven with people's general psychological difficulties. When poor people seek psychological help from social service agencies they do not distinguish financial and personal troubles. Administrators in these agencies may not define their roles as prescribing psychological counseling, but their clients clearly perceive them in that way.

Place of Residence and Region

The only consistent relationship between size of place of residence and the source of help used is a greater tendency for people living in less urban areas to seek help from the clergy. While such a relationship is evident in both survey years, the basic urban-rural difference was more striking in 1976, when people from rural areas, small towns, and smaller cities were distinctly more likely than those in suburban and metropolitan areas to mention using the clergy as a help resource. In 1957, people living in rural areas were actually less likely than metropolitan residents to have consulted a minister or priest. Although differences in the potential availability of other help sources presumably account in part for this difference (though no other significant rural-urban differences in the use of sources in 1976 are apparent in table 5.30), a more compelling explanation might emphasize the more dominant role played by the church as an institution in the nonmetropolitan and rural communities of America in comparison with suburbia and large central cities. In these less densely populated communities, not only are clergy more readily perceived as personal acquaintances, but also their use is more likely to be socially acceptable and supported by a long tradition. A significant interaction with education provides at least some indirect support for this assumption. The grade-school educated living in less densely populated areas are those especially likely to mention clergy as a help resource. If we assume that the grade-school educated are those who are more tradition-oriented, then these findings underscore the greater importance of the clergy in more traditional nonurban areas of the country.

In contrast, other rural-urban differences in the choice of particular help sources are significant only for 1957. A generation ago people in rural areas or in small towns were more likely than people in other areas to make use of lawyers and doctors; people in suburbs were more likely than others to use psychiatrists or psychologists and people in metropolitan areas were more likely than others to use marriage counselors or other mental health resources. We thus had a differential use of specific resources in different areas probably because each area had distinctive services available for mental health problems. Over the generation there evidently was a diffusion of resources of all kinds which then made each type of residential area in 1976 more alike in the types of resources its inhabitants turned to. By 1976, efforts to increase access to or information about mental health resources to residents of communities of all sizes had met with at least a modicum of success. While we have interpreted these findings in terms of changes that made factors predisposing toward choosing a help source more equitable across all residential areas, we cannot avoid another interpretation of these findings. There may have been some shift in the psychological approach to help-seeking so that "social climates" supporting the use of more specialized sources of mental health care are as likely today to be found in rural areas or small towns as in our metropolitan or suburban areas.

Although fewer regional[14] than rural-urban differences are apparent in table 5.30, they are not at all consistent with the pattern of decreasing differences from 1957 to 1976 among respondents from places of residence with different densities. In fact, the opposite seems to be true with respect to people's utilization of psychiatrists and psychologists. While in 1957 there were two regions that were particularly high (the Pacific states) and low (West North Central) in their use of psychiatrists and psychologists, by 1976 these two regions were even more distinctively high and low, and some other regions had also become distinctive. In 1976, New England, Middle-Atlantic, and Mountain states' residents were also very high users of these sources, while border states' residents were very low. Thus, while our data suggest that rural-urban differences in the use of psychiatric care have dissipated somewhat during the two decades, regional differences in factors which serve to facilitate or hinder the choice of a psychiatrist or psy-

[14]See footnote 3 on p. 60 of chapter 3 for detailed list of states grouped in each region.

chologist have, if anything, become even more distinct over that period.

While all regions showed a 1957 to 1976 increase in the use of "other mental health" professions, this was not true for the use of psychiatrists and psychologists, for which the West North Central regions and the Border states showed no such increase. In 1976, these two regions instead showed increased use of the clergy (Border states) or doctors (West North Central) over the generation. Thus, these two regions might well have not shown any increase in the availability of the specialized mental health professions from 1957 to 1976, and the clergy or the medical profession was called on to fill that gap. We shall test that hypothesis more directly in chapter 8.

Religion and Church Attendance

As indicated in table 5.30, both religion and church attendance show relatively consistent relationships in both survey years as to the use of two particular sources of help—the clergy and psychiatrists or psychologists—and the pattern of those relationships suggests that these two major types of professional helpers may be somewhat "substitutable" for certain religious groups and for high and low church attenders. This phenomenon is clearest for Jews who in both survey years were both the lowest users of the clergy (10 percent in 1976) and, with one exception, the highest users of psychiatrists or psychologists (59 percent in 1976). The reverse is also quite clear among Fundamentalists, who were among the highest utilizers of the clergy (61 percent in 1976) but among the lowest utilizers of psychologists or psychiatrists (14 percent in 1976). Other groups showed similar patterns—other Protestants (the dominant constituents are Episcopalians and Congregationalists) showed the pattern of Jews, while Catholics showed the pattern of Fundamentalists, especially in the latter's low rate of usage of psychiatrists or psychologists. What accounts for this phenomenon? The Jews, Episcopalians, and Congregationalists on the one hand were low users of the clergy and high users of the mental health specialists, while the Fundamentalists and to a lesser extent the Catholics were high users of the clergy and low users of psychiatrists or psychologists. One can only speculate that Jews, Episcopalians, and Congregationalists are people for whom religious group affiliation is less controlled by religious dogma and more adapted to their own personal interpretation of beliefs and religious practices. Futhermore, they tend to be upper-middle-class groups (with the exception of the Presbyterians, these groups in our sample report the highest family incomes)[15] for whom the era of psychology dawned

[15]A control for income, however, does not destroy the differential effect we are discussing. Low-income Jews and "other Protestant groups" were also low users of the clergy and high users of psychiatrists or psychologists.

sooner than it did for other groups. In the previous volume, we saw that Jews are particularly inclined to utilize informal help rather than prayer as a way to cope with personal problems—a pattern we interpreted to be a result of a psychological style typical of pace-setters in the society.

By contrast, Fundamentalists and Catholics often have highly structured religious obligations and commitments. Confession as an institution reinforces the role of the priest as the source of tension-release for Catholics. Personal but public participation in rituals are also part of some Fundamentalist services. At any rate, these highly doctrinaire religions provide explicit means of maintaining the moral life. They teach their followers to structure personal difficulties in moral rather than in psychological terms and hence to seek moral rather than psychological counselors for their crises.

The pattern of relationships of church attendance to seeking out the clergy versus psychiatrists or psychologists is compatible with what we noted previously about religion differences. In both 1957 and 1976, regular church attenders predictably indicated that they more often sought help from clergy than did infrequent church attenders. In turn, the latter, especially in 1976, were significantly more likely to have sought psychiatrists or psychologists, suggesting once again a potential "substitutability" of clergy and psychiatrists as providers of professional care for emotional problems.

Other than these relationships, however, there are no consistent differences in the types of help sought between either different religious groups or high and low church attenders. Significant relationships are evident in table 5.30 between religion and the use of physicians (Baptists in 1957 were relatively high, Jews and those with no preference in 1976 were particularly low) and between church attendance and consulting a marriage counselor (low church attenders were more likely to seek such help), but in each case these relationships disappear when sex, age, and education are controlled. Thus, significant relationships between religion or church attendance and the choice of a particular help source were few in number, quite specific, and consistent across the two surveys.

Region of Birth and Rural-Urban Background

Although neither differences by region nor urbanicity of childhood residence is significantly related to the second decision point in the self-referral process—the use of help among those that defined a problem in mental health terms (see pp. 127–128)—they are apparent at the third decision point—the particular professional resource chosen. For example, although neither relationship was significant in 1957, by 1976 people raised in rural areas were distinctly more likely than those growing up in urban areas to report having sought help from a clergyman (ranging from 50 percent among those raised in the country to 31 percent among those reared in a large city), with people born in the Border states being particularly likely and those born in the East and West particularly unlikely to have sought such religious counsel. Once again, a hint of "substitutability" is evident in two patterns: In both years those growing up in urban areas (low users of the clergy) indicate that they sought help from a mental health specialist to a greater extent than did adults from rural backgrounds; and also in both years those born in the East and West (low users of the clergy) were significantly more likely than those from the South and Midwest to have consulted a psychiatrist or psychologist. The only other significant differences involving urban-rural background or region of birth (for example, a greater tendency in 1976 for those born in the West or Midwest, rather than the South, to have consulted an "other mental health source") are no longer evident when age and education are controlled.

Summary

We have now completed our demographic analysis of the help-seeking process initiated earlier in this chapter by investigating relationships between our array of social and demographic characteristics and the choice of a particular help resource—the third stage in the self-referral process. Let us attempt to integrate those findings within the general framework presented earlier, which distinguished between psychological and facilitating factors and suggested possible differences in expected patterns of change based on that distinction.

Our very general assumption was that facilitating factors are assumed to prompt not only the decision to seek help, but also the choice of a particular type of help source. Most of the findings presented here are consistent with that assumption. We also had two hypotheses about how to interpret change or lack of change in factors related to help-seeking patterns in 1957 and 1976. One stated that facilitating factors in help-seeking are especially susceptible to social change. The other stated that some social characteristics may shift in implication as "psychological" or "facilitating" factors—being more or less relevant to psychological decisions as opposed to nonpsychological ones. We assumed that structuring a problem in the first place as a mental health problem is influenced largely by "psychological" factors, but both the decision to seek help and the decision about whom to consult are largely nonpsychological because they are greatly affected by availability, accessibility, and knowledge of resources.

Let us consider this latter hypothesis first. Although our examination of factors relevant at the first two decision points revealed a few relationships consistent with the assumption that a given characteristic may differentially reflect psychological or facilitating factors at different points in the decision process, relationships observed for the third stage of self-referral provide little additional evidence for the proposition. The only characteristics that generate relationships consistent with that assumption are sex and age, variables which in 1957 were relevant only to defining a problem in mental health terms. In 1976, however, both sex and age were related to the use of physicians among those who had gone for help, and age differences are also apparent among those who sought consultation with miscellaneous mental health sources.

The other general hypothesis that factors which serve primarily to facilitate or hinder the use of formal help are more susceptible to change than psychological orientations and motivational factors derives considerable additional support from relationships involving this third decision point. Notable among the significant sociodemographic differences which appeared in 1957, but which were no longer evident in 1976, are several involving family income and size of place of residence. Thus, ability to pay and differences in the availability of various resources to residents of urban and rural areas played a less significant role in the choice of a particular help source in 1976 than they did in 1957. These were clearly facilitating factors that were amenable to change.

All changes in the relevance of sociodemographic characteristics to this third decision point do not, however, reflect a decline in the significance of facilitating factors, since a number of relationships which were not evident or statistically reliable in 1957 emerged more clearly in 1976. The greater use of doctors by women and older people in 1976 has already been mentioned in this regard, and a heavier use of physicians by the less educated was also significant only in 1976. Similarly, a clear tendency for high-income people to make greater use of marriage counseling, regional differences in the use of psychiatric care, and geographical background differences in consulting the clergy all clearly emerged only in 1976.

Overall then, while there was some evidence suggesting a decline in the significance of facilitating factors for the choice of certain kinds of help resources, there were several instances in which there was no change in the significance of facilitating factors, and some in which there was evidence of increased relevance. Although the choice of psychiatric care was less conditioned by the ability to pay, it did vary considerably by region. Marriage counseling (for which health insurance coverage is rarely available) was now largely the treatment of choice primarily among the affluent. Rural-urban differences which so often reflect community differences in available resources or information, and hence would facilitate or hinder the choice of where to go for help, were still very much in evidence. Social background differences which serve to make certain resources (for example, clergy) more psychologically accessible were now even more relevant. Older people were even more reliant on doctors than they once were, probably because of costs which Medicaid and Medicare cover. All and all, it would be difficult to argue that we have made the whole range of resources for help-seeking equally available to all groups of people by social policies instituted in the years intervening between our studies.

While we have interpreted many of the preceding results as changes or lack of changes in nonpsychological, facilitating factors, we must realize that some of them may also be interpreted as changes or lack of changes in psychological factors. For example, while rural-urban, regional background, and even income differences clearly may result from differences in available facilities (see chapter 8) or information about facilities, these social characteristics also reflect social climate differences. Thus, people living in the suburbs or in small cities might learn that going to the clergy is declassé and going to a psychiatrist is the approved style of help-seeking. Rural people may get the opposite message. Regional and income groups also have their own social norms for help-seeking. In fact, in our analysis of the first two decisions in the self-referral process—structuring a problem for help and deciding to go for help—we ended up concluding that urban-rural and regional differences in 1976 compared to 1957 appear to reflect psychological factors which either promote or militate against the definition of problems as relevant for help rather than factors which influence the translation of such problem definitions into an actual decision to seek help. While the 1976 relationships of place of residence or region to the selection of certain resources must indicate vestiges of remaining differences in the types of resources available in different size communities and in different regions of the country, we must be aware that these differences may also reflect the "psychological" availability of various sources (clergymen and physicians, psychiatrists, and mental health agencies) that take on different roles in different communities throughout the nation. Their attractiveness to people is very much regulated by the prevailing social norms which validate their use.

Variations in socialization and social norms supporting the use of certain types of formal resources are also likely to underly differences among religious groups and people raised in different areas of the nation. While differences among these various groups in their general psychological orientations toward problems have already been noted, such trends as the greater use of clergy by Fundamentalists and those born in the border states, and the greater choice of psychiatric care by Jews and people born in the East or West, suggest that these variables also reflect the inculcation of values and norms about the appropriateness of consulting a given type of help source or of general help-seeking behaviors.

By contrast, only income, church attendance, and urban-rural background conform to the hypothesized pattern of strictly facilitating variables, with no relation to problem definition, but with some relation to either the decision to go for help, the particular resource chosen, or both. The declining significance of ability to pay in the selection of psychiatric care has already been noted, and it may well be that the modest difference which remains is more a function of differences among income groups in norms supporting the psychiatric choice than of income per se. On the other hand, the consistently greater choice of the clergy in preference to psychiatrists or psychologists among regular church attenders suggests the continued importance of two critical social phenomena: (1) people will select resources with whom they have social contact and acquaintance; and (2) people will select those professional resources they deem appropriate to their social and institutional memberships or commitments. Although one might conceivably expect that variations in the help-seeking decisions among people raised in communities of different sizes would be most relevant to mental health problem definition, urban-rural background differences are in fact evident only in the choice of a particular help source. Essentially, persons from nonurban backgrounds make considerable use of clergy (as do those currently living in such communities) and are not likely to consult mental health sources—choices that appear to reflect once again socialization and social norms that predispose them to the choice of religious rather than psychological counsel.

Finally, as previously noted, community tenure, father's occupation, broken-home background, and marital status are all more relevant to the initial definition of a problem as relevant for professional help than they are to either the decision to go for help or the particular resource chosen. Thus, the geographically mobile versus the nonmobile, adult children of professionals versus adult children of farmers, people from intact versus maritally-disrupted childhood homes, and the divorced versus other marital groups all appear to differ more in the psychological orientations that make them receptive to defining problems in mental health terms than in the resources available to them, in their information, or in social norms relevant to their decisions about whether to go for help or whom to consult.

Summary

In this extensive chapter, we have covered two major topics: the readiness for self-referral to a professional helper for psychological problems and patterns of help-seeking among those who have sought help. For each, year differences were emphasized, as were sex, age, and education comparisons that were consistent for both 1957 and 1976. Other social and demographic characteristics were also examined in multivariate analyses of these phenomena.

READINESS FOR SELF-REFERRAL

From 1957 to 1976 there was a substantial increase in the proportion of the adult population who report seeking professional help for personal problems (14 percent to 26 percent) and some decrease in the proportion who felt that they could always handle these problems by themselves (44 percent to 35 percent). Within this shift, there has been a greater convergence among different socioeconomic groups in their actual use of some kind of help, once they define a personal problem as relevant for help. These results suggest that governmental attempts to make professional help more accessible to all strata of society have met with some success, but there remains a considerable proportion of the population who are very much committed to managing life by themselves.

Where once most people could only view professional help-seeking as an alternative to a hypothetical but not to an actual personal problem, in 1976 people seemed more ready to see their own lives as presenting problems that could potentially use such help. Stigmatization of professional help-seeking has clearly been greatly reduced.

In both survey years, people who were especially oriented to help-seeking expressed their own subjective distress in a variety of ways. Distress about work, however, seemed singularly insulated from a help-seeking attitude. People who reported having experienced many anxiety symptoms or feelings of an impending nervous breakdown were even more likely in 1976 to have been among help-seekers than they were in 1957. Severe psychological distress thus got referred to a help source more quickly than it once did.

Certain groups consistently showed greater readiness for professional help: women more than men; younger more than older people; educated more than less educated people. One disconcerting result about the minimally educated was that in 1976 they seemed as resistant to help-seeking as they did in 1957, in spite of the general cultural shift toward acceptance of professional help as a legitimate coping strategy for personal problems.

Other social group comparisons also presented stable findings in the 1957 and 1976 analyses of the readiness for self-referral. Especially high readiness to seek professional help was found among: people from urban areas; residents of the Pacific states; Jews; frequent church attenders; divorced men and women; adults who experienced parental divorce while they were growing up; adults whose fathers were professionals. These findings stimulated three interpretations about people who are especially inclined to seek professional help: they experience consistent social stress in their lives; they have a well-developed psychological orientation to their own experience; they receive reference-group support for selecting professional help as a coping strategy.

While there were consistent rural-urban and regional differences in the general readiness for self-referral, the importance of these geographic distinctions applied to a different decision point about help-seeking in 1976 than it did in 1957. Where they once seemed to reflect differential facilitating factors (available or accessible resources, and information about these resources), in 1976 they seemed more relevant to psychological factors underlying people's tendency to define personal problems as help-relevant.

PEOPLE WHO HAVE GONE FOR HELP

People in 1976 who went for professional help with a personal problem characterized the help they sought differently from their counterparts of 1957:

1. They were more likely to have sought help for a situational problem.
2. They were more likely to have selected a specialized mental health resource (psychiatrist or psychologist, marriage counselor, and other mental health professionals) over a general help source (doctor, clergyman, or lawyer), although they turned to all resources much more often.
3. They were more likely to be aware of the referral process, being particularly more alerted to referrals by family or friends.
4. They were more likely to see the counsel of psychologists and psychiatrists as helpful, but were more qualified in their appraisals of help received from the clergy (seeing it less often as either very helpful or unhelpful).
5. They were more likely to view the supportiveness of the counsel they received as the basis of the help that was offered.

Since women are more frequent professional help-seekers than men, they consult more help sources of many types, but only among the young do women consult psychiatrists and psychologists more than men. The heavier use of these specialists by younger women and older men seems to be balanced by a heavier use of the clergy by younger men and older women. Old people, in general, are not frequent help-seekers, even from clergy.

Although the more educated utilize all resources more than the less educated, among those who have sought help the college-educated show a higher rate of use only of psychiatrists and psychologists.

Demographic comparisons in the type of help source sought revealed the following important results: Fundamentalists and Catholics are particularly oriented to the clergy as a help source, especially in contrast to their orientation to psychiatrists or psychologists; Jews and certain Protestant groups (especially Congregationalists) show the reverse pattern. Wealthier people clearly are particularly oriented to psychological specialists. Geographic location (place of residence and region) is still as critical to determining choices of certain professional resources as it was twenty years ago. This finding seems clearly interpretable as a difference in social climates existing in these locations that psychologically motivated people to seek one source or another.

Chapter 6

PEOPLE WHO COULD HAVE USED HELP

IN THIS CHAPTER, we turn our attention to a critical group—those who recognized that a professional source could have helped them with a problem and yet did not avail themselves of such help. Because these respondents are presumably psychologically accessible to the use of formal resources, the reactions of this critical group promise to clarify subtle factors that may be obstacles to the help-seeking process.

Recall from chapter 5 that all respondents who reported never having sought professional help for a personal problem were subsequently asked the following question: "Can you think of anything that has happened to you, any problems you've had in the past, where going to someone like this [i.e., doctors, ministers, psychiatrists, marriage counselors, social agencies, and clinics, previously established as help sources to whom one might turn with a personal problem] might have helped you in any way?" Those responding "yes" were then asked the following series of questions:

1. What do you have in mind—what was it about?
2. What did you do about it?

3. Who do you think might have helped you with that?
4. Why do you suppose that you didn't go for help?

As noted in chapter 5 (table 5.1), about one in ten adults—9 percent of the total sample in 1957 and 11 percent in 1976—responded affirmatively to the filter question in this series; that is, they could think of a problem in the past for which they feel professional counsel would have helped in some way. By examining their answers to the four subsequent questions listed above, we are able to identify factors that may stand in the way of using formal resources. First, we shall look at the types of personal problems this group thought needed some professional attention, and the kinds of resources they thought could have helped. By comparing these responses to problems and sources mentioned by those who had actually gone for help, we shall infer some of the factors which account for their different behavior at the second decision point in the self-referral process. Second, we shall consider reasons reported by these respondents for not having sought formal help. Third, we shall describe the methods actually used by these people to handle personal problems in lieu of seeking professional counsel. We shall give particular emphasis to patterns of stability and change in these relationships, a concern which gives rise to the fundamental question underlying the analyses presented in this chapter: To what extent were factors underlying membership in this "critical group" essentially the same in 1976 as they were two decades earlier?

Problems Perceived as Relevant for Professional Help

The major problem areas seen as relevant for seeking professional counsel by those who said that they could have used such help are presented in table 6.1 along with a parallel tabulation for those who actually went for help. Two comparisons in table 6.1 are important. First, problems mentioned by people who felt they could have sought professional help in 1976 may be compared with those mentioned by people who felt that they could have used such help in 1957. This comparison emphasizes possible changes in the types of problems that were less likely to be translated into an actual decision to go for help. Second, by comparing the types of problems faced by people who thought they could have used help with those who actually did seek help, it may be possible to infer reasons why the latter group went for help while the former did not. Moreover, by being alert to these latter contrasts separately for 1957 and 1976, we should again be able to de-

TABLE 6.1

Problem Areas Seen as Relevant for Help by People Who Went for Help and Those Who Could Have Used Help (by year)

	Could Have Used Help		Used Help	
Problem Area	1957 (%)	1976 (%)	1957 (%)	1976 (%)
Spouse; marriage	51	40	42	40
Child; relationship with child	4	5	12	10
Other family relationship—parents, in-laws, etc.	6	4	5	3
Job or school problems; vocational choice	4	5	6	4
Nonjob adjustment problems in the self (general adjustment, specific symptoms, etc.)	14	17	19	22
Situational problems involving other people (e.g., death or illness of a loved one) causing extreme psychological reaction	6	13	6	11
Nonpsychological situational problems	6	5	8	11
Other problem areas	4	5	4	5
Nothing specific; a lot of little things; can't remember	3	2	2	1
Not ascertained	4	10	1	4
Total	—a	—a	—a	—a
Total Number	222	243	345	580

a Indicates that percentages total to more than 100 percent because some respondents gave more than one response.

tect any possible changes in relationships between the nature of problems faced and the decision to seek or not to seek professional help.

Our comparison of those who "could have used help" in 1957 and 1976 suggests that the types of problems seen as relevant for professional help are similar in the two survey years, with a few notable exceptions. Although marriage problems are those most frequently cited in both survey years, those who said they could have used help in 1976 were significantly less likely to mention such problems than their counterparts in 1957. And, while this decline is especially acute among divorced or separated respondents (96 percent of these previously married adults who in 1957 said that they could have used formal help mentioned their marital difficulties, compared with only 74 percent in 1976), it is not wholly a function of demographic shifts in marital status between the two surveys. This suggests that there was a greater willingness to translate perceived marital problems into actual help-seeking in 1976 than there was in 1957.

The group who felt they could have used help in 1976 reported a higher proportion of situational problems involving other people and a higher proportion of nonascertained or noncodable responses. Note, however, that in both cases similar increases are apparent among those who had gone for help, thus implying that such changes had no particular significance for understanding the help-seeking decisions of the group of interest here.

Further insight about such decisions can be gained, however, by examining more directly differences between the kinds of personal problems reported by people who said they could have used help and those who actually sought it. Once again, similarities in the particular problem areas mentioned are more striking than differences, but some intriguing differences do appear, especially when these findings are analyzed separately within each year. In 1957, marriage problems were significantly more prominent among the difficulties reported by those who said that they could have used help than they were in the difficulties reported by those who did use help, but as a result of the significant decline noted above, by 1976 people who could have used help were no more likely to mention marital difficulties than those who actually sought help. Or, conceiving of the data in yet another way, only 56 percent of those in 1957 who defined a marriage problem as relevant for professional help actually sought such help, whereas in 1976 over 70 percent did. Thus, we have further evidence that psychological or other factors that inhibit the referral of marital difficulties to professional resources were apparently much less influential in 1976.

In contrast, other significant differences in the types of problems reported by these two groups either persisted or were actually greater in 1976. A consistent difference evident in both survey years is a higher frequency of problems involving children among those who actually went for help, presumably due to the fact that "many people who become aware of difficulty with children do so only after some outside source (school or court) has brought it to their attention and also referred them to sources of professional help" (Gurin et al., 1960, p. 346). Similarly, that "general adjustment problems" more often led to the use of professional help in both years may reflect two different possibilities. First, those who actually went for help might have had more serious problems, ones that were more easily labeled as adjustment problems. Or, having gone for help, they might have more readily learned to label their problem as an adjustment problem. Therapists often do train their clients to see problems in personal adjustment terms.

Perhaps more informative is the reporting of more nonpsychological situational problems among those who did receive professional counsel than among those who said that they could have used such help, a difference significant only in 1976. Conceivably, problems of this type encountered in 1957 (or before) were more often defined as "inappropriate" for referral to a professional resource and were therefore viewed as relevant for such help only in retrospect. By 1976, however, 84 percent of such situational problems were actually referred for professional counsel (compared with two-thirds in 1957), suggesting that people confronted with such problems are now much more likely to consider them appropriate for professional attention.

Sources of Help Suggested

Table 6.2 presents two sets of comparisons. The first compares 1957 to 1976 with regard to the professional sources suggested as possibly helpful by people who said that they could have used help. The second compares within each year professional sources suggested by those who said they could have used help with actual resources used by people who did go for help.

Differences from 1957 to 1976 in the potential sources of help suggested by people who could have used help essentially parallel the differences noted in chapter 5 for changes from 1957 to 1976 in the type of resources actually used by those who went for help—that is, there is a greater preponderance of mental health professionals among the sources mentioned in 1976. While less than 30 percent of those who said they could have used help in 1957 suggested a mental health source as potentially helpful, by 1976 over 40 percent of this critical group suggested a mental health professional. In contrast to the pattern evident among those who sought help, however, this increase is significant only for the "other mental health source" category, reflecting the fact that those who did not actually go for help were understandably somewhat vaguer in specifying a particular type of mental health professional (the most frequent response being "a counselor") than those who consulted a particular mental health specialist. Nevertheless, another significant year difference—the less frequent mention of "other" sources by those in 1976 who said they could have used help—implies that people who could have but didn't seek help in 1976 were somewhat more specific in their conceptions of potential professional resources than their counterparts in 1957.

Perhaps the most striking comparison of all, however, is one that shows no significant year difference at all—the proportions of people who said they could have used help but who did not mention a source at all. Fully one-fifth of those people who said that they could have used help in both survey years did not mention a specific professional

TABLE 6.2

Comparison of Sources of Help Used by People Who Have Used Help and Sources Suggested by Those Who Could Have Used Help (by year)

	Could Have Used Help		Used Help	
Source of Help	1957 (%)	1976 (%)	1957 (%)	1976 (%)
Clergy	34		42	
		27	·	39
Doctor	9		29	
		7		21
Psychiatrist or psychologist	14		17	
		17		29
Marriage counselor; marriage clinic	14		4	
		16		8
Other mental health source (specialist or agency)	2		10	
		13		20
Social service agency (nonmental health)	—		4	
		1		3
Lawyer	3		6	
		—		2
Family, friends	5		—	
		6		—
Other	10		10	
		5		4
Don't know	12		—	
		7		—
Not ascertained	8		—	
		13		—
Total	—[a]		—[a]	
		—[a]		—[a]
Total Number	222		345	
		243		580

NOTE: A dash indicates that the percentage is less than one-half of 1 percent.

[a] Indicates that percentages total to more than 100 percent because some respondents gave more than one response.

resource (one in four if we include those who mentioned only an informal help source). This consistent vagueness or uncertainty about professional help sources available which permeates the responses of people who did not seek help in 1957 and 1976 may merely indicate that they were never in fact close enough to going for help to have considered appropriate help sources. Alternatively, however, this vagueness in specification of help resources may reflect real ignorance and lack of sophistication among this group about available sources of professional assistance. If so, it may well be that this vagueness in knowledge about where to go for help is the major characteristic which distinguishes this critical group from the group who actually did seek help.

Because so many people in both 1957 and 1976 who said that they could have used help did not specify a source, one must be cautious in comparing their responses with those who actually went for help. The former group might be expected to mention any potential source of help less often than the latter. In a few cases, this suspicion is indeed confirmed—clergymen, doctors, and lawyers are all mentioned significantly more often in both survey years by people who sought help than by those who did not but said they could have used help. A similar difference appears for social service agencies, but the difference disappears when education is controlled.

Some distinct interactions by year in the differential mention of three other types of professional resources—psychiatrists/psychologists, marriage counselors, and "other" mental health sources—by these two groups (one of which runs counter to the direction expected) yield important information. First, while those who did and did not seek help were about equally likely to mention a psychiatrist or psychologist in 1957, by 1976 these psychiatric specialists were mentioned more often by people who actually went for help. Thus, people who defined a problem as relevant for psychiatric care were significantly more likely in 1976 (81 percent) than those in 1957 (66 percent) to have actually sought help from a psychiatrist. Second, although ostensibly the relationships observed in table 6.2 differ substantially (that is, they are opposite in direction), the same may be said for the mention of marriage counselors, who, in both years, are suggested more often by people who said they could have used help than by those who went for help. However, the relationship is significantly weaker in 1976 than in 1957 (in 1957 people who "could have used help" are almost four times more likely to mention a marriage counselor than those who did seek help, but only twice as likely in 1976). The majority (56 percent) of those in 1976 who considered a problem appropriate for marital counseling actually consulted a marriage counselor or clinic, compared with less than one-third (29 percent) in 1957. Third, in both survey years, people who sought help were more likely to mention "other" mental health sources than those who could have used help, but the gap is significantly smaller in 1976 (declining from a ratio of five to one in 1957 to less than two to one in 1976). There was a substantial increase between the two surveys in the mention of these miscellaneous mental health resources among those who could have used help. As a result, the proportion of those mentioning another mental health source who had in fact sought such help had actually declined between 1957 and 1976 (from 89 percent to 79 percent), although the decrease is not statistically significant.

The comparisons between the resources used by people who went for help in contrast to potential resources suggested by those who did not are useful indicators of possible barriers in the help-seeking process. These latter relationships suggest once again a probable decline between 1957 and 1976 in the influence of factors hindering the utilization of mental health professionals. While those who resisted seeking help in 1957 were as likely to mention a mental health professional as were those who actually went for help, the latter were significantly more likely to mention such professionals in 1976. In fact, three-fourths of those mentioning a mental health professional in 1976 were actual help-seekers (compared to only 61 percent in 1957). Marriage counselors—still more often suggested as a possible source than actually used in 1976—may constitute the major exception (although as noted previously, even that difference represents a significant decline from 1957). It may well be that the term "marriage counselor" continues to be used more as a vague catch-all category than to indicate a specific professional resource (see Gurin et al., 1960, p. 349), although we suspect that the "other mental health source" category increasingly serves this function. There may, indeed, remain some formidable barriers to the use of marriage counselors and clinics, one of which was implied in chapter 5, in which we presented evidence suggesting that the gap between low and high income groups in the use of marriage counseling had apparently widened between 1957 and 1976 (see Kulka et al., 1979).

Why People Do Not Go for Help

Rather than speculate further about possible factors underlying the behavior and motivations of those who did not seek help, let us now turn to a more direct examination of the explicit reasons offered by people who did not go for professional help even though they felt they could have used such assistance. Table 6.3 indicates the proportion of those who could have used help that mentioned each type of reason in 1957 and 1976. Although some of the differences in the problems and resources mentioned by this critical group might lead us to expect substantial changes between 1957 and 1976 in reasons given for not seeking help, the predominant pattern evident in table 6.3 is, on the contrary, remarkably consistent.

In fact, only one statistically reliable year difference appears: those who could have used help in 1976 are significantly less likely to cite their lack of knowledge about the means of getting professional help (for example, "didn't know how to go about it," "didn't know about such places," "didn't know what to do," or "didn't know a doctor, minister, or so forth") as a reason for not going for help. That particular difference is consistent with data presented in chapter 5 which suggest that having access to channels of help or information about available resources plays a less important role in the decision to use

TABLE 6.3

*Reasons Given for Not Going for Help by People Who Feel
They Could Have Used Some Help (by year)*

	Year of Interview	
	1957	1976
Reasons for Not Going for Help	(%)	(%)
Self-help—worked it out myself (ourselves)	25	31
Lack of knowledge about means—didn't know how to go about it	19	12
Shame, stigma, hesitancy—ashamed to talk about it	14	15
Didn't think it would help	7	9
Temporizing—felt it would work out itself	6	6
Didn't realize need at the time	5	10
Problem involved other person who refused to go for help	5	7
Expense	4	7
Other	8	4
Not ascertained; don't know	15	11
Total	—[a]	—[a]
Total Number	222	243

[a] Indicates that percentages total to more than 100 percent because some respondents gave more than one response.

professional help in 1976 than in 1957. And, to the extent that this is true, substantial efforts over the past quarter of a century to increase the availability of mental health services and to increase the public's awareness of the existence of such services have apparently been successful.

While none of the other year differences evident in table 6.3 are statistically significant, three comparisons nevertheless merit attention. First, people who said they could have used help in 1976 were more likely ($p < .09$) than in 1957 to indicate that they failed to seek help because they did not realize the need at the time. Thus, they defined their problems as relevant for professional help only in retrospect. While respondents in this category constitute only 10 percent of those who could have used help, they are nevertheless worthy of note. The critical obstacle to help-seeking for these people came at the first stage in the self-referral process (problem definition) rather than at the second (the decision to seek help). Assuming that these respondents are on average somewhat more ready than others to avail themselves of formal resources, an increase in the proportion giving this response could be conceived as reflecting a modest decrease in actual resistance to the use of professional help among those who said they could have used help in the past. Second, among those people who said they could have used help, the most popular reason for not going for help in both survey years was that the respondent solved or attempted to solve the problem him/herself ("self-help" in table 6.3.)

While such responses may reflect the continuing presence of "irrational" resistance to the use of formal resources, much like the self-help category of readiness for self-referral, "self-help" in this context may often represent an affirmative choice. Admitting that a problem was relevant for professional help does not necessarily imply that the problem in fact required assistance, and in that sense working out a problem by oneself does not automatically imply resistance to the use of formal help. Additional analyses of people who attempted to solve their problems by themselves, presented later in this chapter, suggest that this latter interpretation has merit.

Third, people in 1976 who could have used such help were as likely as those in 1957 to mention shame or stigma as a reason for not seeking professional assistance. This result is somewhat surprising since many findings in chapters 4 and 5 strongly imply the existence in 1976 of a social climate more supportive of the use of professional resources as a means of dealing with emotional problems and less inclined to stigmatize such problems as symptoms of personal inadequacy or weakness. In both survey years, about one out of seven people who were presumably ready for such help refused to go because of what others might think (for example, "ashamed to talk about it," "didn't feel like talking about it," "felt funny about seeing someone"). Thus, while table 6.3 provides some evidence consistent with a greater knowledge about the use of formal resources in 1976 than in 1957, we are unable to find any evidence of a concomitant decline in the influence of fears about social disapproval in the explicit reasons offered by respondents for not having gone for help.

SOURCES OF HELP RELATED TO REASONS FOR NOT GOING FOR HELP

We can gain a more differentiated view of potential points of resistance to professional help-seeking by examining relationships between the types of formal resources suggested by people who said that they could have used help and their reasons for not going (see table 6.4). Although the number of cases involved in many of these relationships are too small to permit reliable comparisons, several intriguing differences emerge. For example, in 1957 people who mentioned a clergyman or laywer as a possible source of help were more likely than others to indicate that they attempted to solve the problem by themselves, implying that many respondents viewed these sources in particular as potentially helpful for the sorts of problems one might otherwise work out by oneself. Although parallel comparisons for 1976 were not significant, results were in the same direction.

Another finding is significant only in 1957: those who suggested a clergyman as a possible source of help were more likely than others to mention stigma or shame as a reason for not going for help. To account for this finding it is important to recall that a major reason cited

TABLE 6.4

Sources of Formal Help Suggested by People Who Could Have Used Help Related to Selected Reasons Given for Not Going for Help

Source of Help Suggested	Self-Help		Lack of Knowledge		Shame or Stigma		Thought Wouldn't Help		Temporizing		Not Realize Need at Time		Problem of Other		Expense		Number of People	
	1957 (%)	1976 (%)	1957 (%)	1976 (%)	1957 (%)	1976 (%)	1957 (%)	1976 (%)	1957 (%)	1976 (%)	1957 (%)	1976 (%)	1957 (%)	1976 (%)	1957 (%)	1976 (%)	1957	1976
Clergy																		
Yes	1	0	36	36	12	11	23	20	7	9	3	6	5	6	5	9	75	66
No	5	9	20	28	23	12	10	13	8	9	8	6	5	11	5	7	147	177
Doctor																		
Yes	5	6	21	25	16	0	16	25	11	13	16	13	5	6	0	6	19	16
No	4	7	26	31	20	13	14	14	7	9	5	5	5	10	5	8	203	227
Psychiatrist or psychologist																		
Yes	16	28	19	23	23	18	10	15	7	5	7	5	10	15	10	5	31	40
No	2	3	26	32	19	11	15	15	7	10	6	6	5	8	4	8	191	208
Marriage counselor; marriage clinic																		
Yes	7	8	30	32	20	13	13	8	0	5	10	5	3	5	7	24	30	38
No	4	6	25	30	19	12	14	16	8	10	5	6	6	10	5	4	192	205
Other mental health source (specialist or agency)																		
Yes	0	??	50	26	25	16	0	7	25	7	0	19	25	10	0	3	4	31
No	5	7	25	31	19	11	14	15	7	9	6	6	5	8	5	7	218	212
Social service agency (nonmental health)																		
Yes	—	0	—	100	—	0	—	0	—	100	—	0	—	0	—	0	—[a]	1
No	4	7	25	31	19	12	14	15	7	9	6	6	5	9	5	8	222	241
Lawyer																		
Yes	0	0	67	100	0	0	33	0	0	100	0	0	0	0	0	0	6	1
No	4	7	24	30	20	12	13	15	7	8	6	6	6	10	5	7	216	242

in chapter 5 for turning to a clergyman for help was the existence of a personal relationship with the clergyman. More often than not this relationship emerges from the respondent's long-term membership in the clergyman's congregation. Such an ongoing relationship, which for some makes it easier to consult with a clergyman for personal problems, evidently becomes a barrier to consultation for others. It is difficult to know under what conditions pastoral counseling becomes an easy choice for people and when a stigmatized choice. Our analysis in a later section in this chapter of differences by religion in reasons given for not seeking help (see table 6.10) suggests that Fundamentalist church members in 1957 and Catholics in 1976 were especially likely to speak of possible disapproval as the reason they did not seek help. Whether these concerns were only in the minds of the respondents or reflected accurate readings of their clergy's attitude cannot be answered. It would of course be ironic if the clergy, in wishing to become even more available for counseling than their traditional roles prescribed, paved the way for it by establishing personal relationships only to find that the very fact of an established personal tie stood in the way of people seeking help. At any rate, stigma for help-seeking is a salient issue for people who thought they needed help for a personal problem from a clergyman but did not seek it.

By contrast, people in both years who said they could have used help from a mental health professional were especially unlikely to mention shame as a source of their hesitancy. The impersonal consultation with a mental health expert evidently makes the choice not very open to perceived disapproval. We suggest that the impersonal style of mental health professionals makes them a more available choice for some people than the clergy who may be more intimately connected to the person's life.

A related difference of particular significance is that people who mention clergy are (predictably) especially unlikely to cite "expense" as a reason for not seeking help. In contrast, the expense of treatment was mentioned more often in both 1957 and 1976 as a reason for not consulting a psychiatrist or psychologist. Although income differences in the actual use of psychiatric care apparently declined somewhat between the two surveys, the greater cost of psychiatric services relative to other sources of care was still apparently of some consequence in the decision to seek such help.

Another interesting difference apparent in both 1957 and 1976 (though significant only in the latter year) was that people who mentioned an "other" mental health specialist or agency were more likely than others to have said that they did not seek such assistance because they did not realize the need at the time. Since the choice of a mental health counselor in such cases has by definition been made in retrospect, this finding serves to confirm an assumption we made earlier—that the "other mental health" category increasingly serves as a vague catch-all category used by those who might well have chosen a different and more specific professional resource if they had actually reached the point of going for help.

In 1957, people who said they could have used help might have also used the "marriage counselor" category in the same general catch-all sense, but people in 1976 evidently had a more specific understanding of that category. We draw these conclusions because people in 1976 who said that they could have used help from a marriage counselor were particularly likely to mention not going because the "problem involved another person who refused to go." A comparable result was not evident in 1957, which suggests that the marriage counselor category was indeed employed more loosely at that time.

SOCIAL CHARACTERISTICS RELATED TO REASONS FOR NOT GOING FOR HELP

Are the specific reasons given by people for not seeking professional help more prevalent in certain sociodemographic subgroups of the population than in others? The answers to this question could have pragmatic implications. If groups offer different reasons for not turning to a professional helper, then any potential mental health program designed to overcome resistances to professional help-seeking must take such differences into account. Tables 6.5 to 6.13 present relationships between selected sociodemographic characteristics and reasons cited for not seeking formal help. Overall, few striking differences appear in either 1957 or 1976, but several are worth noting, including a few in which one might reasonably have expected significant differences among subgroups to appear. First, we shall describe sex, age, and education differences in reasons for not going for help, emphasizing significant differences highlighted by our multivariate analyses which examined each of these social characteristics as well as year differences simultaneously. Then, we shall examine responses of other sociodemographic groups to the question of why they did not go for help, emphasizing differences which are independent of controls for sex, age, education, and year.

Sex

Although men and women offer similar reasons for not having sought help (see table 6.5), they do differ in some of their reports of resistance to formal help-seeking. The most striking difference in table 6.5 is apparent only in 1976, when more men than women tried to solve the problem by themselves. This difference also reflects a significant 1957 to 1976 increase in offering a "self-help" explanation by men, an increase which is not evident for women. Because the findings do not persist in multivariate analyses, we suggest that the differences observed are more a function of age and education disparities

TABLE 6.5

Relationship of Sex to Reasons Given for Not Going for Help by People Who Feel They Could Have Used Help (by year)

	Men		Women	
Reasons for Not Going for Help	1957 (%)	1976 (%)	1957 (%)	1976 (%)
Self-help	26	39	25	25
Lack of knowledge about means	15	10	22	13
Shame or stigma	9	11	17	17
Didn't think it would help	5	13	8	6
Temporizing—felt it would work itself out	9	7	4	5
Didn't realize need at time	8	9	4	10
Problem involved other person who refused help	4	4	6	10
Expense	1	4	6	8
Other	9	5	7	3
Not ascertained; don't know	19	9	13	12
Total	—[a]	—[a]	—[a]	—[a]
Total Number	78	97	144	146

[a] Indicates that percentages total to more than 100 percent because some respondents gave more than one response.

between men and women in the two years than of sex role norm shifts.

Two more persistent interactions involving differences between men and women do emerge from our multivariate analyses. First, sex differences in mentioning lack of knowledge about ways of getting help as a reason for not actually seeking it vary strikingly by education (see table 6.6). Essentially, among the less educated in both survey years men were less likely than women to cite lack of knowledge as a reason for not consulting a formal help source, while college-educated men (especially in 1957) were more likely than college-educated women to cite lack of knowledge as a barrier to help-seeking. Although in several respects this is a puzzling result, it probably stems largely from college-educated women's special sophistication about and direct ac-

TABLE 6.6

*Sex and Education Related to Mentioning Lack of Knowledge
as a Reason for Not Going for Help (by year)*

Sex/Educational Level	1957		1976	
	Percentage	Number	Percentage	Number
Grade school				
Men	13	24	0	6
Women	24	42	20	10
High school				
Men	6	32	5	42
Women	22	81	13	87
College				
Men	32	22	16	49
Women	14	21	12	49

cess to a broad range of professional help sources. Second, slightly more men than women in 1976, but not in 1957, said they had been reluctant to go for help because they didn't think it would help. For a person to say that he/she could have used help in the past but at that time did not think it could help is an admission of an error in judgment. That it is more characteristic of men in 1976 than men in 1957, and women in both years, suggests that men may have become increasingly ready to at least consider the possibility of help-seeking as a way to handle their problems. Where they once categorically denied the usefulness of professional help for themselves, perhaps they can now admit that it might have had some merit, even though at the time they needed help they did not think so.

Two other trends apparent in table 6.5 are worthy of mention because they are evident in both survey years, although statistically reliable in neither. First, women are somewhat more likely than men to mention possible stigma or shame as a reason for not consulting a professional resource. This finding is consistent with evidence presented in earlier chapters suggesting that women are more sensitive than men to social concerns and influences. Second, in both 1957 and 1976 more women than men raised the issue of expense as a reason for not seeking help, a finding which reflects the greater probability of women being financially dependent on men. Since women in 1976 were presumably somewhat less likely to be so dependent, the fact that this relationship was somewhat weaker in 1976 lends further credence to this interpretation.

Age

Table 6.7 indicates that people of different ages are even more similar to each other in reasons given for not seeking help than the two

TABLE 6.7

Relationship Between Age and Reasons Given for Not Going for Help by People Who Feel They Could Have Used Help (by year)

Reasons for Not Going for Help	21 to 29		30 to 39		40 to 49		50 to 59		60 to 64		65 and over	
	1957 (%)	1976 (%)	1957 (%)	1976 (%)	1957 (%)	1976 (%)	1957 (%)	1976 (%)	1957 (%)	1976 (%)	1957 (%)	1976 (%)
Self-help	29	33	21	29	19	24	33	20	36	25	22	20
Lack of knowledge about means	15	11	19	8	22	9	21	15	27	25	22	24
Shame or stigma	12	17	12	8	24	9	3	25	18	8	13	12
Didn't think it would help	4	17	11	9	8	18	6	10	0	8	9	12
Temporizing—felt it would work itself out	0	6	13	8	14	3	0	10	0	17	0	28
Didn't realize need at time	10	7	5	3	3	12	3	15	0	0	4	0
Problem involved other person who refused help	10	12	2	6	5	6	6	5	0	8	4	12
Expense	4	4	8	15	0	6	6	0	0	8	0	4
Other	6	9	5	2	8	12	9	10	9	8	17	8
Not ascertained; don't know	15	11	14	12	11	18	18	5	9	17	17	4
Total	—[a]	—[a]	—[a]	—[a]	—[a]	—[a]	—[a]	—[a]	—[a]	—[a]	—[a]	—[a]
Total Number	52	86	63	67	37	33	33	20	11	12	23	25

[a] Indicates that percentages total to more than 100 percent because some respondents gave more than one response.

TABLE 6.8

Relationship Between Education and Reasons Given for Not Going for Help by People Who Could Have Used Help (by year)

					Education					
	Grade School		Some High School		High School Graduate		Some College		College Graduate	
Reasons for Not Going for Help	1957 (%)	1976 (%)	1957 (%)	1976 (%)	1957 (%)	1976 (%)	1957 (%)	1976 (%)	1957 (%)	1976 (%)
Self-help	21	6	32	18	23	31	23	44	29	32
Lack of knowledge about means	20	13	13	18	22	7	27	16	19	12
Shame or stigma	12	25	23	18	20	14	9	7	14	20
Didn't think it would help	5	25	11	13	5	10	14	5	5	2
Temporizing—felt it would work itself out	6	0	6	3	5	9	5	2	10	10
Didn't realize need at time	2	6	6	8	12	7	0	14	5	12
Problem involved other person who refused help	8	6	0	8	5	10	9	7	5	2
Expense	3	6	4	11	8	4	0	9	0	5
Other	8	0	6	3	10	3	9	2	5	10
Not ascertained; don't know	26	19	9	8	12	13	9	7	10	12
Total	—a	—a	—a	—a	—a	—a	—a	—a	—a	—a
Total Number	66	16	53	38	60	91	22	57	21	41

a Indicates that percentages total to more than 100 percent because some respondents gave more than one response.

TABLE 6.9

Relationship Between Income and Reasons Given for Not Going for Help by People Who Could Have Used Help (by year)

| | Income In 1976 Dollars | | | | | | | | | | | |
| | Under 4,000 | | 4,000 to 7,999 | | 8,000 to 9,999 | | 10,000 to 12,499 | | 12,500 to 19,999 | | 20,000 and over | |
Reasons for Not Going for Help	1957 (%)	1976 (%)	1957 (%)	1976 (%)	1957 (%)	1976 (%)	1957 (%)	1976 (%)	1957 (%)	1976 (%)	1957 (%)	1976 (%)
Self-help	28	10	22	18	27	18	24	43	21	41	55	35
Lack of knowledge about means	18	14	20	18	19	11	19	20	23	4	18	19
Shame or stigma	10	19	22	13	14	14	5	10	19	4	0	19
Didn't think it would help	8	24	8	21	5	14	5	10	9	13	0	13
Temporizing—felt it would work itself out	3	5	2	13	3	4	14	10	9	7	9	4
Didn't realize need at time	3	10	4	3	8	7	5	3	9	9	0	4
Problem involved other person who refused help	0	5	8	11	8	21	5	10	9	9	0	3
Expense	0	14	10	5	8	7	0	13	5	4	0	4
Other	8	0	14	5	0	7	5	7	2	6	9	4
Not ascertained; don't know	30	10	6	18	14	11	16	0	9	13	18	10
Total	—[a]	—[a]	—[a]	—[a]	—[a]	—[a]	—[a]	—[a]	—[a]	—[a]	—[a]	—[a]
Total Number	40	21	51	38	37	28	37	30	43	68	11	48

[a] Indicates that percentages total to more than 100 percent because some respondents gave more than one response.

TABLE 6.10

Relationship Between Religion and Reasons Given for Not Going for Help by People Who Could Have Used Help (by year)

	Religion							
	Baptists, Fundamentalist		All Other Protestant		Catholic		Other	
Reasons for Not Going for Help	1957 (%)	1976 (%)	1957 (%)	1976 (%)	1957 (%)	1976 (%)	1957 (%)	1976 (%)
Self-help	23	22	25	38	34	33	20	25
Lack of knowledge about means	21	15	17	11	24	4	13	20
Shame or stigma	22	15	7	9	11	19	13	20
Didn't think it would help	11	5	2	10	5	9	13	15
Temporizing—felt it would work itself out	6	6	9	8	3	5	0	3
Didn't realize need at time	6	11	2	9	16	12	0	5
Problem involved other person who refused help	3	6	4	11	8	9	13	0
Expense	1	11	9	4	3	2	0	13
Other	3	3	10	4	13	2	7	8
Not ascertained; don't know	14	14	21	9	3	16	20	5
Total	—[a]	—[a]	—[a]	—[a]	—[a]	—[a]	—[a]	—[a]
Total Number	88	65	81	80	38	57	15	40

[a] Indicates that percentages total to more than 100 percent because some respondents gave more than one response.

TABLE 6.11

Differences by Religion in Reporting Shame or Stigma as Reason for Not Seeking Help From Clergy and From a Mental Health Professional[a] (by year)

Religion	Rejected Seeking Help From the Clergy				Rejected Seeking Help From a Mental Health Professional			
	1957		1976		1957		1976	
	Number	Percentage	Percentage	Number	Number	Percentage	Percentage	Number
Baptists/Fundamentalists	33	39	24	21	20	5	4	22
Other Protestants	19	10	12	25	18	11	9	33
Catholic	19	10	28	18	9	22	21	24
Other	2	0	0	2	5	20	21	19

[a] Psychologists, psychiatrists, marriage counselors, and other mental health professionals combined.

TABLE 6.12

Relationship Between Church Attendance and Reasons Given for Not Going for Help by People Who Could Have Used Help (by year)

Reasons for Not Going for Help	Church Attendance									
	More Than Once a Week		Once a Week		A Few Times a Month		A Few Times a Year		Never	
	1957 (%)	1976 (%)	1957 (%)	1976 (%)	1957 (%)	1976 (%)	1957 (%)	1976 (%)	1957 (%)	1976 (%)
Self-help	15	16	28	30	27	40	25	34	29	25
Lack of knowledge about means	15	5	22	17	22	11	18	8	13	14
Shame or stigma	30	21	7	9	16	9	13	21	13	14
Didn't think it would help	11	11	8	15	8	6	2	5	13	13
Temporizing—felt it would work itself out	0	5	7	2	4	6	10	6	4	7
Didn't realize need at time	4	11	8	13	2	9	5	10	8	7
Problem involved other person who refused help	0	11	5	9	6	14	5	6	4	4
Expense	0	5	5	0	4	6	7	7	0	13
Other	7	5	7	2	12	3	3	2	13	5
Not ascertained; don't know	26	16	8	11	12	6	18	15	17	9
Total	—[a]	—[a]	—[a]	—[a]	—[a]	—[a]	—[a]	—[a]	—[a]	—[a]
Total Number	27	19	60	46	49	35	60	83	24	56

NOTE: A dash indicates that the percentage is less than one-half of 1 percent.

[a] Indicates that percentages total to more than 100 percent because some respondents gave more than one response.

TABLE 6.13

Relationship Between Region and Reasons Given for Not Going for Help
by People Who Could Have Used Help (by year)

	Region							
	Northeast		Midwest		West		South	
Reasons for Not Going for Help	1957 (%)	1976 (%)	1957 (%)	1976 (%)	1957 (%)	1976 (%)	1957 (%)	1976 (%)
Self-help	32	23	28	32	19	38	23	27
Lack of knowledge about means	24	8	20	10	14	15	19	14
Shame or stigma	11	20	14	15	11	12	17	15
Didn't think it would help	0	10	8	13	6	3	11	10
Temporizing—felt it would work itself out	11	0	3	6	8	3	5	11
Didn't realize need at time	3	13	3	10	17	8	4	3
Problem involved other person who refused help	5	15	6	4	6	10	4	4
Expense	3	5	5	3	11	7	1	11
Other	8	8	8	3	11	3	6	3
Not ascertained; don't know	11	13	19	13	8	8	17	11
Total	—a	—a	—a	—a	—a	—a	—a	—a
Total Number	38	40	64	69	36	60	84	74

NOTE: A dash indicates that the percentage is less than one-half of 1 percent.

[a] Indicates that percentages total to more than 100 percent because some respondents gave more than one response.

sexes are. In fact, no significant age differences at all emerged as independent of sex, education, and survey year from our multivariate analyses, and no significant interactions involving age were apparent. For example, although older people in 1976 were more likely than younger adults to mention not seeking professional help because of lack of knowledge about how to go about it or because they felt that such assistance wouldn't help, in each case the relationship disappears when education is controlled.

Education

On the whole, the reasons given by people in different education groups for not seeking help are also quite similar. Nevertheless, a few distinctive trends may be seen in table 6.8 and are worthy of note.

The most obvious differences vary for each year. In 1957, considerably more of the grade-school-educated respondents gave no reason for not going for help (that is, were "not ascertained") or said that they did not know why they did not go for help. By 1976, these education differences were no longer statistically reliable. In contrast, two reliable differences occurred only in 1976: less-educated people said they thought that such assistance would not in fact be helpful; more-educated people were more likely to attempt to solve a problem themselves rather than seek professional help. Let us discuss each.

It seems so self-evident that less-educated respondents would be particularly likely to have had misgivings about the presumed effectiveness of professional help, that we think the more critical question is, why should this trend have emerged only in 1976? Perhaps because of the increased awareness among the less educated of professional help-seeking as an alternative, they were more likely in 1976 to speak of rejecting it because they thought it ineffective, whereas in 1957 they were more likely to cite nothing at all (not ascertained or don't know, as indicated in table 6.8). Whatever the reasons, any program directed toward overcoming resistance to help-seeking among less educated groups must take this present skepticism into account. It may be one step ahead of complete dismissal that existed in 1957 of even thinking about professional help, but skepticism is still an obstacle.

The greater reliance on self-help among college-educated adults in 1976 is of great interest because it represents a striking reversal of a major finding reported in chapter 5. Recall that on our index of readiness for self-referral, highly educated respondents were distinctly less likely to adopt a self-help position—that is, to indicate that they could always handle problems by themselves—than were less educated respondents, and this education difference was sharper in 1976 than in 1957. Among those who defined problems as relevant for professional help but did not actually go, the mention of self-help—having attempted to solve or take care of the problem by oneself—was significantly more prominent among the highly educated. In part, this reversal reflects education differences in response style. More educated people with a self-help orientation essentially "know better" than to respond in absolutes, that is, to assert that they have never had or ever would have a problem appropriate for professional help. Also plausible, however, is that this pattern reflects a real social class difference that influences attitudes and values about self-reliance in solving one's problems and affects help-seeking decisions. For many of the less educated, a self-help position may be so much a part of a defensive ideology that it may prevent them from ever considering the idea of help-seeking. For some of the more educated, the self-help orientation may come after they consider help-seeking but reject it in favor of self-help. If so, future educational efforts directed toward overcoming resistances to help-seeking might proceed differently among the less- and more-educated. Among the less-educated these efforts should emphasize potential benefits of seeking formal help in order to overcome an apparently deep-seated and wide-spread self-help ideology. Among the more-educated, efforts would focus on circumstances where reliance on self-help was inappropriate. Such efforts should disseminate more specific information about the types of problems and the stages in the problem-solving process at which the use of a professional resource is likely to be beneficial. This is not to say that the self-help position is always inappropriate. Indeed, policy makers have to consider carefully when professional intervention may interfere with effective coping that people in severe distress can engage in themselves, or through their natural support systems.

Income

Only one consistent difference appears in table 6.9, which compares reasons mentioned for not seeking help by respondents in different income categories, and even that difference was evident only in 1976. Independent of sex, age, and education, higher-income people are more likely to indicate that they attempted to solve a problem by themselves rather than seek professional help. Since this relationship is independent of education, it serves to remind us that reliance on self-help is at least facilitated by the availability of financial resources. Undoubtedly people with higher incomes at least believe they can alter certain situational difficulties by their own efforts, while people with lower incomes may believe they are more restricted in what they are able to do by themselves.

Although people from lower income groups are slightly more likely to mention an economic barrier to help-seeking, that relationship existed only in 1957 and was only marginally significant ($p < .08$). Furthermore, even that relationship disappears when sex, age, and education are controlled. A result described earlier—that people in both survey years who said that they could have used psychiatric help are more likely than others to mention expense as a reason for not going—serves to emphasize the fact that economic resources are not entirely incidental to the help-seeking process. Nevertheless, the lack of a consistent relationship with that category suggests that such differences reflect something more than simply being able to afford or not afford professional help. Part of the reason that lower-income people are not especially likely to view expense of treatment as a problem is that those who may not be able to afford the services of professional resources that require more money generally do not even consider such sources for themselves. Moreover, "expense" is, of course, a relative term and being able *psychologically* to "afford" the services of a psychiatrist or psychologist may not be all that strongly related to family income level, especially since, regardless of income level, cost is rarely of highest priority when a person is suffering greatly from an emotional problem.

Religion

Because of the small number of cases involved in these analyses, the nine categories of religion used in previous chapters have been reduced to only four in table 6.10 (Baptists/Fundamentalists, all other Protestant groups, Catholics, and other). Baptists and Fundamentalists are grouped together because they share a highly individualistic orientation to religious experience with a conservative reliance on the Bible. They also share characteristics such as a relatively low income and high concentration in the South. The other Protestant groups, while admittedly heterogenous, may be described as more secular.

Regardless of how one examines relationships between religious beliefs and reasons for not seeking help, few consistent differences are evident, and only one seems to be important.

Let us mention some trends first. Catholics in both 1957 and 1976 were slightly more likely, while Baptists and Fundamentalists were somewhat less likely, to rely on self-help in lieu of formal help. These differences, however, are not statistically reliable for either survey year. Secondly, Catholics in 1957 were somewhat more likely than others to say that they did not go for help because they did not realize the need at the time, but this trend disappeared when our multivariate controls were applied and, in any case, was no longer evident in 1976. Two other trends vary more systematically by year. First, while all religious groups were about equally likely in 1957 to mention their lack of knowledge as a reason for not seeking help, Catholic respondents in 1976 were particularly *unlikely* to perceive their own ignorance about resources as a deterrent to their obtaining help. This result undoubtedly reflects the fact that Catholics in 1976 tended to express greater interest than others in resources whose access is presumably less problematic—clergy and physicians. Secondly, Baptists and Fundamentalists in 1957 were less likely than others to mention an economic barrier to help-seeking, but by 1976 people in these particular

Protestant groups were actually more likely than others to cite expense as an inhibiting factor. This is a somewhat puzzling result since Baptists and Fundamentalists who in 1976 said they could have used help from a professional did not mention "expensive" resources (psychiatrists or psychologists) more frequently than they did in 1957. The change may reflect cultural differences in the perceived ratio of the costs and benefits of certain types of professional treatment.

Analyses of considerable importance compare religious groups in how much they speak of possible stigmatization or shame as a reason for not going to a professional resource. In both 1957 and 1976, "other Protestant groups" were particularly unlikely to cite this category. Included in this category are many Protestant denominations which are especially secular in their orientation to mental health. Many of them made the psychological counselor role part of the minister's function. This encouraged members not only to seek out the minister for personal problems without fear of moral condemnation, but it also paved the way for seeking out other professional resources. The other Christian churches (Baptists, Fundamentalists, and Catholics) have had a more distinctive religious or moral commitment to "healthy" behavior—which makes psychological consultation with a religious leader or other professional less acceptable behavior. The role of the Catholic priest as an intermediary with God, particularly through confession, is at some odds with the role of priest as psychological consultant.

Although not significant in multivariate analyses, a trend of considerable interest, seen in table 6.10, is a decrement in reporting shame or stigma as a reason for not going for help among the Baptists, Fundamentalists, and an increment among Catholics.[1] This suggests that there may have been a diminution in implicit sanctions against psychological counsel among Baptists and Fundamentalists but an increase in such sanctions among Catholics. In table 6.11, we also see that this shift applies to obstacles to seeing the clergy and not to consulting mental health professionals. With the rapid secularization of Catholicism during the past generation, there may have developed a special ambivalence about consulting a priest whose role, while becoming more psychological in orientation, still retains the critical function of confessor. The role of the priest in American Catholicism is in considerable transition, which makes old images of moral absolver and new images of therapist difficult to blend in Catholic attitudes. The younger generation raised in a more secular environment may be less inhibited about consulting the priest because of lessened apprehension of shameful disclosure. The image of the priest as friend rather than intermediary may have become more paramount and less tinged with old moral norms.

---

[1] There is also an increase in "other" religions but it includes such a heterogeneous group, that we shall ignore it in our present discussion.

Church Attendance

From table 6.12, it is apparent that regular and less frequent church-attenders in both 1957 and 1976 were very similar in the kinds of reasons they offered for not having gone for help. No significant relationships between church attendance and reasons for having rejected seeking help were evident in either survey year, although our multivariate analyses revealed one consistent trend (which achieves significance for the combined sample): especially religious church-attenders (those who go more than once a week) more often mention stigma or shame as a reason for having rejected professional help than either regular or infrequent church attenders. Since the very religious are also more likely than others to mention the clergy as a potential help source, this finding is consistent with data presented earlier which implied that fear of social disapproval may play a particularly salient role in people's reluctance to seek help from ministers and priests. In fact, the few highly religious people in 1957 and 1976 who said they could have used help from a mental health specialist did not particularly cite shame or stigma as the reason for not going. This corroborates a general theme we were suggesting. As some people develop a more familiar relationship with their clergy, there may be some increased anxiety about consulting them for personal problems. Many people feel that to unburden a personal problem on certain people is a violation of their relationship, especially if the basis of that relationship is with respect to nonpersonal matters. Those who are strongly religious perhaps treat their clergyman as a religious counselor and find discussing marital, interpersonal, or other psychological problems a violation of that perceived role relationship.

Region

We find nothing particularly different in the reasons for not seeking help given by people living in different regions of the country (see table 6.13), with one intriguing exception. In 1957, residents of the western part of the nation (specifically the Pacific states) were especially likely to indicate that they did not seek help because they did not realize the need at the time. Although this difference was not large and was no longer apparent by 1976, it is consistent with evidence presented in chapter 5 which implied that people residing in the West are subject to a social climate especially supportive of professional help-seeking. If going for help is "the thing to do" in one's social group, then there would be few obstacles to seeking help if the need was perceived. A logical explanation for people who live in such a milieu and recognize that they could have used help in the past is that they were not cognizant of a personal problem at the time difficulties were experienced.

Place of Residence

Urban and rural residents were remarkably similar in the reasons they gave for not seeking professional help (table 6.14). The problem of "shame" as a deterrent to seeking help was voiced somewhat more frequently by respondents who lived in small towns (presumably reflecting realistic fears about public exposure and social disapproval by small town residents). But this result, which does not quite reach statistical significance ($p< .07$), was evident only in 1957, and disappeared when controls for sex, age, and education were taken into account. The only other noteworthy trend reflects a significant interaction by year which is independent of these controls. Consistent with the overall trend reported in table 6.3, people in 1976 in all residential groups were less likely than in 1957 to cite lack of knowledge as a reason for not seeking such assistance, with one notable exception. Suburbanites in 1976 were actually more likely to mention lack of knowledge than their counterparts twenty years earlier. This makes sense when we also realize that 60 percent of the suburban residents who said that they could have used help were likely to mention the mental health professions, compared to only 39 percent in 1957. These professionals were presumably somewhat more difficult to know about and gain access to than resources such as clergymen and physicians.

How These People Handle Their Problems

A final way of examining the behavioral patterns of those who rejected professional help is to inquire about what they actually did about problems for which they believed help was relevant. If they did not make use of formal sources of help, how did they handle these problems? There are, of course, many different ways that people may handle problems they face in life and nearly as many ways of classifying such strategies. One such theoretical classification found useful in the 1960 monograph (Gurin, et al.) emphasized the distinction between *active* or *coping* ways of handling problems—those which directly involve "problem-solving" activity—and *passive* responses to problems—those which do *not* directly involve problem-solving. In Book 1, we employed an activity-passivity dimension to describe strategies that all respondents used for handling worries and periods of unhappiness. In this chapter, this dimension is used to describe coping-passive differences in the methods used by people who attempted to handle alone problems for which they later felt they could have used professional help.

TABLE 6.14

Relationship Between Size Place of Residence and Reasons Given for Not Going for Help by People Who Could Have Used Help (by year)

	Size of Place of Residence									
	Metropolitan Areas		Suburbs		Small Cities		Towns		Rural Areas	
Reason for Not Going for Help	1957 (%)	1976 (%)	1957 (%)	1976 (%)	1957 (%)	1976 (%)	1957 (%)	1976 (%)	1957 (%)	1976 (%)
Self-help	26	42	27	23	31	30	27	31	21	30
Lack of knowledge about means	21	8	12	23	19	6	23	8	20	18
Shame or stigma	9	8	15	14	4	17	25	14	12	18
Didn't think it would help	3	17	6	6	8	9	6	7	10	11
Temporizing—felt it would work itself out	9	0	6	6	4	9	4	11	7	2
Didn't realize need at time	9	8	6	9	4	6	4	10	5	9
Problem involved other person who refused help	6	13	9	9	8	2	4	10	3	7
Expense	6	0	9	9	0	7	2	4	4	11
Other	6	0	15	6	12	2	4	5	7	4
Not ascertained; don't know	9	4	12	9	19	19	12	15	20	4
Total	—[a]	—[a]	—[a]	—[a]	—[a]	—[a]	—[a]	—[a]	—[a]	—[a]
Total Number	34	24	33	35	26	54	52	74	77	56

[a] Indicates that percentages total to more than 100 percent because some respondents gave more than one response.

Table 6.15 presents by year the distributions of ways that people actually handled these problems, grouped according to the coping-passive dimension, with "prayer" considered separately. Overall, methods used by people to handle personal problems in lieu of seeking professional help tend to be similar in the two survey years, but a few striking differences appear.

Compared to their counterparts in 1957, respondents in 1976 who said that they could have used help more frequently reported having handled the problem by a passive means: "denial or displacement"—by attempting to do or think about something else to "take one's mind off it"—or by "doing nothing." In 1976, nearly half of these people reported one of these passive reactions to the problem compared to about one-third in 1957. This increased reliance on passive reactions to personal problems in 1976 was offset primarily by significant decreases in two kinds of coping reactions—withdrawal from the difficult situation (including mostly people who handled a marital problem by divorce or separation) and seeking help from formal resources other than the types of mental health sources referred to in the question.

Although this might be interpreted as an alarming trend toward

TABLE 6.15

Methods Used by People to Handle Personal Problems for Which They Feel They Could Have Used Some Help (by year)

	Year of Interview	
Methods of Handling Problems	1957 (%)	1976 (%)
Passive Reactions		
Denial or displacement—forgot it; did something else	1	4
Did nothing	32	42
Coping Reactions		
Attempts at coping—tried to work it out myself (or together with another person involved in problems)	26	27
Withdrawal from situation—left home; separated	13	7
Sought help from informal sources—family, friends, etc.	9	13
Sought help from formal sources (nonmental health)	8	<1
Prayer	3	2
Other	3	2
Not Ascertained	9	7
Total	—a	—a
Total Number	222	243

a Indicates that percentages total to more than 100 percent because some respondents gave more than one response.

more "primitive" modes of problem solving, it is important to note that even methods categorized as coping responses essentially imply a kind of "muddling through" rather than a clear reliance on strong internal resources. Moreover, although we cannot answer directly questions about how distressed these people were when they thought they needed help, one gathers from these and other data presented in this chapter that the problems experienced by people in 1976 who said that they could have used help may have been somewhat less serious than the difficulties faced by those who found themselves in the same position twenty years ago. Consistent with this interpretation is a decline in the frequency with which marital problems were mentioned and an increase in the mention of situational problems among this group, as reported early in this chapter (see table 6.1). If this analysis is valid, the implications of the changes toward greater passivity in 1976 would appear to be less alarming. Time does heal wounds. Reactions to the death of a loved one can be overwhelming, but with the passage of time, the event may often be absorbed without active coping. Such a statement is less applicable to marital problems, which were cited more often by the people in 1957 who said they could have used help.

Summary

In this chapter, we have presented an intensive examination of a relatively small group of respondents—people who recognized the need for professional help at some point in their lives but yet never sought formal help—whose responses nevertheless serve to further our understanding of the help-seeking process. Principally, some of the major factors that militate against the use of formal help resources should appear most clearly among those who did not go for help even though they were aware that such help was relevant to their problems. Moreover, while the proportion of respondents from the total sample who comprise this group was essentially the same in both survey years (about one in ten), changes noted in previous chapters led us to expect that significant changes in the help-seeking attitudes and behaviors of this critical group would also be found.

Initially, comparisons between those who could have used help in 1957 and 1976, and between these two groups and those who actually went for help in the two survey years, revealed that these groups were similar in the types of problems they experienced and in the professional sources they used or said that they might have used, although certain intriguing differences were observed. People viewing both marital difficulties and nonpsychological situational problems as relevant for formal help were more likely in 1976 to actually refer such problems to a professional, suggesting that people confronted with such problems were no longer as reticent about conceiving of them as appropriate for professional attention. Consistent with a major trend noted in the previous chapter, in 1976 mental health professionals were more often indicated as possibly helpful by people who said that they could have used help; and people in 1976 who defined a problem as relevant for either psychiatric help or marital counseling were significantly more likely to have actually sought such assistance. A more consistent and striking difference, however, is that those who did not seek help were distinctly more vague and indefinite both in specifying the locus of the problem and in indicating what resources they might have used if they had gone for help. This vagueness and uncertainty, particularly about where to go for help, were characteristics distinguishing this critical group who "almost" went for help from the group who actually did, and may have acted as important deterrents to seeking professional help.

In the explicit reasons given by this group for not having sought help, the only significant survey year difference observed was that lack of knowledge about where to go or what to do in order to get professional help was less often mentioned in 1976 than two decades earlier. In both years, treatment expense was mentioned as an obstacle, particularly by people who considered utilizing a psychiatrist or psychologist. And in both years, an equal number of people mentioned shame or stigma as the reason for their hesitancy to seek help.

This last result is important. While few people mentioned fears of social disapproval as a factor in rejecting formal help, we might have expected a decline in such responses. Analyses of correlates of this reason for avoiding help were not very informative, except for two sets of findings about religion. Fear of disapproval of help-seeking was more often mentioned by people who suggested a clergyman as a potential source of help and less often by people who were members of the more secularized Protestant churches. These results suggest that the important counseling role that clergy play in American life may at times be impeded by people's feelings of discomfort about talking over personal issues with a person whose major image is as a moral authority. As groups become clearly secularized, this may become less of a problem, but it may also be an even greater problem if there remain some conflicts in the role of the priest as psychologist or as moral leader. We suggest that such role conflict may have recently been exacerbated in the secularization of Catholicism over this past generation. From 1957 to 1976, Catholics showed an increase in the report of shame or stigma as reasons they did not consult a priest when they thought they needed help.

Different demographic subgroups also tended to be similar in the reasons they gave for not having gone for help, although certain note-

worthy differences were observed. For example, highly educated people were more likely to attempt to solve a problem themselves rather
than seek professional help, while skepticism about the potential value of professional help more often served as a deterrent to seeking
help among less-educated people.

In most cases, the methods these people did use to handle their
problems were essentially passive—"doing nothing" being predominant—and the general pattern of change observed reflected a greater
use of passive methods for handling personal problems in 1976. Rather than being a matter for great concern, however, this trend may indicate that the problems experienced by people in 1976 who felt that
they could have used help may have been somewhat less serious than
the difficulties of those who "almost" went for help in 1957. If so,
these data provide encouraging evidence that deeply distressed people
(those most in need of help) were more likely in 1976 to have actually
gone for help rather than being hesitant to do so.

Chapter 7

SEEKING FORMAL HELP FOR CRISES

IN OUR ANALYSIS of formal help-seeking we have relied on a set of measures that defines the motivation for seeking help in terms of "personal problems." Used in both the hypothetical (chapter 4) and direct (chapters 5 and 6) questions about professional help-seeking, the term "personal problem(s)" was further defined as being "very unhappy or nervous or irritable all the time," or having "problems getting along in a marriage, or personal problems with a child or job." Clearly implied in this elaboration was that the problem was related to a person's own malfunctioning. An increasingly popular alternative viewpoint conceives of psychological distress not as an internal reflection of one's own personal or interpersonal malfunctioning, but as reaction to some external stress, as a reaction to something that "happens" to a person.

This distinction between defining problems as a function of internal versus external factors was discussed in the 1960 monograph in connection with the different types of difficulties elicited by the phrase, "nervous breakdown" (Gurin, et al., 1960, pp. 38–39). However, the report of the earlier survey gave only rudimentary treatment to the implications of that distinction for formal help-seeking behavior, because the "nervous breakdown" questions did not readily lend themselves to such an analysis. Hence, in the 1976 survey we added a set of questions specifically designed to measure the use of professional and informal resources in response to external stresses or crises:

Over their lives most people have something bad happen to them or to someone they love. By that I mean things like getting sick, losing a job, or being in trouble with the police. Or like when someone dies, leaves, or disappoints you. Or maybe just something important you wanted to happen didn't happen . . .

1. When things like these happened to you, have there been times when you found it very hard to handle? That is, when you couldn't sleep, or stayed away from people, or felt so depressed or nervous that you couldn't do much of anything?
2. (If answered "Yes" to 1.) Now think about the last time you felt that way.
3. (If answered "No" to 1.) Now think about the last time something really bad happened.
4. When things like that happen some people like to talk it over with other people . . .[1] (Respondent is handed a card listing the following titles: psychiatrist, psychologist, social worker, counselor, doctor, nurse, clergyman, teacher, police, lawyer, and other professionals) . . . Did you talk to any of these people about that matter? Again (intervening question referred to list of informal sources), for each person, choose the one description that fits them best. If more than one person you talked to fits the same description, please tell me.

In this chapter, we will emphasize the nature of formal help-seeking reported "the last time something really bad happened." When the basis for seeking help is defined in this way, as a response to an external crisis, 39 percent of our respondents interviewed in 1976 reported having sought professional help compared with only 26 percent on the readiness for self-referral index. Given this sizeable difference, let us first examine the relationship between these two measures (see table 7.1). Since the "personal problem" and the crisis event referred to need not be the same, there should have been considerable divergence in the way people responded. Nevertheless, there is a significant relationship between readiness for self-referral and the use of formal resources in a crisis situation. As one might expect, those who sought professional help for a personal problem were much more likely than others to report having consulted a formal resource the last time something "really bad" happened to them. Sixty percent of those who sought help for a personal problem also reported seeking help for their last crisis; only one-third (30 to 35 percent) of those in each other

[1] This procedure was used to get measures of informal social support discussed in chapter 3. It was also an approximation of the frequency of stressful life events (see Book 1, chapter 2 for a discussion of this measure).

TABLE 7.1

Readiness for Self-Referral Related to Use of Formal Help
When Bad Things Happen (1976 only)

	Used Formal Help When Bad Things Happened?				
			Not		
Readiness for	Yes	No	Ascertained	Total	
Self-Referral	(%)	(%)	(%)	(%)	Number
Has Used Help	60	39	1	100	580
Could Have Used Help	30	70	—	100	243
Might Need Help	35	65	—	100	491
Self-Help	31	69	—	100	664
Strong Self-Help	33	67	—	100	150
Not Ascertained	24	67	9	100	136
All	39	60	1	100%	2,264

NOTE: A dash indicates the percentage is less than one-half of 1 percent.

category of self-referral, none of whom had consulted a professional with a "personal problem," had in fact done so in response to an external source of stress. It is important to note that those in the strong self-help group were as likely to have done so as those who could have used help. Hence, readiness for self-referral as a total index is not very strongly related to this more broadly based index of formal help-seeking.

Four Types of Formal Help-Seeking Patterns

By using help-seeking information from both sets of questions—one asking about personal problems, the other about external crises—we can identify four types of help-seeking patterns. These are noted in table 7.2 and include those who used formal help for both a personal problem and a crisis (16 percent); those who used help only for a personal problem (10 percent); those who used help only for a crisis (22 percent); and those who used help for neither. Note first that less than half of all respondents interviewed in 1976 had *not* sought professional help for either a personal problem, their last (major) crisis, or both. Note also that more than one in five respondents (22 percent) reported never having sought professional help for a personal problem, but later in the interview did report having consulted a formal help source the last time something "really bad" happened. This latter group, which almost doubles our estimate of the proportion of those who had sought professional help (from 26 percent to 48 percent), is of particular interest. We shall look more closely at this group in order to isolate

TABLE 7.2

*Patterns of Formal Help Used for a Personal Problem and
When Bad Thing Happened (1976 only)*

Help-Seeking Pattern	Percentage
Used help for *both* a personal problem and when bad thing happened	16
Used formal help *only* for a personal problem	10
Used formal help *only* when bad thing happened	22
Used formal help for *neither*	46
Not ascertained	6
Total	100%
Total Number	2,264

some general factors which may account for their admission to having used professional help in response to our questions about external stresses.

First, let us examine possible differences in the types of difficulties ("bad things") mentioned by the four types of groups in response to the "crisis" question. Although table 7.3 shows considerable variation among these groups, health problems (either their own or those of someone else) were especially prominent among the difficulties of those reporting the use of formal help only when questioned about crises. Fully 40 percent of the problems reported by this group involved health. Viewed another way, 48 percent of all reported crises involving health problems were mentioned by people who sought professional help only in response to crises, although that group represents only about one-fifth of the total sample. Similarly 45 percent of all legal complications were reported by that group. Health and legal problems were also frequently mentioned by respondents who said they sought professional help to both sets of questions. These latter respondents, however, were also especially likely to report mental health or adjustment difficulties, problem areas infrequently mentioned by those reporting use of help only in response to the crisis question.

Therefore, differences in the types of problems encountered by these groups account in part for their different patterns of reporting. Health problems and legal difficulties, especially in contrast to interpersonal or personal adjustment problems, are evidently less likely to be defined as "personal problems" (that is, as due to personal or interpersonal deficits or malfunctioning), and more easily defined as a "bad thing happening." However, a substantial number of people who went for professional help only for a crisis mentioned problems which were clearly psychological in nature. In combination, nearly as many people in this critical group mentioned a death, interpersonal difficulty, or adjustment problem (43 percent) as they did a legal or health

TABLE 7.3

Type of Crisis Mentioned by Four Types of Formal Help Seeking Patterns
(1976 only)

	Used Formal Help For:			
Type of Crisis	Both Personal Problem and Crisis (%)	Personal Problem Only (%)	Crisis Only (%)	Neither Problem Nor Crisis (%)
Economic or material	2	3	3	3
Work-related	4	11	5	8
School-related	1	2	1	1
Legal difficulty	6	3	6	1
Interpersonal situation	31	29	11	21
Death of someone close	19	28	29	35
Physical health or injury	22	10	40	9
Mental health or adjustment	11	6	2	2
Other	1	1	—	1
Don't know, not ascertained	3	4	3	9
Never had bad thing happen	—	3	—	10
Total	100%	100%	100%	100%
Total Number	349	228	501	1,043

NOTE: A dash indicates the precentage is less than one-half of 1 percent.

problem (46 percent). Moreover, even health and legal problems frequently have a psychological component or serious psychological consequences. This is consistent with the fact that these types of problems are also mentioned (though less frequently) by people who sought professional help for a "personal problem." Thus, in addition to some probable differences in the actual problems encountered by the "crisis only" group, differences in the ways in which they define their problems must also play an important role in their reporting the use of help only for a crisis and not for a personal problem. For example, people who consult someone during a period of mourning may see that consultation as a way to cope with an event that happened to the person, and not as a personal problem. Consequently, the person rejects the idea that he/she has sought help for a personal problem, but can speak of that consultation as a response to a crisis.

Some additional insight about the nature of these help-seeking groups may be gained by examining table 7.4, in which sex, age, and education are related to the four types of professional help-seeking patterns. Men and women are equally likely to be found among those who report consulting a professional only in response to the "crisis" question, or, for that matter, only in response to the "personal problem" series. Women are significantly more likely than men, however,

TABLE 7.4

Sex, Age, and Education Differences in Types of Formal Help Seeking Patterns (1976 only)

			Used Formal Help For:				
Social Characteristic[a]	Both Personal Problem and Crisis (%)	Personal Problem Only (%)	Crisis Only (%)	Neither Problem (%)	Not Ascertained (%)	Total Percentage	Total Number
Sex							
Men	12	10	22	50	6	100	960
Women	18	10	22	43	7	100	1,304
Age							
21 to 29	15	13	15	52	5	100	553
30 to 39	20	12	20	44	4	100	463
40 to 49	20	12	21	42	5	100	341
50 to 59	16	10	26	41	7	100	342
60 to 64	13	6	32	45	4	100	166
65 and over	8	4	28	49	11	100	397
Education							
Grade school	11	5	24	51	9	100	380
Some high school	18	9	20	46	7	100	347
High school graduate	15	11	24	45	5	100	766
Some college	18	11	23	44	4	100	411
College graduate	18	14	17	46	5	100	347

[a] The "not ascertained" respondents on each demographic variable were omitted from this table.

to report using formal help in responding to both sets of questions. More distinctive differences are apparent among age groups in table 7.4. Essentially, while the use of formal help for a personal problem (either alone or in conjunction with seeking professional assistance for a stressful event) tends to decline with age, as observed in chapter 5, reported use of a professional resource only when something "really bad" happened shows a significant *increase* with age, reflecting primarily the greater prevalence of health problems among older people. Education differences in help-seeking as reflected in table 7.4 manifest yet a different pattern. Although, as emphasized in chapter 5, education still bears a relatively strong positive relationship to the use of formal resources for a personal problem, a visual collapsing of columns 1 and 3 in table 7.4 reveals that education is not significantly related to the use of professional help "when bad things happen." In particular, people of different levels of education are about equally likely to report using formal assistance only in response to the crisis question.

Overall, then, two noteworthy and related factors distinguish people who reported seeking professional help only when the question about the action was presented as a response to an "external" event or stress: They tend to be older and more frequently mention physical ill health or injury as the reason for help-seeking.

Sources of Help Used for Crises

The professional persons approached for help in reaction to crises ("when something [really] bad happened") are listed in table 7.5, first as percentages among those who actually sought formal help (net use) and then as percentages of the total sample (gross or absolute use). Consistent with, though not entirely explained by, the frequent mention of health or injury problems (33 percent) as the "last (really) bad thing" that happened, over half of those who sought professional help consulted a physician. As might be anticipated, 56 percent of the crises for which doctors were consulted related to health or injury, and another 22 percent involved the death of someone close. Problems in dealing or coping with death (which constitute one-fourth of the crises mentioned) also account in part for the frequent consultation of clergy by those who sought help (over one-third), since two-thirds of persons who mentioned death consulted a clergyman and almost half (47 percent) of the problems brought to clergy involved a death. Combining all categories (across multiple mentions), 21 percent of those who sought formal help (8 percent of the total sample) consulted a "mental health professional"—a psychiatrist, psychologist, social

TABLE 7.5

Sources of Formal Help Used by People Who Have Sought Professional Help for a Crisis (1976 only)

Source of Help	Among People Who Sought Help (%)	Total Sample (%)
Clergy	35	13
Doctor	52	20
Nurse	8	3
Psychiatrist	10	4
Psychologist	4	2
Social worker	5	2
Counselor or other mental health source	7	3
Lawyer	16	6
Police	7	3
Teacher	3	1
Other	5	2
Total	—[a]	—[a]
Total Number	882	2,264

[a] Indicates that columns total more than 100 percent (or more than the percentage who sought professional help) because some respondents mentioned more than one source.

worker, counselor, or other mental health practitioner. Predictably, over half (53 percent) of the mental health or adjustment problems and 44 percent of interpersonal difficulties mentioned by this group were brought to a mental health professional, but over 25 percent of economic or material, work-related, school-related, and legal problems also entailed a "mental health" consultation. Another 16 percent of those going for help sought assistance from a lawyer. In part this was for explicit legal advice (57 percent of those citing direct legal difficulties consulted a lawyer) but lawyers were also consulted for help with interpersonal (for example, marital) difficulties (34 percent of the crises brought to attorneys), deaths (15 percent), and even health, economic or work problems.

Table 7.6 provides a comparison of the sources of help utilized in crises by two groups: those who sought formal help for both a personal problem and the last time something bad happened and those who sought formal help only for their most recent crisis. As might be predicted from the differences in problems mentioned by these two groups (see table 7.3), people who reported seeking help only for a stressful life event are significantly more likely to mention consulting a physician or nurse, and significantly less likely to have gone to any of the mental health professionals or to a clergyman.[2] Although one-third of this group consulted a clergyman and another 10 percent

[2] Differences for the latter and the social worker category are marginal ($p < .06$).

TABLE 7.6

*Sources of Formal Help Used by People for Crises by
Two Types of Formal Help Seekers (1976 only)*

	Type of Formal Help Seeker	
Sources of Help for Crisis	Sought Formal Help for Both Personal Problems and Crisis (%)	Sought Formal Help for Crisis Only (%)
Clergy	38	32
Doctor	47	56
Nurse	7	10
Psychiatrist	20	3
Psychologist	7	1
Social worker	7	4
Counselor or other mental health source	14	3
Lawyer	15	17
Police	7	8
Teacher	1	4
Other	3	6
Total	—[a]	—[a]
Total Number	349	501

[a] Indicates that columns total more than 100 percent because some respondents mentioned more than one source.

called on a mental health professional, they may have approached this consultation on somewhat different terms than someone who sought a parallel consultation but structured it as a potential personal problem. Seeking help for crisis is a new way to think of mental health consultation and may require a new way to structure appropriate problems and appropriate therapies. Our guess is that even people who seek aid from mental health experts in a crisis but do not see it as a consultation for a "personal problem" are seeking therapy that is short term and supportive rather than therapy that is extensive and directed toward personal change.

Table 7.7, which contrasts the sources of help used for a personal problem with the sources consulted as result of a recent life crisis, serves to accentuate the observations we have been making. Since the questions employed to elicit mentions of different formal resources for these two types of problems vary in ways which make detailed category comparisons unreliable, only a comparison of general categories is possible. Nevertheless, it is still apparent that the questions about stressful life events elicit a substantially higher proportion of physicians and lawyers than the personal problem questions. The latter are more often answered by reference to a psychiatrist, psychologist, or other mental health professional, and, to a lesser extent, clergy.

Table 7.8 examines this comparison in yet another way and provides

TABLE 7.7

Sources of Formal Help for a "Personal Problem" and Recent
Crisis Among Those Who Sought Help (1976 only)

Source of Help	For Personal Problem (%)	For Recent Crisis (%)
Clergy	39	35
Doctor	21	52
Psychiatrist or Psychologist	29	13
Other mental health source	27	12
Lawyer	2	16
Other Professional	10	21
Total	—[a]	—[a]
Total Number	580	882

[a] Indicates that columns total more than 100 percent because some respondents mentioned more than one source.

some additional information about the significance of characterizing problems as "personal problems" or as crises. Table 7.8 presents the percentages of the total population who report each type of source of help in response to the question about personal problems (column 1), in response to the question about crises (column 2), and in responses to either or both of the questions (column 3). These percentages can be used to obtain estimates of the differential use of these various professionals in the 1976 sample. A comparison of the first two columns merely substantiates the differences noted in table 7.7, but comparisons of columns 1 with 3, and 2 with 3 provide additional information of considerable value. They indicate the extent to which one might underestimate the absolute frequency of use of each type of professional source by asking about formal help-seeking only for personal problems or only for crises. Although some differences are obviously much larger than others, only the total estimated proportion of those consulting lawyers would probably be obtained using only one of the two measures.

Since the "personal problems" question presumably measures life-time prevalence (while the point of reference and time frame for the crisis question is more ambiguous), discrepancies between the "personal problems" and "either/both" estimates are of great interest. The four-fold increase in the estimated proportion of those consulting a physician is the most dramatic discrepancy, of course, but the percentage of those who report seeking help from clergy almost doubles, and appreciable increases in the proportions consulting each of the other formal sources are evident as well. In particular, even the estimated proportion of those consulting any mental health professional—a primary datum objective of the "personal problems" question—increases

TABLE 7.8
Sources of Formal Help Used for a Personal Problem in Total Sample
(1976 only)

	Sought Professional Help for:		
Source of Help	Personal Problem (%)	Recent Crisis (%)	Either/Both (%)
Clergy	10	13	19
Doctor	6	20	23
Psychiatrist or Psychologist	7	5	10
Other mental health source	7	5	10
Lawyer	1	6	6
Other Professional	3	8	10
Did not use formal help	74	61	52
Total	—a	—a	—a
Total Number	2,264	2,264	2,264

a Indicates that columns total more than 100 percent because some respondents mentioned more than one source.

by one-third (from 12 percent when only the "personal problems" question is asked to 16 percent when sources mentioned in response to the crisis question are added).

Although a substantial number of the "bad things" reported in response to the life events question are not in literal terms "mental health" problems, those referred to a mental health professional presumably are, as are many of those for which a clergyman was consulted. As noted earlier, even a fair number of the problems referred to a physician or a lawyer are related as much to psychological or personal issues as they are to health or legal matters. Thus, to varying degrees within each professional help source category, at least part of the increase accrued as a result of attention to sources emerging from the crisis question represents a "corrective" increase in our estimate of the proportion of adults who have ever sought professional help for a psychological problem. While the total estimate presented earlier in this chapter (48 percent, derived from table 7.2) is undoubtedly too high, it is also clear that substantially more adults in 1976 had talked to a professional help source about a psychological difficulty than the 26 percent who reported having consulted a professional with a "personal problem" (chapter 5). Conservatively, assuming that a third of those consulting clergy, all of those seeing a mental health source, and none of those consulting a doctor, lawyer, or other professional only for their last crisis had a psychological problem, *at least one-third of adults in 1976 had sought professional counsel for a difficulty that can be viewed as a "mental health" problem.*

We sought more information about this group of people and especially those among them who sought help for a "mental health" prob- .

TABLE 7.9

Nature of Recent Life Crisis Mentioned by People Who Sought Help from Clergy and Mental Health Sources for Both Personal Problem and Crisis, Personal Problem Only, and Crisis Only (1976 only)

Types of Crisis	Sought Help from Clergy for:			Sought Help from Mental Health Source for:		
	Both Personal Problem and Crisis (%)	Personal Problem Only (%)	Crisis Only (%)	Both Personal Problem and Crisis (%)	Personal Problem Only (%)	Crisis Only (%)
Economic or material	1	4	1	2	2	5
Work-related	2	8	2	5	13	8
School-related	1	2	<1	1	2	3
Legal difficulty	1	2	1	5	5	11
Interpersonal situation	34	29	17	49	26	27
Death of someone close	33	22	54	10	25	11
Physical health or injury	14	19	21	10	14	19
Mental health or adjustment	8	6	1	15	8	12
Other	1	1	1	1	1	<1
Don't know; not ascertained	5	7	2	2	4	5
Total	100%	100%	100%	100%	100%	100%
Total Number	97	129	207	112	168	75

lem described as a "bad thing that happened" but not as a personal problem. We continued the assumption that those consulting either a mental health source or the clergy were seeking formal help for a "mental health" problem. We then conducted additional analyses parallel to those described in tables 7.3 and 7.4 in order to examine potential differences between people who reported seeking help from such professionals only for their most recent life crisis and those who consulted them for a "personal problem." Presented in table 7.9 are the types of difficulties mentioned in response to the "crisis" question by people consulting these two types of professional resources. The respondents are grouped according to whether they mentioned the professional for help with personal problems, for crises, or for both. Some distinctive differences among these groups appear. Among those consulting clergy, those who reported talking to a minister, rabbi, or priest only for a recent stressful event were distinctly more likely than others to mention the death of someone close (over half did) and less often mentioned either an interpersonal difficulty or a psychological adjustment problem. That experiencing the death of someone close frequently creates problems of psychological adjustment is undeniable, but death is also the classic example of a stressful life event. Thus, it is not surprising that many people who sought religious counsel in connection with a death did not also view it as a consultation about a "personal problem."

As one might expect, consulting a mental health professional for a "personal problem" as opposed to a "crisis" also involved different types of problems, but these differences were somewhat less clear cut. Essentially, in comparison with those who reported seeing a mental health specialist in answer to both sets of questions, those consulting a psychological counselor only for their most recent life crisis were much less likely to have gone for an interpersonal conflict and significantly more likely to have done so for a financial or material matter or a legal problem. Again, economic or legal difficulties—even those producing an extreme psychological reaction—are those most easily described as situational rather than "personal" problems. Interpersonal crises, while they can be structured as situational problems, more often engage people in an inward looking examination of possible personal inadequacies that precipitate stress.

Table 7.10 extends this examination further by presenting relationships between sex, age, and education and patterns of seeking help from clergy and mental health sources for personal problems only or for recent stressful life events, or for both. Among those seeking help from clergy, we observe a quite familiar pattern—a significant positive correlation between age and reports of seeking help from a minister or priest only in a time of crisis (notably a death, based on table 7.9). Thus, a major distinguishing characteristic of those who did not report seeking religious counsel for a personal problem but did so in connec-

TABLE 7.10
Sex, Age, and Education Related to Seeking Help from Clergy and Mental Health Sources for a Personal Problem, Recent Life Crisis, or Both (1976 only)

Social Characteristic[a]	Sought Help from Clergy for:			Sought Help from Mental Health Source for:			Total Number
	Both Personal Problem and Crisis (%)	Personal Problem Only (%)	Crisis Only (%)	Both Personal Problem and Crisis (%)	Personal Problem Only (%)	Crisis Only (%)	
Sex							
Men	3	5	8	4	7	3	960
Women	5	6	-10	6	8	4	1,304
Age							
21 to 29	4	8	4	6	9	4	553
30 to 39	4	6	7	8	9	4	463
40 to 49	6	8	10	5	11	3	341
50 to 59	5	5	11	4	6	3	342
60 to 64	5	4	16	2	7	4	166
65+	3	3	13	2	2	2	397
Education							
Grade school	3	4	11	2	3	2	380
Some high school	6	5	8	6	6	4	347
High school graduate	4	7	10	4	7	3	766
Some college	5	6	9	5	9	4	411
College graduate	5	4	8	10	14	4	347

[a]The "not ascertained" respondents on each demographic variable were omitted from this table.

tion with a recent "crisis" is that they were older. In contrast, no significant sex or educational differences in patterns of using clergy are evident in table 7.10.

Differences presented on the right side of table 7.10 reveal even less about those who reported seeking aid only from a mental health specialist in response to the "external stress" question, in that none of the relationships presented are significant. Although younger people were somewhat more likely to have consulted a mental health professional for a personal problem, those who called on a mental health specialist for a crisis were not significantly younger or older. Similar comparisons of men and women, or people in various educational groups yielded no distinctive patterns in the use of mental health specialists for crises. Overall, then, those who reported seeking mental health treatment, but only when asked about a crisis, were not distinguishable at all by these basic demographic comparisons, and only modestly so by the types of problems they mentioned. We conclude that subtle psychological factors are involved in whether people structure a problem for which they seek mental health consultation as a personal problem or as a response to a crisis. One of these factors might very well be the way the mental health practitioner diagnosed or structured the problem for the person. Another may be how long-term the difficulty was. Kelley's (1973) analysis of attribution phenomena would suggest that people who see that they have a distinctive long-term failure might make a "personal" causal attribution to their problem. People who see that their problem was only in response to one situation might make a situational causal attribution to their problem. Interpersonal difficulties thus can be structured as either personal or situational depending on how long-term or how distinctive the difficulties are. Being overwhelmed by the death of a loved one would probably be structured as a response to stress if the reaction occurs within a short period following the death; it would more probably be structured as a personal problem if the mourning reaction continues over a long period.

Summary

In this chapter, we provide a somewhat different perspective from our previous analysis of the use of formal help for personal problems by presenting a fairly global examination of the use of professional resources in times of crises or "when bad things happen." Underlying these analyses is the assumption that psychological distress may be conceived either as a "personal problem"—as an outgrowth of one's own personal or interpersonal malfunctioning—or as collapse in the face of external stress, and that survey reports of professional help-seeking will vary significantly according to which conception under-lies the particular question asked. Although the distinction is clearly not as sharp as implied at the beginning of this chapter, a great deal of the evidence presented here is consistent with that assumption.

People who use formal help for a "personal problem," also tend to use formal help "when bad things happen." The responses are indeed strongly related, but they are hardly synonymous. Accounting for for-mal help-seeking only as a response to a "personal problem" will not provide a complete picture of the nature of professional help-seeking for psychological problems. Substantially more people reported the use of professional help for their most recent life crisis (39 percent) than for a personal problem (26 percent), and over half of the former were not included among the latter. And although many of these "ad-ditions" reported seeking help for ostensibly "nonpsychological" problems (health and legal difficulties) and resources (doctors and lawyers), a substantial number of these transactions did involve psy-chological problems and/or psychological counselors, suggesting that differences in the ways in which similar problems are defined plays a significant role in "underreporting" the use of formal resources for psychological problems. Overall, at least a third of American adults in 1976 had sought professional help for a psychological problem either structured as a "personal problem" or as a reaction to a crisis. Other than type of problem reported, age was the only factor which clearly distinguished those who reported having consulted a formal helper for a crisis but at the same time failed to do so when the difficulty was characterized as a "personal problem"; such respondents tended to be older. Among people who sought professional aid only for crises, however, older people were not any more likely than young adults to consult a mental health professional. We suggest that both the analysis provided by the professional consulted and the longevity of the pre-senting problem will affect whether a person attributes a mental health problem to personal malfunctioning or to a situational crisis.

Chapter 8

COMMUNITY MENTAL HEALTH RESOURCES AND HELP-SEEKING

IN the preceding chapters we have considered the relationship between individuals' psychological and social characteristics and their attitudes toward and actual use of professional help for personal problems and crises. In the present chapter we consider the effect of a different kind of variable on these same outcomes for the 1976 sample—the availability of resources in one's community.

The President's Commission on Mental Health, reporting on its comprehensive investigation of resources, concluded that:

> The mental health services system which currently exists is still in a state of evolution. It combines public and private personnel, facilities, and financing without clearly established lines of responsibility or accountability.
>
> For some Americans this system represents few problems. They are able to obtain the care they need.

For too many Americans this does not occur. Despite improvements in the system, there are millions who remain unserved, underserved, or inappropriately served.

   * Because of *where they live* or because of *financial barriers*, far too many Americans have no access to mental health care.

   * Because the services available to them are limited or not sufficiently responsive to their individual circumstances, far too many Americans do not receive the *kind* of care they need.

   * Because of their age, sex, race, cultural background or the nature of their disability, far too many Americans do not have access to personnel trained to respond to their special needs.

         (President's Commission on Mental Health, 1978, Vol. 1, p. 2)

This chapter will provide some information that will both corroborate and raise questions about these assertions from the standpoint of users and potential users of facilities. We will be exploring the extent to which people living in counties that have many rather than few facilities and those that have larger rather than smaller expenditures for mental health services, are more or less likely to use professional help or are more or less oriented toward the use of professional help for problems or crises. Our answers will not be unequivocal.

We entered our analyses with some preconceptions about how the relative availability of mental health resources in a community might affect the self-referral process at several different points. First, the fact that a community has relatively great resources, we conjectured, reflects a sophisticated attitudinal climate among its residents with regard to mental health issues. For a good proportion of people in such communities, problems are likely to be defined within a mental health frame. In addition, the relative availability of different resources should affect not only the decision to seek help, but also the decision about what kind of help to seek. Even if an individual living in a remote rural area should define a problem in mental health terms, he or she may go to a clergyperson or family physician rather than to a more specially trained mental health expert, because such specialists are simply not available within a reasonable traveling distance.

Access to resources will probably not affect all individuals to exactly the same degree. We might anticipate that more sophisticated and perhaps more affluent people would find help even when their local communities do not offer many resources. We might also expect that severity of stress would mediate the effects of resource availability. While people with relatively minor problems would likely be inhibited by the limited availability of resources, people who see themselves in serious trouble would likely seek help even if it meant traveling outside of their immediate communities.

In 1957, the study staff had access to information from another study sponsored by the Joint Commission (Robinson, DeMarche, and Wagle, 1960) which made possible limited analysis of the effects of resource availability on people's readiness to use and their actual use of professional help. These data consisted of ratings for each county in the United States against different kinds of mental health resources: (1) the presence of a mental health clinic service within the county (rated "yes" or "no"); (2) the presence of psychiatric beds in general hospitals, excluding federal institutions (rated "yes" or "no"); and (3) the prevalence of psychiatrists in the county (rated on a six-point scale, reflecting the ratio of psychiatrists to population, which varied from zero to one psychiatrist per 7,499 persons). These three ratings were combined to form an overall patterned index of resource availability.

Since the primary sampling unit for the Survey Research Center is the county, these data resources were well suited to our purposes. Respondents were each assigned the resource availability code for their respective counties. Because in metropolitan areas a county does not always provide an accurate indication of the resources available to residents, this analysis was further restricted to nonmetropolitan (non-SMSA) counties.

Our analysis of the effect of resource availability in 1976 is not completely parallel to the one conducted in 1957. The analysis in 1957 was crude. We had access to a much fuller range of information about mental health facilities in 1976 and hence shifted the strategy to accommodate these data. And while the same limitation of relying on county designation for respondents living in metropolitan areas still holds—that is, data for the entire metropolitan area may more accurately represent the breadth of facilities available to people living in secondary counties within that metropolitan area—we have chosen to include metropolitan cities and their suburbs in our analysis by county, and subsequently control for degree of urbanization as a factor in interpreting the meaning of resource availability. We did so, because preliminary analysis that categorized metropolitan area residents according to SMSA units[1] and the resources available to respondents in such units revealed that by and large this way of aggregating resources did not produce patterns of findings that differed dramatically from those using county level aggregation.

Overall, we constructed six separate measures of resource availability for examination in this chapter, although we focus closely on three: per capita number of agencies, per capita staff hours, and per capita mental health expenditures in a county. Let us describe how the measures, these focal measures in particular, evolved in our analyses.

[1] Standard Metropolitan Statistical Areas; geographical units focused around a small or large metropolitan area as the basis of aggregation.

Measures of Mental Health Resources Available in Counties

Information about the availability of resources in counties throughout the nation was derived from data tapes accumulated and compiled by the National Institute of Mental Health.[2] In order to survey relevant policy-related information about mental health facilities in the country, the Institute had compiled a list of all known mental health-related facilities in 1976, and had asked each to supply information about its services for that year. Critical to our analyses were data about numbers of facilities, the number of staff hours listed by these facilities, and how these hours were distributed among different types of professionals. We initially selected for analysis only those counties from which our respondents had been sampled, but we later added counties which contained administrative headquarters for component facilities within our sample counties. The latter augmentation was necessary to achieve an accurate estimate of staff hours and expenditures, which were not entirely collected on a facility by facility basis. If facilities were components of a larger organization, information on staff hours and expenditures was not available at the facility level. For example, staff hours and expenditures for a sub-unit of a community mental health center were not reported for that specific facility, but only as a component of total staff hours or expenditures for all units of that center, which were summed and reported only for the administrative headquarters of the center. Since these sub-units had no separate entries for expenditures and professional services, whenever the relevant administrative center was located in a county other than the one in which the respondents in our sample resided, it was necessary to abstract that information from an adjoining county, even though that county itself did not appear in our sample.

NUMBER OF MENTAL HEALTH FACILITIES IN RESPONDENTS' COUNTIES

The NIMH listing of public and private facilities included a wide array of possible agencies. The Institute made an attempt·to compile an exhaustive listing of all possible mental facilities in the country. There is no way to estimate its success except by saying that there is probably no better compilation anywhere. Since it was too difficult to make at-a-distance judgments about whether or not a given facility served as a viable resource for a person in psychological trouble and desiring help, we eliminated only a few facilities that were clearly either too remote alternatives (e.g., hospitals for the criminally insane;

    [2] We wish to acknowledge the assistance of Michael Witkin and Rosalyn Bass in procuring this information and in interpreting their coding. In addition, nowhere were David Klingel's acute and persistent skills in data management more indispensable than in the unraveling of these data into usable indices for our analyses.

detoxification units) or too vaguely designated to be useful (e.g., "other general hospital units" or "other mental health facilities"). The remaining facilities listed were coded into six types:

1. Psychiatric hospitals for adults (long-term inpatient service)
2. Emergency mental health services (short-term acute care)
3. Outpatient mental health services (This does *not* include psychotherapists in private practice.)
4. Comprehensive, federally funded, community mental health centers
5. Community support services (predominantly day treatment centers and halfway houses)
6. Child or adolescent treatment services (predominantly residential treatment centers for children)

Two summary indices were developed: the total number of agencies that represent outpatient services (3 and 4 above) in a county; and the number of all mental health agencies in the county (1 through 6 above). These summary indices plus the number of federally-funded community mental health centers (4 above) constitute the major analytic variables for this chapter. We focus especially on the total number of mental health facilities for the county. Each measure was subsequently converted to per capita units based on 1975 county population estimates derived from the *County and City Data Book, 1977* (1978). For each respondent in our sample, these three measures of per capita facilities in his/her county were assigned as measures of resources available to him/her. Each measure was then divided into quartiles for ease of analysis. All respondents in a given county were assigned the same resource code values, and all of our analyses were conducted at the respondent level. While the number of community mental health centers is correlated only .34 and .32 with the number of outpatient services and the total number of agencies, respectively, these latter two indices are correlated .83 in our national sample. These and other intercorrelations of the indices evolved for assessing available resources are presented in table 8.1.

MENTAL HEALTH EXPENDITURES AND PROFESSIONAL STAFF HOURS IN RESPONDENTS' COUNTIES

The Biometry Branch of the National Institute of Mental Health also attempted to accumulate for the year 1976 estimates of dollar expenditures and staff hours for mental health in all agencies reporting to its survey. Some agencies, of course, did not report. If more than 40 percent of the agencies in a given county did not report staff hours or expenditures, these counties were not assigned values for these measures. If a county had at least 60 percent of agencies reporting expenditures or staff hours, any agency with missing data was assigned the mean value of staff hours or expenditures from those agencies which

TABLE 8.1

Intercorrelation of Per Capita Quartile Measures of Facilities in Counties

	(1)	(2)	(3)	(4)	(5)	(6)
1. Federally-Funded Community Mental Health Centers		.34[a]	.32	.33	.42	.25
2. Outpatient Clinics	(2,264)		.83	.48	.57	.44
3. Total Facilities (inpatient plus outpatient)	(2,264)	(2,264)		.56	.60	.57
4. Expenditures for Mental Health Care	(1,812)	(1,812)	(1,812)		.85	.92
5. Psychotherapists' Hours of Service	(2,053)	(2,053)	(2,053)	(1,812)		.85
6. Total Professional Staff Hours of Service	(2,053)	(2,053)	(2,053)	(1,812)	(1,812)	

NOTE: Correlations indicated above the diagonal; NS below the diagonal.

[a] Computed for respondents, consequently each county is weighted in these calculations proportionately to its representation in the total sample.

did report. As noted earlier, if a given facility was a component of a larger agency, such information was aggregated under the administrative "master" of this organization. If a "master" was located in a county different than that of a component agency included in the sample, the component was assigned values from the out-of-county master. We reasoned that availability of resources did not often stop at county lines when such cross-county aggregation occurred. If two or more components in a county within the sample had a common administrative master in another county, that master's expenditures and staff hours were entered into the total for the designated county only once.

Staff hours were accumulated separately for psychiatrists, psychologists, social workers, and other thearapeutic workers (e.g., occupational thearapists). Preliminary analysis indicated that the correlations among hours reported for these various types of professional workers were extremely high. For these analyses, therefore, we accumulated professional hours in two ways: (1) total number of therapeutic staff hours for professionals who had explicit advanced training in psychotherapy (psychiatrists, psychologists, and social workers); and (2) number of total staff hours, including psychotherapists and other supportive professional staff (recreational and occupational workers). The first sum we will call psychotherapists' hours of service, and the second, total professional staff hours of service. Per capita psychotherapists' hours of service and per capita total professional staff hours of service were established by dividing these totals by the population estimate for each county.

The intercorrelations among these six different measures of the availability of resources in counties where our sample survey respondents lived are listed in table 8.1. We note in particular the very high correlation between outpatient clinics and total facilities, which include both outpatient and inpatient services, and the very high correlations between both of the staff hours measures and expenditures. For this reason we focus in our analyses in this chapter on only three measures of resource availability: (1) per capita outpatient services in the county, (2) per capita total mental health services in the county, and (3) per capita mental health expenditures in the county.

Although the correlation between outpatient services and total services is high, the two will be dealt with separately because there is obviously a great conceptual difference between a measure based only on outpatient services and one that includes inpatient services as well. Outpatient services are facilities that may be most directly relevant for help-seeking or self-referrals. Nevertheless, in accounting for inpatient services as well in a total facilities measure, we are also more likely to account at least in part for the availability of psychotherapists in private practice. Staff for inpatient services generally includes many professionals in private practice in the community, another set of resources available to people which are not accounted for in any of the analyses reported in this chapter, because such estimates were not easily available. Therefore, an estimate of the total number of facilities in a community which includes inpatient services may better reflect the actual availability of nonhospitalized referral possibilities in the area since it encompasses not only outpatient institutional services but private options for clients as well.

Are Mental Health Resources Distributed Differentially in Different Demographic Groups?

The final report of the President's Commission on Mental Health (1978) emphasized the view that certain groups are underserved by mental health facilities in our country. In our analyses, one way to assess the extent to which that is true is to see whether or not certain groups in our sample appear particularly low in the availability of such resources, as indexed by the measures we have generated in our analyses. Therefore, in tables 8.2 and 8.3, we present sociodemographic differences in per capita resources for each of the measures. Table 8.2 presents demographic differences in per capita availability of: community mental health centers; mental health outpatient services; and total mental health facilities. Analysis of the availability of community mental health centers is of special interest because these

TABLE 8.2

Sociodemographic Differences in the Per Capita Availability of Community Mental Health Centers,[a] Mental Health Outpatient Services, and Total Mental Health Facilities in Counties of Respondent's Residence[b]

Sociodemographic Characteristics	Per Capita Availability of Community Mental Health Centers[a]				Per Capita Availability of Mental Health Outpatient Services					Per Capita Availability of Total Mental Health Facilities				
	Total Number	Low[c] (%)	High[c] (%)	Total Percentage	Low (%)	Moderately Low (%)	Moderately High (%)	High (%)	Total Percentage	Low (%)	Moderately Low (%)	Moderately High (%)	High (%)	Per
Age														
21 to 34	814	46	54	100	20	24	30	26	100	14	28	26	32	
35 to 54	698	48	52	100	20	26	26	28	100	16	30	24	30	
55 plus	750	44	52	100	20	20	31	29	100	15	25	30	30	
Education														
Grade School	386	53	47	100	27	21	29	23	100	24	26	24	26	
High School	1,113	47	53	100	19	23	28	30	100	14	27	27	32	
College	758	45	55	100	19	25	30	26	100	11	29	28	32	
Place of Residence														
Metropolitan Area	116	7	93	100	0	30	38	32	100	0	37	28	35	
Suburbs	350	42	58	100	19	43	32	6	100	10	48	36	6	
Small City	461	43	57	100	24	31	27	18	100	7	35	30	28	
Town	732	45	55	100	16	18	33	33	100	14	21	28	37	
Rural Area	550	70	30	100	30	10	20	40	100	30	14	16	40	
Race														
White	1,953	49	51	100	20	22	29	28	100	14	28	26	32	
Black	245	39	61	100	23	27	26	24	100	19	20	29	32	
Relative Income														
Low	578	46	54	100	22	21	31	26	100	16	27	27	30	
Moderate	921	48	52	100	21	23	27	29	100	16	26	26	31	
High	608	47	53	100	18	27	28	27	100	11	30	26	32	
Region														
Northeast	461	43	57	100	7	14	52	27	100	7	15	40	38	
E. N. Central	371	59	41	100	19	34	27	20	100	10	47	18	25	
W. N. Central	191	66	34	100	37	10	3	50	100	21	23	15	41	
South	544	52	48	100	34	21	24	21	100	31	13	31	25	
Border	172	37	63	100	36	9	9	46	100	20	31	3	46	
West	314	28	72	100	0	42	35	23	100	0	45	30	25	

[a] Federally funded.

[b] Since these are computed as the bases of respondents in the sample, the compilation weights the relationship proportionately to the representation of counties in the total sample.

[c] Because of skewed distribution, only a median split was sensible for the per capita availability of federally funded community mental health centers.

TABLE 8.3

Sociodemographic Differences in the Per Capita Mental Health Expenditures, and Total Supportive Staff Hours in Counties of Respondents' Residence[a]

Sociodemographic Characteristics	Per Capita Mental Health Expenditures						Per Capita Total Professional Staff Hours					
	Total Number	Low (%)	Moderately Low (%)	Moderately High (%)	High (%)	Total Percentage	Total Number	Low (%)	Moderately Low (%)	Moderately High (%)	High (%)	Total Percentage
Age												
21 to 34	645	24	29	26	23	100	741	22	29	27	22	100
35 to 54	555	26	25	24	25	100	637	26	28	22	24	100
55 plus	610	29	24	23	24	100	673	28	23	24	25	100
Education												
Grade School	312	[35]	21	28	16	100	344	[35]	20	23	22	100
High School	909	27	25	25	23	100	1,014	27	25	25	24	100
College	580	[20]	29	21	30	100	682	[18]	33	23	26	100
Place of Residence												
Metropolitan Area	136	[0]	34	20	[46]	100	166	[0]	30	28	[42]	100
Suburbs	265	26	28	20	26	100	331	22	30	23	25	100
Small City	320	9	27	36	28	100	396	5	46	29	20	100
Town	628	22	34	25	19	100	678	25	29	28	18	100
Rural Area	463	[52]	8	18	22	100	482	[53]	4	14	29	100
Race												
White	1,582	27	25	23	25	100	1,751	26	26	24	24	100
Black	186	23	26	26	25	100	238	26	28	21	25	100
Relative Income												
Low	472	28	26	24	22	100	521	28	25	23	24	100
Moderate	728	27	25	26	22	100	829	27	26	26	21	100
High	476	22	27	21	30	100	559	19	31	23	27	100
Region												
Northeast	445	[7]	11	31	[51]	100	461	[9]	10	28	[53]	100
E. N. Central	367	36	29	22	13	100	371	33	14	39	14	100
W. N. Central	191	52	25	0	23	100	191	34	34	9	23	100
South	399	33	22	24	22	100	544	37	26	18	19	100
Border	172	28	12	58	2	100	172	37	—	41	22	100
West	238	12	[66]	9	13	100	314	9	[76]	11	4	100

[a] Since these are computed on the bases of respondents in the sample, the compilation weights the relationship proportionately to the representation of counties in the total sample.

federally-funded facilities were created since the 1957 study in partial response to the issue of underservice that was emphasized by the Joint Commission on Mental Illness and Health (1961). In table 8.3, we present per capita mental health expenditures and total professional staff hours by the various demographic subgroups.

The following characteristics of our respondents are examined in those tables: age; education; place of residence; race; relative income (broken down into low, moderate, and high on the basis of the distribution of family income in 1976); region (collapsed into six categories, with Middle Atlantic states placed with the New England states as the Northeast, and the Mountain states with the Pacific states as the West). Age and race were isolated for analysis as significant demographic characteristics because of the President's Commission's concern about lack of services for the elderly and racial minorities in the United States. Education and relative income differences were examined to see whether or not lower status groups in our society are as likely to have resources available to them as the more advantaged groups in our society. Place of residence and regional differences were considered in order to see whether or not more densely populated areas are particularly advantageous and whether certain areas of our country are particularly handicapped with respect to the allocation of facilities.

Tables 8.2 and 8.3 clearly indicate that there is no remarkable disadvantage for the elderly or low income groups with regard to the differential distribution of resources as measured. By contrast, the other four demographic characteristics indicate some evidence of differential distribution of resources among groups. We find, for example, that the less educated in our society clearly are living in counties with a low per capita availability of resources to a greater extent than the more educated. The relationship is clearest for per capita expenditures for mental health care and for per capita staff hours of service. Thirty-five percent of grade school-educated people in our society live in counties which are especially low in per capita mental health expenditures in comparison with only 20 percent of the college educated. Parallel results are shown for per capita availability of services, although they are less dramatic. In examining race differences in the per capita availability of resources we find no indication that blacks are more likely to live in counties which are particularly low in mental health resources. In fact, if anything, blacks are more likely than whites to live in counties with a high availability of community mental health facilities. Since our assessments are made on a county basis, this kind of analysis may not reveal real differences in the availability of resources for black and white populations within urban centers in our society. Furthermore, there may be psychological barriers to the use of certain agencies in the county, a factor which we clearly do not assess with these measures. From these data, however, we observe no evidence to suggest a disadvantage for black respondents in the physical availability of resources for mental health care. Similarly, there is no evidence of such a disadvantage for low-income groups in our society.

Two characteristics which do show considerable variation on our measures of availability are place of residence and region. The results indicated in tables 8.2 and 8.3 suggest that rural areas have a particularly low level of per capita resources in terms of mental health facilities available, expenditures, and staff hours. By contrast, metropolitan areas are particularly advantaged. Few metropolitan areas indeed are very low in per capita expenditures or per capita facilities available to their residents. These results are explicable by the fact that about 10 percent of our population live in counties which have no facilities available to them. These people, assigned to the lowest quartile of facilities, expenditures, and staff hours are residents of extremely rural areas of the country.

Regional differences in facilities are more complex. Residents of the northeastern part of the country clearly live in counties with high per capita mental health expenditures and per capita professional staff hours, as can be seen in table 8.3. The western region has a strong representation of moderately low (second quartile) per capita mental health expenditures and staff hours. This latter result is important because in some of our analyses we will find that curvilinear effects are partially due to the overrepresentation of western counties' residents in this second quartile of facilities. With regard to the availability of facilities, we find different regions of the country included in the lowest quartile of per capita availability of community mental health centers, mental health outpatient services, and total facilities. One consistent regional difference exists: residents of the Solid South are highly represented in the lowest quartile of these measures. Based on these analyses, then, we should be particularly alert to the possibility that residents of the western and southern regions of the country may be contributing to some of the overall relationships that we observe between per capita facility availability and the use (both actual and potential) of facilities by people in the nation.

Considering the results presented in tables 8.2 and 8.3 as a whole, it ·hould be clear that in our later analyses of the relationship of facilities to psychological readiness for help and the actual use of help we must institute certain controls. Particularly important for those analyses will be controls for place of residence, education, and region.

Are Mental Health Resources Distributed Differentially
Among People Who View Their Mental Health Negatively as
Opposed to People Who View Their Mental Health
Positively?

In the best of all possible worlds it might be thought that mental
health resources would be available in counties where people "need
them." From that ideal perspective, it would be preferable that the
availability of mental health resources be negatively correlated with
perceived psychological health. Facilities would be located and money
spent for mental health resources in places where people are most in
distress. By the same token, one would hope that where community
facilities are available to people in distress, that over time those people
would come to feel better. From that viewpoint, one would expect
some positive correlation between resources available and psychological health. Because of this conflicting set of hypotheses about the likely relationship between the resources in a community and the mental
health of that community, we are not surprised to find that by and
large there was no relationship between a number of measures of subjective well-being and measures of per capita resources available in the
counties where our respondents lived.

Eight measures from our analysis of subjective mental health presented in Book 1 were correlated with these various measures of resource availability. These subjective measures were: happiness; feelings of an impending nervous breakdown; self-esteem; psychological
anxiety; depression/zest; future morale; frequency of bad things happening; frequency of feeling overwhelmed. Only for the latter measure was there any indication of a relationship between a measure of
subjective well-being and per capita availability of resources in the
community. In that instance, people who said they were sometimes or
frequently overwhelmed when bad things happened to them are more
likely to reside in counties where there is a very high availability of
outpatient services. Nevertheless, even that relationship was modest,
and because of the large number of insignificant findings in this analysis, we feel that the result should not be emphasized. If one accepts
the result at face value, however, one might conclude that people who
are overwhelmed by their life experiences are more likely to reside in
areas which provide adequate services to them. In general, we would
conclude that in American society today there is no clear relationship
of perceived psychological distress and mental health resources.

The Relationship of Availability of Resources to Help-Seeking Attitudes and Behaviors

MEASURES OF HELP-SEEKING ATTITUDES/BEHAVIOR

In this section, we will analyze the relationship between our major measures of availability of resources and various ways people structure their attitudes and behavior toward help-seeking. Seven measures of help-seeking attitudes and behaviors discussed in preceding chapters are used in this analysis.

We have attempted to select measures that reflect different points on the continuum from being ready to seek help to either actual help-seeking or encountering barriers to such help-seeking. These measures are described below.

Would Go to Mental Health Professional If Had Problem

From our analysis of the hypothetical use of mental health professionals we selected one measure—the readiness of a person to seek such help for a problem that he/she might have. That problem was described as having persisted for a while, resulting in unhappiness or trouble in marriage or with a child. In other words, the problem was posed as a serious one, and the question asked about the ways the person saw to handle such a problem. For the present analysis, we measured only whether or not the person spontaneously mentioned professional mental health alternatives for dealing with such a problem.

Defines a Past Problem as Help-Relevant

In analysis of readiness for self-referral, one measure included not only people who had actually sought help for a personal problem but also those who thought they could have benefited by such help. Together, these two groups of people were categorized as having defined a past problem as relevant for professional help.

Actually Consulted a Mental Health Expert (If Problem Defined as Help-Relevant)

If a person defines a problem as relevant for help, did he/she actually go for help? This was a major focus of chapter 5, but for our analysis of available facilities we wanted to look primarily at people who selected a mental health resource for problem solution. Excluded from this analysis were people who selected the clergy as a resource in times of difficulty. We explicitly exclude them because our assessment of available facilities does not include the church or clergy associated with the church as potential resources. The clergy and mental health professionals probably complement each other in this function, but they depend on quite different community structures. We did, however, include people who do not identify an expert consulted beyond mentioning that he/she was a doctor. Doctors need not necessarily be psychiatrists, but some people probably did not make this distinction. Furthermore, even if the doctor were a family physician, we expect that he/she is still viewed as someone who can cope with a mental health problem in a "professional" way.

Professionals Sought for Personal Problems

For the total population, we also wished to see how many actually sought a mental health expert at one time or another, and how many consulted the clergy in search of a problem solution. For this measure, the total population is used as the base, and hence it reflects the gross use of a mental health resource expert or the clergy for help with personal problems.

Differential Use of Resources Among Help-Seekers

In addition to the gross use of a mental health expert as opposed to the clergy for help with personal problems, we also wanted to assess the relative use of these groups among people who have sought help. Such a measure of net use employed as its base only those people who actually sought help for personal problems.

Mental Health Expert Sought for Either Personal Problem or Crisis (or Both)

To derive a more complete assessment of people's use of mental health experts, we included not only those people who had mentioned a mental health expert in the measure "Professionals Sought for Personal Problems," but also those who failed to mention a mental health expert in response to the question about personal problems and yet mentioned a mental health source in response to a question about crises or bad things that happen to a person. Our analyses in chapter 7 suggested that a number of people mentioned seeing a mental health expert only in response to crisis. Therefore, this measure combines mentions of seeking psychological counsel with respect to either personal problems or crises. In that sense, this measure provides our most complete assessment of mental health consultation. We will be using this measure extensively in later sections of the chapter.

Reasons for Not Going

The final measure used is an assessment of the reasons people gave for not going if they thought they could have used help but yet did not go. The analysis presented in chapter 6 indicated that two major reasons that people gave for not going when they felt that they could have used help were lack of knowledge about resources and fear of stigma (or shame) attached to seeking help from such resources.

Therefore, we examine these two types of responses in analyses presented in this chapter, since both appear important with regard to an analysis of the availability of resources. Presumably, the greater the resources available in a community, the greater likelihood that a person should be aware of their availability. There may also be some optimal level of resource availability which makes their use less likely to be stigmatized.

AVAILABILITY OF FACILITIES AND HELP-SEEKING ATTITUDES/BEHAVIORS

In table 8.4 the per capita availability of both outpatient and total services in a county is plotted against the seven measures of help-seeking attitudes and behaviors. The pattern of results indicates only modest relationships between availability of resources and various measures of help-seeking attitudes and behaviors. The basic relationship which is apparent primarily differentiates the lowest category of available resources from all other degrees of availability. That is, people with the least available resources tend to be less oriented toward help-seeking and are less likely to seek help than other people, although this is clearly not the case for all measures. We find no relationship whatsoever between per capita availability of services and whether a person has actually sought help from a mental health expert once he/she has defined a past problem as help-relevant. This lack of relationship contrasts strikingly with findings in 1957 when availability of resources showed a stronger relationship to actual use of help than the tendency to adopt a mental health definition of a problem, while the latter relationship is clearly more striking in 1976. The pattern established in that earlier study, that resources affect problem definition somewhat but actual use of help more strongly, made eminently good sense as evidence that availability of resources was a facilitating factor which translated psychological readiness into action. The fact that the pattern observed in 1976 does not follow that logic is puzzling, but we will postpone any attempt at explanation until we have applied certain controls to these data to determine whether this pattern persists.

For all other measures, there is some indication based on one or the other measure of availability (of either outpatient or total mental health services) that very low availability of facilities contributes to a weak help-seeking orientation, in either attitudes or behaviors. People who reside in counties in the lowest quartile of service availability tend not to view the mental health professional as a potential resource for a hypothetical problem, tend not to define a past problem as relevant for such help, do not seek help from mental health specialists, and if they do seek help, tend to seek help from the clergy rather than a mental health expert. They tend not to seek help from a mental

TABLE 8.4

Relationship of Per Capita Availability of Outpatient Services and Total Mental Health Services to Respondents' Help-Seeking Attitudes and Behaviors

Measure of Help-Seeking Attitude/Behavior	Per Capita Availability of Outpatient Services in County				Per Capita Availability of Total Mental Health Services in County			
	Low (%)	Moderately Low (%)	Moderately High (%)	High (%)	Low (%)	Moderately Low (%)	Moderately High (%)	High (%)
Would go to mental health professional if had problem: Yes	17	21	18	17	11	22	18	18
Defines a past problem as relevant for help: Yes	31	42	40	31	26	43	37	35
If defines a past problem as help-relevant, actually sought help from a mental health expert:[a] Yes	59 (N=92)	56 (N=167)	62 (N=185)	57 (N=139)	58 (N=57)	61 (N=193)	55 (N=156)	58 (N=177)
Sought help for a personal problem from a professional:								
Mental health expert[a]	12	17	18	13	10	19	14	15
Clergy	10	8	10	8	8	9	9	9
Other	1	3	1	1	1	3	2	1
Total	23 (N=104)	28 (N=146)	29 (N=185)	22 (N=130)	19 (N=63)	31 (N=188)	25 (N=145)	25 (N=169)
If sought help for a personal problem, source of help:								
Mental health expert[a]	52	64	62	61	52	63	59	61
Clergy	42 (N=104)	30 (N=146)	34 (N=185)	35 (N=130)	44 (N=63)	31 (N=188)	36 (N=145)	36 (N=169)
Sought help from a mental health expert[b] for a personal problem and/or a crisis: Yes	16	22	21	15	14	22	19	17
If could have used help but did not go, reason:								
Lack of knowledge	18	9	6	11	16	11	8	9
Shame	23 (N=39)	4 (N=79)	11 (N=81)	16 (N=63)	12 (N=25)	11 (N=81)	14 (N=77)	10 (N=79)
Total Number	459	533	653	619	337	624	599	704

NOTE: Numbers in parentheses are total number of persons in each group.

[a] Includes "doctor."

health expert for either a crisis or a personal problem. When people in this lowest quartile did not seek help when they felt that they should have, they are especially aware of their lack of knowledge as a cause for not going, and there is some indication that they did anticipate potential stigma or shame in going. In combination, these results appear sensible if one thinks of high availability of resources as constituting not only a direct facilitating factor in defining problems and in seeking help, but also an indirect factor contributing to the social climate which influences viewing a problem in psychological terms or not feeling ashamed about seeking help for such problems.

The lowest category on the availability index encompasses communities in which there are essentially no mental health resources at all, as well as those which have minimal resources. It seems possible that the large shift toward readiness to seek help between this category and the next highest represents a critical threshold effect. That is, it may well be that when no resources are available to people they cling to denial or rely on informal mechanisms for support in solving personal problems. When some resources become available, they may be especially responsive to a change in attitudinal climate and intensify that change so that that readiness for self-referral is greatly increased.

A surprising finding is in the distributions presented in table 8.4. While the largest differences occur between the lowest level of resources and the next category, increasing resources beyond the first stage either result in no further increase in mental health orientation or help-seeking behavior, or in a few instances actually reduce help-seeking. As a result, the overall relationship between resources and help-seeking attitudes and behaviors is curvilinear. These results are clearest for defining a past problem as relevant for help and in seeking help from mental health experts, whether one limits the analysis only to personal problems or whether one combines personal problems and crises as a basis for seeking help. Why the addition of higher levels of resources should be accompanied by a decline in help-seeking orientations is a mystery, but merits some speculation. Three explanations seem plausible. First, the provision of facilities beyond a certain threshold may represent a response to political and population density pressures rather than to the actual needs of a community; second, when facilities proliferate they may well become bureaucratized and thus deliver less direct service; and third, when the number of facilities available is increased beyond a certain point, this may involve provision of services for very specialized populations and a corresponding neglect of the general population. Since we will observe later that controls for education, region, and place of residence dramatically influence these results, we favor the first explanation. At any rate, we derive clear evidence from table 8.4 that exceedingly low resource availability is associated with a weak orientation toward help-seeking and to low actual use of help-seeking strategies.

MENTAL HEALTH EXPENDITURES AND HELP-SEEKING ATTITUDES/BEHAVIORS

Table 8.5 plots the relationship of per capita mental health expenditures in respondents' counties to help-seeking attitudes and behaviors. For each one of the measures presented we have some indication that low expenditures correlate with a negative attitude toward help-seeking and/or failure to use professional resources for problems. In some instances, those living in counties with the very highest level of expenditures for mental health services manifest the most positive attitude toward help-seeking and the greatest use of mental health experts.

Specifically, the clearest results are: (1) people residing in counties where expenditures for mental health are extremely low are least likely to define a past problem as relevant for help, are least likely to select a mental health source for a problem or a crisis in their lives, and are most likely to cite lack of knowledge as a basis for not seeking help if they thought they could have used help; (2) people who live in a county where per capita expenditures for mental health services are highest are most likely to say they would seek professional help for a mental health problem, are most likely to actually seek help if they have had a problem that required such help, are most likely to have consulted a mental health specialist, are least likely to have consulted the clergy, and are least likely to mention lack of knowledge as a basis for not seeking help if they thought they could have used it but did not go. That pattern of results is consistent with a rational model which suggests that when facilities increase in a community, people are socialized into positive attitudes toward help-seeking when problems arise and to the actual use of professional help. The only slight contradiction to this pattern is that people who reside in counties with the highest expenditures for mental health services also cite shame as a basis for not going if they believed they could have used help.

It is important to note that these results do not show any evidence of the striking curvilinear relationship that we observed in analysis of the relationship between availability of facilities and help-seeking attitudes and behaviors. Given this discrepancy, it is possible that expenditures represent a more direct assessment of actual level of service provided to people in a community than our tallies of the number of facilities available. In contrast, the number of facilities available may be more a reflection of the organizational or political structure of a community than of the service delivery potential of a county.

CONTROLLING FOR PLACE OF RESIDENCE, REGION, AND EDUCATION
AS FACTORS THAT MODERATE THE RELATIONSHIP BETWEEN
RESOURCES AND HELP-SEEKING ORIENTATIONS

Knowing that the availability of services, measured either as expenditures and staff hours or the number of agencies available in a commu-

TABLE 8.5

Relationship of Per Capita Mental Health Expenditures in Respondents' County to Respondents' Help-Seeking Attitudes and Behaviors

Measure of Help-Seeking Attitude/Behavior	Per Capita Mental Health Expenditures in County			
	Low (%)	Moderately Low (%)	Moderately High (%)	High (%)
Would go to a mental health professional if had problem: Yes	15	18	17	20
Defines a past problem as relevant for help: Yes	30	38	39	37
If defines a past problem as help-relevant, actually sought help from mental health expert[a]	58	57	57	64
	(N=92)	(N=129)	(N=112)	(N=126)
Sought help for a personal problem from a professional				
Mental health expert[a]	11	16	15	18
Clergy	10	9	11	7
Other	1	1	2	2
Total	22	26	28	27
If sought help for a personal problem, source of help:				
Mental health expert[a]	52	62	54	70
Clergy	44	33	41	28
	(N=243)	(N=177)	(N=169)	(N=164)
Sought help from a mental health expert[b] for a personal problem and/or a crisis: Yes	14	22	17	21
If could have used help but did not seek it, reason:				
Lack of knowledge	16	6	14	2
Shame	12	3	16	22
	(N=43)	(N=63)	(N=50)	(N=46)
Total Number	474	463	433	442

NOTE: Numbers in parentheses are total number of persons in each group.

[a] Includes "doctor."

[b] Includes "doctor" for personal problem, but not for crisis.

nity, are a function of the educational level and population density of a community and the region of the country in which it is embedded, we wish now to explore the correlation between service availability and help-seeking orientations while controlling for these factors. For this analysis we selected the measure assessing the use of a mental health expert for either a personal problem or a crisis, since it provides the most complete assessment of mental health consultation by our respondents. In examining correlations between such consultation and resources, controlling for each of the critical factors isolated earlier (education, region, and place of residence), we found that for relationships between expenditures and mental health consultation, and between number of facilities and mental health consultation, a number of results described earlier essentially disappear when controls are introduced.

For example, we found that for high school-educated people, the relationship between per capita expenditures and seeking mental health consultation disappears completely, whereas a slight relationship still remains among grade school-educated respondents. Similarly, the relationship is not apparent for people residing in the South and the West, nor for those residing in suburbs. Such controls have an even more devastating effect on the relationship between number of facilities available in a county and whether mental health experts were sought for problems or crises. That relationship completely disappears not only for people in the suburbs but also for those in small cities. Furthermore, since there are no "lowest quartile" counties for people in metropolitan areas, no relationship is evident there either.

Because of the different perspective one derives from applying these controls to relationships between either expenditures or number of facilities and use of mental health resources, we ran log-linear cross-classification analyses for each of these relationships employing controls for education, region, and place of residence as additional classifications. These analyses indicate that the hypothesized effect of service availability on mental health consultation was not needed in the most parsimonious model able to reproduce the observed frequencies. Evidently, educational, regional, and residential differences in mental health consultation largely account for the fact that indices of the availability of resources are related to mental health consultation in the analyses presented in tables 8.4 and 8.5.

In examining parameters for the "saturated model" (the one that accounts for all possible simple and interactive effects for explaining expenditures and mental health consultation), however, we noted a fairly large and significant interactive effect, which, while not needed in the more parsimonious model, represents a nontrivial effect in the overall table. The corresponding relationship is represented in table 8.6. That table indicates that in rural areas of the country, especially when we control for region, higher expenditures for mental health services are correlated with a higher rate of consultation with mental

TABLE 8.6

Relationship of High versus Low Per Capita Expenditures in Respondent's County to Use of Mental Health Expert Among Rural versus Nonrural Residents (by region)

Region	Rural Residents Using Mental Health Experts Among				Nonrural Residents Using Mental Health Experts Among			
	Low Expenditure Counties		High Expenditure Counties		Low Expenditure Counties		High Expenditure Counties	
	Number	Percentage	Number	Percentage	Number	Percentage	Number	Percentage
Northeast	24	12	62	16	56	16	303	22
East North Central	44	5	22	23	197	20	106	24
West North Central	54	4	26	12	90	16	18	17
Solid South	90	12	58	14	127	23	124	13
Border States	36	3	15	7	33	24	88	18
West	28	32	3	33	157	25	50	24

health specialists. Although these results are strongest within certain areas of the country, they are in the right direction in each of the regions. By contrast, the direction of this relationship is not consistent for nonrural residents as can be seen in table 8.6.

These findings are important. They suggest that in less populated regions of the country, expenditures for mental health facilities may have a very direct impact on the use of mental health services. This may be so because in rural areas the introduction or increased buildup of facilities constitutes a more dramatic and important feature of the social organization of the community. In sparsely populated areas, one thinks twice about expending resources for mental health care, and thus residents of such areas may be grossly underserviced. In nonrural areas, however, the social climate characteristic of a particular region or of the educational level of people in the area are perhaps more important factors influencing who uses mental health experts.

We do not wish to argue that the provision of facilities does not make a difference in nonrural areas. We merely suggest that the presence of adequate or inadequate facilities in a nonrural community is part and parcel of the social fabric of the area. That fabric includes other factors facilitating help-seeking—for example, reference groups issues for people with higher education or general social climate pressures in different regions of the country. In nonrural areas, one would expect greater lobbying for mental health facilities by the more highly educated. For example, the Northeast has a long-standing tradition of favorable attitudes toward mental health consultation, and it also is a place where extensive facilities are available. Thus, one cannot easily extract the contribution that the presence of facilities would have in such regions without the presence of these environmental factors.

From these analyses, we conclude that the mere presence of facilities may make a difference in rural areas of the country, but in nonrural areas, other forces such as reference group issues are more critical for self-referral. In previous chapters we described the West as a region strongly oriented toward mental health, and people in metropolitan areas as being particularly inclined toward use of help. Based on the data presented here, we conclude that these patterns do not simply reflect the greater availability of services in this region or in metropolitan areas. Rather, there appears to be something about the West and something about the atmosphere in urbanized areas that predisposes people to mental health consultation over and above the presence of adequate (or high) resources.

RESOURCES AS CONDITIONERS FOR THE RELATIONSHIP
OF SEEING PROBLEMS IN ONE'S LIFE AND SEEKING HELP

While the direct effects of facilities and mental health expenditures on people's help-seeking propensities and behaviors seem minimal, further analyses of these assessments of resources as conditioners of the relationship between seeing a problem and actually seeking help, are more substantial. In chapter 5 we saw that people who described themselves as having certain psychological difficulties were especially likely to seek professional help. Those subjective measures most clearly related to help-seeking were: seeing problems in one's family roles, experiencing psychological anxiety, and having felt an impending nervous breakdown at some point in one's life. Earlier, these measures were related to help-seeking behaviors controlling for sex, age, education, and year differences. A number of other measures were also related to help-seeking but only weakly. Therefore, in this chapter we ask whether or not the presence of more rather than fewer mental health facilities or expenditures in one's county increases the likelihood that a person would translate experiences of psychological distress into actual help-seeking behavior.

This question was explored by correlating selected measures of subjective well-being with our major measure of seeking help from a mental health specialist—whether or not the person saw a mental health expert for a personal problem or crisis (or both). The following measures were selected from our battery of measures of subjective well-being:

1. Measures of *low morale:* unhappiness, worrying, dissatisfaction, and depression (see Veroff, Douvan, and Kulka, 1981, chapter 2)
2. Measures of *self-perception:* low self-esteem and low sense of efficacy (see Veroff, Douvan and Kulka, 1981, chapter 3)
3. Measures of *strain:* having felt an impending nervous breakdown and psychological anxiety (see Veroff, Douvan and Kulka, 1981, chapters 2 and 7)
4. Measures of *family role difficulties:* experiencing marital unhappiness, experiencing marital conflict, feelings of marital inadequacy, experiencing problems with children, feelings of parental inadequacy (see Veroff, Douvan and Kulka, 1981, chapters 4 and 5).

These different measures represent a broad range of psychological feelings that could be related to seeking help from mental health experts. The correlation between each of these measures of subjective adjustment and consulting a mental health expert was run separately within different quartiles of per capita total facilities available in a county and also within different quartiles of per capita mental health expenditures. Overall, in these analyses, we were looking for patterns of correlations which suggest that increasing facilities or expenditures in a county result in higher correlations between a person's subjective feelings of distress or a problem and seeking help from a mental health professional. By and large we observed no change in the pattern of correlations with increased facilities or expenditures, except in a few notable instances. Table 8.7 presents correlations between select-

TABLE 8.7

Correlations of Selected Measures of Subjective Mental Health with Consultation of Mental Health Expert[a]
(by availability of per capita facilities)

Measure of Subjective Mental Health	Availability of Per Capita Facilities							
	Low		Moderately Low		Moderately High		High	
	Number	r	Number	r	Number	r	Number	r
Unhappiness	333		617		585		690	
		.07		.08		.12[b]		.11[b]
Feelings of Nervous Breakdown	336		620		598		703	
		.26[c]		.32[c]		.32[d]		.29[c]
Worrying	319		587		560		669	
		.04		.12[b]		.17[c]		.17[c]
Problems with Children	259		453		424		516	
		.03		.07		.23[c]		.13[b]
Parental Inadequacies	258		466		436		519	
		.04		.11[e]		.14[b]		.19[c]

[a] For either personal problem or crisis.
[b] p<.01
[c] p<.0001
[d] p<.001
[e] p<.05

TABLE 8.8

Correlations of Selected Measures of Subjective Adjustment with Consultation of Mental Health Expert[a]
(by per capita mental health expenditure)

Measure of Subjective Mental Health	Per Capita Mental Health Expenditures							
	Low		Moderately Low		Moderately High		High	
	Number	r	Number	r	Number	r	Number	r
Unhappiness	467		458		422		436	
		.11[b]		.08		.11[b]		.13[c]
Feelings of Nervous Breakdown	421		460		432		442	
		.31[d]		.29[d]		.29[d]		.28[d]
Psychological Anxiety	462		457		429		439	
		.07		.11[b]		.16[c]		.18[e]
Low Feelings of Personal Efficacy	448		430		414		413	
		.01		.01		.00		.14[c]

[a] For either personal problem or crisis.
[b] p<.05
[c] p<.01
[d] p<.0001
[e] p<.001

ed measures of subjective adjustment and consultation of mental health specialist experts within different levels of per capita number of facilities available, and table 8.8 provides parallel correlations for different levels of mental health expenditures. In each table, one can see that for reports of unhappiness and for the measure most highly correlated with help-seeking (feelings of an impending nervous breakdown), there is no change in their relationship pattern with consulting a mental health expert at different levels of resource availability. Feeling unhappy about one's life is only moderately correlated with consulting a mental health specialist at each of the levels of availability, and having felt that one might have a nervous breakdown is fairly strongly related to consulting a mental health expert at each of the levels of resources. Evidently, something other than availability of resources in a community influences whether or not people who have low morale seek mental health consultation for their problems. Clearly, the availability of mental health resources does not appreciably affect that relationship. Likewise, availability does not affect the relationship of feeling impending nervous breakdowns with help-seeking. Apparently, if one feels desperate or helpless in facing a problem, so much so that one senses a potential "nervous breakdown," then one is likely to seek help no matter how many or how few facilities are available in the community. In other words, for both problems of personal morale and feelings of desperation available facilities do not critically affect help-seeking. One seeks help in desperate moments wherever one can get it, and for the few people who seek help in times of unhappiness, the extent of resources available in a community does not seem to be a facilitating factor.

We do, however, find an increased tendency to translate perceived problems with children and feelings of inadequacy as a parent into actual help-seeking behaviors when more facilities are available. Moreover, a similar pattern of results is apparent for people who say they worry a great deal. Since one of the major bases of worry reported by respondents is concern about children, this pattern of findings may indicate that the increased proliferation of facilities in a community tends to stimulate consultation with specialists concerned with family issues, particularly those involving children.

Associated with increased mental health expenditures in a county, (table 8.8) we observe increased correlations between subjective distress and mental health consultation for two other measures. One of these is our index of psychological anxiety: when mental health expenditures in a county are very high there is apparently a greater tendency to translate symptoms of psychological anxiety into seeking psychological counsel. The other relationship involves the measure of personal efficacy: only at the highest level of county expenditures is there a relationship between low feelings of efficacy and help-seeking. These results suggest that as expenditures in a county go up, greater numbers of people confronted with a sense of helplessness or anxiety see mental health consultation as a possible avenue for helping to resolve their difficulties. When mental health expenditures in a county are relatively low, there tends to be little or no translation of these uncertainties into mental health consultation.

It appears that when mental expenditures are at a very high level, people tend to seek consultation for certain problems that people in counties where facilities are less available view as inappropriate for help-seeking. It is as if there were a critical threshold for available mental health resources in a community which represents the point where more varied and more specific problems become relevant for help. For half of the fourteen measures of subjective distress that we related to mental health consultation within different levels of resource availability, the highest correlation between distress and help-seeking appeared in the highest quartile of availability. By chance, one would expect only one quarter of the correlations to be highest in this quartile. This suggests that when mental health facilities are readily available in a community, a greater variety of psychological problems will be brought to the mental health consultants.

Precisely how this process occurs is not clear. When specialized resources such as family counseling agencies or clinics for alcoholics evolve in communities that already have adequate general facilities, explicit recruiting procedures are often set up in the community to advertise or promote these services. In turn, such recruitment efforts can strengthen the link between specific felt needs and use of these resources. In communities where facilities are overburdened, however, recruitment would likely be minimal. Such communities are most likely to be found in counties low in available resources, where the connection between overall (and differential) felt needs and mental health consultation is indeed somewhat weaker.

In summary, when mental health resources measured as per capita facilities are relatively more available to people, we find a greater translation of family concerns into actual help-seeking behavior. When per capita mental health expenditures become greater in a community, we find a corresponding increase in translating concerns about one's own efficacy or uncertainties into mental health consultation. Both of these trends suggest that as mental health resources increase, more diverse types of problems become relevant for help-seeking actions.

RELATIONSHIP OF EDUCATION TO HELP-SEEKING CONTROLLING FOR PER CAPITA RESOURCES AVAILABLE

Because there is both a relationship between education and help-seeking in general, and a relationship between education and resource availability (as noted in tables 8.2 and 8.3), we were interested in addressing an important question which may have implications for public policy: Are educated people more likely to seek help than less educated people regardless of the level of mental health resources available in a community? In *Americans View Their Mental Health*, the findings suggested that in 1957 more educated people were indeed seeking help regardless of the availability of facilities. It was argued that more educated people in our society not only have the financial wherewithal to seek help beyond the confines of their particular community, but they also have the knowledge and sophistication to achieve maximum access to whatever facilities are available in their communities. Such findings imply that the consistently observed relationship between education and help-seeking should be highest where facilities are least available.

Consequently, we examined the correlation between education and mental health consultation within different levels of available resources. Controlling for per capita mental health facilities in a county, we find that indeed, going from lowest to highest quartile, correlations manifest a pattern of change in the predicted direction. These results are reported in table 8.9. For different levels of per capita facilities available in a county, the pattern of correlations indicates a striking decline from .21 to .04 as the availability of facilities increases. While there is a declining correlation from the lowest to the third quartile per captia mental health facilities (from .11 to .06), the correlation rises to .17 in the highest quartile. Except for correlation evident

TABLE 8.9

Correlation of Education of Respondent to Consultation of Mental Health Expert[a] in Counties Differing in Mental Health Per Capita Resources

Level of Per Capita Mental Health Resources	Number	Correlation (r) of Education with Consulting Mental Health Experts
For Available Facilities		
Low	337	.21[b]
Moderately low	618	.19[b]
Moderately high	596	.09[c]
High	700	.04
For Mental Health Expenditures		
Low	471	.11[c]
Moderately low	458	.08
Moderately high	432	.06
High	440	.17[d]

[a] For either personal problem or crisis.

[b] $p < .0001$

[c] $p < .05$

[d] $p < .001$

in the highest quartile in expenditures, the pattern of results presented in table 8.9 suggests that education becomes a less important pre-
dictor of the use of mental health consultations as mental health resources become more available. In a society where we wish to equalize
the availability of resources for people in different social strata, this
pattern is reassuring.

The one result contrary to the general pattern is that within communities with high expenditures for mental health resources there is a
relatively high correlation between education and mental health consultation. It may be that as expenditures become extremely high, new
programs are introduced which are more avant-garde in nature. As a
result, the more highly educated once again become primary consum-
ers. If in a given community, for example, a mental health center es-
tablishes a special program for singles, it is likely that the college educated would be more aware of its existence and more likely to take
advantage of it.

In spite of this one discrepant correlation, the general pattern seems
important: the higher the level of resources available in a community,
the greater the tendency for the less educated as well as the more
educated to take advantage of them.

Summary

Per capita expenditures and facilities for mental health care in the
counties of residence for the 1976 sample were related to various help-
seeking attitudes and behaviors and were found to be positively correlated, but not strikingly so. There was a tendency for people residing
in communities with low resources, in terms of either expenditures or
number of facilities available, to be less oriented toward professional
help and to have actually sought help less often. Only for the measure
of per capita expenditures in a county, however, did we find any indication that people residing in counties where per capita resources
were extremely high have particularly strong help-seeking
orientations.

Since both high per capita expenditures and high per capita facilities are also more commonly found in the communities of the higher
educated, in nonrural areas, and in certain regions of the country, it
was important that we control these demographic characteristics in
examining the relationship between facilities and help-seeking behaviors. In a crucial test of the correlation between per capita facilities
and seeking help from a mental health expert for either personal problems or crises, we found that these control factors largely accounted
for the direct relationship between per capita resources and the use of

mental health specialists. However, one interaction that remained when controls were taken into account suggested that over and above these region, education, and place of residence effects, differences in expenditures for mental health resources in rural areas were related to seeking mental health consultation, a pattern which was not evident for nonrural areas. In general, however, the results presented suggest that the availability of facilities is very much connected to and embedded within regional and population density differences. Furthermore, educational reference groups constitute important mediating climates which provide a context for understanding how the resources available in a community become associated with help-seeking orientations.

Over and above these complex interactions, we also found two additional noteworthy effects of increasing mental health facilities within a county: (1) increased resources are related to an increase in the correlation between certain feelings of subjective distress and mental health consultation; and (2) increased resources tend to dissipate the relationship between education and mental health consultation. These results are significant because they suggest that in expanding mental health resources within a community, we may also increase the range of problems that people see as relevant for help-seeking, as well as the range of people who avail themselves of professional help for the problems they experience.

Chapter 9

CONCLUSIONS

THE LEGITIMACY and use of professional help for personal problems increased notably over the twenty-year period between our studies. People in 1976 were much more likely to mention spontaneously a professional help source as a way to cope with a hypothetical personal problem. More important, in 1957, some 14 percent of the population said they had sought professional help at some point in their lives; by 1976 the proportion had nearly doubled (26 percent). The proportion varied for different subgroups in the population, reaching a high of 32 percent among college graduates.

Professional help is broadly defined in our studies; it includes any help source having expertise rather than a personal relationship to the help-seeker. So, for example, it includes medical doctors, lawyers, and clergy as well as psychiatrists, psychologists, social workers, and counselors.

The decision to seek help from an outside expert requires a certain psychological readiness. Readiness is a willingness to admit vulnerability in the self—to admit, that is, that a problem might arise which was critically upsetting and outstripped one's capacities for managing and resolving distress. In the questions, we asked people not only whether they had used professional help but also whether they could imagine having a problem for which they might look to an outside professional for help. We allowed for legitimate "self-help" responses in all questions by providing a self-help alternative. Self-help answers declined from 44 percent to 35 percent over the twenty years. While this is a significant decrease, it is nonetheless remarkable that in 1976 a full third of adults in our psychologically-oriented society could not conceive of themselves as ever encountering an overwhelming problem or a state of stress that would lead them to consult a professional helper broadly defined. One cannot but be impressed with the size of this trenchantly self-assured group. These were people who must have possessed very great personal resources or powers of psychological denial or were members of social milieus so supportive that they were certain they could manage any problem with the personal and informal resources available to them.

The authors, in *Americans View Their Mental Health,* revealed in their research report clear bias toward professional help-seeking as the reasonable, optimal response to personal problems of adjustment and stress. In this view they reflected their times and the dominant thrust of expert opinion. We were, in 1957, at the threshold of the "era of psychology" and we were, in characteristic American style, optimistic about our new technology. If people could only come to see that personal and interpersonal problems of living were, like all problems, susceptible to rational analysis and the application of the methods of science; if they could be educated to make use of experts who employed the knowledge and techniques of psychology, they would be able to achieve resolution of their problems, avoid disruptive failures in their personal and interpersonal negotiations, and live fuller and more satisfying lives.

The view, as we say, reflected the times. But times change. Between 1957 and 1976, we acquired a good deal of experience with the application of psychological knowledge, and we have been chastened by the experience. We have come to recognize that "human engineering" is not so simple as the analogy with the physical sciences implies. Some human problems are intractable, at least at this stage of knowledge in the "human sciences" and perhaps even in the foreseeable future. Solving one source of distress, we discover, may lead to new problems (which historians and critics of social science have described in florid detail). Over and above these experiences which served to dampen early enthusiasm, the mental health specialists themselves have been compelled to recognize that realization of their original vision would perforce have required turning a quarter or a third of the population into psychological experts! If we all used experts whenever we were troubled, a large part of the world would have to be turned into experts. Even the mental health establishment came to see that there might be a better way. In the last seven to ten years that establishment has turned to encouraging self-help groups, peer counseling, and the development of paraprofessional and community (as opposed to professional) resources. It may be, we came to see, that people can handle most problems of life on their own if they have the help and support of caring family and friends. The goal of community mental health programs should perhaps be to encourage indigenous resources, to strengthen people's own powers to navigate through life's complex problems. Professionals, in this view, would stand by to offer assistance where needed but would assume that people can manage their own lives if they have the resources and knowledge and support that make their efforts meaningful.

Indeed, in 1976, we found that resources people used for crises they experienced rarely consisted of formal helpers alone. Most people turned to family or friends for aid and support, sometimes in conjunction with a formal helper. Only 3 percent relied only on "professionals." Nevertheless there were 13 percent of Americans who used neither formal nor informal help in their last time of crisis. This group, along with 7 percent of the population in 1976 identified as "loners" (people who are self-help oriented and denied talking over worries with anyone at all), may be of special concern to practitioners who wish to serve isolated people in distress. Nevertheless, even among these groups there may be some people whose commitment to autonomous coping serves them well.

Reflecting attitudes prevalent in our own times, therefore, we view "self help" respondents in a less pessimistic light than we once did. To be sure, some of them are probably utilizing primitive and denying defenses because they have no strength or resources to solve personal problems even if they were to admit them. Some of these people may have paid a heavy price for denial in physical symptoms or a narrowing of life experience. But others who think that they would never have need of professional counseling obviously base their self-assurance on an optimism about their own resources based on past experience, a sense of their rootedness in a community of friends and family members who provide help, comfort, and counsel, or both. Many in the self-help group recognize professional help as a reasonable choice for people facing problems they cannot handle. They have, in other words, knowledge of professional help as an alternative. But they do not feel they would ever need such help in their own dealings with life and life's problems.

In a later report, we shall present a more refined analysis of the self-help group. It is sufficient for our present purpose to note that the group is large—though not as large in 1976 as it was in 1957—and that its size alone can be taken as a sign that the era of psychology has not swept our culture with quite the total force that popular writing might lead us to expect. It can also, we think, be taken as a sign that community and connectedness are still forces in the lives of at least a significant segment of our population. Most people do use informal resources, such as family and friends, to help them in troubled times. For many of these people, such resources supplement formal helpers. For others, these resources are sufficient for any problems they can imagine confronting.

To tap people's knowledge about and acceptance of professional resources—aside from whether they expected they would even need or use them—we asked a hypothetical question about professional help as a reasonable alternative for a person facing an unmanageable crisis. Some people who would not themselves ever use professional help nonetheless recognized it as a legitimate choice. The relationship between the two responses was, however, closer in 1976 than it was in 1957, and we interpret this as an indication that stigma associated with seeking help has decreased. If help-seeking was considered a reasonable and available option, it was more likely in 1976 to translate directly to readiness to exercise the option. Fears of social disapproval apparently no longer blocked the way if one recognized the alternative at all.

A finding reported in chapter 5—that people who said they did not seek professional help when they might have because they felt a sense of embarrassment or shame about doing so were more likely to be thinking of clergy rather than psychiatrists or psychologists—casts an interesting light on the issue of stigma. Embarrassment about seeking help from one's priest, minister, or rabbi can be thought of as a response to self-exposure in a relationship which is personal, in which one has a stake in maintaining face because one respects and reveres the other (the clergy) and wishes to continue the relationship. We do not want to bare our negative characteristics to people when we hope to hold on to their respect and continuing regard. When, on the other hand, we have a problem or flaw serious enough to require self-disclosure, we seek out a stranger, a professional with whom we have no personal relationship. In these circumstances, apparently, shame, embarrassment, and loss of face do not inhibit self-disclosure.

Respondents who actually experienced serious crises (such as divorce), unhappiness, or symptoms of distress (particularly anxiety and apprehension about a nervous breakdown) more often used professional help and were less likely to assert that they would never face a problem they could not handle on their own. Many of these results were clearer in 1976 than they were in 1957, suggesting that people in really serious trouble are being much better served.

The original conception of forces affecting the process of help-seeking employed in these studies distinguished not only internal psychological factors such as the willingness to see oneself as potentially vulnerable, but also external facilitating factors such as the availability of professional resources. A number of changes in demographic relationships to help-seeking between 1957 and 1976 indicate clearly that facilitating factors have markedly increased in those twenty years. The most important of these changes concerns income: while in 1957 we found a clear relationship between income and use of professional help, the relationship disappeared in 1976. Cost of care no longer inhibits the use of professional help. Clearly the programs and policies initiated by the federal government to enlarge and broaden access to mental health care have been successful. The poor as well as the rich now use professional help if they think it will be helpful. Furthermore, in the last chapter we found that in 1976 increasing mental health resources within a county increased the range of problems that people see as relevant for seeking professional help, as well as the range of people who avail themselves of such help. Improving mental health resources seems to have its most direct impact in rural areas.

Certain population subgroups show greater readiness than others to seek professional help in both 1957 and 1976: women more than men; younger more than older people; educated more than less educated people. Especially high readiness was found in: people from urban areas; residents of the Pacific states; Jews; frequent church attenders; divorced men and women; adults who experienced parental divorce while they were growing up; adults whose fathers were professionals. Three interpretations are offered about the subgroups who are especially likely to seek professional help: they experience consistent social stress in their lives; they have a well developed psychological orientation; and they have reference group support for choosing professional help as a means of coping with stress.

People who used professional help characterized that help differently in 1957 and 1976. In 1976 they were more likely to:

1. Seek help for situational problems and equally likely to use such help for interpersonal or personal problems.
2. Select a specialized mental health resource (psychiatrist/psychologist, marriage counselor, and other mental health professionals) in preference to a general help source (doctor, clergyman, or lawyer), although they turned to *all* resources much more often than did help-seekers in 1957.
3. Be aware of the referral process, being particularly more susceptible to referrals by family or friends than was true in 1957.
4. View the counsel of psychologists and psychiatrists as helpful, but to be more qualified in appraisals of help received from clergy (seeing it less often as either very helpful or unhelpful).
5. Recognize supportiveness as the basis of the effectiveness of the help they obtained.

Since women are more frequent professional help-seekers than men, they consult more help sources of many types, but only among the young do women consult psychiatrists and psychologists more than men do. The heavier use of these specialists by younger women and older men seems to be balanced by a heavier use of clergy by younger men and older women. Old people, in general, do not often seek help, even from clergy.

Although the more educated utilize all resources more than the less educated, among those who have sought help, the college educated only show a higher rate of utilizing psychiatrists and psychologists.

Demographic comparisons in the type of help sought revealed the following important results for both 1957 and 1976: Fundamentalists and Catholics were particularly oriented to clergy as a help source, especially in contrast to their disinclination to use psychiatrists or psychologists; Jews and certain Protestant groups (especially Episcopalians, Congregationalists) showed the reverse pattern. Wealthier people clearly were particularly oriented to psychological specialists. Geographic location (place of residence and region) was as critical in determining choice of certain professional resources as it was in 1957. This finding now seems clearly interpretable as reflecting differences in social climates of these locations that psychologically influence people to seek one source or another.

More than a small proportion of men and women in 1976 sought help for situational problems—certainly more than did so in 1957. This was further reinforced by our analyses of what people did about "bad things that happen to them." Many sought professional help for external crises, more indeed than did for personal problems. Thus, our analysis of professional help-seeking is considerably expanded by having people focus not just on personal problems but on external crises. It has become more and more acceptable for the expert to intervene in such crises—whether it be the clergy for illness or death, the doctor during a grave illness, or the psychologist for difficulties encountered on a job or in a relationship.

We have indeed become more positive about consulting the expert for all kinds of personal issues, so much so that we now find among help-seekers some people who see professional consultation as a way to expand their potential rather than primarily as a way to alleviate psychological distress. We find, for example, that people who consider themselves different from others, as having strong points, and whose self-perceptions are ambivalent rather than merely negative are particularly ready to seek professional help. This pattern suggests that many people use a relationship with a professional as a way to explore and expand their personalities rather than as a way to undo painful or thoroughly negative feelings about themselves. This new view of professional help-seeking may represent a luxury available to an affluent society. It will in all likelihood continue to be a prevalent view as we make the goal of self-fulfillment more dominant in our hierarchy of values.

Not all of our help-seeking occurs in formal channels. We reported in Book 1 that talking to someone about troubles is Americans' dominant mode of coping. We are very social animals. Prayer, once a common response to periods of unhappiness, is now less often used; talking through worries or unhappiness is now more often used.

In this volume we find that in times of crisis we are also most likely to turn to informal resources, though formal resources are also engaged. Thirty-nine percent of American adults in 1976 said they used both formal and informal resources when asked about their most recent life crisis. Only three percent of the population used only a formal resource for problems. Nothing in our data indicates that having a larger rather than a smaller network is correlated with better subjective mental health.

There is a remarkable difference between the available support for crises experienced by men and women. Women are much more likely to have a large available support system. There was no indication that this difference has changed since 1957. Sex role expectations run deep: men are inclined to be autonomous and not to admit to vulnerabilities. If there is anything to the view that the sharing of problems with others not only binds people to one another but may at some level help a person cope with the problem, then it is clear that considerable effort should be directed toward breaking down men's inhibitions about the intimate sharing of difficulties.

Appendix A

1976 INTERVIEW
SCHEDULE

GUIDE FOR DETECTING QUESTIONS IN THE 1976
INTERVIEW SCHEDULE THAT WERE ALSO PART
OF THE 1957 INTERVIEW SCHEDULE

Question prefix	Information Designated about 1957 Interview
*	Identical question asked in the 1957 study
*⅓	Identical question asked of one-third of the 1957 sample
*(M)	Identical question asked of men only in the 1957 sample
*(M)⅓	Identical question asked of one-third of men only in the 1957 sample
*(H)	Identical question asked of housewives only in the 1957 sample
#	Approximate question asked in the 1957 study
#(W)	Approximate question asked of women only in the 1957 sample

¹X, Y, Z represented random two-thirds of the total 1976 sample.

*Introduction: Read to *Everyone*

The Survey Research Center has been asked to make a study of the stresses and strains of modern living. There have been a lot of changes in our way of living over the past fifty years or so. These changes have brought this country to the highest standard of living in the world. But a great many people are concerned about whether or not there are problems involved in the rapid pace of our present life. Doctors, educators, religious leaders, and other experts are interested in finding out how people feel about this question.

Of course this interview is completely voluntary. If we should come to any question you don't want to answer, let me know and we'll skip over it. I think you'll find the questions interesting and will want to give them careful thought.

TIME NOW_____

Section A: Leisure and Social Support

One of the things we'd like to know is how people spend their time.

*A1. For instance—how do you usually spend your time when your work is done—what kind of things do you do, both at home and away from home?_____

_____
_____
_____
_____

*A2. Are you a member of any (other) clubs and organizations—like a lodge, PTA, a community group, or any other kind of group?

1. YES   5. NO ──────→ GO TO A3

*A2a. What are they?_____

_____
_____

A3. (CARD A) How much of your free time do you usually spend doing things to help or please other people? Would you say that you spend *most, a lot, some, a little,* or *none* of your free time doing such things?

| 1. MOST | 2. A LOT | 3. SOME | 4. A LITTLE | 5. NONE |

A4. Do you wish that you spent *more* of your free time doing things to help or please other people, *less time,* or do you *like it the way it is?*

| 1. MORE TIME | 5. LESS TIME | 3. LIKE IT IS |

A5. (CARD A) Next, how much of your free time do you spend doing things that challenge you? Would you say that you spend *most, a lot, some, a little,* or *none* of your free time doing such things?

| 1. MOST | 2. A LOT | 3. SOME | 4. A LITTLE | 5. NONE |

A6. Do you wish that you spent *more* of your free time doing things that challenge you, *less time,* or do you *like it the way it is?*

| 1. MORE TIME | 5. LESS TIME | 3. LIKE IT IS |

A7. Now a couple of questions about neighbors. About how many of your neighbors do you know well enough to visit or call on? Would you say you have *many, several, a few,* or *none* that you know well enough to visit or call on?

| 1. MANY | 2. SEVERAL | 4. A FEW | 5. NONE | 7. R SAYS HAS *NO* NEIGHBORS |

TURN TO A9

A8. (CARD B) About how often do you visit with any of your neighbors, either at their homes or at your own? (Would you say *more than once a week, once a week, a few times a month, once a month,* or *less than once a month?*)

| MORE 1. THAN ONCE A WEEK | ONCE 2. A WEEK | A FEW 3. TIMES A MONTH | ONCE 4. A MONTH | LESS 5. THAN ONCE A MONTH | 6. NEVER |

*A9. (CARD B) Here are a few questions about your friends and relatives. First, about how often do you get together with friends or relatives—I mean things like going out together or visiting each other's homes? (Would you say *more than once a week, once a week, a few times a month, once a month,* or *less than once a month?*)

| MORE 1. THAN ONCE A WEEK | ONCE 2. A WEEK | A FEW 3. TIMES A MONTH | ONCE 4. A MONTH | LESS 5. THAN ONCE A MONTH | 6. NEVER |

A10. Now, think of the friends and relatives you feel free to talk with about your worries and problems or can count on for advice and help—would you say you have *many, several, a few,* or *no* such friends or relatives?

| 1. MANY | 2. SEVERAL | 4. A FEW | 5. NONE |

A11. (CARD C) How often, if ever, have you talked with friends or relatives about your problems when you were worried or asked them for advice or help—*very often, often, sometimes, rarely,* or *never?*

| 1. VERY OFTEN | 2. OFTEN | 3. SOMETIMES | 4. RARELY | 5. NEVER |

*A12.   Do you feel you have as many friends as you want, or would you like to have more friends?

1. AS MANY FRIENDS AS WANTS	5. WOULD LIKE MORE FRIENDS

A13.   INTERVIEWER CHECKPOINT

☐ 1. COVER SHEET IS FORM "X" OR "Y" ⟶ TURN TO SECTION B
☐ 2. COVER SHEET IS FORM "Z" ⟶ TURN TO SECTION C

Section B: Picture Stories

*Another thing we want to find out is what people think of situations that may come up in life. I'm going to show you some pictures of these situations and ask you to think of stories to go with them. The situations won't be clearly one thing or another—so feel free to think of any story you want to. *(SHOW SET OF MALE PICTURES TO MEN; FEMALE PICTURES TO WOMEN.)*

(SHOW PICTURE 1)

*For example, here's the first picture. I'd like you to spend a few moments thinking of a story to go with it. To get at the story you're thinking of I'll ask you questions like: Who are these people? What do they want? and so on. Just answer with anything that comes to mind. There are no right or wrong answers.

*B1.   Who are these people? What are they doing?_____

_____

*B1a.   What has led up to this—what went on before?_____

_____

*B1b.   What do they want—how do they feel?_____

_____

*B1c.   What will happen—how will it end?_____

_____

(SHOW PICTURE 2)

*B2.   Who are these people? What are they doing?_____

_____

*B2a.   What has led up to this—what went on before?_____

_____

*B2b.   What do they want—how do they feel?_____

_____

_____

_____

*B2c.   What will happen—how will it end?_____

_____

_____

_____

(SHOW PICTURE 3)

*B3.   Who are these people? What are they doing?_____

_____

_____

_____

*B3a.   What has led up to this—what went on before?_____

_____

_____

_____

*B3b.   What do they want—how do they feel?_____

_____

_____

_____

*B3c.   What will happen—how will it end?_____

_____

_____

_____

(SHOW PICTURE 4)

*B4.   Who is this person? What is (he/she) doing?_____

_____

_____

_____

*B4a.   What has led up to this—what went on before?_____

_____

_____

_____

*B4b.   What does (he/she) want—how does (he/she) feel?_____

_____

_____

_____

*B4c.   What will happen—how will it end?_____

_____

_____

_____

(SHOW PICTURE 5)

*B5. Who are these people? What are they doing?_____

_____
_____
_____

*B5a. What has led up to this—what went on before?_____

_____
_____
_____

*B5b. What do they want—how do they feel?_____

_____
_____
_____

*B5c. What will happen—how will it end?_____

_____
_____
_____

(SHOW PICTURE 6)

*B6. Who are these people? What are they doing?_____

_____
_____
_____

*B6a. What has led up to this—what went on before?_____

_____
_____
_____

*B6b. What do they want—how do they feel?_____

_____
_____
_____

*B6c. What will happen—how will it end?_____

_____
_____
_____

Section C: Worries and Unhappiness

One of the things we're interested in is what people think about these days.

*C1. Everybody has some things he worries about more or less. What kinds of things do you
worry about most?

_____
_____
_____

*C2. Do you worry about such things a lot, or not very much? _____

_____

_____

*C3. If something is on your mind that's bothering you or worrying you, and you don't know what to do about it, what do you usually do?

_____

_____

*C4. INTERVIEWER CHECKPOINT

☐ 1. R MENTIONS "TALK IT OVER"—
       PERSON MENTIONED ⟶ TURN TO C5
   ☐ 2. R MENTIONS "TALK IT OVER"—PERSON *NOT* MENTIONED
     ☐ 3. R DOESN'T MENTION "TALK IT OVER" ⟶ GO TO C4b

C4a. Who do you talk it over with?
     (RELATIONSHIP TO R)

_____

_____

TURN TO C5

C4b. Do you ever talk it over with anyone?

| 1. YES; DEPENDS | 5. NO |

TURN TO C5

C4c. Who is that?
     (RELATIONSHIP TO R)

_____

_____

TURN TO C5

*C5. Now I'd like you to think about your whole life—how things are now, how they were ten years ago, how they were when you were a little (boy/girl). What do you think of as the happiest time of your life? (IF R MENTIONS SINGLE EVENT, PROBE: I don't mean just a particular day or single happening, but a whole period of your life.)

_____

_____

(IF R MENTIONS "PRESENT" TIME AS HAPPIEST OR BOTH A PRESENT AND PAST TIME.)
*C5a. Why is this a happy time—what are some of the things that you feel pretty happy about these days? (PROBE FOR FULL RESPONSES.)

_____

_____

_____

GO TO C6

(IF R MENTIONS "PAST" TIME ONLY AS HAPPIEST.)
*C5b. How about the way things are today—what are some of the things you feel pretty happy about these days? (PROBE FOR FULL RESPONSES.)

_____

_____

_____

*C6. Everyone has things about their life they're not completely happy about. What are some of the things that you're not too happy about these days? (PROBE FOR FULL RESPONSES.)

_____
_____
_____
_____
_____
_____

*C7. Thinking now of the way things were in the *past*, what do you think of as the most unhappy time of your life? (PROBE FOR WHOLE PERIOD OF R'S LIFE.)

_____
_____

    *C7a. Why do you think of that as an unhappy time? (Can you tell me more about that time?)

    _____
    _____
    _____
    _____
    _____
    _____

*C8. Taking things all together, how would you say things are these days—would you say you're *very happy, pretty happy,* or *not too happy* these days?

| 1. VERY HAPPY | 3. PRETTY HAPPY | 5. NOT TOO HAPPY |

*C9. Compared to your life today, how do you think things will be 5 or 10 years from now—do you think things will be happier for you than they are now, not quite as happy, or what?

_____
_____

C10. Compared to your life today, how were things 5 or 6 years ago—were things happier for you then than they are now, not quite as happy, or what?

_____
_____

*C11. One of the things we'd like to know, is how people face the unhappy periods in their lives. Thinking of unhappiness you've had to face, what are some of the things that have helped you in those times?

_____
_____
_____

Section D: Self-Perceptions

Now, we'd like to ask you some other questions about yourself.

*D1. People are the same in many ways, but no two people are exactly alike. What are some of the ways in which you're different from most other people?

_____
_____
_____

*D2. Many people when they think about their children, would like them to be different from themselves in some ways. If you had a (son/daughter—SAME SEX AS R), how would you like (him/her) to be different from you?

_____
_____
_____

*D3. How about your good points? What would you say were your strongest points?

_____
_____
_____
_____

(P. 1, RESPONDENT BOOKLET) Now I'd like you to look at the first page of this booklet which tells about some of the ways in which different people describe themselves. After each statement, would you please check the category that applies to you. Please let me know when you have finished this page.

(HAND R THE RESPONDENT BOOKLET TURNED TO D4 AND D5. AFTER R FILLS OUT AND RE-TURNS IT, TURN TO D6.)

> INTERVIEWER: IF R HAS A READING OR SEEING PROBLEM, USE THE QUESTION-NAIRE AS USUAL: READ EACH STATEMENT AND THE RESPONSE CATEGORIES AND CHECK R'S CHOICE.

SAMPLE OF PAGE 1
RESPONDENT BOOKLET

D4. How often do you feel:	A LITTLE OR NONE OF THE TIME	SOME OF THE TIME	A GOOD PART OF THE TIME	ALL OR MOST OF THE TIME
a. My mind is as clear as it used to be.				
b. I find it easy to do the things I used to.				
c. My life is interesting.				
d. I feel that I am useful and needed.				
e. My life is pretty full.				
f. I feel hopeful about the future.				

D5. How often are these true for you:	OFTEN TRUE	SOMETIMES TRUE	RARELY TRUE	NEVER TRUE
a. I feel that I am a person of worth, at least as much as others.				
b. I am able to do things as well as most other people.				
c. On the whole, I feel good about myself.				

TURN TO D6

D6. When you make plans ahead, do you usually get to *carry out things the way you expected*, or do things usually come up to make you *change your plans?*

1. THINGS WORK OUT AS EXPECTED	5. HAVE TO CHANGE PLANS	8. DON'T KNOW

D7.   Some people feel they *can run their lives* much the way they want to; others feel the *problems of life are sometimes too big* for them. Which one are you most like?

| 1. CAN RUN OWN LIFE | 5. PROBLEMS OF LIFE TOO BIG | 8. DON'T KNOW |

D8.   In general, how satisfying do you find the way you're spending your life these days? Would you call it *completely satisfying, pretty satisfying* or *not very satisfying?*

| 1. COMPLETELY SATISFYING | 3. PRETTY SATISFYING | 5. NOT VERY SATISFYING | 8. DON'T KNOW |

D9.   INTERVIEWER CHECKPOINT

☐ 1. COVER SHEET IS FORM "X" ⟶ TURN TO SECTION F
☐ 2. COVER SHEET IS FORM "Y" OR "Z" ⟶ TURN TO SECTION E

Section E: Personal Preferences

Now I'd like to ask you about your preferences for certain things. Keep in mind that there are no right or wrong answers.

E1.   (CARD D) Which of the three things on this card is *truest* for you—I would like to have more friends, I would like to do better at what I try, or I would like to have more people pay attention to my point of view?

| 1. I WOULD LIKE TO HAVE MORE FRIENDS |

| 2. I WOULD LIKE TO DO BETTER AT WHAT I TRY |

| 3. I WOULD LIKE TO HAVE MORE PEOPLE PAY ATTENTION TO MY POINT OF VIEW |

E2.   (CARD D) Which of these three is *least* true for you?

| 1. I WOULD LIKE TO HAVE MORE FRIENDS |

| 2. I WOULD LIKE TO DO BETTER AT WHAT I TRY |

| 3. I WOULD LIKE TO HAVE MORE PEOPLE PAY ATTENTION TO MY POINT OF VIEW |

E3.   (CARD E) Now looking at the next card—what kind of job would you want the *most*—a job where you had to think for yourself, a job where the people you work with are a nice group, or a job where you have a lot to say in what's going on?

| 1. A JOB WHERE YOU HAD TO THINK FOR YOURSELF |

| 2. A JOB WHERE THE PEOPLE YOU WORK WITH ARE A NICE GROUP |

| 3. A JOB WHERE YOU HAVE A LOT TO SAY IN WHAT'S GOING ON |

E4. (CARD E) Which of these three would you want *least?*

> 1. A JOB WHERE YOU HAD TO THINK FOR YOURSELF

> 2. A JOB WHERE THE PEOPLE YOU WORK WITH ARE A NICE GROUP

> 3. A JOB WHERE YOU HAVE A LOT TO SAY IN WHAT'S GOING ON

E5. Now I'll read some statements people use to describe other people. Suppose you were to hear them. Which of the following would you *most* like to overhear about yourself—(his/her) opinion carries a lot of weight among people who know (him/her), *or* people like to live next door to (him/her)?

> 1. (HIS/HER) OPINION CARRIES A LOT OF WEIGHT

> 2. PEOPLE LIKE TO LIVE NEXT DOOR TO (HIM/HER)

E6. Now which of these would you rather hear about yourself—other people like (him/her) very much, *or* (he/she) can do anything (he/she) sets (his/her) mind on doing?

> 1. OTHER PEOPLE LIKE (HIM/HER) VERY MUCH

> 2. (HE/SHE) CAN DO ANYTHING (HE/SHE) SETS (HIS/HER) MIND ON DOING

E7. Now these two. (He/She) is fun to have at a party, *or* people like to go to (him/her) for advice on important matters?

> 1. (HE/SHE) IS FUN TO HAVE AT A PARTY

> 2. PEOPLE LIKE TO GO TO (HIM/HER) FOR ADVICE ON IMPORTANT MATTERS

> INTERVIEWER: QUESTIONS E8–E10 SHOULD BE ASKED OF *EVERYONE,* REGARDLESS OF WORK, PARENTAL, OR MARITAL STATUS.

E8. Now, for each pair of statements I read, please tell me which one you would rather overhear *a friend* say about you. First, which of these—(he/she) is a fine (father/mother), *or* (he/she) is excellent at the work (he/she) does?

> 1. (HE/SHE) IS A FINE (FATHER/MOTHER)

> 2. (HE/SHE) IS EXCELLENT AT THE WORK (HE/SHE) DOES

E9. How about these two—(he/she) is a fine (father/mother), *or* (he/she) is a fine (husband/wife)?

> 1. (HE/SHE) IS A FINE (FATHER/MOTHER)

> 2. (HE/SHE) IS A FINE (HUSBAND/WIFE)

E10. And which of these two would you rather overhear—(he/she) is a fine (husband/wife),
      or (he/she) is excellent at the work (he/she) does?

> 1. (HE/SHE) IS A FINE (HUSBAND/WIFE)

> 2. (HE/SHE) IS EXCELLENT AT THE WORK (HE/SHE) DOES

Section F: Marriage

Now I'd like to ask you some questions about marriage.

*F1. First thinking about a (man's/woman's—SAME SEX AS RESPONDENT) life. How is a
      (man's/woman's—SAME SEX AS RESPONDENT) life changed by being married?
      (PROBE FOR FEELINGS.)
      _____
      _____
      _____
      _____

*½ F2. Suppose all you knew about a (man/woman—SAME SEX AS RESPONDENT) was that
      (he/she) didn't want to get married. What would you guess (he/she) was like? (PROBE
      FOR FULL RESPONSES.)

> IF ANSWER IN TERMS OF NEVER ASKED, NEVER MET A PERSON TO MARRY, ETC.:
> Well, suppose (he/she) had plenty of chances to get married, but just didn't want to?

      _____
      _____
      _____
      _____

F3. How about a (man/woman—OPPOSITE SEX FROM RESPONDENT)? Suppose all you
      knew about a (man/woman) was that (he/she) didn't want to get married. What would
      you guess (he/she) was like? (PROBE FOR FULL RESPONSES.)

> IF ANSWER IN TERMS OF NEVER ASKED, NEVER MET A PERSON TO MARRY, ETC.:
> Well, suppose (he/she) had plenty of chances to get married, but just didn't want to?

      _____
      _____
      _____
      _____

*F4. Are you married, separated, divorced, widowed, or have you never been married?

> ☐ R VOLUNTEERS THAT (HE/SHE) IS LIVING WITH SOMEONE OF OPPOSITE
> SEX (ALSO CHECK APPROPRIATE BOX BELOW AND FOLLOW SKIP
> INSTRUCTION.)

1. MARRIED, (INCLUDING SPOUSE AWAY IN SERVICE)	2. SEPARATED	3. DIVORCED	4. WIDOWED	5. NEVER MARRIED, SINGLE
TURN TO F5	TURN TO F17		TURN TO F23	TURN TO F27

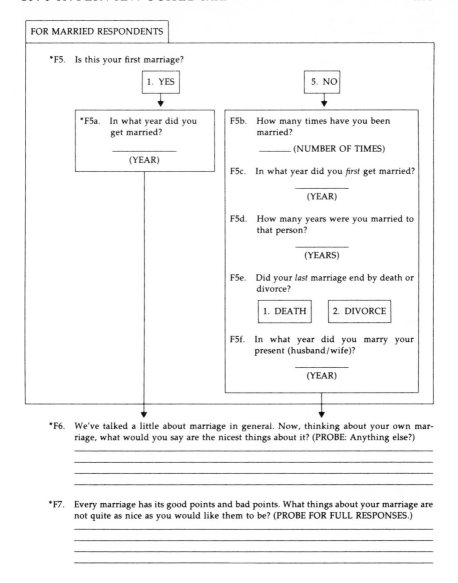

FOR MARRIED RESPONDENTS

*F5.   Is this your first marriage?

1. YES

5. NO

*F5a.   In what year did you get married?

_____
(YEAR)

F5b.   How many times have you been married?

_____ (NUMBER OF TIMES)

F5c.   In what year did you *first* get married?

_____
(YEAR)

F5d.   How many years were you married to that person?

_____
(YEARS)

F5e.   Did your *last* marriage end by death or divorce?

1. DEATH   2. DIVORCE

F5f.   In what year did you marry your present (husband/wife)?

_____
(YEAR)

*F6.   We've talked a little about marriage in general. Now, thinking about your own marriage, what would you say are the nicest things about it? (PROBE: Anything else?)

_____
_____
_____
_____

*F7.   Every marriage has its good points and bad points. What things about your marriage are not quite as nice as you would like them to be? (PROBE FOR FULL RESPONSES.)

_____
_____
_____
_____

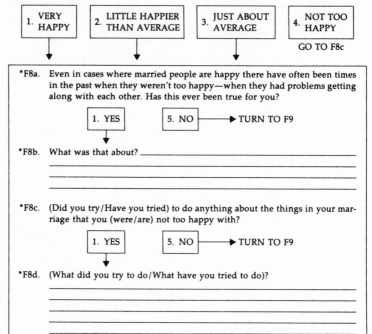

FOR MARRIED RESPONDENTS

*F8. Taking things all together, how would you describe your marriage—would you say your marriage was *very happy, a little happier than average, just about average,* or *not too happy?*

| 1. VERY HAPPY | 2. LITTLE HAPPIER THAN AVERAGE | 3. JUST ABOUT AVERAGE | 4. NOT TOO HAPPY |

GO TO F8c

*F8a. Even in cases where married people are happy there have often been times in the past when they weren't too happy—when they had problems getting along with each other. Has this ever been true for you?

1. YES   5. NO ──────► TURN TO F9

*F8b. What was that about? _____
_____
_____

*F8c. (Did you try/Have you tried) to do anything about the things in your marriage that you (were/are) not too happy with?

1. YES   5. NO ──────► TURN TO F9

*F8d. (What did you try to do/What have you tried to do)?
_____
_____
_____
_____

FOR MARRIED RESPONDENTS

*F9. Many (men/women—SAME SEX AS RESPONDENT) feel that they're not as good (husbands/wives) as they would like to be. Have you ever felt this way?

1. YES   5. NO ──────► GO TO F10

*F9a. What kinds of things make you feel this way? (PROBE FOR FULL RESPONSES.)
_____
_____
_____

*F9b. Do you feel this way a lot of times, or only once in a while?
_____
_____
_____

F10. Now I'm going to read you a couple of things that married couples sometimes do together.

(CARD F) First, how often have you and your (husband/wife) chatted with one another in the past 2 weeks? Would you say *many times, sometimes, hardly ever,* or *never?*

| 1. MANY TIMES | 2. SOMETIMES | 3. HARDLY EVER | 4. NEVER |

F11. (CARD F) How about: Been physically affectionate with one another? How often have you and your (husband/wife) been physically affectionate with one another in the past 2 weeks? (Would you say *many times, sometimes, hardly ever,* or *never?*

| 1. MANY TIMES | 2. SOMETIMES | 3. HARDLY EVER | 4. NEVER |

FOR MARRIED RESPONDENTS

F12. We are also interested in work that has to be done around the house—like cooking, cleaning and laundry. Who would you say does *more* of the housework in your family— you, your (husband/wife) or both about equal?

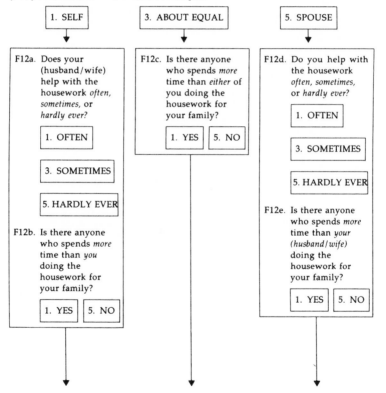

(RESPONDENT BOOKLET) Now would you look at this list which tells about troubles and complaints some people have. (HAND R RESPONDENT BOOKLET, F13, AND PENCIL.) For each one, would you check the answer which tells how often you have had this trouble or complaint: *often, sometimes, rarely,* or *never.* Please let me know when you have finished this page. (WHEN R RETURNS BOOKLET, TURN TO F14.)

SAMPLE OF
RESPONDENT BOOKLET

F13. How often have you:

	OFTEN	SOMETIMES	RARELY	NEVER
a. Been irritated with or resentful toward what your spouse did or didn't do.				
b. Been upset about how you and your spouse were getting along in the sexual part of your life.				
c. Wished your spouse talked more about how (he/she) feels or thinks.				
d. Felt tense from fighting, arguing or disagreeing with your spouse.				
e. Wished that your spouse understood you better.				

TURN TO F14

FOR MARRIED RESPONDENTS

F14. Some married people think of themselves as two separate people who make a life together. Others think of themselves as a couple, it being very hard to describe one person without the other. Which best describes your marriage—the "two separate people" way, or the "couple" way?

1. TWO SEPARATE PEOPLE   5. COUPLE

F15. All and all, who would you say gets more out of being married—you, your (husband/wife), or both about equal?

1. SELF   5. SPOUSE   3. ABOUT EQUAL

F16. Some people think that divorce is often the best solution when people can't seem to work out their marriage problems. Other people think divorce is never the best solution. Would you say divorce is *often, sometimes, rarely,* or *never* the best solution?

1. OFTEN   2. SOMETIMES   3. RARELY   4. NEVER

TURN TO SECTION G

FOR DIVORCED/SEPARATED RESPONDENTS

F17. In what year were you (divorced/separated)? (IF R HAS BEEN DIVORCED MORE THAN ONCE, RECORD LAST TIME ONLY.)

_____ YEAR

F18. In what year did you marry that person?

_____ YEAR

*F19. We've talked a little about marriages in general. Now, thinking about your own marriage, what were some of the problems in your marriage? (PROBE UNLESS R IS RESISTANT.)

_____
_____
_____
_____

*F20. What did you and your (husband/wife) try to do to work things out? (IF R MENTIONS TALKING TO SOMEONE, PROBE FOR WHOM.)

_____
_____
_____
_____

F21. Was that your first marriage?

| 1. YES | | 5. NO |

TURN TO F22

F21a. How many times have you been married?

_____ NUMBER OF TIMES

F21b. Did any of your other marriages end in divorce?

| 1. YES | | 5. NO |

F21c. In what year did you *first* get married?

_____ YEAR

F21d. How many years were you married to that person?

_____ YEARS

FOR DIVORCED/SEPARATED RESPONDENTS

F22. Do you think you'll ever marry again?

| 1. YES | 3. MAYBE; PROBABLY | 5. NO | 8. DON'T KNOW |

TURN TO SECTION G

F22a. Do you have specific plans to marry in the near future?

| 1. YES | | 5. NO |

F22b. What are the main reasons you don't think you'll marry again?

_____
_____
_____
_____

TURN TO SECTION G

FOR WIDOWED RESPONDENTS

F23. In what year did your (husband/wife) die? (MOST RECENT SPOUSE IF WIDOWED MORE THAN ONCE.)

_____ YEAR

F24. In what year did you and (he/she) get married?

_____ YEAR

F25. When your (husband/wife) died what helped you the most? (PROBE FOR MORE THAN ONE SOURCE.)

_____
_____
_____
_____
_____
_____

F26. Was that your first marriage?

| 1. YES | 5. NO |

TURN TO SECTION G

> F26a. How many times have you been married?
>
> _____ NUMBER OF TIMES
>
> F26b. In what year did you *first* get married?
>
> _____ YEAR
>
> F26c. How many years were you married to that person?
>
> _____ YEARS

TURN TO SECTION G

FOR SINGLE, NEVER MARRIED RESPONDENTS

F27. Do you think you'll ever get married?

| 1. YES | MAYBE; 3. DEPENDS; PROBABLY | 5. NO | 8. DON'T KNOW |

TURN TO SECTION G

> F27a. Do you have specific plans to marry in the near future?
>
> | 1. YES | 5. NO |

> F27b. What are the main reasons you think you won't get married?
>
> _____
> _____
> _____
> _____

TURN TO SECTION G

Section G: Parenthood

(ASK EVERYONE)

And now I'd like to ask you some questions about children.

*G1.   First, thinking about a (man's/woman's—SAME SEX AS RESPONDENT) life, how is a (man's/woman's—SAME SEX AS RESPONDENT) life changed by having children? (PROBE FOR FEELINGS.)

_____
_____
_____
_____

*G2.   What would you say is the nicest thing about having children? (PROBE FOR FULL RESPONSES.)

_____
_____
_____
_____

G3.   How do you feel about couples who decide to have no children at all?

_____
_____
_____
_____

G4.   INTERVIEWER CHECKPOINT

☐ 1. R IS MARRIED OR NEVER MARRIED ⟶ TURN TO G5
☐ 2. R IS SINGLE, NEVER MARRIED ⟶ TURN TO SECTION H

*G5. Do you have any children?

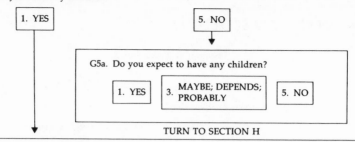

| 1. YES | | 5. NO |

G5a. Do you expect to have any children?

| 1. YES | 3. MAYBE; DEPENDS; PROBABLY | 5. NO |

TURN TO SECTION H

*G5b. How many children have you had? _____ NUMBER OF CHILDREN

*G5c. Would you tell me whether they're boys or girls, how old they are, and whether they're living with you or away from home?
(WRITE DOWN IN ORDER OF MENTION)

CHILD NUMBER	SEX	AGE	CHILD LIVES WITH R, AWAY, OR IS DEAD?		
1			1. WITH R	2. AWAY	3. DEAD
2			1. WITH R	2. AWAY	3. DEAD
3			1. WITH R	2. AWAY	3. DEAD
4			1. WITH R	2. AWAY	3. DEAD
5			1. WITH R	2. AWAY	3. DEAD
6			1. WITH R	2. AWAY	3. DEAD
7			1. WITH R	2. AWAY	3. DEAD
8			1. WITH R	2. AWAY	3. DEAD

G5d. Are there any other children you have helped to raise who you may not have mentioned—like a child who died, an adopted child, or a child from a previous marriage?

| 1. YES | | 5. NO | → TURN TO G6 |

G5e. Would you tell me whether they're boys or girls, how old they are, and whether they're living with you or someplace else?
(WRITE DOWN IN ORDER OF MENTION)

CHILD NUMBER	SEX	AGE	CHILD LIVES WITH R, AWAY, OR IS DEAD?		
1			1. WITH R	2. AWAY	3. DEAD
2			1. WITH R	2. AWAY	3. DEAD
3			1. WITH R	2. AWAY	3. DEAD
4			1. WITH R	2. AWAY	3. DEAD
5			1. WITH R	2. AWAY	3. DEAD
6			1. WITH R	2. AWAY	3. DEAD
7			1. WITH R	2. AWAY	3. DEAD
8			1. WITH R	2. AWAY	3. DEAD

G6. In what year did you first become a parent?

_____ YEAR

*G7. Do you expect to have any more children?

| 1. YES | | 3. MAYBE; DEPENDS; PROBABLY | | 5. NO |

*G8. Most parents have had some problems in raising their children. What are the main problems you've had in raising your child(ren)? (PROBE FOR FULL RESPONSES.)

_____
_____
_____
_____
_____
_____

*G9. Many (men/women—SAME SEX AS RESPONDENT) feel that they're not as good (fathers/mothers—SAME SEX AS RESPONDENT) as they would like to be. Have you ever felt this way?

| 1. YES | | 5. NO | ⟶ TURN TO G10

*G9a. What kinds of things have made you feel this way? (PROBE FOR FULL RESPONSES.)

_____
_____
_____

*G9b. Have you felt this way a lot of times, or only once in a while?

_____
_____

G10. Some people say that having children does not leave them enough time for other things they want to do. Would you say that having children prevents (prevented) you from doing things you want(ed) to do *often, sometimes, rarely,* or *never?*

| 1. OFTEN | | 2. SOMETIMES | | 3. RARELY | | 4. NEVER |

G11. Some people say that having children brings a husband and wife closer together. Others feel that having children makes a husband and wife less close. How do you feel about that? Do you feel that children have brought you and your (husband/wife) *closer together* or *farther apart?*

| 1. CLOSER TOGETHER | | 5. FARTHER APART | | 3. SOME OF BOTH | | 6. NO DIFFERENCE |

G12.   INTERVIEWER CHECKPOINT: R IS:

☐ 1. *CURRENTLY MARRIED* WITH CHILD(REN) UNDER 12 LIVING IN HOUSEHOLD
☐ 2. *NOT* CURRENTLY MARRIED *OR* HAS NO CHILD(REN) UNDER 12 LIVING IN HOUSEHOLD ──────▶ TURN TO SECTION H

G13.   Who in your family would you say spends *more* time taking care of the child(ren)—you, your (husband/wife) or both about equal?

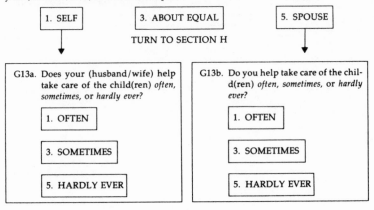

| 1. SELF | 3. ABOUT EQUAL | 5. SPOUSE |

TURN TO SECTION H

G13a. Does your (husband/wife) help take care of the child(ren) *often, sometimes,* or *hardly ever?*

1. OFTEN

3. SOMETIMES

5. HARDLY EVER

G13b. Do you help take care of the child(ren) *often, sometimes,* or *hardly ever?*

1. OFTEN

3. SOMETIMES

5. HARDLY EVER

#H1.   Now I'd like to talk to you about your work. Are you working now, unemployed,

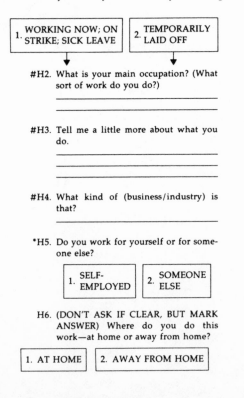

| 1. WORKING NOW; ON STRIKE; SICK LEAVE | 2. TEMPORARILY LAID OFF |

#H2.   What is your main occupation? (What sort of work do you do?)

_____
_____

#H3.   Tell me a little more about what you do.

_____
_____
_____

#H4.   What kind of (business/industry) is that?

_____

*H5.   Do you work for yourself or for someone else?

| 1. SELF-EMPLOYED | 2. SOMEONE ELSE |

H6.   (DON'T ASK IF CLEAR, BUT MARK ANSWER) Where do you do this work—at home or away from home?

| 1. AT HOME | 2. AWAY FROM HOME |

H7. About how many hours do you work on your job in the average week?

_____ HOURS A WEEK

TURN TO H16

4. UNEMPLOYED

H8. Have you ever done any work for pay?

| 1. YES | | 5. NO |———▶TURN TO H43

#H8a. What was your occupation on your last regular job? (What sort of work did you do?)

_____

_____

#H8b. Tell me a little more about what you did.

_____

_____

#H8c. What kind of (business/industry) was that?

_____

#H8d. Did you work for yourself or for someone else?

1. SELF-EMPLOYED	2. SOMEONE ELSE

H8e. About how many hours did you work on your last job in the average week?

_____ HOURS A WEEK

TURN TO H40

retired, (a housewife), (a student), or what?

5. RETIRED	6. PERMANENTLY DISABLED

GO TO H10

H9. Have you ever done any work for pay?

| 1. YES | 5. NO |——▶ TURN TO SECTION J

#H10. What was your main occupation before you (retired/became disabled)? (What sort of work did you do?)

_____

_____

#H11. Tell me a little more about what you did.

_____

_____

#H12. What kind of (business/industry) was that?

_____

#H13. Did you work for yourself or for someone else?

1. SELF-EMPLOYED	2. SOMEONE ELSE

H14. INTERVIEWER CHECKPOINT

☐ 1. R IS RETIRED ⟶ TURN TO H44

☐ 2. R IS DISABLED

H14a. Are you doing *any* work for pay at the present time?

1. YES	5. NO

GO BACK TO H2 "WORKING NOW"   TURN TO SECTION J

7. HOUSEWIFE	8. STUDENT

#H15. Are you doing *any* work for pay at the present time?

1. YES	5. NO

GO BACK TO H2 "WORKING NOW"

H15a. Have you ever done any work for pay?

1. YES	5. NO

GO TO H15d

H15b. When did you leave your last regular job? (IF LESS THAN TWO YEARS, GET MONTH.)

_____ YEAR   _____ MONTH

H15c. What happened—why did you leave it?

_____

_____

_____

_____

H15d. INTERVIEWER CHECKPOINT

☐ 1. R IS HOUSEWIFE ⟶ TURN
                            TO H49

☐ 2. R IS STUDENT ⟶ TURN TO
                          SECTION J

ASK ALL PEOPLE WORKING FULL OR PART TIME

*(M)H16. How long have you been doing this kind of work?

_____ YEARS

*H17. Taking into consideration all the things about your job, how satisfied or dissatisfied are
you with it?

_____
_____
_____

*H18. What things do you particularly like about the job? _____

_____
_____
_____

*H19. What things don't you like about the job? _____

_____
_____
_____

*H20. Regardless of how much you like your job, is there any other kind of work you'd rather
be doing?

| 1. YES | | 5. NO | ⟶ TURN TO H21

*H20a. What is that? _____

_____
_____

ASK ALL PEOPLE WORKING FULL OR PART TIME

H21. Taking everything into consideration, how likely is it that you will make a genuine effort to find a new job within the next year—*very likely, somewhat likely,* or *not at all likely?*

| 1. VERY LIKELY | | 3. SOMEWHAT LIKELY | | 5. NOT AT ALL LIKELY |

*(M)H22. If you didn't have to work to make a living, do you think you would work anyway?
#(W)

| 1. YES | | 3. MAYBE; PROBABLY | | 5. NO | | 8. DON'T KNOW |

GO TO H23

*H22a. What would be your reasons
for going on working?

_____
_____
_____

H22b. Why would you *not* continue
to work?

_____
_____
_____

*(M)H23. Have you ever had any problems with your work—times when you couldn't work or weren't getting along on the job, or didn't know what kind of work you wanted to do?

| 1. YES | | 5. NO | ⟶ GO TO H24 |

*(M)H23a. What was that about? _____

_____

_____

_____

H24. Do you feel that the demands of your work ever interfere with the demands of your family?

| 1. YES | | 3. SOMETIMES | | 5. NO |

ASK ALL PEOPLE WORKING FULL OR PART TIME

H25. Next are some things that might describe a person's job. First, how much does your job allow you to make a lot of decisions on your own? Would you say *a lot, somewhat, a little, or not at all?*

| 1. A LOT | | 2. SOMEWHAT | | 3. A LITTLE | | 4. NOT AT ALL |

H26. How much say do you have over what happens on your job? Would you say *a lot, some, a little,* or *none?*

| 1. A LOT | | 2. SOME | | 3. A LITTLE | | 4. NONE |

(CARD G) Here are some more things that might describe a person's job. Please tell me *how true* each is of *your* (main) job, using one of the answers on this card.

	VERY TRUE (1)	SOMEWHAT TRUE (2)	NOT VERY TRUE (3)	NOT AT ALL TRUE (4)
H27. The first one is: The work is interesting. Is this *very true, somewhat true, not very true* or *not at all true* of your job?				
H28. The next one is: I am given a lot of chances to talk with the people I work with. (Is this *very true, somewhat true, not very true* or *not at all true* of your job?)				
H29. I am given a chance to do the things I do best. (Is this *very true, somewhat true, not very true* or *not at all true* of your job?)				

*(M)½H30. What does it take to do a really good job at the kind of work you do?

_____

_____

ASK ALL PEOPLE WORKING FULL OR PART TIME

*(M)½H31. How much *ability* do you think it takes to do a really good job at the kind of work you do?

_____

_____

*(M)½H32. How good would you say you are at doing this kind of work—would you say you were *very good, a little better than average, just average,* or *not very good?*

| 1. VERY GOOD | 2. A LITTLE BETTER THAN AVERAGE | 3. JUST AVERAGE | 4. NOT VERY GOOD |

*(M)H33. Do you have any people working under (for) you?

| 1. YES | | 5. NO |———▶ GO TO H34

*(M)H33a. How many?

_____ NUMBER OF PEOPLE

H34. INTERVIEWER CHECKPOINT

☐ 1. R IS SELF-EMPLOYED————▶ TURN TO H37
☐ 2. R IS *NOT* SELF-EMPLOYED————▶ TURN TO H35

WORKING FULL OR PART TIME

(IF R IS *NOT* SELF-EMPLOYED)

*(M) H35. Do you work under anyone—a supervisor or anyone in charge of your work?

| 1. YES | | 5. NO |———▶ GO TO H36

*(M)H35a. Just how much does (he/she) have to do with you and your work?

_____

*(M) H36. Outside of the people working over you or under you, do you work with any other person or people?

| 1. YES | | 5. NO |———▶ GO TO H37

*(M)H36a. How do you like the people you work with? _____

_____

H37. INTERVIEWER CHECKPOINT

☐ 1. R IS MALE ———▶ TURN TO SECTION J
2. R IS FEMALE

*(H)H38. Different people feel differently about taking care of a home—I don't mean taking care of the children, but things like cooking and sewing and keeping house. Some women look on these things as just a job that has to be done—other women really enjoy them. How do you feel about this?

_____

_____

WOMEN WORKING FULL OR PART TIME

H39.   INTERVIEWER CHECKPOINT

□ 1. R HAS CHILD(REN) UNDER 12 LIVING IN HOUSEHOLD
□ 2. R HAS *NO* CHILD(REN) UNDER 12 LIVING IN
     HOUSEHOLD ⟶ TURN TO SECTION J

H39a.   How (are the children/is the child) taken care of while you are at work?
_____
_____

H39b.   (IF R MENTIONS SCHOOL *ONLY*) What about the time (he/she isn't) (they aren't) in school?
_____
_____

TURN TO SECTION J

R IS UNEMPLOYED

---

*H40.   When did you leave your last job? _____

*H41.   What happened—why did you leave it? (DON'T PROBE IF R IS RESISTANT.)
_____
_____
_____

*H42.   Do you expect to have much trouble getting another job?

| 1. YES | | 5. NO |

H43.   Have you been looking for work during the past month?

| 1. YES | | 5. NO | ⟶ GO TO H43b

H43a. What have you been doing in the last month to find work?
_____
_____
_____

TURN TO SECTION J

H43b. Do you want a regular job now, either full or part-time?

| 1. YES | 3. MAYBE—IT DEPENDS | 5. NO | 8. DON'T KNOW |

H43c. What are the reasons you are not looking for work? (DON'T PROBE IF R IS RESISTANT.)
_____
_____
_____

H43d. Do you intend to look for work of any kind in the next 12 months?

| 1. YES | 5. NO |

| 3. DEPENDS | 8. DON'T KNOW |

TURN TO SECTION J

R IS RETIRED

H44. In what year did you retire? (IF LESS THAN TWO YEARS, PROBE: In what month was that?)

_____ YEAR   _____ MONTH

*H45. Why did you retire? _____
_____

H45a. (IF NOT CLEAR) Did you have to retire, or is this something that you wanted to do?
_____

*H46. In what way has retirement made a difference in your life?
_____
_____
_____

*H46a. Could you tell me more about these changes and what they have meant in your life?
_____
_____
_____

*H47. When you think of the days when you were working, what do you miss most?
_____
_____
_____

H48. Are you doing *any* work for pay at the present time?

| 1. YES | | 5. NO | → TURN TO SECTION J |

TURN *BACK* TO H2
"WORKING NOW"

R IS A HOUSEWIFE

*H49. Different people feel differently about taking care of a home—I don't mean taking care of the children, but things like cooking and sewing and keeping house. Some women look on these things as just a job that has to be done—other women really enjoy them. How do you feel about this?
_____
_____
_____

*H50. Have you ever wanted a career?

| 1. YES | | 5. NO | → GO TO H51 |

*H50a. What kind of career? _____
_____
_____

H51. What are the main reasons you aren't working at present?
_____
_____
_____

*H52.   Are you planning to go to work in the future?

┌──────────────┐   ┌──────────────┐
│   1. YES   │   │   5. NO   ├──────► TURN TO SECTION J
└──────────────┘   └──────────────┘
        │
        ▼

┌───┐
│ *H52a.   Women have different reasons for working. What would be your main rea- │
│   sons for working? (PROBE FOR FULL RESPONSES.)   │
│   _____ │
│   _____ │
│   _____ │
│   _____ │
│   │
│   │
│ *H52b.   What kind of work do you think you will do? _____ │
│   _____ │
│   _____ │
│   _____ │
│   │
│ H52c.   Are you looking for work at the present time?   │
│   ┌──────────────┐   ┌──────────────┐   │
│   │   1. YES   │   │   5. NO   │   │
│   └──────────────┘   └──────────────┘   │
└───┘

TURN TO SECTION J

Section J: Role Comparisons

J1.   (CARD H) Here is a list of things that many people look for or want out of life. Please
      study the list carefully, then tell me which *two* of these things are *most* important to you
      in *your* life.

      (CHECK TWO)

┌──────────────────────────────┐   ┌──────────────────────────────────┐
│ 01. SENSE OF BELONGING   │   │ 06. FUN AND ENJOYMENT IN LIFE   │
└──────────────────────────────┘   └──────────────────────────────────┘

┌──────────────────────────────┐   ┌──────────────────────────────────┐
│ 02. EXCITEMENT   │   │ 07. SECURITY   │
└──────────────────────────────┘   └──────────────────────────────────┘

┌──────────────────────────────┐   ┌──────────────────────────────────┐
│ 03. WARM RELATIONSHIPS WITH OTHERS │   │ 08. SELF-RESPECT   │
└──────────────────────────────┘   └──────────────────────────────────┘

┌──────────────────────────────┐   ┌──────────────────────────────────┐
│ 04. SELF-FULFILLMENT   │   │ .09. A SENSE OF ACCOMPLISHMENT   │
└──────────────────────────────┘   └──────────────────────────────────┘

┌──────────────────────────────┐
│ 05. BEING WELL-RESPECTED   │
└──────────────────────────────┘

J2.   (CARD H) And of these two, which *one* is *most* important to you in your life?

      (CHECK ONE)

┌──────────────────────────────┐   ┌──────────────────────────────────┐
│ 01. SENSE OF BELONGING   │   │ 06. FUN AND ENJOYMENT IN LIFE   │
└──────────────────────────────┘   └──────────────────────────────────┘

┌──────────────────────────────┐   ┌──────────────────────────────────┐
│ 02. EXCITEMENT   │   │ 07. SECURITY   │
└──────────────────────────────┘   └──────────────────────────────────┘

┌──────────────────────────────┐   ┌──────────────────────────────────┐
│ 03. WARM RELATIONSHIPS WITH OTHERS │   │ 08. SELF-RESPECT   │
└──────────────────────────────┘   └──────────────────────────────────┘

┌──────────────────────────────┐   ┌──────────────────────────────────┐
│ 04. SELF-FULFILLMENT   │   │ 09. A SENSE OF ACCOMPLISHMENT   │
└──────────────────────────────┘   └──────────────────────────────────┘

┌──────────────────────────────┐
│ 05. BEING WELL-RESPECTED   │
└──────────────────────────────┘

NOTE TO INTERVIEWER: COPY HERE THE VALUE SELECTED BY R IN J2: _____ . SUBSTITUTE THIS PHRASE FOR "MOST IMPORTANT VALUE" IN QUESTIONS J3a-J3e.

J3. (CARD J) Now I'd like to ask you how much various things in your life either have led or would lead to (MOST IMPORTANT VALUE).

QUESTIONS J3a-J3e SHOULD BE ASKED OF *EVERYONE*	VERY LITTLE (1)	A LITTLE (2)	SOME (3)	A LOT (4)	A GREAT DEAL (5)
a. First, how much have the things you do in your *leisure* time led to (MOST IMPORTANT VALUE) in your life— *(very little, a little, some, a lot,* or *a great deal)?*					
b. How much has the work you do in and around the house led to (MOST IMPORTANT VALUE) in your life— *(very little, a little, some, a lot,* or *a great deal)?*					
c. How much (has/would/did) *work at a job* (led/lead) to (MOST IMPORTANT VALUE) in your life?					
d. How about being married? How much (has/would/did) *being married* (led/lead) to (MOST IMPORTANT VALUE) in your life?					
e. What about being a (father/mother)? How much (has/would) being a parent (led/lead) to (MOST IMPORTANT VALUE) in your life?					

J4. (CARD K) Some things in our lives are very satisfying to one person, while another may not find them satisfying at all. I'd like to ask how much satisfaction you have gotten or would get from some of these different things.

QUESTIONS J4a-J4e SHOULD BE ASKED OF *EVERYONE*	GREAT SATIS- FACTION (1)	SOME SATIS- FACTION (2)	LITTLE SATIS- FACTION (3)	NO SATIS- FACTION (4)
a. First, consider the *things you do in your leisure time.* All in all, would you say you have gotten *great* satisfaction, *some* satisfaction, *a little* satisfaction, or *no* satisfaction from the things that you do in your leisure time?				
b. How about the *work you do in and around the house?* (Would you say you have gotten *great, some, a little,* or *no* satisfaction?)				
c. How much satisfaction (have you gotten/would you get/did you get) out of work at a job?				
d. What about *being married?* How much satisfaction (have you gotten/would you get/did you get) from being married?				
e. How much satisfaction (have you gotten/would you get/did you get) out of being a (father/ mother)?				

Section K: Symptoms

*Now, some questions about your health.

*K1.   Do you have any particular physical or health trouble?

1. YES		5. NO	→ GO TO K2

*K1a.   What is that? _____

_____
_____
_____
_____

*K2.   (RESPONDENT BOOKLET) Here is a list which tells about different troubles and complaints people have. After each one would you check the answer which tells how often you have had this trouble or complaint. Please let me know when you have finished the page. (HAND RESPONDENT BOOKLET TURNED TO Qs K2 AND K3, AND PENCIL.) (AFTER R FILLS OUT AND RETURNS BOOKLET, TURN TO K4.)

*K2. How often have you had the following?	NEARLY ALL THE TIME	PRETTY OFTEN	NOT VERY MUCH	NEVER
*a. Do you ever have any trouble getting to sleep or staying asleep?				
*b. Have you ever been bothered by nervousness, feeling fidgety and tense?				
*c. Are you ever troubled by headaches or pains in the head?				
*d. Do you have loss of appetite?				
*e. How often are you bothered by having an upset stomach?				
*f. Do you find it difficult to get up in the morning?				

*K3. How often have you had the following?	MANY TIMES	SOME-TIMES	HARDLY EVER	NEVER
*a. Has any ill health affected the amount of work you do?				
*b. Have you ever been bothered by shortness of breath when you were not exercising or working hard?				
*c. Have you ever been bothered by your heart beating hard?				
*d. Do you ever drink more than you should?				
*e. Have you ever had spells of dizziness?				
*f. Are you ever bothered by nightmares?				
*g. Do you tend to lose weight when you have something important bothering you?				
*h. Do your hands ever tremble enough to bother you?				
*i. Are you troubled by your hands sweating so that you feel damp and clammy?				
*j. Have there ever been times when you couldn't take care of things because you just couldn't get going?				
k. When you feel worried, tense or nervous, do you ever drink alcoholic beverages to help you handle things?				
l. Have there ever been problems between you and anyone in your family (spouse, parent, child, or other close relative) because you drank alcoholic beverages?				
m. When you feel worried, tense or nervous, do you ever take medicines or drugs to help you handle things?				

TURN TO K4

*K4. Here are some more questions like those you've filled out. This time just answer "Yes" or "No." Do you feel you are bothered by all sorts of pains and ailments in different parts of your body?

| 1. YES | | 5. NO |

*K5. For the most part, do you feel healthy enough to carry out the things that you would like to do?

| 1. YES | | 5. NO |

*K6. Have you ever felt that you were going to have a nervous breakdown?

| 1. YES | | 5. NO |——▶ TURN TO K7

*K6a. Could you tell me about when you felt this way? What was it about?
_____
_____
_____

*K6b. What did you do about it?
_____
_____

K7. (CARD M) Now here is something different. I have some statements here that describe the way some people are and feel. I'll read them one at a time and you just tell me how true they are for you—whether they're *very true* for you, *pretty true*, *not very true*, or *not true at all*.

	VERY TRUE (1)	PRETTY TRUE (2)	NOT VERY TRUE (3)	NOT TRUE AT ALL (4)
*K7a. I have always felt pretty sure my life would work out the way I wanted it to.				
K7b. No one cares much what happens to me.				
*K7c. I often wish that people would listen to me more.				
*K7d. I often wish that people liked me more than they do.				
K7e. These days I really don't know who I can count on for help.				

Section M: Formal Help-Seeking

Problems often come up in life. Sometimes they're personal problems—people are very unhappy, or nervous and irritable all the time. Sometimes they're problems in a marriage—a husband and wife just can't get along with each other. Or, sometimes it's a personal problem with a child or a job. I'd like to ask you a few questions now about what you think a person might do to handle problems like these.

*M1. For instance, let's suppose you had a lot of personal problems and you're very unhappy all the time. Let's suppose you've been that way for a long time, and it isn't getting any better. What do you think you'd do about it?

_____
_____
_____
_____

M2. INTERVIEWER CHECKPOINT

☐ 1. R IS CURRENTLY MARRIED
☐ 2. R IS NOT CURRENTLY MARRIED ⟶ TURN TO M4

*M3. Suppose it was a problem in your marriage—you and your (husband/wife) just couldn't get along with each other. What do you think you would do about it?

_____
_____
_____

ASK EVERYONE

*M4. Sometimes when people have problems like this, they go someplace for help. Sometimes they go to a doctor or a minister. Sometimes they go to a special place for handling personal problems—like a psychiatrist or a marriage counselor, or social agency or clinic. How about you—have you ever gone anywhere like that for advice and help with any personal problems?

| 1. YES | | 5. NO | ➤ TURN TO M5 |

*M4a. What was that about? _____
_____
_____
_____

*M4b. Where did you go for help? _____
_____
_____
_____

*M4c. INTERVIEWER CHECKPOINT

☐ 1. IN M4b R MENTIONS PERSON *ONLY*
☐ 2. IN M4b R MENTIONS PLACE ──────➤ GO TO M4e

*M4d. Is that person connected with an agency, place, or other organization?

| 1. YES | | 5. NO | ➤ TURN TO M4f |

*M4e. Can you tell me the type of place it was? _____
_____
_____

#M4f. How did you know to go there? That is, how did you know about that (person/place)?
_____
_____
_____
_____

*M4g. What did they do—how did they try to help you? _____
_____
_____
_____

*M4h. How did it turn out—do you think it helped you in any way?
_____
_____
_____

TURN TO M6

IF R SAID "NO" TO M4

*M5. Can you think of anything that's happened to you, any problems you've had in the past, where going to someone like this might have helped you in any way?

| 1. YES | | 5. NO |

*M5a. What do you have in mind—what was it about?

_____
_____
_____
_____
_____

*M5b. What did you do about it?

_____
_____
_____

*M5c. Who do you think might have helped you with that?

_____
_____
_____
_____

*M5d. Why do you suppose that you didn't go for help?

_____
_____
_____
_____

*M5e. Do you think you could ever have a personal problem that got so bad that you might want to go someplace for help—or do you think you could always handle things like that yourself?

_____
_____
_____

TURN TO M6

TURN TO M6

ASK EVERYONE

M6. Has any member of your family or a close friend ever gone to a special place for handling personal problems—like a psychiatrist or a marriage counselor, or a social agency or clinic?

| 1. YES | | 5. NO |

M7. Over their lives most people have something bad happen to them or to someone they love. By that I mean things like getting sick, losing a job, or being in trouble with the police. Or like when someone dies, leaves, or disappoints you. Or maybe just something important you wanted to happen didn't happen. Compared with most other people you know, have *things like this* happened to you *a lot, some, not much,* or *hardly ever*?

| 1. A LOT | 2. SOME | 3. NOT MUCH | 4. HARDLY EVER |

M8. When things like these have happened to you, have there been times when you found it very hard to handle? That is, when you couldn't sleep, or stayed away from people, or felt so depressed or nervous that you couldn't do much of anything?

1. YES	5. NO

*M8a. Would you say you felt that way *many times, sometimes,* or just *once in a while?*

1. MANY TIMES

3. SOMETIMES

5. JUST ONCE IN A WHILE

M8b. Now think about the last time you felt that way. What was it about?

_____
_____
_____
_____

M8c. Now think about the last time something really bad happened to you. What was it about?

_____
_____
_____
_____
_____
_____

M8d. How long ago did that happen?

_____ | YEARS | MONTHS | WEEKS | DAYS | AGO | IT'S HAPPENING RIGHT NOW
NUMBER

(CHECK ONE)

M9. (CARD N) When things like that happen some people like to talk it over with other people. (HAND R CARD.) Did you talk to any of *these* people about that matter? For each person, choose the *one* description that fits them best. If more than one person you talked to fits the *same* description (like friend or relative), please tell me.

	□ CHECK HERE IF R SAYS "TALKED TO NO ONE" ON THE LIST. THEN TURN TO M10 *PERSON:*	M9a. Is that person male or female?
CARD N A. HUSBAND B. WIFE C. SON D. DAUGHTER E. FATHER F. MOTHER G. BROTHER H. SISTER I. OTHER RELATIVE OR FAMILY MEMBER (PLEASE SPECIFY) J. FRIEND K. NEIGHBOR L. CO-WORKER	1.	1. MALE 2. FEMALE
	2.	1. MALE 2. FEMALE
	3.	1. MALE 2. FEMALE
	4.	1. MALE 2. FEMALE
	5.	1. MALE 2. FEMALE
	6.	1. MALE 2. FEMALE
	7.	1. MALE 2. FEMALE
	8.	1. MALE 2. FEMALE

M9b. Is (he/she) older than you are, younger, or about the same?	M9c. (CARD P) Which of the things on this card happened when you talked with (him/her)? You can choose *more than one*. (CHECK ALL THAT APPLY.) a. listened to me b. cheered or comforted me c. talked things out d. told me who else to see e. showed me a new way to look at things f. gave me advice g. helped me take action	M9d. How much did it help to talk? Would you say it: helped a lot? helped some? or was it not much help?
1. OLDER 5. YOUNGER 3. SAME	a b c d e f g	1. A LOT 3. SOME 5. NOT MUCH
1. OLDER 5. YOUNGER 3. SAME	a b c d e f g	1. A LOT 3. SOME 5. NOT MUCH
1. OLDER 5. YOUNGER 3. SAME	a b c d e f g	1. A LOT 3. SOME 5. NOT MUCH
1. OLDER 5. YOUNGER 3. SAME	a b c d e f g	1. A LOT 3. SOME 5. NOT MUCH
1. OLDER 5. YOUNGER 3. SAME	a b c d e f g	1. A LOT 3. SOME 5. NOT MUCH
1. OLDER 5. YOUNGER 3. SAME	a b c d e f g	1. A LOT 3. SOME 5. NOT MUCH
1. OLDER 5. YOUNGER 3. SAME	a b c d e f g	1. A LOT 3. SOME 5. NOT MUCH
1. OLDER 5. YOUNGER 3. SAME	a b c d e f g	1. A LOT 3. SOME 5. NOT MUCH

M10. (CARD S) Now how about these people? Did you talk to any of these people about that matter? Again, for each person, choose the *one* description that fits them best. If more than one person you talked to fits the same description, please tell me.

CARD S	☐ CHECK HERE IF R SAYS "TALKED TO NO ONE" ON THE LIST. THEN TURN TO SECTION N OCCUPATION OF *PROFESSIONAL:*	M10a. Is that person connected with an agency, clinic, or other organization?			M10b. (IF YES TO M10a) Do you remember the name of the place, or the kind of place it was? (What is it?) (ENTER NAME OR TYPE OF PLACE)
M. PSYCHIATRIST					
N. PSYCHOLOGIST	1.	1. YES	5. NO	8. DK	
O. SOCIAL WORKER	2.	1. YES	5. NO	8. DK	
P. COUNSELOR	3.	1. YES	5. NO	8. DK	
Q. DOCTOR	4.	1. YES	5. NO	8. DK	
R. NURSE	5.	1. YES	5. NO	8. DK	
S. CLERGYMAN	6.	1. YES	5. NO	8. DK	
T. TEACHER	7.	1. YES	5. NO	8. DK	
U. POLICE	8.	1. YES	5. NO	8. DK	
V. LAWYER					
W. OTHER PROFESSIONAL (PLEASE SPECIFY)					

M10c. How did you know to go to that person?	M10d. (CARD P) Which of the things on this card happened when you talked with that person? You can choose *more than one*. (CHECK ALL THAT APPLY.) a. listened to me b. cheered or comforted me c. talked things out d. told me who else to see e. showed me a new way to look at things f. gave me advice g. helped me take action	M10e. How much did it help to talk? Would you say it: helped a lot? helped some? or was it not much help?
	a b c d e f g	1. A LOT 3. SOME 5. NOT MUCH
	a b c d e f g	1. A LOT 3. SOME 5. NOT MUCH
	a b c d e f g	1. A LOT 3. SOME 5. NOT MUCH
	a b c d e f g	1. A LOT 3. SOME 5. NOT MUCH
	a b c d e f g	1. A LOT 3. SOME 5. NOT MUCH
	a b c d e f g	1. A LOT 3. SOME 5. NOT MUCH
	a b c d e f g	1. A LOT 3. SOME 5. NOT MUCH
	a b c d e f g	1. A LOT 3. SOME 5. NOT MUCH

Section N: Personal Data

Now we have finished the regular part of the interview. We need a few facts about you, like age, education, and so on, so that we can compare the ideas of men with those of women, older people with younger people, and one group with another.

#N1. First, what is your date of birth? _____ / _____ / _____
                                              MONTH   DAY   YEAR

*N2. Where were you born?

    STATE (OR COUNTRY IF NOT U.S.A.)_____

N3. And where did you live mostly while you were growing up?

    STATE (OR COUNTRY IF NOT U.S.A.)_____

*N4. Were you brought up mostly in the country, in a town, in a small city, or in a large city?

| 1. COUNTRY | 2. TOWN | 3. SMALL CITY | 4. LARGE CITY |

N5. What was your religious background when you were growing up—Protestant, Roman Catholic, Jewish, or something else?

| PROTESTANT | 200. ROMAN CATHOLIC | 300. JEWISH | 800. NONE, NO PREFERENCE | OTHER: SPECIFY _____ _____ |

GO TO N6

N5a. What church or denomination was that?

    _____

N6. What is the original nationality of your family on your father's side? (IF R SAYS, "AMERICAN," PROBE: What was it before coming to the United States?)

    _____ ORIGINAL NATIONALITY

N7. How many brothers and sisters did you have while you were growing up?

    _____ NUMBER | 00. NONE | → GO TO N8

    N7a. Were you the oldest, the youngest, or what?

    | 1. OLDEST | 5. YOUNGEST | 3. IN BETWEEN |

*N8. Did you always live together with both of your *real* parents up to the time you were 16 years old?

| 1. YES | | 5. NO |

TURN TO N9

*N8a. What happened? _____

_____

*N8b. How old were you when it happened?

_____ YEARS OLD

N8c. Who was the head of your family or household most of the time while you were growing up?

| 1. FATHER | 2. MOTHER | OTHER MALE:

_____
(SPECIFY) | OTHER FEMALE:

_____
(SPECIFY) |

*N9. (ASK N9–N13 ABOUT FATHER OR OTHER HEAD MENTIONED IN N8c.) Now a few questions about your father (the person who was head of your family while you were growing up). First, what kind of work did (he/she) do for a living while you were growing up? (What was (his/her) main occupation?)

_____

#N10. Can you tell me a little more about what (he/she) did on (his/her) job?

_____

_____

#N11. What kind of (business/industry) was that? _____

_____

#N12. Did (he/she) work for (himself/herself), or for someone else?

| 1. SELF-EMPLOYED | | 2. SOMEONE ELSE |

N13. What was the highest grade of school or year of college (he/she) completed?

GRADES OF SCHOOL													COLLEGE				
00	01	02	03	04	05	06	07	08	09	10	11	12	13	14	15	16	17+

TURN TO N14

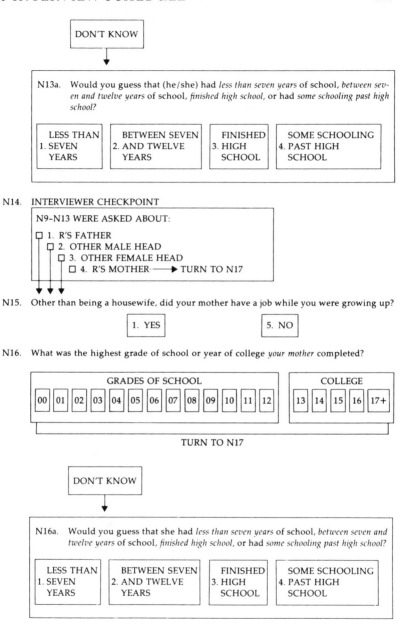

DON'T KNOW

N13a.   Would you guess that (he/she) had *less than seven years* of school, *between seven and twelve years* of school, *finished high school*, or had *some schooling past high school?*

| LESS THAN 1. SEVEN YEARS | BETWEEN SEVEN 2. AND TWELVE YEARS | FINISHED 3. HIGH SCHOOL | SOME SCHOOLING 4. PAST HIGH SCHOOL |

N14.   INTERVIEWER CHECKPOINT

N9–N13 WERE ASKED ABOUT:

☐ 1. R'S FATHER
  ☐ 2. OTHER MALE HEAD
    ☐ 3. OTHER FEMALE HEAD
      ☐ 4. R'S MOTHER ──→ TURN TO N17

N15.   Other than being a housewife, did your mother have a job while you were growing up?

1. YES   5. NO

N16.   What was the highest grade of school or year of college *your mother* completed?

GRADES OF SCHOOL													COLLEGE				
00	01	02	03	04	05	06	07	08	09	10	11	12	13	14	15	16	17+

TURN TO N17

DON'T KNOW

N16a.   Would you guess that she had *less than seven years* of school, *between seven and twelve years* of school, *finished high school*, or had *some schooling past high school?*

| LESS THAN 1. SEVEN YEARS | BETWEEN SEVEN 2. AND TWELVE YEARS | FINISHED 3. HIGH SCHOOL | SOME SCHOOLING 4. PAST HIGH SCHOOL |

#N17.   What is the highest grade of school or year of college you have completed?

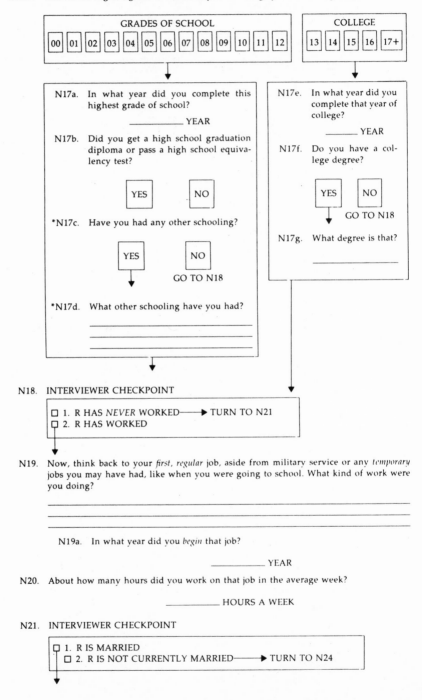

GRADES OF SCHOOL	COLLEGE
00 01 02 03 04 05 06 07 08 09 10 11 12	13 14 15 16 17+

N17a.   In what year did you complete this highest grade of school?

_____ YEAR

N17b.   Did you get a high school graduation diploma or pass a high school equivalency test?

YES   NO

*N17c. Have you had any other schooling?

YES   NO

GO TO N18

*N17d. What other schooling have you had?

_____
_____
_____

N17e.   In what year did you complete that year of college?

_____ YEAR

N17f.   Do you have a college degree?

YES   NO

GO TO N18

N17g.   What degree is that?

_____

N18.   INTERVIEWER CHECKPOINT

☐ 1. R HAS *NEVER* WORKED ——► TURN TO N21
☐ 2. R HAS WORKED

N19.   Now, think back to your *first, regular* job, aside from military service or any *temporary* jobs you may have had, like when you were going to school. What kind of work were you doing?

_____
_____
_____

N19a.   In what year did you *begin* that job?

_____ YEAR

N20.   About how many hours did you work on that job in the average week?

_____ HOURS A WEEK

N21.   INTERVIEWER CHECKPOINT

☐ 1. R IS MARRIED
☐ 2. R IS NOT CURRENTLY MARRIED ——► TURN TO N24

N22. And what is the highest grade of school or year of college your (husband/wife) has completed?

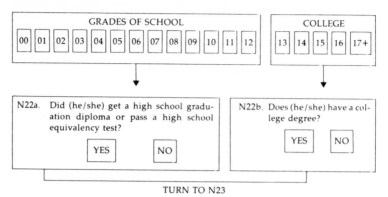

GRADES OF SCHOOL	COLLEGE
00 01 02 03 04 05 06 07 08 09 10 11 12	13 14 15 16 17+

N22a. Did (he/she) get a high school graduation diploma or pass a high school equivalency test?

YES   NO

N22b. Does (he/she) have a college degree?

YES   NO

TURN TO N23

#N23. Is your (husband/wife) doing any work for pay at the present time?

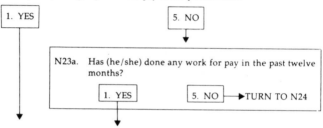

1. YES   5. NO

N23a. Has (he/she) done any work for pay in the past twelve months?

1. YES   5. NO → TURN TO N24

*N23b. What kind of work (does/did) (he/she) do? (What [is/was] [his/her] main occupation?)

_____

#N23c. Please tell me a little more about what (he/she) (does/did) on (his/her) job.

_____

_____

#N23d. What kind of (business/industry) is that?

_____

N23e. (Does/Did) (he/she) work for (himself/herself) or for someone else?

1. SELF-EMPLOYED   2. SOMEONE ELSE

(IF R IS *MALE* WITH CHILD(REN) UNDER 12 LIVING IN HOUSEHOLD)
N23f. How (are the children/is the child) taken care of while your wife is at work?

_____

_____

N23g. (IF R MENTIONS IN SCHOOL *ONLY*) What about the time ([he/she] isn't/ they aren't) in school?

_____

_____

#N24. (CARD T) In this survey of people all over the country, we are trying to get a clear picture of people's financial situations. Taking into consideration all sources of income, about what do you think your total income will be this year (1976) for yourself and your immediate family? Just give me the letter on the card.

01	A. LESS THAN $1,000	07	G. $6,000–$6,999	13	M. $12,500–$14,999
02	B. $1,000–$1,999	08	H. $7,000–$7,999	14	N. $15,000–$17,499
03	C. $2,000–$2,999	09	I. $8,000–$8,999	15	O. $17,500–$19,999
04	D. $3,000–$3,999	10	J. $9,000–$9,999	16	P. $20,000–$24,999
05	E. $4,000–$4,999	11	K. $10,000–$10,999	17	Q. $25,000–$34,999
06	F. $5,000–$5,999	12	L. $11,000–$12,499	18	R. $35,000 AND OVER

N25. (CARD T) How much of this total will you yourself earn this year? (Just give me the letter on the card.)

01	A	04	D	07	G	10	J	13	M	16	P
02	B	05	E	08	H	11	K	14	N	17	Q
03	C	06	F	09	I	12	L	15	O	18	R

#N26. Is your current religious preference Protestant, Roman Catholic, Jewish or something else?

PROTESTANT	200. ROMAN CATHOLIC	300. JEWISH	800. NONE, NO PREFERENCE	OTHER: SPECIFY _____

TURN TO N27

#N26a. What church or denomination is that? _____

*N27. About how often do you usually attend religious services?

1. MORE THAN ONCE A WEEK	2. ONCE A WEEK	3. TWO OR THREE TIMES A MONTH	4. ONCE A MONTH	5. A FEW TIMES A YEAR OR LESS	6. NEVER

N28. How long have you lived in (INSERT NAME OF PRESENT COMMUNITY OR OF TOWNSHIP IF RURAL)_____ ? (IF LESS THAN TWO YEARS, GET NUMBER OF MONTHS.)

_____ YEARS _____ MONTHS, OR SINCE: _____

N29. And finally, how many telephones, counting extensions, do you have in your (house/apartment)?

0	1	2	3	4	5	MORE THAN 5, SPECIFY _____

TIME NOW _____

This completes the interview. Thank you very much for your help. When we have finished this survey we would like to send you some of our findings as a way of thanking you for your time. (HAND R A REPORT REQUEST CARD AND EXPLAIN ITS USE. BE SURE TO WRITE IN "MODERN LIVING" AS THE PROJECT.) We may also want to come back in a few months to talk with you or another member of your family to see if any of your opinions or your situation have changed.

Section S: Interviewer Observation

*S1. Respondent's sex is: | 1. MALE | 2. FEMALE |

#S2. Respondent's racial or ethnic group is:

| 1. WHITE | 2. BLACK | 3. ORIENTAL | 4. CHICANO; PUERTO RICAN; MEXICAN- OR SPANISH-AMERICAN |

| 5. AMERICAN INDIAN | OTHER (SPECIFY): _____ |

S3. Other persons present at interview were (CHECK MORE THAN ONE BOX IF NECESSARY):

| NONE | CHILDREN UNDER 6 | OLDER CHILDREN | SPOUSE | OTHER RELATIVES | OTHER ADULTS |

GO TO S5

S4. How much do you feel the presence of other person(s) influenced the answers given by respondent?

| 1. A GREAT DEAL | 2. SOME | 3. VERY LITTLE | 4. NONE |

#S5. Overall, how great was R's interest in the interview?

| 1. VERY HIGH | 2. ABOVE AVERAGE | 3. AVERAGE | 4. BELOW AVERAGE | 5. VERY LOW |

S6. Did the respondent seem to find the interview too long?

| 1. YES | 5. NO |

S7. Type of structure in which family lives?

| 01. TRAILER |

| 02. DETACHED SINGLE FAMILY HOUSE |

| 03. 2-FAMILY HOUSE, 2 UNITS SIDE BY SIDE |

| 04. 2-FAMILY HOUSE, 2 UNITS ONE ABOVE THE OTHER |

| 05. DETACHED 3-4 FAMILY HOUSE |

| 06. ROW HOUSE (3 OR MORE UNITS IN AN ATTACHED ROW) |

07. APARTMENT HOUSE (5 OR MORE UNITS, 3 STORIES OR LESS)

08. APARTMENT HOUSE (5 OR MORE UNITS, 4 STORIES OR MORE)

09. APARTMENT IN A PARTLY COMMERCIAL STRUCTURE

10. OTHER: _____
    (SPECIFY)

S8. Number of stories in the structure, not counting basement:

    [1] [2] [3] MORE THAN 3: _____
                              (SPECIFY)

S9. COPY INFORMATION FROM COVER SHEET

	*(a) Household member by relationship to Head	(b) Sex	(c) Age	(e) Enter "R" to Identify Respondent
PERSONS 21 YEARS OR OLDER				
PERSONS UNDER 21				

S10. *THUMBNAIL SKETCH:*

Appendix B

SAMPLE DESIGN
AND SAMPLING
VARIABILITY

SAMPLE DESIGNS FOR THE 1957 AND 1976 SURVEYS

The sample designs for the two surveys have a high degree of correspondence, each being a national multistage, area probability sample of housing units and adults at a particular time. Each is a study of persons twenty-one years of age or older living in housing units within the coterminous United States, exclusive of housing units on military reservations.[1] In the first stage of sampling, the two studies included the twelve major metropolitan areas of the United States in addition to a selection of other metropolitan areas and nonmetropolitan counties or county groups. The samples progressed along the same path of stratification and selection from the first to the final stage of

[1] In both surveys, the Survey Research Center used the dwelling unit definition formulated by the U.S. Bureau of the Census and reported in *1950 Census of Housing*, Vol. I, Part I, Washington, D.C.: U.S. Government Printing Office, 1953, p. XVI. Persons living in a dwelling unit comprise a household. Persons in nondwelling unit quarters—such as large rooming houses, residential clubs, transient accomodations, barracks for workers, accommodations for inmates of institutions, and general hospitals—were excluded from both studies.

sampling. In the last two stages, clusters of approximately four housing units were identified, and from each sample household one eligible person was objectively selected to be interviewed (Kish, 1949). If,
after repeated calls, no one was at home or the designated respondent
was not at home or refused to be interviewed, no substitution was
made. Further details of the sample designs are presented by Gurin et
al. (1960) and Kish and Hess (1965) for the 1957 and 1976 surveys,
respectively.

Differences in the two samples occur in both the number of sample
areas and in the number of designated respondents. For the 1957 survey, the metropolitan areas and counties, exclusive of the twelve major
areas, were assigned to fifty-four strata, while in 1976 that number was
increased to sixty-two. Each stratum was represented by one primary
area selected with probability proportionate to the population reported in the preceding census, bringing the total number of sample areas
to sixty-six in 1957 and to seventy-four in 1976. Thirty of the fifty-four
primary areas in the 1957 sample were also in the 1976 sample. The
remainder of the study population was represented by twenty-four
sample areas in 1957 and thirty-two in 1976. Population growth over
the two decades explains in part the rationale for increasing the number of sample areas. A further consideration was to effect some improvement in the precision of regional estimates from the Survey Research Center sample. The 1957 survey was designed to yield about
2,500 interviews, the second survey about 2,300 respondents. The
overall sampling rates for housing units were one in 16,360 for the
first study and one in 20,960 for the second. The achieved numbers of
interviews were 2,460 in 1957 and 2,264 in 1976, with response rates of
84 and 71 percent, respectively.

Although each household had an equal chance of selection into the
sample, adults within households had different probabilities of selection according to the number of eligible persons within the household. That is, the chance of a person being selected for interview was
inversely proportional to the number of eligible household members.
Thus, to counter the biasing effects of these inequalities, data for each
respondent should be weighted by the number of eligible persons in
the housing unit. However, the use of such variable weights to calculate sample estimates increases the complexities of data processing to
some degree, and experience has shown that the preponderance of
dwellings with one to three eligible members (and particularly those
with two eligible members) is so large that weighted results generally
closely resemble unweighted results.

As a precaution in this study, however, both weighted and unweighted estimates for a number of variables of primary importance to
the research were examined. Specifically, weighted and unweighted
percentage distributions for the twenty-four subjective adjustment
measures selected for demographic analysis in chapter 8 in Book 1

were compared for both the 1957 and 1976 samples. In all cases, differences between weighted and unweighted percentages are well within sampling error, usually differing by less than one percentage point. Although similar coxmparisons on demographic variables (such as those presented in table 1.1 in chapter 1) yield somewhat larger differences, estimation of distributions on such variables was not a primary goal of the research. Consequently, the bias resulting from the use of unweighted data was judged to be negligible, and all analyses presented in this report are based on unweighted data.

SAMPLING ERROR

Errors in Sample Survey Estimates

Properly conducted, sample interview surveys yield useful estimates, but they do not yield exact values. Errors and biases arise from several sources. These include sampling errors and nonsampling errors, which in turn include interviewer errors and biases, response errors, nonresponse bias, and processing errors. By design, sampling variability can be estimated from the sample data. Other types of errors are not as readily recognized and measured. Even though data collection procedures can be designed to measure interviewer variability, that type of design is infrequently employed and was not a part of these surveys. Comparisons with estimates from other sources, or record checks, may reveal the magnitude of response errors. While nonresponse (failure to obtain an interview with a designed respondent) can be counted, the effects often remain unknown.

With some types of sample estimates, such as aggregates, it is essential to make adjustments for missing data in order to avoid serious underestimates of population totals or to avoid distorted estimates of the distribution of the population by economic and demographic variables. When attitudes and opinions are the primary research interest, however, frequently little is known about population parameters, and researchers have been reluctant to assume that nonrespondents share the same opinions and attitudes as their responding neighbors. Therefore, data in this report were not adjusted for total or item nonresponse.

Factors Affecting the Size of Sampling Errors

If a list of all household members meeting criteria for eligibility had been available and a simple random sample of those persons had been selected, the calculation of sampling errors would be greatly simplified. When simple random sampling has been used to choose respondents, the sampling error of estimated percentages depends on two major factors: the magnitude of the percentage and the number of respondents. Since a simple random sample of eligible persons could not be achieved, the samples were clustered in a limited number of geographic locations. This clustering lowers data collection costs but yields higher sampling errors than a simple random sample would yield. At the same time, the 1957 and 1976 samples were both highly stratified—a technique that tends to lower sampling errors. Moreover, some variables of research interest may not be evenly distributed among eligible persons, so in some cases the sample may have too many or too few of certain classes of respondents.

The formulas used to calculate sampling errors for this report take into consideration the various factors affecting the precision of sample estimates (Kish and Hess, 1965). All of the factors affect the final outcome of sample estimates and their sampling errors in unknown ways. Therefore, it must be recognized that values presented in tables B.1 and B.2 offer guidance to the interpretation of sampling error but do not give the exact sampling error for a specific percentage or percentage difference.

Estimating Sampling Error of Percentages

This discussion is limited to sampling errors of percentages because many survey findings are presented as percentages, and their sampling errors are more easily summarized than the sampling errors of more complex estimates. If the latter are required, it is best to calculate the sampling variability of the particular estimates being analyzed.

Sample statistics reflect random variations which arise in interviewing only a fraction of the population. The distribution of individuals selected for a sample will usually differ from that of the population. As a result, the proportion of respondents having a given attitude, opinion, or some other characteristic will usually be somewhat larger or smaller, by an unknown amount, than the population value—the values that would have been obtained if the entire population had been interviewed using the same survey instrument and data collection procedures during the same time period. The population value

TABLE B.1
Approximate Sampling Errors of Percentages[a] (in percentages)

Reported Percentages	Number of Interviews												
	2,500	2,250	2,000	1,750	1,500	1,250	1,000	750	500	400	300	200	100
50	2.4	2.5	2.6	2.8	3.0	3.2	3.5	3.9	4.8	5.2	5.9	7.1	9.8
30 or 70	2.2	2.3	2.4	2.6	2.7	2.9	3.2	3.6	4.4	4.8	5.4	6.5	9.0
20 or 80	1.9	2.0	2.1	2.2	2.4	2.5	2.8	3.2	3.8	4.2	4.7	5.7	7.8
10 or 90	1.4	1.5	1.6	1.7	1.8	1.9	2.1	2.4	2.9	3.1	3.5	4.3	5.9
5 or 95	1.1	1.1	1.2	1.2	1.3	1.4	1.5	1.7	2.1	2.3	2.6	3.1	4.3

[a] The figures in this table represent *two* standard errors. Hence, for most items the chances are 95 in 100 that the value being estimated lies within a range equal to the reported percentage, plus or minus the sampling error.

TABLE B.2

Approximate Sampling Errors of Difference[a] (in percentages)

Size of Subgroups	For Percentages from 35 percent to 65 percent								
	2,000	1,500	1,000	700	500	400	300	200	100
2,000	3.6	3.9	4.3	4.8	5.4	5.8	6.4	7.5	10.1
1,500		4.2	4.6	5.0	5.6	6.0	6.6	7.7	10.2
1,000			4.9	5.4	5.9	6.3	6.8	7.9	10.4
700				5.8	6.3	6.6	7.2	8.2	10.6
500					6.7	7.1	7.6	8.6	10.9
400						7.4	7.9	8.8	11.1
300							8.3	9.2	11.4
200								10.0	12.1
100									13.9

Size of Subgroups	For Percentages around 20 percent to 80 percent								
2,000	2.9	3.1	3.4	3.8	4.3	4.6	5.1	6.0	8.1
1,500		3.3	3.7	4.0	4.5	4.8	5.3	6.2	8.2
1,000			4.0	4.3	4.7	5.0	5.5	6.3	8.3
700				4.6	5.0	5.3	5.7	6.6	8.5
500					5.4	5.6	6.1	6.8	8.7
400						5.9	6.3	7.0	8.9
300							6.7	7.3	9.1
200								8.0	9.7
100									11.1

Size of Subgroups	For Percentages around 10 percent to 90 percent								
2,000	2.1	2.3	2.6	2.9	3.2	3.5	3.8	4.5	6.1
1,500		2.5	2.7	3.0	3.4	3.6	4.0	4.6	6.1
1,000			3.0	3.2	3.5	3.8	4.1	4.8	6.2
700				3.5	3.8	4.0	4.3	4.9	6.4
500					4.0	4.2	4.5	5.1	6.5
400						4.4	4.7	5.3	6.7
300							5.0	5.5	6.9
200								6.0	7.3
100									8.3

Size of Subgroups	For Percentages around 5 percent to 95 percent								
2,000	1.6	1.7	1.9	2.1	2.3	2.5	2.8	3.3	4.4
1,500		1.8	2.0	2.2	2.4	2.6	2.9	3.4	4.5
1,000			2.2	2.3	2.6	2.7	3.0	3.5	4.5
700				2.5	2.7	2.9	3.1	3.6	4.6
500					2.9	3.1	3.3	3.7	4.8
400						3.2	3.4	3.8	4.8
300							3.6	4.0	5.0
200								4.4	5.3
100									6.0

[a] The values shown are the differences required for significance (two standard errors) in comparisons of percentages derived from two different surveys and from two different subgroups of the same survey.

may differ from the "true value" because of nonsampling errors which would affect an attempt at complete enumeration as well as a sample survey.

The sampling error is a measure of the expected variation of a sample statistic from the corresponding population value. It does not measure the actual error of a particular estimate but leads to statements in terms of confidence intervals that are correct in a specified proportion of cases over the long run. The estimates of sampling errors presented in table B.1 are *two standard errors*, a measure frequently chosen in social research to obtain a 95 percent level of confidence. A statement that the range of sampling error on either side of the sample value includes the population value will be correct 95 times out of 100 in the long run and incorrect 5 times out of 100. If a greater degree of confidence is required, a wider range should be used. Most of the time, however, the actual error of sampling will be less than the sampling error just described. In about 68 cases out of every 100, a range of one-half of the sampling error on either side of the sample estimate can be expected to include the population value.

To illustrate, the survey estimate that 25 percent of the 578 low-income people in 1976 had sought professional help for a personal problem is subject to a sampling error of about 3.9 (by interpolation from table B.1). Thus, the statement that the interval 21.1 to 28.9 percent includes the population value has 95 in 100 chances of being correct. The chances are 68 in 100 that the range 23.0 to 27.0 percent includes the population value. It is impractical to calculate the sampling error for every sample estimate when there are hundreds of such statistics. Hence, the sampling errors presented in table B.1 are average values derived from a large number of calculations for the two samples taken in 1957 and 1976. Some of the survey statistics calculated had larger and some had smaller sampling errors than those shown in the table. The estimates of sampling errors themselves are subject to the vagaries of sampling. Therefore, the approximate sampling errors provided in table B.1 should be regarded as just that—approximations. If more precise estimates of sampling error are required, calculations of sampling error should be made for the specific statistic. In particular, regional estimates and those for domains that concentrate in a limited number of primary areas, standard metropolitan sampling areas (SMSA's) or non-SMSA's may be subject to higher sampling errors than those presented in table B.1. Special calculations could be made for such estimates.

Sampling Error of Differences

Of greater interest than the sampling error of percentages is the sampling error of the differences between percentages for two different surveys or from two different subgroups of the same survey. Factors affecting individual percentages affect their differences in a similar but more complex manner. The sampling errors of many comparisons within each of the surveys and between the two surveys were calculated using formulas that take those complexities into account (Kish and Hess, 1965). The average values given in table B.2 may be used for either type of comparison, although, on the basis of comparisons made in this and some previous studies conducted at the Survey Research Center, there is a tendency for sampling errors of year-to-year differences in the same group (for example, men) to be somewhat smaller than those applicable to differences between two groups from the same survey (for example, men and women). The table is not appropriate when overlapping subgroups (the same respondents appearing in both subgroups) are compared. The sampling error of that kind of estimate may be calculated, however, when the need is established.

An illustration may aid in understanding table B.2 and its uses. Let us suppose that we are interested in the difference between the 25 percent of 578 low-income people in 1976 and the 11 percent of 666 poor adults in 1957 who had sought professional help for a personal problem. By inspecting the section of table B.2 for percentages around 20 percent and locating the intersection of the row for 700 and the column for 500, we see that the average sampling error (two standard errors) is 5.0 percent. Since the observed difference of 14 percent far exceeds the average sampling error, we may confidently say the chances are at least 95 in 100 that in the population as a whole, and not only for our samples, low-income people in 1976 were substantially more likely to have sought professional help than were poorer adults in 1957.

Appendix C

STRATEGIES OF MULTIVARIATE ANALYSIS

THROUGHOUT THIS BOOK, log-linear and hierarchical models, as described by Goodman (1978) and others (Bishop, Fienberg, and Holland, 1975; Davis, 1974; Fienberg, 1977; Reynolds, 1977), are routinely used for significance tests in multivariate contingency tables, most commonly in multivariate analyses involving sex, age, education, and year—the standard filter or control variables used to differentiate respondents in each chapter of the book. Our use of log-linear analysis in this regard follows the general lead of Davis (1975) and the Duncans (Duncan, 1975; Duncan and Duncan, 1978; Duncan and Evers, 1975), who demonstrate the substantial analytic rigor to be gained by using log-linear models for studying social change by survey replication.

In the current research, our choice of the log-linear approach was guided by two major considerations. First, log-linear and hierarchical models represent a powerful system of novel techniques for analyzing *qualitative* or *categorical* data, and *Americans View Their Mental Health* (perhaps to a greater extent than any national survey conducted either before or since) is almost entirely an investigation of categorical data, since it relies heavily on open-ended questions or codes and a concomitant presentation of results in both bivariate and multivariate contingency tables.

Second, the log-linear analysis approach is especially well suited to address several key multivariate research questions of particular interest in the replication study. As noted by Davis (1974), the system provides at least three important significance tests not previously readily available to the average researcher: (1) tests for the significance of a partial association (e.g., whether or not a year difference vanishes when education is controlled), regardless of the number of categories or level of measurement in the associated variables or controls; (2) a test for the significance of interactions (specifications) where the control variable has many categories, including higher-order interactions involving a combination of control variables; and (3) general significance tests which permit relatively succinct statements about the structure and nature of relationships in a multivariate contingency table, including tests of significance for log-linear effect coefficients corresponding to specific cells in a table. Hence, log-linear and hierarchical models are especially useful for answering questions such as: (1) to what extent are significant changes in attitudes, behaviors, and characteristics observed between the two survey years due to shifts in demographic characteristics (e.g., age and education) of the population over that period; (2) to what extent do such changes vary in intensity within various population (e.g., educational) subgroups; and (3) to what extent have there been significant changes in the nature or strength of relationships between the two survey years (e.g., are various significant subgroups of the population becoming more or less alike in their attitudes and behaviors)?

Based on its capacity to address these major analytic questions, it is perhaps not surprising that log-linear hierarchical modeling systems have gradually emerged as a favored means of analyzing qualitative data in survey replications (see, however, Davis, 1975; Grizzle, Starmer, and Koch, 1969). Nevertheless, the development of log-linear analysis has been far from a one-man effort, a factor which has predictably resulted in substantial differences in both notation and strategy. In general, the statistical analyses described in this research follow the Goodman (1978) system, using the ECTA computer program developed and distributed by Fay and Goodman, but even among those using the Goodman system, there are important differences in strategy, interpretation, and presentation, and the present research is no exception. Consequently, this appendix will illustrate the specific log-linear hierarchical analysis strategies used in this research by providing several examples of the types of analyses used throughout the book so that the interested reader may better understand the analytic assumptions which underlie the major multivariate conclusions stated in the text. For a detailed and comprehensive exposition of the fundamental concepts and techniques underlying the Goodman system (including alternative analytic strategies), the reader is referred to the literature cited previously.

Central to the log-linear method is a sequential modeling process, by which the researcher attempts to explain what is going on in a multiway contingency table. Based on hypotheses about the relationships among variables in the table, the researcher employs an iterative procedure to calculate maximum likelihood estimates of the expected frequencies in each cell of the table. The process involves a series of decisions which ultimately permit determining which dimensions of a contingency table (e.g., relationships among variables) are necessary and sufficient to reproduce the observed cell frequencies; i.e., how much a given table can be collapsed without sacrificing important information. The maximum likelihood-ratio chi-square ($LR\chi^2$) statistic is used to assess the goodness of fit between cell frequencies expected under a given model and those actually observed. A nonsignificant (e.g., $p > .05$) $LR\chi^2$, indicating little discrepancy between expected and observed frequencies, implies that a model fits the data well. By deriving a "best-fitting" model for a given table, researchers are able to determine which of several possible relationships represented in the table must be taken into account in order to explain the data structure; or, more specifically, whether an effect of interest is included in that model.

Although several basic approaches for selecting a "best-fitting" model (i.e., a model which most accurately and parsimoniously fits the structure of data in a contingency table) have been proposed in the literature, the basic selection strategies used in this research involve a "bracketing" process, whereby researchers fit models of uniform order (e.g., all marginal [univariate], all bivariate, or all trivariate relationships) to find a model with terms of r-1 that fits the data poorly (i.e., yields a significant $LR\chi^2$) and a model with terms of order r that fits the data too well (i.e., yields a nonsignificant $LR\chi^2$ and has several unnecessary parameters).[1]

Under the assumption that the simplest, best-fitting model falls somewhere within the region bracketed by these two models which do and do not fit the data well (since the bracketing process tells us that at least one r-level effect but no effect more complex than level r is needed to describe cell frequencies), one then employs either a forward (stepwise-up) selection procedure, whereby one adds terms one at a time to the model with terms r-1 until the model fits, or a backward (stepwise-down) elimination of redundant terms from the model

---

[1]For example, for a given table with three or more variables, a model containing all third-order (trivariate) terms (i.e., all interactions of variables taken three at a time) might fit the data too well (e.g., $p > .25$), while a model with all second-order (bivariate) terms (all associations between variables taken two at a time) yields a significant difference between observed frequencies and those expected under the model.

with terms of order *r* until no more terms can be excluded without significantly decreasing the fit, or a combination of both, to find an intermediate model containing one or more terms of order *r*. Once no more terms of order *r* can be added or deleted, a similar stepwise-down procedure is executed to insure that no effects of order *r*-1 or *r*-2 are unnecessary.

In this research, both forward selection and backward elimination procedures were used in model fitting, generally in combination. In addition, two possible criteria of "fit" were employed: one absolute and one relative. Under the first criterion, a model was said to fit if the discrepancy between the model and actual data was not statistically significant at a prespecified alpha level, arbitrarily chosen at .05 for this study. A second criterion emphasizes instead significant improvement or reduction in fit compared with a base model, based on a test of significance for the difference between likelihood-ratio chi-square statistics for the two models in question, again with an alpha level set at .05. Under the first criterion, terms are added until researchers obtain a model yielding a $LR\chi^2$ greater than .05 or deleted until the associated $LR\chi^2$ drops below .05. Under the second criterion, however, terms that result in a significant improvement in fit ($p < .05$) over a base model are sequentially added, even after achieving a model with a $LR\chi^2$ greater than .05, until no further terms can be added that produce a significant improvement in fit, or, in a stepwise-down procedure, are deleted until no further terms can be eliminated without resulting in a significant reduction in fit.

Regardless of how a best-fitting model is derived, however, for most survey data analyses it is necessary to supplement these basic significance tests used in model selection with some additional tests of significance and descriptive statistics to simplify the interpretation of statistical findings based on log-linear analysis. In essence, the model-fitting process alerts us to the existence of statistically significant effects, but tells us nothing about the nature, direction, or magnitude of those relationships. To aid in our interpretation of complex multivariate tables, log-linear effect coefficients—equivalent to Goodman's (1978) lambdas (λ) and taus (τ) and Fienberg's (1977) "u-terms" were computed for each final model using the ECTA program. Since these log-linear effect coefficients are similar to analysis of variance effects, we are able to test whether they are statistically different from zero. By attending to the pattern of statistically significant λ coefficients associated with a given relationship, we are better able to describe the direction of that association, or, in the case of a higher-order interaction, we are better able to specify the precise nature of that interaction.

However, even these statistics are limited in their capacity to convey the magnitude of these relationships (cf. Page, 1977). The particular utility of calculating and interpreting odds ratios—to which log-linear effect coefficients bear a direct functional relationship—for that purpose has been amply demonstrated by Page (1977) and Duncan and Duncan (1978). However, in the interest of continuity with the previous reporting of the 1957 data (Gurin, Veroff, and Feld, 1960), we decided to provide conventional percentage tables rather than adopt the odds ratio approach.

Let us turn now to some specific examples of our use of log-linear and hierarchical models for multivariate contingency table analysis in this book. Basically, three distinct types of analysis were conducted: (1) five-variable log-linear analyses of the cross-classification of key dependent measures in each chapter by sex, age, education, and year (except for measures assessed only in 1976, which reduced the problem to a four-dimension cross-classification); (2) three-variable analyses of the cross-classification of multiple indicators of subjective mental health and selected social characteristics by year; and (3) six-variable analyses of the cross-classifications of these same indicators of subjective adjustment and selected social characteristics by sex, age, education, and year.

Example 1: A Five-Variable Table

Table C.1 presents the results of the log-linear analysis of the classification of readiness for self-referral (R) by sex (S), age (A), education (E), and year (Y). All models assume (R) as the dependent variable and thereby routinely fit the marginals (SAEY), the relationships among all independent variables. The purpose here in finding a best-fitting model is to ascertain whether sex, age, education, and year differences in readiness for self-referral, or higher order interactions among these predictors, are necessary to describe adequately the pattern of frequencies in a cross-classification table of these variables. In general, the criterion of selection in these tables is the most parsimonious model (over and above a base model which includes all relationships among the independent variables) which generates expected frequencies which do not significantly deviate from those actually observed (e.g., yields a LRχ^2 with $p > .05$).

We first present the models with terms of uniform order used to bracket models with terms of r (in this case the model which includes all bivariate relationships involving R) and r-1 (a model including only the univariate marginal for R). Next, by backward (step-wise down) elimination we tried to eliminate terms of order r (bivariates) one at a time to determine which if any terms were expendable. Having established that none of the bivariate terms could be omitted without falling below our prespecified criterion, the model including all bivariate relationsips involving (R) could have been designated "best-

TABLE C.1

*Log-Linear Hierarchical Models of Effects of Sex (S),
Age (A), Education (E), and Year (Y) on
"Readiness for Self-Referral" (R)*

Fitted Models (all include SAEY)	$LR\chi^2$	df	p
1. (R)	641.01	175	.000
2. (RS) (RA) (RE) (RY)	168.16	145	.091
3. (RS) (RA) (RE)	267.27	150	.000
4. (RS) (RA) (RY)	252.83	155	.000
5. (RS) (RE) (RY)	291.11	155	.000
6. (RA) (RE) (RY)	232.25	150	.000
7. (RSA) (RE) (RY)	163.52	135	.048
8. (RSE) (RS) (RY)	152.78	135	.141
9. (RSY) (RA) (RE)	165.58	140	.069
10. (RAE) (RS) (RY)	154.22	125	.039
11. (RAY) (RS) (RE)	152.66	135	.142
12. (REY) (RS) (RA)	142.14	135	.320
13. (REY) (RA)	206.39	140	.000
14. (REY) (RS)	264.49	145	.000
Differences			
$\chi^2(H_2)-\chi^2(H_7)$	4.64	10	$p>.50$
$\chi^2(H_2)-\chi^2(H_8)$	15.38	10	$p>.10$
$\chi^2(H_2)-\chi^2(H_9)$	2.58	5	$p>.50$
$\chi^2(H_2)-\chi^2(H_{10})$	13.94	20	$p>.50$
$\chi^2(H_2)-\chi^2(H_{11})$	15.50	10	$p>.10$
$\chi^2(H_2)-\chi^2(H_{12})$	26.02	10	$p<.005$
$\chi^2(H_{12})-\chi^2(H_{13})$	64.25	5	$p<.001$
$\chi^2(H_{12})-\chi^2(H_{14})$	122.35	10	$p<.001$

fitting model." However, because that model did not really fit the observed data very well ($p < .09$) and because previous analyses had suggested the presence of an education X year interaction on readiness for self-referral, four additional models adding terms of order $r+1$ (three variable interactions) one at a time were fitted to determine whether any of these resulted in a significant improvement in fit over the base model. Finally, having established that one (and only one) such model did in fact result in a significant improvement in fit, two additional models, each omitting one of the remaining bivariate relationships, were fitted to determine whether or not they remained really necessary.

The best-fitting model derived from this process is (REY) (RS) (RA), indicating that sex and age are both significantly related to readiness for self-referral independent of education and year, while the relationship of education to readiness differs significantly by year (or, alternatively, year changes in self-referral differ significantly by education).

TABLE C.2

Estimates of Log-Linear Parameters (λs) Describing the Effects of Sex (S), Age (A), Education (E), and Year (Y) on "Readiness for Self-Referral (R)[a]

Predictor	Readiness for Self-Referral					
	Has Used Help	Could Have Used Help	Might Need Help	Self-Help	Strong Self-Help	Not Ascertained
Sex						
Male[b]	−.200[d]	−.120	−.008	.106[d]	.175[e]	.047
	(.048)[c]	(.065)	(.041)	(.038)	(.068)	(.074)
Age						
21–34	.152[e]	.349[d]	.054	−.039	−.360[d]	−.156
	(.073)	(.096)	(.064)	(.058)	(.110)	(.113)
35–54	.219[d]	−.003	.013	−.108	−.023	−.098
	(.061)	(.087)	(.055)	(.051)	(.090)	(.099)
55 and over	−.371[d]	−.346[d]	−.067	.147[d]	.383[d]	.255[e]
	(.069)	(.093)	(.056)	(.051)	(.087)	(.100)
Education						
Grade School	−.373[d]	−.260	−.070	.107	.254[e]	.342[d]
	(.078)	(.108)	(.067)	(.060)	(.108)	(.111)
High School	−.016	.060	−.088	−.014	.072	−.015
	(.058)	(.077)	(.050)	(.045)	(.079)	(.087)
College	.389[d]	.199[e]	.158[d]	−.093	−.326[d]	−.327[d]
	(.065)	(.089)	(.057)	(.054)	(.099)	(.112)
Year						
1957[b]	−.298[d]	.005	.118[d]	.074[e]	.151[e]	−.050
	(.048)	(.065)	(.041)	(.038)	(.068)	(.074)
Education × Year (1957[b])						
Grade School	−.171[e]	.259[e]	−.048	−.131[e]	.045	.045
	(.078)	(.108)	(.067)	(.060)	(.108)	(.111)
High School	−.001	−.139	−.004	−.008	.102	.049
	(.058)	(.077)	(.050)	(.045)	(.079)	(.087)
College	.172[d]	−.120	.051	.139[c]	−.147	−.094
	(.065)	(.089)	(.057)	(.054)	(.099)	(.112)

[a] Based on best-fitting model from table C.1: (REY) (RS) (RA) (SAEY).

[b] Since sex and year are two-level variables, parameter estimates for females and 1976 respondents are identical to those for males and 1957 respondents, but opposite in sign.

[c] Numbers in parentheses are standard errors of the lambda coefficients.

[d] $p < .01$.

[e] $p < .05$.

Having established the significance to these main and interactive effects of sex, age, education, and year on readiness for self-referral, log-linear effect parameter estimates for this best-fitting model (H_{12}) were computed and examined to determine the precise nature or direction of these significant effects. Table C.2 presents estimates of Goodman's lambda (λ) parameters and their standard errors for each of the effects included in that model.

These results, which are presented in table 5.5 of chapter 5, indicate that: (1) men are less likely to seek professional help and more likely to adopt a self-help position than women; (2) young people are more likely to consult a professional and less likely to endorse self-help than older adults; (3) grade school-educated people are less likely to seek formal help (and, parenthetically, more likely to be "not ascertained" on this measure) than the college educated; and (4) adults in 1957 were less likely to use formal help for a personal problem than men and women in 1976. The main effects for education and year must be qualified, however, because they are couched within a significant education × year interaction, which indicates that these main effects are conditional. Throughout this book such main effects are reported and interpreted only when the lambda coefficients corresponding to these relationships are statistically significant at the .01 level, a criterion which is met by each of these effects. In addition, however, the parameters describing a significant education × year interaction in table C.2 reflect (as noted in chapter 5) that: (1) the relationship between education and having actually gone for help is significantly weaker in 1976 than in 1957; while (2) the gap between grade school- and college-educated adults in assuming a self-help position is wider in 1976 than in 1957.

Example 2: A Three-Variable Table

Two other types of log-linear analyses were used primarily in relating several subjective adjustment and sociodemographic variables to readiness for self-referral and stages of self-referral. Multivariate analyses of these variables proceeded in two distinct stages: (1) a three-variable analysis of the cross-classification of the help-seeking variable of interest by an adjustment indicator or social characteristic and year, to determine whether the relationship between that indicator or characteristic and help-seeking differed significantly by year; and (2) a six-variable analysis of these same three variables along with sex, age, education and year, to assess whether or not the basic bivariate relationship persists when the latter predictors are controlled and/or whether such relationships differ significantly by sex, age, education, and year (this time with the other predictors held constant).

An example of the first type of analysis is shown in table C.3, which presents the results of a three-variable log-linear analysis of the cross-classification of use of help (among those defining a problem in mental health terms) by family income and year. In this case, a model which includes all bivariate relationships (notably those between use of help and income and year, respectively) generates frequencies which differ significantly from those observed, implying that a year ×

TABLE C.3
Log-Linear Hierarchical Models of
Effects of Income (I) and Year (Y) on
"Use of Help Among Those Defining a
Problem in Mental Health Terms" (U)

Fitted Models	LRχ^2	df	f
1. (U) (IY)	33.05	11	.001
2. (UI) (UY) (IY)	13.45	5	.019
3. (UIY)	—	—	—

income interaction is required to fit the data well. The nature of that interaction is indicated by the parameter estimates for the saturated model (UIY) presented in table C.4. Main effects for year and income indicate that people in 1957 who had defined a problem in mental health terms were less likely to have actually sought help than comparable adults in 1976, and that among those defining a problem as relevant for formal help, high income people are more likely to actually consult a professional resource. The significant interaction reflects the fact, however, that this income difference was statistically significant only in 1957. In 1976, no reliable relationship was apparent between income and the use of help among those defining a problem in mental health terms.

Example 3: A Six-Variable Table

As noted, six-variable analyses were conducted to determine whether or not relationships between subjective adjustment indicators or demographic characteristics and aspects of professional help-seeking behavior (including interactions by year) persisted when sex, age, and education were controlled and to determine whether or not such relationships were conditioned by sex, age, and/or education. Table C.5 presents the results of a log-linear analysis of the cross-classification of "use of help" (among those defining a problem in mental health terms) by income (I), sex (S), age (A), education (E), and year (Y). Recall that a previous three-variable analysis of the cross-classification of "use of help" by income and year, summarized in table C.3, revealed a statistically significant income by year interaction, whereby only in 1957 did income show a significant positive association with use of help among those who defined a problem as relevant for professional help.

Since the relationship of "use of help" and income is that of foremost interest in table C.5, marginals specifying all relationships be-

TABLE C.4
Estimates of Log-Linear Parameters (λs)
Describing the Effects of Income (I) and
Year (Y) on "Use of Help Among
Those Defining a Problem in
Mental Health Terms" (U)[a]

Predictor	Used Help	
Income		
<$4,000	−.038	(.075)[b]
$4,000 to 7,999	.011	(.062)
$8,000 to 9,999	−.095	(.072)
$10,000 to 12,499	−.126	(.072)
$12,500 to 19,999	.041	(.058)
$20,000 and over	.206[d]	(.084)
Year		
1957[c]	−.102[e]	(.032)
Income × Year (1957[c])		
<$4,000	−.199[e]	(.075)
$4,000 to 7,999	−.017	(.062)
$8,000 to 9,999	.008	(.072)
$10,000 to 12,499	−.072	(.072)
$12,500 to 19,999	.103	(.058)
$20,000 and over	.177[d]	(.084)

[a] Based on saturated model: (UIY).

[b] Numbers in parentheses are standard errors of the lambda coefficients.

[c] Since year is a two-level variable, parameter estimates for 1976 respondents are identical to those for 1957 respondents, but opposite in sign.

[d] $p < .05$.

[e] $p < .01$.

tween use of help and the four control variables (USAEY) and between income and these same variables (ISAEY) are routinely fitted for all models in these six-variable analyses. Table C.5 shows that a model specifying only these "constant" terms fits the observed pattern of frequencies in this table quite well, and that adding the bivariate relationship between income and use of help does not significantly improve that fit. Thus, we noted in chapter 5 that even the relationship between income and the use of professional help (among those defining a problem as relevant for formal help) evident in 1957 disappears when sex, age, and education are controlled, the latter, in particular, also being a strong correlate of professional help-seeking.

A different example of a six-variable problem is presented in table C.6, which presents a similar analysis of the cross-classification of "readiness for self-referral" (R) by "having felt an impending nervous breakdown" (N), sex (S), age (A), education (E), and year (Y). Once again, since our focus is on the nervous breakdown-readiness relationship, two "constant" terms are fit—(RSAEY) and (NSAEY). Using the

TABLE C.5

*Log-Linear Hierarchical Models of Effects of
Income (I), Sex (S), Age (A), Education (E),
and Year (Y) on "Use of Help Among Those
Defining a Problem in Mental Health Terms" (U)*

Fitted Models	$LR\chi^2$	df	f
1. (USAEY) (ISAEY)	197.47	180	.177
2. (UI) (USAEY) (ISAEY)	193.40	175	.162
Difference $\chi^2(H_1)-\chi^2(H_2)$	4.07	5	>.50

TABLE C.6

*Log-Linear Hierarchical Models of Effects of
"Impending Nervous Breakdown" (N), Sex (S),
Age (A), Education (E), and Year (Y) on
"Readiness for Self-Referral" (R)*

Fitted Models (all models fit: RSAEY and NSAEY)	$LR\chi^2$	df	p
1. (RSAEY) (NSAEY)	524.85	180	.000
2. (RN)	196.65	175	.126
3. (RNS)	195.92	170	.084
4. (RNA)	183.86	165	.150
5. (RNE)	179.43	165	.209
6. (RNY)	185.36	170	.199
7. (RNY) (RNS)	184.61	165	.141
8. (RNY) (RNA)	172.51	160	.236
9. (RNY) (RNE)	169.16	160	.294
Differences			
$\chi^2(H_2)-\chi^2(H_3)$	0.73	5	>.50
$\chi^2(H_2)-\chi^2(H_4)$	12.79	10	>.30
$\chi^2(H_2)-\chi^2(H_5)$	17.72	10	>.05
$\chi^2(H_2)-\chi^2(H_6)$	11.29	5	<.05
$\chi^2(H_6)-\chi^2(H_7)$	0.75	5	>.05
$\chi^2(H_6)-\chi^2(H_8)$	12.85	10	>.05
$\chi^2(H_6)-\chi^2(H_9)$	16.20	10	>.05

bracketing procedure described previously, we determine that a model including only the "constant" terms (H_1) fits quite poorly, while the model containing only the bivariate relationship (H_2) fits the data fairly well. However, because a previous three-variable analysis of these variables, similar to that summarized in table C.3, suggested the presence of a significant nervous breakdown by year interaction, three-way interactions were added to model H_2 one at a time (H_3-H_6), to test for significant improvement in fit over the base model. After establishing that one such model (H_6) does result in a significant improvement in fit over the base model (H_2), each of the remaining trivariates (H_7-H_9) is added in turn to the new base model (H_6) to determine whether or not any of these more complex models result in a significant improvement in fit over model H_6. Since none of these do, model H_6—which specifies the suspected nervous breakdown by year interaction—is designated the best-fitting model. Based on our examination of the log-linear effect parameter estimates (not presented here) for model H_6 in table C.6, we were able to specify in chapter 5 that people who reported having felt an impending nervous breakdown in 1976 were much more likely than people who reported such feelings in 1957 to accept the possibility that they might have a problem that required professional help.

References

Aday, L.A. and Eichhorn, R. L. *The Utilization of Health Services: Indices and Correlates.* DHEW pub. no. (HSM) 73-3003 (Rockville, Md.: National Center for Health Services Research and Development, 1972).

Andersen, R. and Newman, J. F. "Societal and Individual Determinants of Medical Care Utilization in the United States," *Milbank Memorial Fund Quarterly,* 51, (1973), 95-124.

Andersen, R., Kravits, J., and Anderson, O. W. *Equity in Health Services: Empirical Analyses in Social Policy* (Cambridge, Mass.: Ballinger, 1975).

Anderson, O. W. and Andersen, R. M. "Patterns of Use of Health Services, " in *Handbook of Medical Sociology,* eds., H. E. Freeman, S. Levine, and L. G. Reeder, 2nd ed. (Englewood Cliffs, N.J.: Prentice-Hall, 1972), pp. 386-406.

Antonovsky, A. "Breakdown: A Needed Fourth Step in the Conceptual Armamentarium of Modern Medicine," *Social Science and Medicine,* 6 (1972) :537-544.

Asser, E. S. "Social Class and Help-Seeking Behavior," *American Journal of Community Psychology* 6 (5), (1978) :465-475.

Bateson, G., et al. "Toward a Theory of Schizophrenia," *Behavioral Science,* 1, (1956):251-264.

Bishop, Y.M.M., Fienberg, S. E., and Holland, P. W. *Discrete Multivariate Analysis: Theory and Practice* (Cambridge, Mass.: MIT Press, 1975).

Blum, J. D. "On Changes in Psychiatric Diagnosis Over Time, "*American Psychologist* 33 (1978):1017-31.

Brown, B. B. "Social and Psychological Correlates of Help-Seeking Behavior Among Urban Adults," *American Journal of Community Psychology* 6(5), (1978):425-439.

Butler, R. N. and Lewis, M. *Aging and Mental Health* (St. Louis, Missouri: C. V. Mosby Co., 1977).

Callaghan, M. E. "Marital Status and Support Seeking" (Ph.D. diss., University of Michigan, 1978).

Caplan, G. *Support Systems and Community Mental Health: Lectures on Concept Development* (New York: Behavioral Publications, 1974).

Cobb, S. "Social Support as a Moderator of Stress, "*Psychosomatic Medicine* 38(5) (1976):300-14.

Davis, J. A. "The Log-Linear Analysis of Survey Replications," in *Social Indicator Models* ed., K. C. Land and S. Spilerman (New York: Russell Sage, 1975), pp. 75-104.

Davis, J. A. "Hierarchical Models for Significance Tests in Multivariate Contingency Tables: An Exegesis of Goodman's Recent Papers," in *Sociological Methodology 1973-1974,* ed. H. L. Costner (San Francisco: Jossey-Bass, 1974) pp. 189-231.

Duncan, O. D. "Measuring Social Change Via Replication of Surveys" in *Social Indicator Models,* ed. K. C. Land and S. Spilerman (New York: Russell Sage, 1975), pp 105-127.

Duncan, B. and Duncan, O. D. *Sex Typing and Social Roles: A Research Report* (New York: Academic Press, 1978).

Duncan, B. and Evers, M. "Measuring Change in Attitudes Toward Women's Work," in *Social Indicator Models,* ed., K. C. Land and S. Spilerman (New York: Russell Sage, 1975), pp. 129-155.

Eisdorfer, C. and Stotsky, B. A. "Intervention, Treatment, and Rehabilitation of Psychiatric Disorders," in *Handbook of the Psychology of Aging,* ed., J. E. Birren and K. W. Schaie (New York: Van Nostrand, 1977), pp. 724-748.

Elinson, J., Padilla, E., and Perkins, M. E. *Public Image of Mental Health Services* (New York: Mental Health Materials Center, Inc., 1967).

Fienberg, S. E. *The Analysis of Cross-Classified Categorical Data* (Cambridge, Mass.: MIT Press, 1977).

Glenn, N. D. "Massification Versus Differentiation: Some Trend Data from National Surveys," *Social Forces* 46(1967):172-180.

Goodman, L. A. *Analyzing Qualitative Categorical Data: Log-Linear Models and Latent Structure Analysis* (Cambridge: Abt, 1978).

Gourash, N. "Help-Seeking: A Review of the Literature," *American Journal of Community Psychology*, 6(5) (1978):413–423.

Gove, W. R. "Sex Differences in Mental Illness Among Adult Men and Women: An Evaluation of Four Questions Raised Regarding the Evidence on the Higher Rates of Women," *Social Science and Medicine* 12B (1978): 187–198.

Greenley, J. R. and Mechanic, D., eds., "Patterns of Seeking Care for Psychological Problems" in, *The Growth of Bureaucratic Medicine*, ed., D. Mechanic. (New York: Wiley-Interscience, 1976), pp. 177–196.

Greenley, J. R. "Social Selection in Seeking Help for Psychological Problems," *Journal of Health and Social Behavior* 17 (1976):249–62.

Grizzle, J. E., Starmer, C. F., and Koch, G. G. "Analysis of Categorical Data by Linear Models," *Biometrics*, 25 (1969):489–504.

Gurin, G., Veroff, J., and Feld, S. C. *Americans View their Mental Health* (New York: Basic Books, 1960).

Gutmann, D. "An Exploration of Ego Configurations in Middle and Later Life," in *Personality in Middle and Later Life*, ed., B. Neugarten (New York: Atherton, 1964), pp. 114–148.

Heller, K. "The Effects of Social Support: Prevention and Treatment Implications," in *Maximizing Treatment Gains: Transfer Enhancement in Psychotherapy.* ed., A. P. Goldsten and F. H. Kanfer (New York: Academic Press, 1979), pp. 353–382.

Huffine, C. L. and Craig, T. J. "Social Factors in the Utilization of an Urban Psychiatric Emergency Service," *Archives of General Psychiatry*, 30 (1974):249–55.

Joint Commission of Mental Illness and Health. *Action for Mental Health* (New York: Basic Books, 1961).

Jung, C. G. "The Stages of Life," in *Modern Man in Search of a Soul*, ed., C. G. Jung, (New York: Harcourt Brace Janovich, 1933), pp. 109–131.

Kadushin, C. *Why People Go to Psychiatrists* (New York: Atherton, 1969).

Kahn, R. and Quinn, R. "Mental Health, Social Support and Metropolitan Problems," Unpublished research proposal, Survey Research Center, Institute of Social Research, Ann Arbor, 1977.

Kelley, H. H. "The Processes of Causal Attribution," *American Psychologist* 28 (1973): 107–28.

Kessler, R. C., Reuter, J. A., and Greenley, J. R. "Sex Differences in the Use of Psychiatric Outpatient Facilities," *Social Forces* 58 (2) (1979) :557–71.

Kish, L. "A Procedure for Objective Respondent Selection Within the Household," *Journal of the American Statistical Association* 44 (1949) :380–87.

Kish, L. and Hess, I. *The Survey Research Center's National Sample of Dwellings* (Ann Arbor, Mich.: Institute for Social Research, University of Michigan, 1965).

Kramer, M., Taube, C. A., and Redick, R. W. "Patterns of Use of Psychiatric Facilities by the Aged: Past, Present, and Future," in *The psychology of adult development and aging*, ed., C. Eisdorfer and M. P. Lawton, (Washington, D.C.: The American Psychological Association, 1973), pp. 428–528.

Kulka, R. A. and Tamir, L. M. "Patterns of Help-Seeking and Formal Support," in E. Douvan (chair), A twenty-year cohort analysis of social support and well being in adults with special emphasis on the elderly. Symposium presented at meetings of the Gerontological Society, Dallas, November, 1978.

Kulka, R. A., Veroff, J. and Douvan, E. "Social Class and the Use of Professional Help for Personal Problems: 1957 and 1976," *Journal of Health and Social Behavior*, 20 (1979) :2–17.

Laing, R. D. *The Politics of Experience* (Baltimore: Penguin Books, 1967).

Lasch, C. *Haven in a Heartless World* (New York: Basic Books, 1977).

Linn, L. "Social Characteristics and Social Interaction in the Utilization of a Psychiatric Outpatient Clinic," *Journal of Health and Social Behavior* 8 (1967) :3–14.

McKinlay, J. "Some Approaches and Problems in the Study of the Use of Services: An Overview," *Journal of Health and Social Behavior* 13 (1972) :115–52.

Mechanic, D. "Illness and Cure," in *Poverty and Health: A Sociological Analysis.* ed., J. Kosa, A. Antonovsky, and I. K. Zola (Cambridge, Mass.: Harvard University Press, 1969), pp. 191–214.

Mechanic, D. "Sociocultural and Social Psychological Factors Affecting Personal Responses to Psychological Disorder," *Journal of Health and Social Behavior* 16 (1975) :393–405.

Mechanic, D. "Stress, Illness, and Illness Behavior," *Journal of Human Stress* 2 (1976):2–6.

Mechanic, D. *Medical Sociology*, 2nd ed. (New York: Free Press, 1978).

Myerhoff, B. *Number Our Days* (New York: Dutton, 1979).

Neugarten, B. L. *Middle Age and Aging* (Chicago: University of Chicago Press, 1968).

Neugarten, B. L. and Gutmann, D. L. "Age-Sex Roles and Personality in Middle Age: A Thematic Apperception Study," in *Middle Age and Aging*, ed. B. L. Neugarten (Chicago: University of Chicago Press, 1968), pp. 58–71.

Page, W. F. "Interpretation of Goodman's Log-Linear Model Effects: An Odds Ratio Approach," *Sociological Methods and Research* 5 (4) (1977) :419–35.

President's Commission on Mental Health *Report to the President for the President's Commission on Mental Health, vol. 1*, Washington, D.C.: U.S. Government Printing Office, 1978.

Reynolds, H. T. *The Analysis of Cross-Classifications* (New York: Free Press, 1977).

Robinson, R., DeMarche, D. F., and Wagle, M. K. *Community Resources in Mental Health* (New York: Basic Books, 1960).

Rosen, B. M. "Mental Health and the Poor: Have the Gaps Between the Poor and 'Nonpoor' Narrowed in the Last Decade?" *Medical Care* 15 (1977) :647–61.

Rosenberg, M. *Society and the Adolescent Self-Image* (Princeton, N.J.: Princeton University Press, 1965).

Ryan, W., ed. *Distress in the City: Essays on the Design and Administration of Urban Mental Health Services* (Cleveland, Ohio: Press of Case Western Reserve University, 1969).

Scheff, T. J. "Users and Nonusers of a Student Psychiatric Clinic," *Journal of Health and Social Behavior*, 7 (1966) :114–21.

Shanas, E. and Maddox, G. L. "Aging, Health and the Organization of Health Resources," in *Handbook of Aging and the Social Sciences*, eds., R. H. Binstock and E. Shanas (New York: Van Nostrand, 1976), pp. 592–618.

Stack, C. *All Our Kin* (New York: Harper & Row, 1974).

Szasz, Thomas S. *The Myth of Mental Illness* (New York: Harper & Row, 1974).

Tamir, L. M. "The Transition to Middle Age: Men in Their Forties," (doctoral diss., Ann Arbor, Mich.: University of Michigan, 1980).

Tischler, G. L., Henisz, J. E., Myers, J. K., and Boswell, D. C. "Utilization and Mental Health Services: I. Patienthood and the Prevalence of Symptomatology in the Community," *Archives of General Psychiatry* 32 (1975) :411–415.

U.S. Department of Commerce. *County and City Data Book, 1977* Washington, D.C.: U.S. Government Printing Office, 1978.

Vanneman, R. and Pampel, F. C. "The American Perception of Class and Status," *American Sociological Review* 42 (3) (1977) :422–37.

Veroff, J., Douvan, E., and Kulka, R. *The Inner American* (New York: Basic Books, 1981).

Veroff, J., et al. "The Use of Thematic Apperception to Assess Motivation in a Nationwide Interview Study," *Psychological Monographs*, 74 (1960) :(whole no. 499).

Zung, W. W. "A Self-Rating Depression Scale," *Archives of General Psychology* 12 (1965): 63–70.

Index